Pumla Gobodo-Madikizela (ed.)

Breaking Intergenerational Cycles of Repetition

A Global Dialogue on Historical Trauma and Memory

Contents

Dedication IX

Acknowledgements X

Foreword
Reconciliation without Magic: Preface Honouring Nelson Mandela............ XI
Donna Orange
Training and Supervising Analyst, New York University

Introduction
Breaking Intergenerational Cycles of Repetition 1
Pumla Gobodo-Madikizela
University of the Free State

Chapter 1
Disrupting the Intergenerational Transmission of Trauma:
Recovering Humanity, Repairing Generations 12
Jeffrey Prager
University of California, Los Angeles

Chapter 2
Rethinking Remorse: The Problem of the Banality of Full Disclosure in
Testimonies from South Africa...27
Juliet Brough Rogers
University of Melbourne

Chapter 3
Towards the Poetic Justice of Reparative Citizenship 49
AJ Barnard-Naudé
University of Cape Town

Chapter 4
"Moving Beyond Violence:" What We Learn from Two Former
Combatants about the Transition from Aggression to Recognition 71
Jessica Benjamin
Psychoanalyst and Clinical Professor, New York University Postdoctoral
Program in Psychotherapy and Psychoanalysis

Chapter 5
Unsettling Empathy: Intercultural Dialogue in the Aftermath of
Historical and Cultural Trauma...90
Björn Krondorfer
Northern Arizona University

Chapter 6
Interrupting Cycles of Repetition: Creating Spaces for Dialogue,
Facing and Mourning the Past 113
Pumla Gobodo-Madikizela
University of the Free State

Chapter 7
Memoryscapes, Spatial Legacies of Conflict, and the Culture of
Historical Reconciliation in 'Post-Conflict' Belfast 135
Graham Dawson
University of Brighton

Chapter 8
The Anglo-Boer War (1899 – 1902) and Its Traumatic
Consequences...160
André Wessels
University of the Free State

Chapter 9
Breaking the Cycles of Repetition? The Cambodian Genocide across
Generations in Anlong Veng..174
Angeliki Kanavou; Kosal Path; Kathleen Doll
University of California, Irvine

Chapter 10
Reflections on Post-Apology Australia: From a Poetics of Reparation to a
Poetics of Survival 194
Rosanne Kennedy
Australian National University

Chapter 11
Ending the Haunting, Halting Whisperings of the Unspoken:
Confronting the Haitian Past in the Literary Works of Agnant, Danticat,
and Trouillot 213
Sarah Davies Cordova
University of Wisconsin-Milwaukee

Chapter 12
Intergenerational Jewish Trauma in the Contemporary
South African Novel 234
Ewald Mengel
University of Vienna, Austria

Chapter 13
Handing Down the Holocaust in Germany: A Reflection on the
Dialogue between Second Generation Descendants of Perpetrators
and Survivors 247
Beata Hammerich, Johannes Pfäfflin, Peter Pogany-Wnendt,
Erda Siebert, Bernd Sonntag
Members of the Study Group on Intergenerational Consequences of the
Holocaust (Cologne)

Chapter 14
Confronting the Past, Engaging the Other in the Present:
Intergenerational Healing Journey of a Holocaust Survivor and
his Children...267
Jeff Kelly Lowenstein, Dunreith Kelly Lowenstein, Edward Lowenstein
Harvard University

Chapter 15
Breaking Cycles of Trauma and Violence: Psychosocial Approaches to
Healing and Reconciliation in Burundi.......................................291
Wendy Lambourne, David Niyonzima
University of Sydney; Trauma Healing and Reconciliation Services,
Burundi

Chapter 16
Breaking Cycles of Trauma through Diversified Pathways to Healing:
Western and Indigenous Approaches with Survivors of Torture and
War 308
Shanee Stepakoff
California Institute of Integral Studies

Chapter 17
Acting Together to Disrupt Cycles of Violence:
Performance and Social Healing..325
Polly Walker
Juniata College, Pennsylvania

Epilogue
"They did not see the bodies": Confronting and Embracing in the Post-Apartheid University...343
Jonathan Jansen
University of the Free State

Author Biographies...**351**

Index...**359**

Dedication

This book is dedicated to the memory of Nelson Mandela.

Acknowledgements

This edited collection is the product of an interdisciplinary conference titled *Engaging the Other: Breaking Intergenerational Cycles of Repetition*, which took place at the University of the Free State in December 2012. The conference was followed by a series of research forums, conversations and symposia to explore what it means for victims, perpetrators and bystanders of past historical trauma to live together in the same country and sometimes as neighbours. Various aspects of the conference and the subsequent research meetings were supported through funding from the University of the Free State, the National Research Foundation, and the Ministerial Special Project on the Future of the Humanities and Social Sciences, which was provided for the Reconstruction and Reconciliation Catalytic Project, and the Fetzer Institute. We gratefully acknowledge the financial support from these organisations.

I would like to thank Jo-Anne Naidoo, who was the Office Manager in our office and research unit, Trauma, Forgiveness and Reconciliation Studies, at the University of the Free State. As member of the organising team and coordinator of the conference, Jo-Anne did a fantastic job of coordinating the complex details of the conference. A superb team of post-graduate students in our unit, Samantha van Schalkwyk, Jessica Taylor and Naleli Morojele, assisted her. Samantha, now Dr van Schalkwyk and Senior Post-doc Fellow, has continued her involvement with the Reconstruction and Reconciliation Catalytic Project. Thanks are also due to the student assistants who worked tirelessly to give support to the conference delegates who came from more than 22 countries.

Most of all, I would like to thank the contributors to this volume for their time and effort in making their contributions and for being available throughout the stages of production in this project. Special thanks to Donna Orange for writing the Foreword for the book, and to Jonathan Jansen for the Epilogue.Finally, I would like to thank the editors for our project at Barbara Budrich. David Newmarch of Grammarline Editing Services provided much needed help in the final stages of the project.

Foreword
Reconciliation without Magic:
Preface Honouring Nelson Mandela

Donna Orange

Faculty and Supervising Analyst
At New York University Postdoctoral Program in Psychoanalysis and Psychotherapy
and at the Institute for the Psychoanalytic Study of Subjectivity, New York

> *The purpose of freedom is to create it for others*
> (N. Mandela, Kani, & James, 2010), p. 270.

Nelson Mandela learned Afrikaans. Neither by chance nor by brilliance, nor in the end by force, did he mitigate the fears of the ruling white minority in apartheid South Africa. He studied their language, their history, their culture and habits, even their sports. He practiced his language skills on his prison warders for many years. When he needed to negotiate in secret the freedom and full equality for his comrades and for all his people, he already spoke fluently[1]. Former New York Times Johannesburg bureau chief John F. Burns reported an act of "particular kindness" from his press conference at Desmond Tutu's residence the day after Mandela came out of prison in 1990:

> …a white reporter stepped forward and identified himself as Clarence Keyter, the chief political correspondent of the Afrikaans-language service of the state-run broadcasting monopoly, SABC. Sensing Mr. Keyter's unease, Mr. Mandela shook the reporter's hand and thanked him, saying that in his last years in prison, when he had been given a radio, he had relied on Mr. Keyter's reports to learn "what was going on in my country." Mr. Keyter, stunned had tears welling in his eyes (Burns, 2013), p. A14.

Such an act of kindness became possible, of course, only because Mandela had devoted years to learning Afrikaans, and then possessed the sensitivity to respond in the moment. Few have noticed, in celebrating the life of "the great reconciliator," his disciplined attention to the specific proficiencies needed

---

[1] Mac Maharaj: "When we went to prison most of us were not speaking Afrikaans. I argued with Mandela about whether we should study the language. He'd say: "Let's do it together." I'd say I'm not interested in this language, first of all it's not even an international language, and second it's the language of the oppressor. He'd reply: "Look, man, we're in for a long struggle, a protracted struggle. It's going to be a war of attrition." He'd say: "How are we going to lead the enemy forces into an ambush? To do that we look at the enemy's commander and try to understand him. To do that, we've got to read his literature, read his poetry. So shall we study Afrikaans?" (various, 2013)

for such peacemaking. To make war skilfully, as he had learned as a young man from Walter Sisulu and Oliver Tambo, demanded planning and preparation and a cool head. To stop war, to overcome hatred and fear, to build a functioning nation—these demanded different skills, and no less unrelenting effort.

I begin with this concrete example—chosen not at random but because language itself both murders and welcomes—to introduce a book full of initiatives for justice and peace from South Africa and all across the world. This moment of Mandela's recent "transition"—I am told that in the world of his origins, dying means he has transitioned into a state from which he can now speak to us more directly than before—gives those he has taught the chance to listen again to what he would be telling us now. In this foreword, I will emphasize several messages I hear coming through his life and words. Without directly summarizing the chapters in this book, I will try to make it clear how these authors' work seems to me to channel Nelson Mandela.

My own voice speaks, of necessity, from a humble place in this foreword. This book's writers describe hard reconciliation—none of what Dietrich Bonhoeffer (Bonhoeffer & Fuller, 1949) called "cheap grace"—after extensive human rights abuses and explosive conflicts, and answer to the insistent demands of transitional justice (Huyse & Salter, 2008). Not only has my indirect contact with this giant of history whom South Africans affectionately call "Madiba", his clan name, or "Tata" (dad)[2] been limited to my three-day visit to Cape Town, including my visit to his cell at Robben Island, and to the District Six museum in Cape Town. Much more, I write from the United States, where the work of confronting our legacy of human rights violations—destruction of indigenous peoples, and hundreds of years of slavery—has scarcely begun. White Americans—who barely realize that we are white because we assume we are simply normal—almost never speak directly of our own crimes.

May the courageous authors in this book find readers in my country, though their focus lies elsewhere. Each of them works with one or several situations of egregious historical violence, and helps us imagine what may be needed to make early steps toward reconciliation and healing. Some authors are theoreticians and teachers, some artists, some organize close to the ground, that is, to the wounded people. Some are themselves the wounded people, or their children, embodying the ghosts of the unconscious (Loewald,

---

[2]   For me a point of contact comes in his original name, Rolihlahla, tree-shaker or troublemaker, so appropriate in his early life, an epithet also applied disparagingly to me by my psychoanalytic teachers. One could only wish to have transformed one's troublemaking as he did.

1960). Each horror seems uniquely atrocious and unsurmountable: Germany's "final solution", Burundi, Cambodia, Haiti, Belfast, the stolen children of the indigenous people of Australia, Israel/Palestine. Each effort can learn from the others.

The book starts and ends in South Africa, with its visionary Truth and Reconciliation Commission (TRC), envisioned by Mandela, led by Desmond Tutu—Mandela's prophetic and passionate counterpart (Krog, 1999)—and in which the editor of this book, Pumla Gobodo-Madikizela, played a significant part. The TRC contributed and disappointed, in the view of most who write in this book, and forms a standard against which other similar approaches measure and challenge themselves. As my colleague Melanie Suchet writes, "I do believe that assuming individual responsibility, as a white South African, for the acts of apartheid committed while I lived under the system, even if not directly committed by me, is a necessary act of collective moral responsibility and part of what the Truth and Reconciliation Commission hoped to achieve in broadcasting the horrors on national television" (Suchet, 2010, p 194). It framed the discussion of alternative attempts at transitional justice in other contexts besides South Africa, and leaves the tremendous open questions that intrigue, even torment, the writers of this book.

What constitutes a "sorry" that truly makes a difference to the people offended, and to their descendants? Is there any kind of apology that actually changes the perpetrator (Gobodo-Madikizela, 2003)? Does it help the victims to know, really know, the sadistic enjoyment of the perpetrator? Is it true, as my colleague Robert Stolorow often says, that "trauma recovery" is an oxymoron, or can people heal enough to interrupt some of the cycles of violence in the next generation, as some of our authors suggest? At the same time, can the achievement of crucial political objectives require so much official forgetting that time bombs sit ticking away, as for example our chapter on Belfast warns? In this question intersect the stories of South Africa, Germany, the United States, and possibly more.

Mandela delegated the problems of human rights abuses to the TRC. He understood his own responsibility as the first president of all South Africans in a specific way, and believed it must fall to others to detail the injustices he had spent his life to overturn. But as several contributors to this book note, South Africa after apartheid has inherited overwhelming economic injustice and continuing mental apartheid, so that the silent rage of so many years has begun to explode. Without faulting Mandela's trade-off—his clarity placed political equality before everything—South Africans now find themselves faced with his unfinished work even as we and they mourn his departure.

In another instance of official forgetting, British and American victors colluded to silence those who would have faced ordinary Germans with their responsibility for the massacre called holocaust or shoah[3]. In April 1945, British filmmakers accompanied the British and American soldiers who liberated Bergen Belsen and eight other concentration camps. They assembled 55 minutes of indescribably gruesome film in which well-fed SS guards were made to bury thousands of horribly emaciated bodies, while similarly very well-fed townspeople from no more than two or three kilometers away were made to watch. From other camps, also right next to towns, the film showed gas chambers and crematoria. In some camps there were survivors to be nursed back to life, survivors too ill to eat or drink, and in others evidence that survivors had been shot on the approach of the Allies. Alfred Hitchcock assembled all this extremely difficult film footage, prepared its narration by Trevor Howard, but then it was buried as too difficult for the German people to see. Someone made the decision that Germany's post-war reconstruction was more important. Only now, in January 2014, has this film become available for anyone who wants to google "Memory of the Camps." As in South Africa, we buried stories of atrocity in the service of important political objectives, but this decision has borne costs.

A third instance: American slavery. Perhaps if we do not say these words, we can all just get along as if we all just fell out of the sky onto the North American continent, intended by a provident god to have the social and economic privileges that we have. Puzzling, then, why people seem resentful about their lower class status. If they would just work harder, stay out of prison, stay in school, they could do as well as my children do. All these bemused reactions make sense when history remains invisible: the atrocities of apartheid, memories of the camps, the daily indignities and violence of slavery.

The contributors to the book, each in his or her own voice, demonstrate that transitional justice requires deliberate hard work, specific skills, and creativity. It belongs to no one approach alone, and has nothing magically transformational about it. Massive evils leave invisible and invasive scars that require the determination and faith that each voice brings. Both the writers and the protagonists in the humbling stories they tell us demonstrate courage that outstrips the traumatic strictures of the horrors they recount. But

---

[3]   I hesitate in naming this disaster, knowing that some object to either choice: holocaust (sacrifice by fire) or shoah (catastrophe). The choice of lower-case indicates its belonging with other historical massacres treated in this book; upper case would have recognized the uniqueness of this deliberate extermination.

let us pause, in this dedication, to consider a few more of the elements that Nelson Mandela brought.

Madiba—here I use his South African name deliberately—accomplished something extraordinary that few have noticed: he articulated in English and acted out in Afrikaans the African communitarian philosophy of *ubuntu*—in the context of the United Nations Declaration of Human Rights. Misunderstood, even by philosophers as prominent as Derrida (Derrida, Mandela & Tlili, 1987), to be writing a new version of Rousseau's social contract theory (a radical western individualism), Mandela instead assumed a fundamental human solidarity with egoistic behavior as a deviation (Bernasconi, 1993). When, in all his early writings, he contrasted law with conscience, he meant that laws like apartheid were unjust because conscience called everyone to struggle for basic human solidarity and equality. Born into the African assumptions, he could learn and love western culture and law without ever accepting its foundational ethics. Like his friend Desmond Tutu—poet Antjie Krog speaks of "the politician and his prophet"—Mandela could speak Western justice ethics while working from their own native communitarian *ubuntu* (we are what we are together).

"This isn't right."[4] Injustice bothered Mandela all his life. As a young man faced with the blatant injustice of more and more rigid apartheid laws, he channelled his rage into physical training and legal education, becoming South Africa's first black attorney, and preparing himself to represent his people in the great trials and in the first truly representative government. For a time he willingly lived in hiding because his country regarded him as a terrorist. In prison, he calmly confronted the small injustices: the differences in food and clothing and privileges. Why should black political prisoners have to wear short pants when Indian and colored prisoners get the dignity of long pants? This isn't right. He served nearly 20 years on Robben Island[5], where his eyesight suffered from working in the limestone quarry without sunglasses, from 1982 to 1988 in Pollsmoor near Cape Town, and two more years at Victor Verster, where he was moved when he contracted tuberculosis from the dank conditions at Pollsmoor. Only once did he erupt in rage, over

---

[4]   According to Richard Stengel (Stengel, 2010), who assisted Mandela in the preparation of his autobiography, *Long Walk to Freedom*, Mandela would often listen quietly to a long conversation, and then insert these words.

[5]   On my 2009 visit to Cape Town, my day free from teaching took me to Mandela's Robben Island cell, seven by eight feet, barely large enough for him to lie down. Our guide, also a former prisoner, explained clearly the differences in diet among the groups of prisoners, and described the daily routine and living conditions. The Africans who took me there asked about our elections and were amazed to meet a white person who had voted for a black man. Some remembered with pride Obama's visit to Robben Island.

an insult to his wife Winnie. "I have mellowed," he told Richard Stengel, who helped him to write his autobiography, "I was very radical as a young man, fighting everybody, using high-flown language" (Stengel, 2010, p. 51). By the time he emerged from prison twenty-seven years later (November, 1962 to February, 1990), he had become the quietly dignified leader of his people.

How did this happen? In prison Mandela learned to value self-control over self-expression. The "man without bitterness" whose measured style reassured white leaders and whose response prevented civil war when Chris Hani was assassinated in 1993, also hid his pain and anger. Just as he considered courage a choice to act in the face of real fear, he chose his calm and measured public style at a personal cost he rarely acknowledged. In prison, besides the "university" formed by his comrades there to study history and political science—particularly his mentor Walter Sisulu and his close friend Ahmed Kathrada—he developed his spiritual resources.

Who belonged to Mandela's internal chorus[6]? An intense sense of justice and human equality seems to have preceded all the voices—for him other elements (non-violence, socialism, etc.) served only as "tactics." He had attended Methodist schools as a child, attended church with family, but kept any religious beliefs very much to himself. African tribal leaders remained important inspirations, but thinkers like Marx and Gandhi, so crucial for others, he refused to consider authoritative. Two voices clearly ring out as influences for him: Shakespeare, and Abraham Lincoln.

When someone brought the works of Shakespeare to Robben Island in 1980 (Stengel, 2010), and asked the prisoners each to choose a favorite passage, Mandela did not hesitate but turned to *Julius Caesar*:

Cowards die many times before their deaths;
The valiant never taste of death but once.
Of all the wonders that I yet have heard
It seems to me most strange that men should fear,
Seeing that death, a necessary end,
Will come when it will come. (Act 2, scene 2).

---

[6]   Sandra Buechler borrows this idea from the chorus of Greek drama: "The internal chorus we bring into our offices every day must be of comfort, and must be sufficiently stimulating, to encourage the creative use of aloneness. The feeling the chorus must give us is that whatever may go on today, with this particular patient, does not define us as analysts...We are not personally and professionally at stake with each new interaction with a patient....An aloneness that doesn't cost us a good connection with ourselves, with our chorus, or with the patient can be used creatively. A creatively used aloneness is not loneliness." (Buechler, 1998, p. 111)

Not only was Shakespeare a resource for him, but he had obviously engaged in the ancient philosophers' meditation on death, the spiritual practice intended to help us to live in the present moment. Mandela often used this exercise to reduce fear, as we can also hear in his closing words at the Rivonia Trial of 1963-64, facing probable hanging:

> During my lifetime I have dedicated myself to this struggle of the African people. I have fought against white domination, and I have fought against black domination. I have cherished the ideal of a democratic and free society in which all persons live together in harmony with equal opportunities. It is an ideal which I hope to live for and to achieve. But if needs be, it is an ideal for which I am prepared to die.

So the meditation on death had begun before the Robben Island years. Shakespeare accompanied him too.

Abraham Lincoln appears in Mandela's image-conscious style of leadership, in his keeping rivals close (Stengel, 2010) and learning their Afrikaans language, and even in his speeches. In the 1993 crucial address to the nation on the death of Chris Hani, even before the first elections that brought him to the presidency, we can hear Lincoln:

> This is a watershed moment for all of us. Our decisions and actions will determine whether we use our pain, our grief, and our outrage to move forward to what is the only lasting solution for our country—an elected government of the people, by the people, and for the people.

We could wish to know more of Mandela's inner life and its inhabitants, but what we do glimpse provides continuity with his public life. His example of deliberate personal growth based on reflection on the example of others offers a way to reflect on the extraordinary work toward justice recounted in this book.

Unexpectedly, Mandela developed his character by the examination of conscience. This spiritual exercise, taught to every monastic novice, one does not expect of a South African political prisoner. He described it, however, in detail in a letter from prison to Winnie, herself imprisoned in 1975. First he set out the values to be sought:

> In judging our progress as individuals we tend to concentrate on external factors such as one's social position, influence and popularity, wealth and standard of education. These are, of course, important in measuring one's success in matters and it is perfectly understandable if many people exert themselves mainly to achieve all these. But internal factors may be even more crucial in assessing one's development as a human being. Honesty, sincerity, simplicity, humility, pure generosity, absence of vanity, readiness to serve others—are the foundation of one's spiritual life. (N. Mandela et al., 2010 p. 271).

To refocus on these matters, however, would require discipline, and he had found himself a method:

> …you may find that the cell is an ideal place to learn to know yourself, to search realistically and regularly the process of your own mind and feelings… Development in matters of this nature is inconceivable without serious introspection, without knowing yourself, your weaknesses and mistakes. At least, if for nothing else, the cell gives you the opportunity to look daily into your entire conduct, to overcome the bad and develop whatever is good in you. Regular meditation, say about 15 minutes a day before you turn in, can be very fruitful in this regard. You may find it difficult at first to pinpoint the negative features in your life, but the 10th attempt may yield rich rewards. Never forget that a saint is a sinner who keeps on trying (pp. 271-272).

His method reminds me that injustice thrives on prejudice and, as Gillian Straker writes, "stereotyped interchanges, which, at the level of their subtly choreographed prosody, interpellate us again and again as the homophobic and racist subjects we would wish not to be" (Straker, 2006, p. 750). She recommends relentless mindfulness as a corrective, much as he did.

He developed a personal style that alternated between understatement and irony. In the face of injustice, he often spoke quietly only three words: that's not right.

Mandela emerged from prison a peacemaker, focused on one goal only, full equality for all South Africans, without retribution toward anyone: the white oppressors, or his African rivals. At his death, John Dramani Mahama, the president of Ghana, wrote of him:

> His utilization of peace as a vehicle of liberation showed Africa that if we were to move beyond the divisiveness caused by colonization, and the pain of our self-inflicted wounds, compassion and forgiveness must play a role in governance. Countries, like people, must acknowledge the trauma they have experienced, and find a way to reconcile, to make what was broken whole again (Mahama, 2013).

Mahami remembers his childhood, imagining that Mandela would never come out of prison. When he did, "we waited for an indescribable rage." Had Mandela wanted retribution, who would not have understood?

Twenty-seven years of his life, gone. Day after day of hard labor in a limestone quarry, chipping away at white rock under a merciless sun—without benefit of protective eyewear—had virtually destroyed his tear ducts, and for years, robbed Mandela even of his ability to cry (Mahama, 2013).

In contrast with the letter to Winnie quoted above, here is another, reflecting the cost of his sacrifices for justice:

Yet there have been moments when that love and happiness, that trust and hope, have turned into pure agony, when conscience and a sense of guilt have ravaged every part of my being, when I have wondered whether any kind of commitment can ever be sufficient excuse for abandoning a young and inexperienced woman [Winnie] in a pitiless desert, literally throwing her into the hands of highwaymen. (Letter of 4 February 1985, pp 148-49, cited in W. Mandela, Benjamin, & Benson, 1985).

But because his suffering, and enormous personal losses, had been for justice, Mandela saw no need for resentment. "To go to prison because of your convictions and be prepared to suffer for what you believe in, is something worthwhile. It is an achievement for a man to do his duty on earth irrespective of the consequences" (Mahama, 2013).

In the face of blatant dishonesty, he tended to say, well, people act in their own self-interest. In his last years he sadly noted that "we have now learned that even those that fought beside us in the struggle for freedom can be corrupted" (Abuya, 2013). Whatever his private suffering, he refused to demonize those who had subjugated his people[7], and as many have noted, invited some of his prison guards to his inauguration as the first president of all South Africans. Oppressors had never crushed his spirit. His critics may argue that government exists to protect people from those who disregard the common good, and that he ought to have done more to structure such protection from gross inequality. His private notes from 1993 show that he knew exactly where the crucial agenda lay:

> Priority is commitment to oppressed.
> Will fall or rise depending on our success or failure to address their needs, to accommodate their aspirations. Specifically we must get them houses and put an end to informal settlements; end unemployment, school crisis, lack of medical facilities (N. Mandela et al., 2010, p. 339).

These responsibilities belong to us who remain, and have been ably and eloquently taken up by the authors of this book. Many of them have, like Mandela, learned languages so that they can reach and be reached by the suffering or oppressing other. These authors' vulnerability, their creativity, their courage, their questions, their humility, their audacity, render them Nelson Mandela's legitimate heirs in the spirit and work of *ubuntu*.

---

[7]   His "people" came to include for him, all who fought injustice. He wrote in 1976 from prison: "The first condition for victory is black unity. Every effort to divide the blacks, to woo and pit one black group against another, must be vigorously repulsed. Our people— African, Colored, Indian and democratic whites—must be united into a single massive and solid wall of resistance, of united mass action" (SL, 191).

References

Abuya, K. (2013). Special Tribute. from http://www.saybrook.edu/rethinkingcomplexity/ posts/12-22-13/special-tribute-nelson-rolihlahla-mandela-great-leader-and-elder-took-stand-humanity

Bernasconi, R. (1993). Politics beyond humanism: Mandela and the struggle against apartheid. In G. Madison (Ed.), *Working through Derrida* (pp. 94-119). Evanston, IL: Northwestern University Press.

Bonhoeffer, D., & Fuller, R. H. (1949). *The cost of discipleship*. New York,: Macmillan.

Buechler, S. (1998). The Analyst's Experience of Loneliness. *Contemp. Psychoanal., 34*(1), 91-113.

Burns, J. (2013, Friday, December 6, 2013). An Act of Kindness on a Day of Adulation. *New York Times,* p. A14.

Derrida, J., Mandela, N., & Tlili, M. (1987). *For Nelson Mandela.* New York: Seaver Books.

Gobodo-Madikizela, P. (2003). *A Human Being Died That Night.* London: Houghton Mifflin.

Huyse, L., & Salter, M. (2008). *Traditional justice and reconciliation after violent conflict: learning from African experiences.* Stockholm: International Idea.

Krog, A. (1999). *Country of my skull: guilt, sorrow, and the limits of forgiveness in the new South Africa* (1st U.S. ed.). New York: Times Books.

Loewald, H. W. (1960). On the Therapeutic Action of Psycho-Analysis. *Int. J. Psycho-Anal., 41*, 16-33.

Mahama, J. (2013, December 6, 2013). He Taught a Continent to Forgive. *New York Times*.

Mandela, N., Kani, J., & James, P. F. (2010). Conversations with myself [sound recording]. New York: Macmillan Audio,.

Mandela, W., Benjamin, A., & Benson, M. (1985). *Part of my soul went with him* (1st American ed.). New York: Norton.

Stengel, R. (2010). *Mandela's Way: Fifteeen Lessons on Life, Love, and Courage*. New York: Crown.

Straker, G. (2006). The Anti-Analytic Third. *Psychoanalytic Review, 93*, 729-753.

Suchet, M. (2010). Searching for the Ethical: Reply to Commentaries. *Psychoanlytic Dialogues, 20*, 191-195.

Various. (2013, December 6, 2013). The Nelson Mandela I Knew. *The Guardian*.

Introduction
Breaking Intergenerational Cycles of Repetition

Pumla Gobodo-Madikizela

How do societies characterised by a history of mass violence work through their traumatic past? In the aftermath of gross violations of human rights and genocide, when people have suffered collective trauma, how does the trauma play out in subsequent generations? How might we map out the arc of historical trauma as a nexus for the interweaving of individual and collective traumatic memories? These are not just rhetorical questions; answers to them are far from obvious. This presents salient challenges for a project that seeks to engage in scholarly reflection on historical trauma and memory as an area of exploration across disciplinary and national boundaries.

I want to begin this introduction with a scene that I witnessed of the re-enactment of violent events that took place in South Africa in the mid-1980s. The re-enactment, which I witnessed in Mlungisi Township in the Eastern Cape, was a game by a group of young girls who were not yet born when the events they were enacting took place. Mlungisi was one of many black residential areas affected by a wave of "necklace" murders committed against those who were suspected of collaborating with the apartheid government security. The "mob justice" meted out against victims involved burning a petrol-soaked tyre that was put around a victim's neck. Victims of this gruesome crime rarely, if ever, had a chance to defend themselves, and soon after being identified as police informers, they were beaten and driven to a spot where these murders took place. There the tyre was thrown around the victim's neck, doused with petrol and set alight. The accusing crowd and bystanders would then circle around the burning body, performing a macabre dance to some singing until the victim died. Here is what I witnessed in 1996 during a visit to Mlungisi to organise the launch of the public hearings of the Truth and Reconciliation Commission in the township:

"Let's play a game." It was strange, almost surreal, to see a group of young girls seven to ten years old laughing and cavorting in the streets of Mlungisi, the same township that between 1986 and 1988 had become the scene of so much misery, a tinderbox of inflamed emotion against the inhumanities of apartheid. But that was before these children were even born. Their squeals and cries were the very embodiment of joy. They looked like little tender shoots of foliage—little blades of life—poking out from under the cooled lava of the township once utterly devastated by apartheid's volcano.

"What game?" the others shouted back, skipping back and forth.

"Let me show you," the first one said. She was about eight and looked as if she might be the informal leader of the group. She began to demonstrate. The other girls did not seem too enthusiastic about this new game. What was wrong with just playing skip? But slowly, they became intrigued.

"It is called the 'necklace' game," the leader said. "This is just going to be pretend 'necklace,' not the real thing," she said. She pushed the other girls aside as if to open up the stage. Rotating through the role of victim, then killers, then bystander, she seemed to my amazement to recall virtually everything that actually happened in a real necklace murder, even though she had not been born when the last necklace killing occurred in Mlungisi Township.

She flailed her arms, screaming in mock anguish as if being pushed around and beaten by an imaginary crowd, swaying back and forth, turning her head from left to right, and begging for mercy with eyes wide open to show mock fright. Then she switched roles and playacted someone going off to find petrol, then another person offering matches, then someone running to demand a car tyre from an imaginary passing motorist.

"Give me your tyre," she ordered with mock hostility. She narrated the part of the motorist dutifully obeying, then the petrol man, then the matches man. Finally, she returned to her victim role, struggling against the make-believe tyre placed around her neck. Nervously, she made a gesture simulating the striking of a match, as if her friends—now a crowd of executioners—had forced her to set herself alight.

As make-believe flames engulfed her, she threw her arms wildly into the air. "Now sing and clap your hands and dance. I'm dying," she said. Her friends started clapping and singing in a discordant rhythm, moving in circles around her "body." Gradually, the high-pitched screams of the girl with the imaginary tyre around her neck faded into a whimper as her life ebbed away. Consumed by the flames, she slowly lowered herself to the ground and "died." It was all make-believe.

None of the girls I saw re-enacting the necklace game that morning had actually witnessed a necklace murder. The unspoken events of the past, however—the silence of Mlungisi's lambs—had become imprinted on their minds. It was not just the outward form of the game, but its inner meaning, and the sense of trauma to communal life that it carried with it. Re-enacting the death dance of the necklace victim may well have been a way of transforming the unspoken memory of it into something more accessible and less fearful for the girls.

This theatrically narrated scene provides an illuminating metaphor for the way in which trauma is passed on intergenerationally in subtle ways through stories or silences, through unarticulated fears and the psychological scars that are often left unacknowledged. It is a dramatic illustration of Prager's notion (in this volume) of how unwittingly subsequent generations "can inhabit a past that preceded them." The symbolic re-enactment may also represent a transformation of traumatic experience into ritual, perhaps a cathartic way of putting into action the struggle to find language that expresses not only the unspoken pain of the past. It is also a response to the crisis of the present, the frustrations, the helplessness, and the disempowerment of people whose lives still cry out for the fruits of transformation that have eluded them and their communities.

Few topics stake a more compelling claim to Humanities research than the legacies of historical trauma – the impact of mass atrocity not only on individuals and groups that experienced the violence directly, but also across multiple generations of the descendants of survivors. Yet the most urgent question of the 21st century is how responses to historical trauma and their intergenerational transmission might be interrupted in post-conflict societies. In this book, scholars respond to, and explore responses to, historical traumas experienced in different cultural contexts, engaging with the question of what transformation and breaking cycles of repetition might mean in a post-conflict environment.

Breaking Intergenerational Cycles of Repetition is a product of an international conference that brought together an interdisciplinary group of scholars, researchers, practitioners and survivors at the University of the Free State (UFS) in December 2012. The conference drew nearly 350 participants from more than twenty-two countries, including survivors from ten post-conflict and post-genocide regions. Papers presented at the conference explored the various ways in which societies and individuals have engaged in processes of "working through" historical traumas, from truth commissions, to using dialogue, cultural practices and the arts.

The reference point for the canons of knowledge on historical trauma and memory has been either the Holocaust or other perspectives inspired by Euro-American case studies. The authors in this volume are uniquely placed as socially engaged scholars in a changing global context who are interested in shifting the lenses to focus on other historical traumas in order to explore new intellectual frontiers in this field.

In Chapter 1, Jeffrey Prager reminds us that trauma "is a memory illness," and thus healing "can only be done in the present." He considers the work of the Truth and Reconciliation Commission (TRC) of South Africa as a process that created a moment in which the traumatic past could be "clearly and sharply demarcated from a new future." Prager is careful not to suggest that the TRC has solved all the challenges of a post-apartheid South Africa. Apartheid's "generational ripples" mean that the task of disrupting the intergenerational transmission of trauma is a formidable one. For Prager, a break with the past means instating "a full-blown humanity for all humans." Elsewhere, he has argued that such a goal requires moving beyond memory in order to enable "a hopeful world of possibility for everyone" (Prager, 2008, p. 418).

There are echoes between Jeffery Prager's views in Chapter 1 about the TRC, and the idea of empathy that develops in encounters between victims and perpetrators in the context of what Shults and Sandage (2008) refer to as "a broader horizon of humanness" (p. 61). Victim-perpetrator encounters at public hearings of the TRC are the subject of Chapter 2 by Juliet Brough Rogers. Brough Rogers focuses her attention on perpetrators' expressions of remorse. One might expect discussion of remorse to follow a predictable line of argument: remorse as an expression of empathy that simultaneously presents the brokenness of the perpetrator and his recognition of the pain of the victim. Remorse, in other words, that is "other"-directed. Brough Rogers, however, wants to disrupt this "clean" view of remorse. Using a psychoanalytic lens, she examines the nature of the "full disclosure" of crimes committed by two of the most notorious torturers in the apartheid government's security forces, Jeffrey Benzien and Eric Taylor. An acknowledgement of enjoyment of the scene of violence, Brough Rogers argues, is an important aspect of giving "full disclosure," and may indicate a form of genuine remorse, albeit an "ugly remorse."

In Chapter 3, Jaco Barnard Naudé reminds us that remorseful apologies by perpetrators of apartheid atrocities and statements of acknowledgement and reconciliation by beneficiaries of apartheid are not enough to assuage the continuing pain of the *still* "dispossessed, the poor and the disenfranchised." He calls attention not so much to past historical trauma, or responses to this trauma and its repercussions in contemporary South Africa, but is concerned, rather, with the crisis of the present – the traumas of the everyday faced by millions of South Africans who, still without the reparations that they were promised, continue to live at the margins of society.

The past of the apartheid era was the most complex moment in the history of South Africa, characterised by spectacular forms of violence. It was a time when black people were relegated to second-class, or even third-class citizenship in their own country, their lives rendered invisible. Blackness was a marker of inferiority, and racial identity a framework that determined not the plurality of human life, but the otherness of the "foreigner" – the one who does not belong – "the discarded," in Jessica Benjamin's (2014) turn of phrase. Despite the change of guard from a white repressive government to a "people's government" of the African National Congress (ANC), for the majority of black people the dream of freedom has not yet been realised. The cruellest of all features of the current era of government leadership in South Africa is the continuing injustice of the failure of service delivery, the collapse of health institutions and the dire state of many schools. It is a paradox, Barnard Naudé observes in Chapter 3, that the ANC "as an agent of reparation, has as yet failed dismally to bring about large scale reparation through structural interventions in the economy." The broken promises of politicians, is a traumatic pain that cuts deep and explodes the sense of hope and optimism that ushered in an imagined South Africa of opportunity. Barnard Naudé says it is time to shed "the cloak of denialism" with which the ANC government has covered up "post-apartheid disasters as if to render them invisible."

Yet when it comes to the question of who ultimately is responsible for reparations, for repairing the irreparable brokenness of the past, and "the 'now' of the irreparable," all South African are responsible. This sense of responsibility, Barnard Naudé argues, involves "a reparative approach to the irreparable" and "a process of becoming-human (again)." This involves "a conception of politics as creative potentiality ... as reparative citizenship [which] is necessarily an inter-generational concept ... that requires us to imagine a future generation to which we will stand accountable not simply for the Apartheid past that lies behind us, but also for the post-apartheid as it becomes a past in the 'now' of the irreparable."

Becoming human, or recognition of the other as a human being, are forms of reparation. These terms often emerge in the context of dialogue between individuals and groups from different "sides" of historical trauma. In Chapter 4, Jessica Benjamin applies a psychoanalytic lens to explore the dialogue captured in the film *Beyond Violence* between a Palestinian man called Bassam, who was imprisoned for resisting the Occupation, and Itamar, a former soldier in the Israeli Army who grew up in a Zionist military home. Benjamin draws from the concepts she developed, including the ideas of recognition and of the "moral third" to explore the men's journey of dialogue that led to their establishing the movement "Combatants for Peace." Benjamin offers the psychoanalytic paradigm of recognition to "conceptual-ize what it means to transform one's view of a previously repudiated other and step into the space of dialogue – a space where both subjects are equally dignified and ethically obligated to respect the other." The power of the transformation of their relationship "beyond violence" is illustrated by the story of the shooting death of Bassam's daughter by an Israeli soldier. Benjamin informs us that despite this incident, Bassam refuses to retaliate with vengeance and instead identifies "with the suffering of those who feel responsible for injury and want to repair it."

Björn Krondorfer continues on this theme of dialogue in Chapter 5. The chapter draws on his work as facilitator of intergroup dialogue in wide-ranging contexts including between Israelis and Palestinians, Israelis and Germans, and third-generation American Jews and non-Jewish Germans. He proposes the term "unsettling empathy" as an ethical *posture* of "shared responsiveness ... that leads to transformation.

The discussion of dialogue as a response to historical trauma is also the subject of Chapter 6. Using a psychoanalytic framework, Pumla Gobodo-Madikizela explores the relationship between remorse and forgiveness based on examples of encounters between victims and perpetrators drawn from the TRC. She argues that remorse, as in forgiving or mourning, involves a reparatory process in which there is an integration of self and other on both internal and external levels. This opens up the possibility of connection between victim and perpetrator and the transformation of the relationship between them. Exploring the empathy-remorse-forgiveness cycle in the context of the TRC, Gobodo-Madikizela argues, "might broaden our understanding of the construction of meaning, and strengthen and enliven psychoanalytic debates about the conditions that facilitate positive change after violence."

Building connections and reconciliation between former enemies after historical trauma is also the subject of Chapter 7. Graham Dawson takes us to the Northern Ireland "Troubles" and strategies aimed at "historical reconciliation" in Belfast, the "post-conflict city" as he refers to it. Dawson goes to the heart of the issues at the forefront of contemporary debates about historical trauma, its aftermath, and its expression in memory and other symbolic forms of expression in places that became the sites of violence – "the cultural landscapes and memoryscapes that construct the meaning of places and their pasts." He engages with questions that are seldom explored in post-conflict contexts, shifting the lens from responses to historical trauma that focus on interpersonal dialogues, to addressing the central question of the complex interplay of the historical, political and traumatic dimensions of memory when former enemies live in the same city as neighbours, and how these memories are transmitted to the next generation.

In Chapter 8, André Wessels brings us back to South Africa and discusses a historical trauma that predated apartheid-era violence, namely the Anglo-

Boer War, or the "South African War" as it is now referred to in recognition of the countless black people, women, men and children, who were also killed in that war; a war waged by the British Empire in colonial times, which, according to Wessels, is "the most extensive and destructive war that has been fought in southern Africa." Wessels' chapter examines the shadow that this war cast on the future, and explores its multigenerational repercussions, including the yearning for re-enactment of the past in violent ways, the yearning to "refight the battles of the past." Why is it, Wessels asks, that despite the important work of the South African TRC, "reconciliation is still a problem in South Africa? Why? Why all the bitterness, the hostility, the unresolved trauma?"

Chapter 9, by Angeliki Kanavo, Kosal Path and Kathleen Doll, is a study based in post-genocide Cambodia in Anlong Veng, a community known to be the last stronghold of the Khmer Rouge. The authors explore the transmission not only of trauma, but also of patterns of unquestioning obedience among former cadres of the Khmer Rouge, and how these patterns have been transmitted to the younger generation within this Khmer stronghold community. Their findings suggest that young people in Anlong Veng have not been critical of the past and of their parents' role in it, and that far from engaging in efforts to break the cycles of the repetition of the violent past, always strong in Anlong Veng, an environment in which cycles of destructiveness have thrived has been nurtured.

The novel as a response to historical trauma is the focus of the next three chapters in the book. Chapter 10, by Rosanne Kennedy, takes a critical look at the public apologies and the discourse of reconciliation in Australia. She calls for new avenues of inquiry, new genres that will allow shifts "from a discourse of reconciliation to one of crisis … and from a poetics of reparation to a poetics of survival." In Chapter 11, Sarah Cordova shows how two female novelists confront the silences around the traumatic period of the Duvalier years in Haiti. In Chapter 12, Ewald Mengel returns us to the South African context, and focuses on trauma novels written by Jewish authors after apartheid. Cordova and Mengel are interested in how the trauma novel is used by the authors symbolically to break the silence and to reclaim a sense of agency and wholeness.

Chapter 13 is by Beata Hammerich, Johannes Pfäfflin, Peter Pogany-Wnendt, Erda Siebert, and Bernd Sonntag, all members of the Psychotherapeutic Study Group for People Affected by the Holocaust (PAKH) who are descendants of Nazi perpetrators and children of Holocaust survivors. The chapter is a reflection on the authors' on-going dialogue about the impact of the Holocaust on their lives, how the themes of trauma, shame and guilt have played out in their lives, and the challenges they faced over the years during their dialogue process.

Chapter 14 is by Jeff Kelly Lowenstein, Dunreith Kelly Lowenstein and Edward Lowenstein. As a four-year-old in Essen, Germany in 1939, Edward Lowenstein was put on the Kindertransport to England to escape the imminent destruction of Jews in Nazi Germany. The chapter is about his journey of return to Essen for the first time in 2012 with two of his sons and his grandson, and how he and the community in the neighbourhood of his former home in Germany have found healing through confronting the Holocaust past and its transgenerational repercussions among both survivors' children and the descendants of perpetrators and bystanders. Both Chapter 13 and 14 are written with a rare honesty that will deepen readers' understanding of what it means for children of survivors and of perpetrators to experience the "memory" of the past, and of the complex journeys of dialogue and the imperative for the inheritors of the past to confront it in order to transcend it and break its cycles of repetition.

Marianne Hirsch (2001; 2012) refers to the emergence of traumatic memory at the level of the second generation as "post memory." She describes "postmemory" as the relationship that descendants of survivors of collective trauma have with their parents' traumatic experiences. "Postmemory" experiences are those that the younger generation "remember" from the images and stories with which they grew up, "but that are so powerful, so monumental, as to constitute memories in their own right" (Hirsch, 2001, p. 16). The importance of Hirsch's analysis, based as it is in the context of exploration of transgenerational trauma within families, is that it opens up the possibility of broadening research in this field beyond individual experience, and provides theoretical insights on what is at play when children "inherit" their parents' traumatic memories. What is still rare in the literature on transgenerational trauma and the Holocaust is research on societal strategies of "social repair" (Prager, 2011) or on dialogue processes as a way of interrupting the transmission of intergenerational cycles of trauma, shame and guilt associated with "memory" of the Holocaust. Chapters 13 and 14 are illustrative examples of what happens when individuals and groups confront this unspeakable past and forge links with people from opposite sides of history in order to transcend its debilitating repercussions.

The chapters in this book represent perspectives from a wide range of disciplinary fields. Historical traumas are discussed that were experienced in different cultural contexts. Thus, we have moved away from what Michael Rothberg (2008) refers to as the "homogenization" of historical trauma (p.

230), and from marginalising traumatic events that have occurred in other part of the globe (Stef Craps & Bret Buelens, 2008). The diversity of voices we have maintained in the book – interdisciplinary voices and transnational voices – finds expression in Chapters 15 and 16. The authors' contributions reflect a consciousness about the importance of using methodologies of healing responses to historical trauma, which are drawn from cultural contexts relevant to the groups in question. In Chapter 15, Wendy Lambourne and David Niyonzima show how integrating cultural practices of healing and reconciliation dialogue in Burundi with Euro-American approaches can facilitate meaningful transformation. In Chapter 16, Shanee Stepakoff discusses a counselling programme developed for different post-conflict regions and refugee centres by combining indigenous approaches with traditional psychological counselling methods.

The last chapter in the book, Chapter 17, by Polly Walker, discusses the use of performance arts in peacebuilding strategies after mass trauma and violence. The link between the arts and trauma was recognised in ancient Greece, where theatre was used as a way of reintegrating returning traumatised soldiers back into society. Jonathan Shay (1995), in his book *Achilles in Vietnam: Combat Trauma and the Undoing of Character*, discusses this sophisticated use of the arts in ancient Greece, and how the arts were brought into dialogue with trauma to help traumatised soldiers to reclaim their sense of humanity and to reconnect in a social world. Connecting with humanity – the humanity of the audience and the humanity of the other – is where the power of the performance arts lies. Used in the context of dealing with historical trauma and responses to it, performance theatre becomes a communicative tool that inspires public conversations not only about trauma and its repercussions in individuals and society, but also about its role as a tool that can be used to draw attention to the manifestation of destructive cycles of repetition of historical trauma in social context. Thus, performance as public narrative can become a "visual conscience of society" (Dorfman, 2006). As Polly Walker observes in her chapter, performance "engages more than verbal, rational analysis: it engages people's bodies, emotions, and sense of spirituality" and opens up the possibility for conversations about the past on multiple levels, including with self and with others.

Consider, for example, South African composer Philip Miller's musical composition, *Rewind: A Cantata for Voice, Tape and Testimony. Rewind* is based on recordings of testimonies of victims and survivors who appeared before the Truth and Reconciliation Commission. In Miller's musical, we encounter the interweaving of stories of victims, perpetrators and bystanders, narrating the different roles they played. One of the stories in Miller's performance is based on the testimony of Nomonde Calata, whose husband was murdered by Eric Taylor, one of the security police who is the subject of Juliet Brough Rogers' discussion in Chapter 2. At the TRC hearing, Nomonde's voice, replayed in Millers' musical production, carried the original intensity of her emotions when she found out about the vicious murder of her husband. At one point during her testimony, she let out a piercing cry that shattered the stillness of the theatre where the hearing was held.

Miller resurrects this wailing voice from the archives of TRC. A soloist then takes up Nomonde's cry and re-presents it through her magnificent and electrifying soprano voice. Several other voices in the choir, with different levels of intensity, male and female voices, sing this wailing cry. The effect is a seamless repetition of this voice-cry that reverberates like a re-enactment of a wound that refuses to be silenced. Miller seems to be telling the audience: This is not yet past. Indeed, at the end of Miller's show at one of the main theatres in Cape Town, the Baxter, a still and dead silence hangs in the hall after the curtain call. The audience, clearly moved by Miller's unsettling stories, leaves the hall in reflective mood.

And here is the power of the creative arts: people did not leave after the performance of *Rewind*. Instead, they gathered around one another – around friends and strangers alike – weeping, talking, being silent and sharing the most tragic, shameful or confusing aspects of this collective past. Through these brief dialogue encounters, members of post-conflict communities can take some first steps into the light of hopefulness – hope, not as an abstract concept, but as a moment imbued with the possibility of deepening reflection that may lead to the kind of acknowledgement that gestures towards action, that inspires a wisps of a fresh breeze that awakens a sense of responsibility for the "'now' of the irreparable." Performance theatre can transform public spaces into sites for ethical engagement, sites for forging human links across time and space with the Other – even an Other responsible for the irreparable.

References

Benjamin, J. (2014). The Discarded and the Dignified. Part 1and 2. Retrieved from http://www.publicseminar.org/2014/12/the-discarded-and-the-dignified-parts-1-and-2/#.VlYWMHYrLIU

Craps, S. & Buelens, G. (2008). Introduction: Post-colonial novels. *Studies in the Novel, 40,* 1-12.

Dorfman, A. (2006). The Missing and Photography: The Uses and Misuses of Photography. In J. Santino (Ed.), Spontaneous Shrines and the Public Memorialization of Death, 255-260. New York: Palgrave Macmillan.

Hirsch, M. (2001). Projected Memory: Holocaust Photographs in Personal and Public Fantacy. In M. Bal, J. Crewe & L. Spitzer (Eds.), *Acts of Memory: Cultural Recall in the Present*. Hanover: University Press of New England.

Hirsch, M. (2012). *The Generation of Postmemory: Writing and Visual Culture After the Holocaust*. Columbia University.

Prager, Jeffrey. 2011. Danger and Deformation: A Social Theory of Trauma. *American Imago, 68*, 425-448.

Rothberg, M. (2008). Decolonising Trauma Studies: A Response. *Studies in the Novel, 40*, 224-234.

Shay, J. (1995). *Achilles in Vietnam: Combat Trauma and the Undoing of Character*. London: Simon & Schuster.

Shults, l., & Sandage, S. (2008). *The Faces of Forgiveness: Searching for Wholeness and Salvation*.

Chapter 1
Disrupting the Intergenerational Transmission of Trauma: Recovering Humanity, Repairing Generations

Jeffrey Prager

University of California, Los Angeles

Introduction

The entire world celebrated the end of apartheid. Since 1994, all eyes have watched hopefully as South Africa has struggled to forge for itself a new path. We have been witness to the nation's efforts to establish a more just society, one not divided by racial distinction or by brutal practices of subordination and exclusion. We have applauded efforts to enact policies for a more inclusive civil society and stable democracy, and to overcome the moral stain of a shameful past. The world has also paid attention to the formidable challenges, setbacks and leadership failures faced by the nation in recent years, and the various economic, political and social challenges with which it has been confronted. But the fact remains that, although it shares many similar problems with other developing countries, the South African political experience is unique.

There is no parallel to this country's efforts to peacefully preserve democracy while explicitly acknowledging that the entire political and social system had been upheld by a system of tyranny and brutality. It was then a democracy maintained through an elaborate system effectively dividing the nation into either real or potential victims and real or potential perpetrators.

And while the narrative accounts of the apartheid regime focus on these features of the past and the patterns of injustices resulting from the system, requiring an ever-developing system of rationalizations and justifications on behalf of black oppression and racially-defined domination, a new account beginning in the early 1990's was coming into view. This version focuses on the ways the *whole* nation suffered as a result of apartheid, producing a modern nation-state locked into an old vision of itself and that finally with the help of the international community was able to break the stranglehold the system of apartheid held on its development.

Twentieth-century South African history continues to be seen through this prism and shapes understanding of contemporary challenges. This narrative does not replace the former one but recognizes the ways in which the entire society—whites, blacks, and coloreds—has been deeply traumatized by the system. Apartheid's harm had been inflicted on all South Africans (though materially and psychically, of course, in different ways). Suspicion and mistrust of the other and the anxiety and fear of harm being done to oneself were common and everyday experiences shared by all. Apartheid, while most directly aimed to restrict the freedoms of South African blacks and coloreds, resulted in a national psychic trauma. No one was exempt from the anti-human premises upon which the system was conceived and no one was exempt from the "apartheid mind" (Gobodo-Madikezela, 2004).

Following the end of apartheid, dramatic efforts were undertaken to implement a new post-racist, post-racial nation especially visible in the establishment of The Truth and Reconciliation Commission (TRC) and the drafting of the new South African Constitution. The TRC in particular constituted a genuinely novel institutional response to overcome the perceived impediments to national self-development. Through it, South Africans were being provided a vehicle to achieve *forgiveness* toward one another and *reconciliation* between all sectors of the population. The political leadership through these measures, especially those identified with the African National Congress but others as well, sought, against great odds, to break a likely cycle of violence, revenge and torture. The goal was to create a South African history in which its racist past might be clearly and sharply differentiated from its post-apartheid present. The TRC constituted the nation's effort to reclaim for itself a common humanity long been denied. Yet despite some remarkable successes, the past still haunts the present.

The Conundrum of Time

A survivor of the European Holocaust describes her worry of passing on her experience to others. She writes, "Hitler is dead. Still, he may yet achieve his goal of destroying us if we internalize the hate, mistrust, and pain, all the inhumanity we were exposed to for so many years…I am afraid we might have come out of it lacking the human capacities we had before…to hope, love, and to trust. Have we acquired the wisdom to prevent such a terrible outcome (cited in Bar-On 1989:5)." In a quite different context, just prior to the collapse of apartheid in South Africa, J. M. Coetzee (1991) writes:

> It is not inconceivable that in the not too distant future, the major protagonists having agreed that apartheid has been 'dismantled,' the era of apartheid will be proclaimed to be over. The unlovely creature will be laid to rest, and joy among nations will be unconfined. But what is it that will be buried? The more cautious among us may want to draw lines between apartheid legislation, which indeed can

be dismantled, apartheid practices, which cannot be dismantled but can be combatted, and apartheid thinking, which is likely to resist coercion, as thinking generally does. The sensible course for future governors of South Africa to follow may be to concentrate on liquidating apartheid practices and to ignore apartheid thinking, allowing the latter to lead whatever forms of subterranean life it chooses as long as it does not emerge in action—treating it, in fact, very much as sin is treated in modern secular societies. Unfortunately, thinking does not always remain in its own compartment: thinking breeds action. There is thus reason to reopen the coffin and remind ourself of what apartheid looks like in the flesh.

Coetzee's point is an important one. In time, South Africans will only know *of* apartheid, not apartheid itself. Each generation will be further removed from its legislation and practices. Currently, more than 40% of the South African population has been born since 1993. The dehumanization that occurred during the apartheid era, certainly for its victims but for the perpetrators as well, will be remembered only through various narrative forms. For a while, there will be first-person accounts. Later, publicly sanctioned and un-sanctioned or non-formal personal narratives will predominate. In time, what will serve as memory will be laws making discrimination by race or ethnicity illegal. But Coetzee, of course, is correct in stating that apartheid thinking, an especially virulent form of racism, doesn't die easily. It generated actions whose consequences were passed on over time and continues to do so.

Racism, shared both by victims and perpetrators, becomes inscribed psychically and even bodily by all social members, and wittingly or unwittingly gets passed on long after the last survivor of the apartheid era dies. As Auerhahn and Laub write (1984), massive traumas, like those suffered at the hands of the apartheid system, continue to shape "the internal representation of reality of several generations, becoming an unconsciously organizing principle passed on by parents and internalized by their children." Each generation stands to receive these past traumas of racialized distinctions and experience new ones as a result of them: thinking becomes action. The result is a **life constricted by perceived difference**, specific perceptions dominated by strong echoes of the past. Long after apartheid's demise, the country is still required to reckon with, what Derek Hook (2008) describes as racism's "psychic density…its extraordinarily affective and often eruptive quality, its visceral or embodied nature, its apparent stubbornness to social, historical, discursive change" (p. 672). Hook (2008) goes on to argue, "This, for South Africa, is the legacy of trauma" (p. 672). Like many other countries who struggle with their own version of a constricted humanity, South Africa continues to confront apartheid's generational ripples: distortion, suspicion, fear, violence and hatred. This describes the formidable task of breaking the cycle: how to insure or instate a full-blown humanity for all humans, what the Holocaust survivor captured as the capacity "to hope, to love, and to trust."

In what follows, three propositions are offered that may stimulate thinking on ways of breaking historical cycles of destructiveness, especially for those who have no specific memories of the trauma itself but also for the "first generation" of PTSD sufferers themselves. I describe *individual* psychological trauma and the challenges it poses for therapeutic treatment—of those who experienced the trauma themselves as well as for their descendants—building upon both my clinical experience as a psychoanalyst and my previous research in psychoanalysis and sociology. From this, I extrapolate to describe particular social mechanisms intended to respond collectively to the damages inflicted by trauma. These strategies of "cure" should always be held against the backdrop of knowing that we are asking of trauma's sufferers and their impacted descendants, in the end, "to forgive the unforgivable (Derrida, 2001)."

1. Trauma is a memory illness. Healing can only be done in the present

Trauma victims, to paraphrase Freud, suffer from their reminiscences. Psychic trauma has its origins in some event or series of events in the past (moments, hours, days, weeks, months, years ago), remembered after the fact. It manifests itself *symptomatically* **in the present**, triggered by a memory that typically remains unconscious. Ordinary timeliness suddenly gives way to timelessness, and the painfulness of the past is felt as if it is occurring now (Stolorow, 2003; Prager, 2006). Trauma, at times, may be felt by the trauma victim as a return to the original moment or moments of danger though, of course, it is not an actual return to the past. Rather some experience *triggers* a reminder of the feelings of helplessness, or fear, or of being overwhelmed, transforming the present from benign to both dangerous and affectively unbearable. The here-and-now is itself felt to be unsafe. Intrusive memory, in short, is the symptom that requires immediate attention. As Cathy Caruth (1991) describes this feature, "The traumatized person, we might say, carries an impossible history within them, or they become themselves the symptom of a history that they cannot entirely possess" (p. 3). Traumatic memories reflect the failure of defensive strategies to contain them. The challenge is how best to "re-tell the lost truths of pain among us" (Laura Brown, cited in Caruth, 1991, p. 8).

Stated differently, trauma, as psychic illness, cannot be known until it surfaces in various symptomatic behavioral forms: suicide, homicide, or other kinds of anti-social behavior, intrusive memory, psychic paralysis or shutting-down, and various expressions of repetitive interpersonal incapacity. The psychological responses of either **fight or flight** unfortunately capture too much of contemporary psychic reality, notably in South Africa but elsewhere as well. Either as an unconscious re-creation of the past or as earnest effort to ward off the memories of the past's painfulness, these can have the unintended effect of helping to create an outer reality that conforms to the dangers of the past and confirms it. The traumatic past continues to intrude on current-day perception and shapes interaction between oneself and others, between parents and their children, and even between oneself and individual representatives of various institutional orders: teachers, bureaucrats, clergy, bosses, politicians, police etc. An interaction with someone in authority, for example, may trigger the memory of having been once demeaned, diminished or endangered. Unmetabolized remorse or guilt for past actions can also complicate interactions in the present, obscuring demands of the present by repetitive efforts to re-do the past. The trauma sufferer holds little or no capacity to distinguish whether the feeling is a product of a present-day interaction or instead a feeling of past abuses, now transposed into the present. Trauma **possesses** the person, the individual is not in possession of his or her history. It is often impossible, as Coetzee comments, for thinking **not** to be transformed into action. "Indirect knowledge," as Jonathan Jansen (2009) characterizes it in his important book *Knowledge in the Blood,* often creates a reality-on-the-ground where the imagined past is re-lived and re-created *as if* it were the present (see also Prager, 2008).

Following the end of apartheid, South African leadership appreciated the necessity to provide an institutional apparatus to combat apartheid's lasting traumatic effect on South Africans. The leaders understood the necessity to insure that power and race relations were simply not inverted; that memory not be employed as a vehicle of revenge and fight, where what was done to one group would now not be done to the other. The Truth and Reconciliation Commission was an inspired effort and, likely, a necessary one, in the words of Coetzee, for "reopening the coffin, and seeing what apartheid looks like in the flesh." It was designed, of course, to promote healing for the first generation, those who had lived and suffered through various traumatic experiences—either as victims or perpetrators—a consequence of the apartheid system. There was no precedent, anywhere in the world, for the form it took—equating truth with justice (and amnesty). It relied on no already existing institutional apparatus—neither governmental nor religious—to achieve its intended goals.

The insight behind the formation of the TRC is a profound one, speaking directly to breaking the cycle of destructiveness a result of a traumatic past. The procedures of the Commission embraced the following postulate: It is not the past that needs to be **forgotten** but, rather, personal memory's hold on the present that requires **disabling**. Without that, traumatic memory fails to lose its affective power or its capacity to dominate present-day interactions and social experience. In the words of the American psychoanalyst Hans Loewald, the TRC sought to transform a sense that individuals are currently haunted and **possessed** by the **ghosts** of the past to the conviction that these new South Africans are **in possession** of their **ancestors** *and* distinct from them. "Those who know ghosts," Loewald (1960) writes, "tell us that they long to be released from their ghost life and led to rest as ancestors. As ancestors they live forth in the present generation, while as ghosts they are compelled to haunt the present generation with their shadow life" (p. 29).

The public testimonies produced as the central feature of the TRC represented recognition that the apartheid past had to be **remembered**; yet it needed to become a memory emotionally distinct from the new Republic's present. The categories of victims and perpetrators had to be **retired** by the end of the hearings; apartheid thinking required demarcation from a post-apartheid citizenry, neither victims nor perpetrators but as post-apartheid survivors of trauma collectively forging a new society and a new politics.

The genius of the TRC was its creation of a **liminal** moment in the history of the nation—neither past nor present nor really public or private; a moment in time that itself had neither past nor a future. For that moment in time, time was suspended. Only when time stood still could a traumatic past be clearly and sharply demarcated from a new future. It was to be a future when all individuals might become in possession of their pasts. All testimony was public, within earshot not only of those who attended the hearings but broadcast by radio to the whole country. It would have been difficult not to hear the proceedings: as such, all of South Africa constituted itself as community of listeners, neither victims nor persecutors but post-apartheid co-equals.

The aspirations of the TRC, of course, were utopian. It is easy to describe in detail the ways in which it failed to achieve these impossible goals. The TRC implicitly understood trauma as a memory affliction dominated by ghosts from the past, and its repair required that apartheid's survivors take possession of their past and experience themselves as free from its hold. As the nation transforms itself by denouncing a shameful past, its citizens similarly need to take possession of their own past and possess it, clearly demarcating themselves from their discriminatory and exploitative ancestors.

Only then can memory loses its hold as a haunting, ghostly presence in the present (See also Gordon, 2008).

2. Traumatic transmission across generation often occurs unconsciously and affectively. Traumatic experiences live beyond those who are the direct recipients. We know how unwittingly new generations, in fact, can *inhabit* a past that preceded them, can be *carriers* of it, can continue to live it, reproduce it, pass it on and, at the same time, imagine or think themselves free from their history. We know that persecution and victimization in one generation, as if being haunted, typically gets acted-out in the next. We know that violence toward and fear of others becomes communicated, both overtly and covertly, between parents and children: that whole sub-cultural communities are constituted on the basis of shared, painful histories on the one side, and fear of violence, retaliation and infiltration, on the other. We know that communities of distrust, alienation and hatred persevere even when legal and institutional measures are implemented to dismantle those collectivities. Paradoxically, even amid good intentions and explicit efforts to protect the next generation from the violence and human destructiveness of the past, the same patterns often prevail. Inhumane re-enactments occur from one human being to another, generation after generation after generation.

How does this transmission occur? Studies of the children of Holocaust survivors reveal some of the unconscious processes at work that keep ghosts of the past alive (Bergmann and Jucovy, 1982; Auerhahn and Laub, 1998; Felsen, 1998; Kogan, 1995; Herzon, 1982; Pynoos, unpublished; Prager, 2003). As a consequence of their parents' experience, children differentiate less completely from their parents, see themselves as protectors of their parents rather than *vice versa*, and tend to inhibit their own impulse to establish independence and autonomy. Identity development, in short, becomes severely hindered because these children have not been able to experience themselves as persons occupying a particular discrete location in time and space. Auerhahn and Laub (1998), for example, in summarizing extensive research on Holocaust survivors and their children write, "We have found that knowledge of psychic trauma weaves through the memories of several generations, making those who know it as secret bearers" (p. 22). The researchers describe how children of survivors develop a sense that their parents often experience their activities of separation, differentiation and individualization as a reactivation of the original trauma. Such responses by their parents support their own identification with their parents' victimization. Their own feelings and needs, it came to be felt, are murdering their parents (Auerhahn and Laub, p. 38). Kogan (1995) writes, "The traumatized parent, in his own frantic search for an object which can be experienced as something which joins together desperate parts of his own personality, turns the child into a container. Thus, instead of fulfilling the role of an internal protective skin, the parent fosters a permeable membrane between himself and the child, through which he transmits depressive and aggressive tendencies which cannot be contained in himself (pp. 251-2)."

Two French psychoanalysts, Nicolas Abraham and Maria Torok (1994), have conceptualized this process of insufficient differentiation between generations by distinguishing between two distinct psychic processes: *introjection* and *incorporation*. For them, the critical role of parents in a child's psychic development is to help enable him or her to structure external experience **with** inner need and desire. This process is described as a process of introjection, taking in the external environment as presented to the child and calibrating it with the features of her own inner world. As they describe, introjection is about the capacity, facilitated by the previous generation, to transform needs and desires into words, to develop a language of self-discovery and self-fashioning and speak it to others. As they write, introjection, by its very nature, ensures independence between generations as it is synonymous with the articulation, through words, of inner desire with an outer world always different, always changing in time, always providing unique vehicles for self-expression. Introjection describes the process by which one generation moves coherently forward in time, facilitated by those from the previous generation who both tolerate and encourage that movement.

But trauma, Abraham and Torok argue, interferes with the spontaneous work of introjection. When traumatic moments intervene, the facilitative environment provided by parents is thwarted. The disarray in the parents' own state of desire—introjection frustrated—passes itself on to the children, who encounter caregivers distracted by their need to protect their secret. The trauma suffered by the one generation and unmetabolized or digested becomes "entombed" as an *unspeakable*—without words—and unconsummated desire, interfering with a capacity to pass on their whole world capable for introjection to the next. When words cannot be found to stand in for the person missing and unavailable to provide protection and guidance, introjection is replaced by the fantasy of incorporation, the insufficient provider now taken wholesale into the psychic life of those who encounter silence. Trauma distorts desire. Incorporation becomes an effort, through magical means, to regain a connection with the person who has failed, in fact, to fulfill their function: facilitating the introjection of desire in an ever-changing world. Introjection might be more familiarly understood as *identification* in contrast to incorporation where, as a result of the fantasy, the parent does **not** encourage or allow separation but (unconsciously) demands obsequiousness; the child experiences little choice but to comply. The subject takes it upon herself to accept the secret as her own, and thus trauma makes its way from one generation to the next. "It is therefore the object's secret that needs to be kept, his shame covered up…The fantasy of incorporation reveals a utopian wish that the memory of the affliction had never existed or, on a deeper level, that the affliction had nothing to inflict (pp. 131,134)."

In this rendering, incorporation cannot be more strongly opposed to the aim of introjection. When an individual enters and speaks among a community of others—articulating personal desire—autonomy and independence is the result. Introjection promotes the creation of a new voice, uttering new words, fulfilling unique desire. Incorporation, in contrast, reinforces the imagined ties to the past as well as dependency on it. "Like a commemorative monument," Abraham and Torok write, "the incorporated object betokens the place, the date, and the circumstances in which desires were banished from introjection: they stand like tombs in the life of the ego" (p. 114).

But importantly, the secret, or the tomb that Abraham and Torok so vividly describe constitutes a foreign body, an alien object. As bearers of the secret, children protect their connection to their traumatized parents and preserve their dependence upon them. To be sure, the secret is a toxic force yet it remains outside "the kernel of the self." It need not distort character; with appropriate conditions, when the secret comes to be revealed, it can be exorcised or eliminated from the inner world, allowing introjection or identification to resume its natural course.

There is an intriguing and suggestive body or research about the children of Holocaust survivors in Israel that bears on these hopeful possibilities. It appears that the descendants of Holocaust survivors in Israel have been more successful in establishing independent lives as compared with similar populations of Jews either in Europe, the United States, or Latin America (Solomon, p. 79). Israel, of course, is a nation whose existence in large measure had been defined as a response to the Holocaust, and innumerable public rites, sites and rituals document the inextricable connection between the nation and the trauma. It might be said that the nation has taken the traumatic secret and assertively sought to expose it. In this sense, it might be speculated, there is far less need for any individual to hold the secret privately, to internalize it, and to unconsciously fear the autonomy and independence that comes from no longer being the secret's bearer.

We are living in an age, throughout the world, of collective remembering, in which political agents and various organized publics are gingerly attempting to find a way of undoing the secrets, passed from one generation to the next, without irreparably opening old wounds. This is no easy process and, it is also true, considerable effort is also being expended to forget and to protect a traumatic past from full-scale exposure. From Chile and Argentina, to the Republic of South Africa and Rwanda, from Serbia, Croatia to Indonesia, these debates about remembering are now central to national politics. The debate in many of these nations has focused on the delicate political balance between remembering, and thereby creating a healthy distance between the present and the past, and forgetting, thereby not bringing to center stage the bitter divisions and experiences that divide the nation. Much of this debate has centered on the political costs incurred when the secret is uncovered, to "reopen the coffin." But there is also much to be said when, through public rites of remembering, mourning, and accountability, traumatic secrets are allowed to see the light of day. Conditions are established, it might be said, to recover childhoods for the children and to enable subsequent generations to claim the world as their own.

3. Traumatic symptoms surface as a result of an in-the-present interpersonal and/or societal failure. I have been suggesting that the repetition of cycles of destructiveness depend on the **intrusion** of memories of a traumatic past—either as mediated in subsequent generations through an over-identification (incorporation) with the generation that preceded them or, for the first generation, by remembering events or experiences that happened earlier in one's life. These incursions powerfully blur the present day from the past. As important as the past figures in all of this, trauma can only be overcome in the present. Freud, in discussing the importance of the transference relationship between patient and therapist for cure to occur, writes "one cannot overcome an enemy who is absent or not within range," and trauma "must be re-created not as an event in the past but as a present-day force...For when all is said and done, it is impossible to destroy anyone *in absentia* or *in effigie* (Freud 1961 [1912], p. 108)."

Intrusive memory, in short, signifies not so much the events of the past that predispose survivors to pass on their experiences repetitively but rather failures occurring in the present. Intrusive memories indicate an instantaneous loss of contact with the present, an experience in which a sense of one's own isolation in the world, the absence of a caring and protective environment and consequently the fear of annihilation have been revived and insufficiently contained. The defensive purposes such memory serves, i.e. never to re-experience the life-threatening experience again, are undermined, and traumatic repetition seems close at hand. The psychoanalyst Heinz Kohut (1984) describes intrusive memory as a reminder of the traumatic experience itself characterized by the absence of empathic contact between self and other. It becomes the principal task of the analyst (as a stand-in for the present-day larger environment), he argues, to provide for the patient, to demonstrate cognitively and affectively the capacity in-the-present to hold, contain and protect the patient's experience, including those that feel to be life-threatening, annihilative, infuriating. And as Winnicott emphasizes, the analyst must be able to sustain the destructive rage that becomes mobilized in the unfolding relationship; rage the patient holds as a contemporary tribute to the profound loss of self-centeredness that was traumatically stolen, and whose loss he or she continues to mourn and yearns to be restored (Winnicott, 1971).

The defensive quality of traumatic memories leads to a rethinking of the narrative account itself, the retelling of the story of what happened. Telling the story constitutes a cognitive acknowledgement of historical wrongs and an effort to demarcate present from past while understanding oneself in relation to that past. Yet one must also be alert to its likely use, person to person, as a form of defensive distancing from the affective or emotional experience and inner personal conflicts of oneself and of others who have been traumatized. Narratives of past wrongs tend to externalize conflict to the outside world and, paradoxically, protect defensive denial, preserve others as villains, and promote oneself as a victim. Moreover, they are easily passed on from one generation to the next, oftentimes, as I have described, generating unintended consequences for subsequent generations. For second and subsequent generations, the narrative can also be employed as a defense against any ambivalent feeling of pleasure that it was they and not I who suffered the trauma. As the case of Israel suggests, it is important for the public sphere or the state to continue to tell the story of from whence the new state came. When the nation acknowledge the past through ritual, rites and memorial sites, it repeatedly articulates for all the citizenry the difference between present and past. In doing so, individuals who comprise the nation are better provided the possibility of freeing themselves from "private" memory, and "to forget" traumatic personal histories.

Public remembering holds an important place in breaking the cycle of destructiveness that trauma so often produces. Yet its achievement requires too the development of new patterns of social interaction in each post-traumatic social institution. Prior categories—victim or perpetrators, white, black or coloured—can no longer be relied upon—even for benign goals—to organize interaction in the present. By working to erase these categorical distinctions from contemporary consciousness, the possibility exists for contemporary interactions not to serve as constant reminders, or triggers, of past traumatic exchanges. New patterns of inclusion and equality require implementation, different from the old racially-based criteria. Since exclusionary and hierarchical principles inevitably operate in all social institutions, it becomes critical to create criteria non-reminiscent of prior principles of inequality. Race and linguistic categories through which the society, in every respect, had been organized now requires wholesale replacement. The challenge for new beginnings, as I have described, is to have a public sphere as container and holder of memories of past wrongs. Every institution in civil society meanwhile resists the temptation to reinforce social distinctions from the past, either in unconscious and unreflective patterns of thought that reproduce the past in the present, or in their own affirmative efforts to "remember" by attempting to undo the past but still employing the same categories of social distinction. When that temptation is not resisted, and when the past injustices and inequities too powerfully effect the thinking of these institutions, the necessary oxygen is provided for those distinctions—either in action or thought—to reproduce themselves from generation to generation.

South Africa is in a unique place to lead the way in these new forms of remembering. As a new Republic, born from the remains of a not-so-distant apartheid, it is possible to build into the civic structure ways of acknowledging its traumatic past. With the TRC as its inspiration, various social institutions can continue to develop their own strategies and vehicles to promote mutual recognition, forgiveness and reconciliation. As this process develops over time, the onus becomes increasingly lifted from each individual to remember on behalf of his or her ancestors. Rather, the social collectivity itself bears that burden.

In sum, what is required is the birth of new social circles—new patterns of relatedness—in each institution, responsive to the on-going, present-day challenges faced in today's world. Post-apartheid South Africa, in short, is confronted not with racial differences, exacerbated over time by the domination of one race over others. Rather, South Africa today contends, in every sphere of social life, with the crisis of mistrust between the citizenry. Past history, of course, bred profound mistrust between members of various groups. But in this post-racialized, post-victimized society, the restoration of trust between human beings becomes the over-riding concern. Each institution needs to confront the problem as it is uniquely expressed within its confines and to implement strategies best designed to achieve greater trust between its members. The answer is new and stronger friendship circles that self-consciously bear little resemblance to apartheid South Africa.

In an important book *Talking to Strangers: Anxieties of Citizenship since Brown v. Board of Education*, Danielle Allen (1994), an American moral philosopher and political theorist, notes that, at least in most modern societies, one of the first lessons taught to children is "don't talk to strangers." Don't trust the world, in other words, because it is a dangerous place. Allen persuasively argues that one's natural sense of trust in others must be contravened through instruction. In the United States, the institution of slavery and racism, as determinative features of its history, intensified the distrust between "whites" and "blacks." For Allen, the constitutional abolition of racial segregation in 1954, unleashed intensifying anxieties of a new post-segregated society and profound national uncertainty about dealing with it. 20th Century South Africa's history, too, had been one of inculcating in its citizenry the unsafety of the world. The apartheid-era succeeded in creating in the real world what the South African elite had most vividly imagined, conjured and feared, namely, racially defined animosities. Now, the challenge is to reverse the causal chain: to treat one another in the world *as if* there is mutual trust. The presence of two distinct groups, "whites" and "blacks" reproduces into the present, in the US and South Africa, the "unsafety of the world". Allen insists that good citizenship in America requires the on-going work of political friendship: a sense of obligation and responsibility to fellow citizens, not unlike those we feel toward our personal friends. This includes an understanding of why we might **not** be trusted by others, just as we might try to imagine why a friend might be angry at us at any given time. Through processes promoting recognition, forgiveness and reconciliation, the "apartheid mind" may in time be overcome. Every contemporary social institution bears responsibility in moving toward that goal. Only then, as I have argued, might the dream of breaking the cycle of destructiveness more decidedly come to pass.

Acknowledgements

I would like to express my thanks to Pumla Gobodo-Madikizela, organizer of the conference Engaaging the Other: Breaking Intergenerational Cycles of Repetition, University of Free State, December 5-8, 2013. for which this chapter was originally prepared and delivered. Many thanks to the fellow participants in the Conference for their helpful comments and responses to the paper. Also, thanks to Matthew Nesvet and Alexander Stein for their insightful suggestions on previous drafts. Thanks, too, to René Valius for research assistance.

References

Abraham, N., & Torok, M. (1994). *The shell and the kernel*, Volume 1, University of Chicago Press.

Allen, D. (2004). *Talking to strangers; Anxieties of citizenship since Brown v. Board of Education*. Chicago: University of Chicago Press.

Auerhahan, N.C., & Laub, D. (1984). Annihilaton and restortation: Post-traumatic memory as pathway and obstacle to recovery. *International Review of Psycho-Analysis,* 11, 327-344.

Auerhahn, N., & Laub, D. (1998). Interngenerational Memory of the Holocaust. *International handbook of multigenerational legacies of trauma*. Danieli, Y. (Ed.). New York: Plenum.

Bar-On, D. (1991). *Legacy of silence: Encounters with children of the Third Reich.* Cambridge, MA.: Harvard University Press.

Bergmann, M., & Jucovy, M. (1982). *Generations of the Holocaust*. New York: Basic Books.

Caruth, C. (1991). Introduction. *American Imago,* 48, 1-3.

Coetzee, J. (1991). The mind of apartheid: Geoffrey Cronjé (1907-). *Social dynamics*, 17, 11-40.

Derrida, J. (2001). *On cosmopolitanism and forgiveness*. London: Routledge.

Freud, S. (1961) [1912] The Dynamics of Transference, *The Standard Edition of the Complete Psychological Works of Sigmund Freud XII*, 108.

Gobodo-Madikizela, P. (2004). A human being died that night: A South African story of forgiveness. Boston: Mariner.

Gordon, A. (2008). *Ghostly matters: Haunting and the sociological imagination.* Minneapolis: University of Minnesota Press.

Herzon, J. (1982). World beyond metaphor: thoughts on the transmission of trauma. In M. Bergmann, & M. Jucovy (Eds.), *Generations of the Holocaust*, New York: Basic Books.

Hook, D. (2008). Fantasmatic transactions: On the persistence of apartheid ideology. *Subjectivity*, 275-297.

Jansen, J. (2009). *Knowledge in the blood: Confronting race and the apartheid past.* Stanford, Calif.: Stanford University Press.

Kogan, I. (1995). *The cry of mute children: A psychoanalytic perspective of the second generation of the Holocaust*. London: Free Association Books.

Kohut, H., & Goldberg, A. (1984). *How does analysis cure?* Chicago: University of Chicago Press.

Loewald, H. (1960). On the Therapeutic Action of Psycho-Analysis. *The International Journal of Psychoanalysis*, (41), 16-33;

Prager, J. (2003). Lost Childhood, Lost Generations: The Intergenerational Transmission of Trauma, *Journal of Human Rights*, 2, 173-181

Prager, J. (2006). Jump-starting timeliness: Trauma, temporality and the redressive commuity, In *Time and memory*, J. Parker, M. Crawford, P. Harris (Eds.), Amsterdam: Koninklijke Brill, 229-2

Prager, J. (2008). "Healing from history: Psychoanalytic considerations on traumatic pasts and social repair. *European journal of social theory*, 11, 405-420

Pynoos, R. (Unpublished). The Transgenerational reprecussions of tramautic expectations.

Solomon, S. Transgernerational effects of the holocaust: The Israeli research Perspective, In The International handbook of multigenerational legacies of trauma, Y. Danieli (ed.), 69-84

Stolorow, R. (2003). Trauma and temporality. *Psychoanalytic psychology*, 20, 158-161.

Winnicott, D. (1971). Playing and reality (pp. 86-94). New York: Basic Books.

Chapter 2
Rethinking Remorse: The Problem of the Banality of Full Disclosure in Testimonies from South Africa

Juliet Brough Rogers

University of Melbourne

Introduction

A remorse that does not disclose the enjoyments, affiliations and excitements of the perpetrator in the execution of violence may be less helpful to victims. When the perpetrator denies or does not acknowledge their own enjoyments in the scene of violence, when a perpetrator only tells the clinical facts, this may be frustrating or even debilitating for the victim in assisting their re-integration into reality in the world. When the perpetrator tells only the facts then the affective witness no longer exists, where the perpetrator does not display who s/he was in the past, that is, where the perpetrator's story reflects very little of the victim's own experience, the re-externalising capacity **for** witnessing is diminished and the agonizing between fantasy and reality for the victim may insist. In this chapter I apply a psychoanalytic discussion of the Amnesty Hearings in the South African Truth and Reconciliation Commission of Jeffrey Benzien and Eric Taylor to consider whether a display of the enjoyments of the perpetrators may be an important part of full disclosure for the victims and may be considered a form of remorse, albeit an ugly one.

The remorse of the perpetrator can be a gift to the victim of trauma, but not always. And the quality of that gift is not as obvious as we might think. As a gesture—or many gestures—remorse can be an acknowledgement of the reality of what happened, as the reality of the death, destruction, humiliation and agonies that the victims endured. The remorse of the perpetrator in this form is an opportunity to legitimate the story of reality, for the trauma victim and for those left behind. However, while remorse is commonly thought of as an emotional experience for the perpetrator who feels sorrow, guilt or responsibility, I suggest here that remorse may consist of all these feelings, but that the remorseful gesture can be so much more, and, I tentatively suggest that for the purposes of social and psychological healing, it should be so much more. Gestures of remorse, to function as a legitimation of the stories of victims, need to entail a witnessing function for the victims that may exceed or even contradict the feelings usually attached to ideas of remorse. In this sense the gestures and the perpetrators may appear less compassionate, less gentle and less desirable than gestures that are traditionally or standardly thought of as remorseful. Gestures of remorse can go further than simple apologies—no matter how heartfelt—and can entail an act of witnessing that holds nothing back of the perpetrator, as a way of holding forth the story of trauma for the victim. A story that, by its very nature as traumatic, is difficult to tell.

In a condition of trauma the symbols used to communicate, the symbols which, when arranged into language, tell the story of history, experience and identity, disintegrate. When this occurs the victim can lose the capacity to witness for themselves. The victims then have no thing to tell, no symbol to exchange with another, no story which can be understood in the world outside themselves. To heal from trauma, this story needs to be—as Dori Laub describes—'re-externalised' (Laub, 1992, p. 69). That is it needs to be told, to be understood, to be accepted into the reality of the day and to bring the victim into that reality so they can live in the present rather than the past. Remorse, as a form of telling all of what the perpetrator did to the victim- to her friends, family and home—can precisely speak to the problem of the acceptance of the victim's story into reality. This is because a full disclosure from perpetrators who were there, as a full disclosure of the violence committed—in all its enjoyments, excitements and even in its banalities—can hold the pieces of the story of what happened out to the world and thus reinforce the victim's story as reality.

The demands of the South African Truth and Reconciliation Commission—in its efforts to gain the 'truth' of what happened through the granting of amnesty only on the condition of perpetrators offering a full disclosure of the violence they committed—were an obvious effort to enable the telling of stories. This form of story-telling is one form of witnessing the violence for victims. But the 'full disclosure' of facts, of participants—even of one's own participation—is not a full disclosure in a psychoanalytic sense of narrative. A full disclosure, as the recounting of facts, is unlikely to provide the victims with the witnessing function required to know or to hold a story of trauma as reality. A full disclosure of facts is not a full disclosure of the fantasies, identifications and excitements that often accompany the practices of violence. That is, facts do not tell the whole story, and are thus an impoverished form of witnessing. Fact telling, without an acknowledgement of what I am calling the "enjoyments" of the perpetrator—as the awful, agonizing and sometimes exciting feelings that Jacques Lacan associates with an experience he calls 'jouissance' (2007, pp. 14-15)—is unlikely to assist the victim feeling like there was a witness to the event who can offer their experience of the perpetrator's violence as a story to the world. Fact telling, as a mode of narrating violence is thus unlikely to provide a witness who can bring the reality of the violence into the reality of the day.

In this paper I'll consider one aspect of remorse—that of narrating the perpetrator's enjoyments in the scene of violence—as a narrative that may be helpful in providing a witnessing, as a form of full disclosure, for the survivors of legally sanctioned (if not actively encouraged) violence. I am not suggesting that all perpetrators enjoy violence in the sense that Lacan considers enjoyment, nor do I suggest that the acknowledgement of enjoyment is the only quality required of a perpetrator to either enact what is often called 'genuine remorse' or 'sincere remorse'. What I suggest is that when perpetrators do experience such an enjoyment—as an enjoyment of the act, the effects, even an enjoyment if the legal sanction and the accompanying accolades—that the experience of this enjoyment, no matter how socially or legally distasteful, is an important offer from a perpetrator as one of the ugliest elements of their act. This acknowledgment of enjoyment is unlikely to endear a perpetrator to a judge or jury, indeed, it is very unlikely to secure a lighter prison sentence and may even contribute to a verdict as "guilty" (see Gobodo-Madikizela, 2002, and Proeve & Tudor, 2010, pp. 78-81, 95-96, 124). Even if it does not influence the legal outcome, it would not be a disclosure which would gain the perpetrator what we have come to call 'forgiveness' or any social capital in a country, like South Africa, where the dominant narrative is of the wrongness of the violences committed under the Apartheid regime. However, it is this very act of showing the ugliness of their actions, I suggest, that can be understood to perform a kind of, what we might call selflessness, that further indicates a form of 'genuine remorse'. A form of remorse that risks a great deal and retains little for the perpetrator's self; but, a remorse that may offer a substance beyond measure for the victim.

I focus in this chapter on two well known cases of the complexities of 'full disclosure' in post-apartheid South Africa. That of the often discussed performance of Jeffrey Benzien at his Amnesty Hearing in Cape Town in 1997, including his reenactment of torture, in many forms, and the responses of his victims at the Hearing and afterwards—particularly that of Ashley Forbes, Gary Kruser, Peter Jacobs and Tony Yengeni. I then consider the case of Eric Taylor—one of the perpetrators in the killing of the men known as the 'Cradock 4'. I examine the subtext and seeming dissatisfactions that emerged in this case, documented in both printed media and in the film Long

Night's Journey into Day (Hoffman & Reid, 2000). There is much, I believe, that the film and the interviews—beyond the official Hearings in these cases—display that was certainly distasteful, but also very helpful in understanding what gestures of remorse may mean beyond the calls for either full disclosure or evidence of sincerity.

Part I—The Importance of Acknowledgment

Before we consider these scenes a distinction needs to be made between victims who were in the scene of violence and those who were not, but were and are nevertheless left behind when a family member or friend is killed. Both, I understand, as victims of the violence, but there is likely to be a difference in their relations with the perpetrators, and, consequently, a difference in what they require from the perpetrators as gestures of remorse. Often victims who were not in the scene of violence require, first and foremost, an acknowledgement of the event's occurrence as a wrong. In examples of apology such as that practiced by Eugene de Kock—as discussed by Pumla Gobodo Madikizela in the context of post-Apartheid South Africa—the function of acknowledgement is possible and often of great solace to survivors. In one of Gobodo-Madikizela's accounts of De Kock's 'remorse' he approached the mothers of two men he had killed and apologized to them. For these women that gesture appears to have forcefully legitimated their reality of loss. Similarly, although without the sentiment, the showing of the police video made of the aftermath of the killing of the Gugulethu Seven in the Truth and Reconciliation Commissions in South Africa offered, at least in one Truth Commissioner's account, a witnessing function for the mothers of those killed. As Commissioner Mary Burton describes, 'they felt so much better' because they knew 'so much more' of what happened. In the context of Northern Ireland during The Troubles the well documented acknowledgment offered to Alan McBride for the wrongness of the killing of his wife in the Shankill Road bombing in 1993 might be similarly understood as a gesture of acknowledgement, but largely as an acknowledgment of wrong and a legitimation of the feelings of pain and loss (Rowan, 2009). This is an acknowledgement, in Martha Minow's terms, of '[the victims'] humanity and the reaffirmation of the utter wrongness of its violation.' (1998, p. 146). These gestures may be crucial as a beginning point, they may also, in Gobodo-Madikizela's account, offer the victims and the perpetrators an avenue for a return to humanity. However, they differ in my discussion of remorse here in that they are not a witnessing function in the ways I highlight in this chapter, and, I believe, are limited in what they can provide victims of trauma beyond a crucial feeling of knowing that they were wronged and that this is also known by others. Thus, while these forms of acknowledgment are undoubtably crucial to healing—as part of the restoration of one's reality into the reality of the day—they are not in conflict with, but sit alongside other possible gestures of remorse, such as the one's I am considering.

In terms of the capacity to provide a witnessing function, there is also a distinction to be made between institutional perpetrators who did not intimately participate in the violence—which is not to say they do/did not benefit from it in ways that further legitimate their lives—including through the acquisition of financial, political and social resources. Acknowledgement of wrong from institutional perpetrators brings a form of moral reality to the event, often for the victim's left behind, and allows for what might be a catharsis that determines the platform for reality in which one was victim and one was perpetrator. This form of acknowledgment also determines that the one(s) left behind were subject to an institutional wrong that need be addressed by the institutions in the present—but isn't always. Arguably, gestures of apology such as that practiced in Australia in 2008 by then Prime Minister Kevin Rudd toward the Indigenous people known as the 'Stolen Generations', a similar apology in 2008 by Prime Minister Stephen Harper in Canada to the First Nations' Peoples for the Indian Residential Schools programs, and perhaps even Former British Prime Minister David Cameron's apology in 2010 to survivors of the 1972 'Bloody Sunday' killings in Northern Ireland, offered an important acknowledgement of reality and the determination of "rightness" and "wrongness" for those who were victims of the practices of these regimes. The experience of violence actioned by perpetrators who were intimately involved in scenes of violence is qualitatively different from that of those who benefited after the fact (and may be still benefiting) and requires a different form of acknowledgment as a different form of remorse. In short, "sorry" and even acknowledgment of wrong may be important in some contexts, but sometimes what is required is confrontation, with the perpetrator, with the full account of the enjoyments that accompanied the act of perpetration. This requirement, I believe, is part of what occurred in the Amnesty Hearing of Jeffrey Benzien in South Africa.

Part II—An Ugly Event

In the now well documented event of the assessment of the application for amnesty of Security Branch Police Operative Jeffrey Benzien during the hearings of the Truth and Reconciliation Commission in South Africa, we see the importance of perpetrator as witness, and also the importance of a particular type of witness; an unpleasant and uncertain witness offering a very unpalatable account of his brutal and ugly work. When Benzien is confronted by four former victims of his torture techniques—Ashley Forbes, Tony Yengeni, Gary Kruser and Peter Jacobs—about what he did to them, and the question of who he is, we see the very specfic demand for a full witness as a full accounting of perpetration and its enjoyments. As Wüstenberg states of an understanding of the meeting of Benzien and his victims 'in the case of Benzien, the personal and inter-personal dimensions of reconciliation hang together; Ashley Forbes needs the recollections of Benzien in order to get more clarity on his own story...' (2009, p. 353). This desire for clarity, as a desire for Benzien as witness, can be heard in Forbes moving account of his disappointment after the Hearing. As Forbes says of his experience of hearing Benzein's account at the Hearing:

> it was also a bit difficult because for numerous reasons he couldn't remember the details. He couldn't remember what had happened. And for us that was a bit important to just, [sic] for him to be able to say that these are the kind of things that we did to people, even if he doesn't remember the detail, but he could have explained the kind of process that we went through, a whole systematic process where you're physically, psychologically, tortured for a long period. And up to the kind of period for three months that I tried to commit suicide...

Forbes commentary on what was a journey, initially from pity for Benzien in his isolation, to seemingly a feeling of frustration at his lack of capacity to be a witness for the victims, indicates powerfully the importance of what Benzien could have offered; a witness as not only someone who can acknowledge what was done, but who can say that **what** Forbes experienced did actually happen. Even though Forbes was there, even though it was done to him, Forbes requires a witness beyond himself. This is why he wants the filling out of 'the kind of things that [they] did to people' and the 'whole systematic process'. His own story is not enough and even his own experience is not enough—he wants Benzien's account because it was '[Benzien who] could have explained the kind of process.' Similarly, one of Benzien's other victims—Gary Kruser—may have found it, in the words of Antjie Krog, 'too much for flesh and feeling: that [his] experience [of torture], which has nearly destroyed his life, made not the slightest imprint on

Benzien's memory' (1998, pp. 94-96). The reality of the experience for the victim needs to be thought to make a mark in reality, and this is sometimes exemplified in the mark it makes on the perpetrator. What Benzien's account suggests is that what he did made no mark on him or perhaps in him, unlike the marks it seems to have left on (physically) and in (psychologically) his victims.

In one sense the particular demands of Benzien's victims seem counter intuitive. Of course Forbes and Kruser know what was done to them. They were there. But such is the nature of trauma that it introduces a doubt about reality, and thus often requires a further witness. Therefore it is Benzein's recounting of the 'whole systematic process', or of the arrest and 'hanging up' of Kruser, that can offer them a narrative, both political and psychological, to fill out the scene for those in the room, and indeed for themselves. Benzien was there too, and Benzien was not tortured or arguably traumatised beyond recollection. Benzien, for them, should be able to remember, to recount. Benzien could meet their partial, fragmented, narratives. Narratives that are so rife with the trauma that torture can inflict. Benzien could offer a sanction to their reality—a reality that is always so tentatively maintained for victims of trauma.

The Reality of Trauma

Victims of trauma struggle to hold onto their own stories, which are fraught with gaps and confusions. These effects are partially caused by their own efforts to hold onto alternative realities and to fix their minds onto objects that are secure—that are reality—for them at that time. This can often render them locked in what we might think of as an exclusive reality, but one which is disabling to their capacity to live in the reality with others. Sometimes for healing to happen their exclusive reality needs to cohere with a public reality, or in Kruser's terms, the reality of their trauma needs to make an 'imprint' on others outside themselves. As Dori Laub says of the healing from trauma:

> a therapeutic process …of re-externalising the event—has to be set in motion. This…can occur and take effect only when one can articulate and transmit the story, literally transfer it to another outside oneself and then take it back again, inside. Telling thus entails a reassertion of **the hegemony of reality** and a re-externalization of the evil that affected and contaminated the trauma victim. (1992 p. 69, my emphasis).

This therapeutic process of re-externalisation does not necessarily need to be with a therapist, it may be through an engagement with what Douglas has called 'narrative jurisprudence' (2011, p. 112), or through what Hackett and Rolston discuss as 'storytelling' (2009, p. 355), as a means to have the story, in Laub's terms reasserted as the hegemony of reality. Benzien may have been able to offer the meeting of Forbes' and Kruser's exclusive realities with his own, if only it had made 'the slightest imprint' or if he had been prepared to share that imprint. But Benzien, for Forbes and for Kruser, could not, or would not, offer the re-externalising of the event, even in his efforts toward 'full disclosure'. I suggest, however, that the much recounted brutality of what Benzein did to, and with, Tony Yengeni at this hearing, may have gone further toward a re-externalisation of the scene of violence—at least as Yengeni may have experienced it—than is often discussed of this scene.

For Antjie Krog this particular meeting of victim and perpetrator 'seizes at the heart of truth and reconciliation—the victim face to face with the perpetrator—and tears it out into the light.' (1998, p. 93). It is this bringing into light the heart of reconciliation that we can understand also as an assertion of the hegemony of reality. Not quite a 'reassertion', as Laub would have it, because the (political and legal) hegemony of Apartheid rule is not the hegemony of South Africa post Apartheid. However, the process of tearing-out-hearts and bringing them to light are precisely what bringing trauma to the reality of the present requires. And sometimes it is brutal. The telling of what happened to Benzien's victims, what he did to them and the details of that damage, if we take Laub's point, could have enabled a transition from the reality of the past in which it was performed to the reality of the day. This means explaining it in all its processes and conditions, in precisely the reality of Apartheid rule which sanctioned and encouraged the torture of Yengeni, Kruser, Forbes, Jacobs and so many more. This reality is what the victims need to have known by others and not, I suggest, clouded in a post Apartheid hegemony that (at least socially) requires Benzien to be apologetic for his actions; to not be the torturer he was.

The victims, in order to have their experience in reality, may require Benzien to be the perpetrator he was—the brutal, ugly and violent perpetrator that enacted the sanctioned violence of the state upon them in its, as Forbes suggests, 'whole systemic process'. They may require him to be the apparatus of the Apartheid regime as both an indication of what they experienced at the hands of the man and at the hands of the state. These are not mutually exclusive under any oppressive regime which employs law's sanction to justify—and law's zealots to enact—its practices. And we can see Forbes' desire to have the 'whole systemic process' brought into light, as part of both the political and personal narrative that Benzien can supply. In supplying this narrative Forbes perceives that it will show why it was that he and they behaved in the victimised manner that they did; why they broke, why they betrayed, why they—and in this example, he—tried to commit suicide.

For Forbes the need for Benzien to be the torturer sanctioned by the Apartheid state, is particularly evident when he wants to counter Benzien's narrative of their 'friendship', with the knowledge that he (Forbes) tried to kill himself during his incarceration. Forbes' suicidal reality seems, on the surface, incongruous with Benzien's description of their: 'not friends as such', but having a 'special relationship' characterized by Forbes' being allowed to go 'playing in the snow along the N1' and eating 'Kentucky Fried Chicken' (TRC, 1997). Torture makes no sense in the context of Kentucky Fried Chicken and 'playing in the snow'. But Forbes remains dissatisfied and, while the factual narratives coincide, Forbes' and Benzien's emotional narratives offer little by way of making sense of what Forbes experienced at the hands of Benzien. It is Yengeni, however, who makes sense of Forbes' reality at the same time as he exhibits his own, with the successful request that 'Benzien demonstrate the wet bag method' (Krog, 1998, p. 93). And it is this demonstration which then offers all Benzien's victims the truth of the torturer from the past as an indication of the reality of the past.

The presentation of the reality of what Forbes, Yengeni and many others experienced at the hands of Benzien was painfully reenacted in two ways in the Benzien Hearing. Firstly when, as du Bois-Pedain describes the events after Benzien agrees to perform the reenactment: 'A volunteer then lies down on his stomach, and Benzien sits on the small of his back. A cushion stands in as the wet bag....' (2007, p. 227). Benzien becomes the torturer again and reenacts the relation, as Krog suggests, 'where he has the power and they the fragility.' (1998, p. 95). Both these enactments return the victims, the audience and the event itself back to the realities of the past. The presentation of the wet bag method is hard to watch and undoubtably awful to experience for Yengeni, the volunteer on the floor at the Hearing, and seemingly for Benzienwho begins to cry while still sitting on the back of the volunteer). The physicality of this scene, its visceral tropes and its disturbance has been much commented on and much condemned. However, I suggest that the scene and the practice of Benzien serves as an important form of disclosure for perpetrators as the perpetrators they were.

The importance of the reenactment is not only as a mode of factual disclosure, or even as gratuitous spectacle to titillate some of the audiences to the Commission, but as an important return for Benzien and Yengeni in to the reality of the past while enabling a reinscription of that past in the hegemony of the day. The same can be said of Benzien's general behavior toward the torture victims who confront him. As Krog says:

> A torturer's success depends on his intimate knowledge of the human psyche. Benzien is connoisseur. Within the first few minutes he manages to manipulate most of his victims back into the role of their previous relationship—where he has the power and they the fragility (1998, p. 95).

This all takes place in the sanctioning eyes of the Commission, that is, this is also a legal scene; one sanctioned in the reality of the (post apartheid) day. To note this is not to suggest, however, that the Commission makes the torture possible—in the most cruel sense of this criticism—but that the Commission, its reality as a legal presence, makes sense of the reenactment. This is because Benzien reenacts the hegemony of the previous regime through his 'techniques' and in doing so goes part way to showing who and what he was, with all the (legal) sanctions. Indeed it is in this moment that we begin to see the 'whole systemic process' at work in how it may have worked on his victims. Benzien as torturer in the Hearing is a form of real flashback to the previous experience for the victims and to the previous regime's system of sanctions and prohibitions. A flashback, however, that is no longer only in the mind of the victims but is now in the mind of audience, the Commission, the public. This is a flashback that has become reexternalised as reality.

The flashback effect of the torture and the torturer, which brings the reality of the past into the reality of the day, is fraught with the ordinary (and important) ambivalences that need be brought to any scenes of violence reenacted in the present. We should ask the questions as **to** what effect this has on the victims? On other victims in the room? Or on the audience as now submitted to such awful knowledge? However, perhaps contentiously, I want to suggest that this reenactment—in all its ugliness—may not have been as brutal and violent in the present as it seems. Contrary to Krog I want to suggest that it may not have been entirely a 'manipulation' without any form of agency on behalf of the victims. To say the victims—Forbes or Yengeni particularly—were not pressing Benzien to show what he did to them, even beyond the 'wet bag' reenactment but right into his 'manipulation', as Krog describes it, or his 'torture' as Henry describes it, in the courtroom is, I suggest, a misreading. Benzien's behavior does not seem unwelcome to the victims, indeed they wish he told more (and perhaps wish he showed more). Even Krog follows her interpretation (assessed as a one-sided power dynamic) with her description of Yengeni's reaction to Benzien's recounting of his betrayal of other comrades under torture as him 'sitting there—as if begging this man to say it all, as if betrayal or cowardice can only make sense to him in the presence of this man' (1998.p. 94, my emphasis). And making sense is the point here. Yengeni makes sense to himself, to this world, to the reality of the day only when the reality of the past is fully recounted in all its sanctions and enjoyments.

I want to be careful not to suggest that this form of sense making is actively desired by the victims. It may be extremely painful and, in the case of Benzien's recounting of Yengeni's betrayal, as Krog says 'For this moment, Yengeni has to pay dearly' (1998.p. 94). Yengeni's political profile as an activist, a courageous freedom fighter who can now hold a leadership position, is at stake. However, it is the excess of this payment, the 'aneconomics' of the moment, in the sense that Derrida might suggest (1992, p. 7) that offers more than perhaps Benzien intended or what Yengeni asked, but nevertheless offers an excess that may be useful or helpful to the victims. Specifically, Yengeni pays dearly but receives an excess of what he seems to desire—to know "what kind of man [Benzien is]?". This is an excess embodied in the spectacle in which Benzien offers himself as torturer and shows the brutality of his methods and his lack of concern for the 'political profile' of Yengeni (a lack of concern that compliments his obvious lack of regard for Yengeni's life in the past). It is this lack in Benzien that exceeds the payment. Yengeni pays, but what is not demanded in the exchange is what Yengeni secures: the gift of a return to reality in which Benzien is shown to be the brutal figure that he was, and Yengeni: a torture victim who was at the mercy of this man who was obviously capable—because now we all see it—of being so brutal, and of disregarding the 'kind of man' that Yengeni was.

In the light of the sense-making needs of victims in the scenes of violence, we can read the question from Yengeni to Benzien 'what kind of man are you?' as not simply, as du Bois-Pedain suggests, a 'clear implication' in respect to the unveiling of a 'personal inclination towards violence and abuse' (2007, p. 227), or in Christodoulidis' frame of this Hearing as an indication of the 'ethics' of communication (2000, p. 181-2). The question may be a plea for the man who tortured him to come forward, for the kind of man he was to be presented, indeed, it is only after this question from Yengeni is answered—in a manner that is more apologetic than explanatory—that Yengeni then demands the demonstration of torture. And then we all see what kind of man Benzien was. Although, now the audience may not be sure if this is, in fact, who he (still) is. This is perhaps where the audience's ambivalence about Benzien, now, can meet Yengeni's own ambivalence. Because, for Yengeni, an apology is not enough.

What we know of Yengeni is that he is certainly ambivalent about Benzien's remorse in its appearance as a form of apology. Yengeni asks his question and then asks for the demonstration of torture even after Benzien has apologized 'to any person or persons to whom [he] has harmed' (TRC, 1997). Benzien as an apologetic man may not be unhelpful as a figure of acknowledgment of wrong, but, if he only performed this role—no matter how sincere—I suggest he would be of little use to Yengeni, and perhaps to his other victims. An apology is no flashback. An apology shows little, if anything, of the scene to the audience. It shows nothing of what was done to Forbes, Yengeni, Jacob, Kruser and others such as Ashley Kriel, who died being tortured by Benzien. This is not to say that the willingness to come forward and say what perpetrators did as an account of fact, is of no use. The importance of information about where bodies are located is another question, and the role of acknowledgment of wrong also has its value—as I discussed above—and can compliment the containing function of the TRC. A function that enables reenactments such as these to be done in the safety of a new hegemonic inscription. One where the legal sanction of torture reenactments may help with offering the context of the torture, while holding it in a forum of transition. That is, while holding it in a context that no longer sanctions anything more than a reenactment in the interests of full disclosure. However, the role of reenactment, the role of perpetrators being something of what they were, is what may be required to enable a full witnessing, as a full disclosure, of what happened in the intimacies of the scene of violence. Benzien, as torturer, as manipulator, as 'connoisseur' of other people's psyches, may be what is required in this Hearing if he is to be a witness, one who can tell something of the 'whole systemic process', for the victims.

Part III – When Fantasy becomes Reality

To extrapolate on the emphasis I place above—on the legal sanction of the Hearing and the demonstration—and the crucial role of (legally sanctioned) perpetrators as witness, I'll examine now the relation between the perpetrator in intimate scenes of violence and the subject (understood through psychoanalysis) who gains its facilities and coordinates for making sense, through a relation between self and Other. This is not any other, but, for Jacques Lacan it is a (big O) Other—as a location inhabited by people, doctrine and decision-makers that exist, for the particular subject, in a location in which it is perceived that 'knowledge'—as the universal and often moral truth—is held and dispensed (Lacan, 2007, pp. 14-17). That is, the Other is not a person, but a location which may be inhabited and is imagined by subjects to hold the capacity to say what is right and wrong, or, in the terms I am discussing, of authoring reality. Of specific concern in instances of intimate violence—this location may be readily and violently inhabited by perpetrators sanctioned by the law of the day.

In situations of violence where torture, detention, death and destruction are enacted at the hands of perpetrators sanctioned by law then the figure of judgment—the figure that haunts the reality of infants and children—emerges from the world of fantasy and is embodied in the living. This is not usually the case. In an ordinary neurotic state the figure in the place of the Other, in psychoanalytic terms, is a fantastical figure because in such a location they neither wield real judgment, nor absolutely know what is good or bad. Beyond the fragile parameters of childhood the ordinary neurotic subject becomes more ambivalent about the force and fundamentalisms of the Other. For the subject not under duress or not in a situation of violence, they only imagine that this knowing and authoritative power is located in someone, and even then they are dubious and tentative about the possibility that anyone, any doctrine, any law or any regime, could be all-knowing. But in intimate and immediate events of violence—perhaps particularly in instances of torture—when perpetrators become able to decide on life or death, torture or release, pain or freedom—then the omniscient judge of our childhood fantasies becomes real. That is, when life and death are truly held in the hands of a perpetrator—such as Benzien—then that perpetrator is often elevated to the position of the Other in a mode that most resembles a psychoanalytic configuration of psychosis (Lacan, 1993). It is then that confusions about reality emerge for the victim of trauma. Indeed, this, we might say, is precisely what trauma is. The characteristic of scenes of violence which produce trauma is that fantasy becomes reality; reality becomes fantasy. What is believed and believable is confused. Simply put, the boundary between one's sense of reality and an external reality becomes uncertain. This confusion is precisely because the figure of judgment of which authored what is considered 'reality'—the figure which previously jostled for place between the parent, the law and self—is externalized and fixed in situations of violence into an all deciding, all powerful perpetrator. In a psychoanalytic sense we can say that—particularly in intimate scenes of violence such as torture—the castrating presence of the paternal figure for the child, who usually exists in the realm of fantasy, becomes not imagined, but real. This is further exacerbated when the perpetrator in scenes of violence is sanctioned by the law of the day, and thus enables the imaginary figure of the omniscient judge of fantasy to be brought into the realm of reality as persecutor and as judge, jury, and as executioner.

The implication of the relocation of fantasy into reality is (at a minimum) twofold. Firstly, it positions the perpetrator as the judge and thus disables, or damages what we might call one's own internal witness. The second effect is that of the relocation of the omniscient judge into the realm of reality. This is what produces a broader confusion as to what is fantasy and what is reality. This relocation dislodges the necessary split between those two registers. Just as what was fantasy becomes reality, reality itself can become fantasy beyond simply the re-positioning of the perpetrator. Having experienced the trauma of the loss of identity at the hands of the now real judge who was supposed to remain a fantasy, one becomes uncertain as to the reality of an event or experience, or we could say that one becomes uncertain of representation itself, in all its necessary definitions, categories and quantifications. As Laub and Lee suggest of the traumatic event:

> [it] produce[s] feelings of absence and of rupture, a loss of representation, an inability to grasp and remember the trauma, and a loss of coherence. Libidinal binding to associative links, to meaning, and to words, as well as to the internal object and to oneself, becomes at least temporarily suspended. There is a profound sense that structure and representation—the ability to tell one's story to oneself or to another—are missing from the survivor's experience. (2003, p. 144).

The combined effect of the omniscience of the perpetrator in the scene of violence becoming a very real judge, while the victim's associative links and experiences are suspended, is that the perpetrator becomes a, if not *the*, crucial witness to the event.

The example of the Hearing of Jeffrey Benzien's application for amnesty, the response of his victims, and Benzien's own accounts, shows us something of firstly the effects of intimate violence, and how what should always remain in the realm of imagination—the absolute judgment of the Other—becomes a real judgment embodied in the figure of the perpetrator. But it also shows us the importance of the perpetrator performing as a witness for the victim. I do not suggest that Benzien was a perfect witness, however. Nor, obviously, that he was a generous or forgivable one. His actions may even have done other forms of harm to the process of 'reconciliation'. But Benzien's actions were not only for the audience or the nation. And we can see in the interactions with him—through the words of Forbes and Yengeni—the desire for a witness, and a few fleeting moments of what might be called relief, for his victims. Benzien's apologies were not, I suggest, particularly valuable for the victims. The form of his remorse might be understood as embodied in the demonstrations of his actions and in his own—arguably unintended—capacity to show himself as a brutal man, who still seemed to be the man he was, the manipulator, the torturer. With this understanding we can allocate him the status of some form of useful witness for the victims.

Part IV – An Ambivalent Remorse

The perpetrator who performs as witness for the victims, in the sense of Benzien's performance, however, is not easy to find. This is because examples of accounts of the perpetrators' visceral realities in the moment of violence are not well told, they are painful to hear, they are likely to be distressing for their victims and for the families of their victims. Short of the fictional accounts and some helpful illustrations from the enjoyments of Dr Miranda in Ariel Dorfman's play Death and Maiden there is little public account of the real enjoyments of perpetrators. Perpetrators tend to protect the judges of the day from their previous personae, (personae which victims are intimately familiar with, of course). Perpetrators before the courts tend to behave toward the judge as they did before the law that sanctioned their violence, as obedient contrite subjects, displaying the personalities their superiors' desire. We can see this identification played out in the sentiment of Nazi War Criminals such as Hans Frank, who, as Lacan commented 'felt remorse stir his soul at the dignified appearance of his judges, especially that of the English judge who he said was "so elegant".' (2006, p. 110). Only when the new judge is in place, for some perpetrators, do we then see their tendency for contrition as another form of obedience. But this very obedience to the new regime—if it holds no residue of the perpetrator's violent enjoyments of the past—can disable their capacity as an effective witness for the victim.

In another case before the TRC in South Africa we can see the problems of a form of remorse that looks to a sanction from the new judge rather than indicating the enjoyments of the sanction of the old judge. In the example of the Hearing on the killing of Mathew Goniwe, Fort Calata, Sparrow Mkhonto and Sicelo Mhlauli—the men known as the 'Cradock 4'—one perpetrator, Eric Taylor, applies for amnesty because, as he states, he believes his actions were 'wrong' (Hoffman, 2000). The story of Taylor's application for amnesty and his rationale are helpfully illuminated in the documentary Long Night's Journey into Day where Taylor justifies a good deal of his contrition over the deeds based on an affiliation with God. He saw himself as enacting God's work in the killing—as he says in the film 'One of the elements of communism is atheism. That is the outstanding point as far as I'm concerned that actually justified the kind of work we were doing' (Hoffman, 2000).

And, the recognition of the unchristianness of his actions, is also, at least in part, what brings him to apply for amnesty. Taylor's Christian-ness informs him and, in a characteristically Christian sentiment, he wants forgiveness from the wives of the men he killed, specifically, from Nomonde Calata and Nyameka Goniwe. The meeting that took place between the women and Taylor, is described by one reporter in this way:

> It seemed to the widows that Taylor envisioned a brief and perfunctory encounter. He seemed to want to apologize, receive absolution, and leave.

> "He was expecting us to say, 'Oh, you are forgiven,' " said Nomonde Calata, Fort's widow. "We made him tell us what happened that day. We didn't come all the way from Cradock just to see his face.'"

> But they all went away unsatisfied.

> The families were unmoved. The meeting lasted five hours, but even after all that time they thought Taylor was holding back, masking the truth. When they parted, the white man and the black women were in tears, but for different reasons. (Maykuth, 1998)

As Nyamaka Goniwe says in Long Night's Journey into Day: 'We need an inside person, we need a witness' and, for her, despite Taylor's supposed efforts toward full disclosure, he is not a witness. And as she says of his testimony 'I can't make peace with that'. (Hoffman, 2000)

Why, we can speculate, can't Nyamaka Goniwe make peace either with Eric Taylor, his actions or his testimony at the hearing of his amnesty application? Of course, the matter of forgiveness and of peace is a profoundly personal one, and Nyamaka Goniwe may have moments of peace beyond the making of the film, or she may have never known peace. We do not know. I do not know. What we can say is that at the time of the hearing the woman who wanted an inside person, a witness, did not find one in Eric Taylor. A man who was there, a man who described what he did, a man who—by the filmmaker's standards—'is tormented by his violent involvement in upholding the apartheid system', a system he believes 'was wrong' (Hoffman, 2000).

If he is tormented about his actions and believes the system wrong, then what is it, we can ask, that Taylor cannot say or do which might give Nyamaka Goniwe peace? The filmmakers of Long Night's Journey into Day may have, perhaps unintentionally, given some insight into what may be of use for Mrs Goniwe. In one interview in the film we get a sense of Taylor's actions at the time of the killing that he does not disclose in the Hearing. Taylor states to the filmmakers that his journey toward admitting his actions to the TRC and applying for amnesty began with his viewing of the film *Mississippi Burning* (Parker, 1988). In this film he saw policemen murder four men in a car—not dissimilarly to the murder of the Cradock 4—and he recognizes himself in this gesture. He identifies with the men and their actions in *Mississippi Burning*. As Taylor discusses, an identification with the killers in the film was his first awakening to the problem of his actions. Taylor's identification with the police in *Mississippi Burning* divulges more than he may care to admit, however. In the film the scene of killing is an excited, frenzied event where the police evidently enjoy the killing. His interview is interspersed with scenes of the film which helpfully illustrate what Taylor does not say. After Taylor notes his identification with the film we are shown by Hoffman the first moment of the shooting in *Mississippi Burning*. It is a nighttime scene and is almost all black, but we hear a gun shot and then a very enthusiastic 'whoah hoh, we're in it now boys' from the policeman, and then some laughing. This, it seems, is how Taylor saw himself, but it is not how he represents himself or his actions in his Amnesty Hearing. In the Hearing he very clinically depicts his assault and burning of the bodies in these words:

> **I hit Mr Calata from behind with this heavy object, approximately where the head joins the neck. He fell to the ground. I cut the petrol pipe from the Honda to pour over Mr Goniwe's and Mr Calata's bodies, and I set both these bodies alight**.

While this may go some way toward a 'full disclosure' as a criteria for amnesty, it does little to disclose his experience at the time of the killing. There is no excitement, no 'boys' who were all in it together, sanctioning even encouraging each other and perhaps even celebrating the kill, as the film depicts later. What we can imagine in hindsight and what Fort Calata and Matthew Goniwe's wives can imagine, is that this man experienced some kind of an excitement and perhaps a collegial pleasure over the killing. His actions were not, given Taylor's identification with the police in *Mississippi Burning*, a clinical matter of a hit on the head, a pouring of petrol and a setting alight. There was a kind of excitement in the scene of violence and there was identification with both law and his colleagues.

Taylor did not receive amnesty for his actions (IOL, 1999). Ostensibly this denial was because he did not disclose the actions of others who were there. He withheld information and did not fulfill the criteria for 'full disclosure' on this basis. As he said: 'I was just talking for myself…I was not going to implicate my colleagues.' (Maykuth, 1998) And here, of course, we see the identification as collegial allegiance with those in the scene. This is an identification which also has its satisfactions, even excitements. As Zizek has noted:

> the only way—to have an intense and fulfilling personal (sexual) relationship is not for the couple to look into each other's eyes...but, while holding hands, to look together outside, at a third point (the Cause for which both are fighting, in which both are engaged). (2002, p. 85).

This is not only a sexual relationship—in the sense of being coital—but a fulfillment which brings the colleagues into a love relationship with each other, a form of 'whoah hoh, we're in it now boys'. A form of relation in which all are gazing and imagining the gaze returned; imagining themselves in the loving sanction of the Apartheid regime—the Cause.

The sanction of the regime, the enjoyment of enacting violence with one's colleagues—in the gaze of the law, the Cause or perhaps God—is certainly one version of a jouissance described by Lacan as an enjoyment through being in the proximity of a form of perfect obedience (or perfect significance); an enjoyment at being in the proximity of knowledge (Lacan, 2007). This, in Lacanian terms, may produce an excitement, but it is an excitement, which, not surprisingly, is hard to articulate in testimonies designed to plead for and secure amnesty. Nevertheless, as I have suggested, articulations such as these, may be thought about as a gesture of remorse. A remorse as accountability of who the person was (and perhaps still is), and a remorse as a kind of selflessness which does not look to the judge, the regime or even to God for the sanction of their actions. This is a remorse which looks only to what the perpetrator was and what s/he did in the scene of violence. A remorse which declares the reality of what the victim would have experienced at the hands of the perpetrator. A remorse which looks only to the victim and what they need, and not toward to the third point—the Cause, the regime, or the judge of the day.

Conclusion

What is the 'making sense' that one can get from a perpetrator who stands for, and arguably believes, in an ideology, a world, a reality that is apposite to that of victim? What could enable the victims to 'make peace' with such a perpetrator? What could such a perpetrator possibly offer? The answers, I suggest, are more than full disclosure as fact, and more than 'genuine remorse' as sorrow, pain or regret. Such disclosures and sentiments are profoundly steeped in the investments and imaginations of the perpetrator and their identifications with the regime—both past and present. What I suggest is required for some victims of intimate violence—even if it is not actively desired—is a witnessing as cathexis from the perpetrator. A witnessing infected with the interpersonal and intersubjective relations and, indeed, fantasies that saturate scenes of violence; a witnessing that sometimes highlights the perpetrators fantasies, in all their identifications and enjoyments. This kind of witnessing is hard to watch, sometimes awful, painful and may even be destructive for some—as Yazir Henry notes of his own experience of watching Benzien: 'I struggled with my anger and resolved not to participate in any further amnesty proceedings' (2000, p. 171). However, what I suggest here, tentatively, uncertainly—with the backing of psychoanalytic thought—is that there may be something necessary for the victims in having the perpetrator be or certainly perform, for a short time and for an audience which already acknowledges the wrongs of the past, exactly who there were in the scene of violence.

The usefulness of the perpetrator enacting the scene of violence as a method of witnessing for the victim is precisely because the perpetrator, who emerges from the primal scene into the reality of the scene of violence, brings with him or her the capacity to author reality. This capacity is not eroded through time for the survivor. Time, in its usual chronological ordering, has no meaning for survivors, who live with the trauma in the present. This is because trauma itself has a timeless quality (Laub, 1992, p. 69) and when it exists in the survivor's exclusive reality—when it cannot be brought into reality in the world—the survivor, in very somatic and cognitive ways, lives in the scene (the past). Because the scene of violence is alive for the victim then the perpetrator too is imagined (by the survivor) to be as in the scene as the survivor, many years later. It is from this location—in the scene—that the perpetrator can bear witness for, or with, the survivor. The perpetrator can acknowledge the reality of the flashback. That is, the perpetrator can perform what no one else can, which is to reflect the victim back to themselves, or perform the function of internal witness from an external position. This is more than a companion function, it is the capacity to sanction what happened as reality, and bring it into the reality of the day for all to see, while definitively placing it in the past—never again.

Any legitimate witnessing of the scene of violence by the perpetrator must, however, ensure that the perpetrator is put back into reality (while the omnipotent judge is put back into the realm of fantasy). The veneration of perpetrators who are apologetic or traumatised themselves is unlikely to help this process. The perpetrator needs to be ugly in the present, disliked and certainly socially and politically judged as such. For this to take place a disclosure of facts is rarely enough. The perpetrator needs to show who they were and disclose their enjoyments, excitements and identifications with, at least some of the affect that was displayed in the execution of the violence. This affect is what the victim endures, what those left behind—such as Nyamaka Goniwe and Nomonde Calata—would suspect, and what Ashley Forbes, Tony Yengeni, Peter Jacobs and Gary Kruser know all too well.

An acknowledgment of the enthusiasms and pleasures of the perpetrator in the scene of violence can enable the victim to show the reality of their experience as a reality for others. In an account of the reality of the perpetrator's enjoyment the victim can say "You were the person that I believed you to be." Which is arguably precisely what Benzien showed in both his demonstration of torture and his reenactments of his power as a torturer. As unpalatable as Benzien was, the retelling of narratives that collapse the enjoyments and affiliations of perpetrators and the particularities of the experience of victims into simplistic or even clinical stories, unilateral truths or cathartic displays can render victims further unable to locate a language to share with the living. The victims experience the enjoyments of the perpetrator in the flesh, and this enjoyment, no matter how ugly, may be an important part of the full disclosure of the perpetrator and constitutes a gesture of remorse not confined to the demands for forgiveness, amnesty or social acceptance. An ugly, but perhaps selfless, form of remorse is a point from which the victim may be able to symbolize the event in the reality of the day, and thus return it to the past, where it belongs.

References

Barta, T. (2008). Sorry, and not sorry in Australia: How the apology to the Stolen Generations buried a history of genocide. *Journal of Genocide Research*, 10 (2), 201-214.

Christodoulidis, E. (2000). Truth and Reconciliation as Risks. *Social and Legal Studies*, 9 (2), 179-204.

Colesbury, R. Zollo, F. (Producers) Parker, A. (Director). (1988). *Mississippi Burning*, [motion picture] United States: Orion Pictures.

Derrida, J. (1992). *Given Time: 1. Counterfeit Money*. (trans.) Peggy Kamuf. Chicago and London: University of Chicago Press.

Dorfman, A, (1991) *Death and the Maiden*, London: Nick Hern Books.

du Bois-Pedain, A. (2007). *Transitional Amnesty in South Africa*. London: Cambridge University Press.

Douglas, L. (2001). *The Memory of Judgment: Making Law and History in the Trials of the Holocaust*. USA: Yale University Press.

Editor (1999, Dec 14). No amnesty for killers of Cradock Four. *IOL News.* Retrieved from IOL http://www.iol.co.za/news/south-africa/no-amnesty-for-killers-of-cradock-four-1.23218#.U7vlZF5Rdg0

Feldman, A. (1999). Commodification and Commensality in Political Violence in South Africa and Northern Ireland. *Etnografica*, III (1), 113-129.

Foucault, M. (1970). *The Order of Things: An Archaeology of the Human Sciences.* New York: Vintage Books.

Gobodo-Madikizela, P. (2004). *A Human Being Died that Night: A South African Woman Confronts the Legacy of Apartheid.* New York: Mariner Books.

Gobodo-Madikizela, P. (2002). Remorse, Forgiveness, and Rehumanization: Stories from South Africa. *Journal of Humanistic Psychology,* 42, 7-32

Hackett, C. & Rolston, B. (2009). The burden of memory: Victims, storytelling and resistance in Northern Ireland, *Memory Studies*, 2, 355-376.

Hatzfeld, J. (2005). *Machete Season: The Killers in Rwanda Speak,* New York: Farrar, Straus and Giroux.

Henry, Y. (2000). 'Where Healing Begins'. In C. Villa-Vicencio & W. Verwoed, W (Eds). *Looking Back, Reaching Forward: Reflections on the Truth and Reconciliation Commission of South Africa*, pp. 166-173. Cape Town: Juta and Company Ltd.

Krog, A. (1998). *Country of My Skull: Guilt, Sorrow and the Limits of Forgiveness in the New South Africa.* New York: Three Rivers Press.

Lacan, J. (1977) *Seminar XI: Four Fundamental Concepts of Psychoanalysis*, Sheridan, A. (trans) Miller, JA. (ed) London: Penguin.

Lacan, J. (1993). *The Seminar of Jacques Lacan, Book III: The Psychoses 1955-1956.* Grigg, R. (trans) Miller, JA, (ed) New York: W.W. Norton & Company.

Lacan, J. (2006). *Ecrits: The First Complete Edition in English*. Fink, B. (trans), New York: W.W. Norton & Company. (first published in French 1966).

Lacan, J. (2007) *The Seminar of Jacques Lacan, Book XVII: The Other Side of Psychoanalysis 1969.* Grigg, R. (trans) W.W. Norton & Company, London, (first published in French, 1991).

Laub, D. (1992) 'Bearing Witness'. In S. Felman & D. Laub, (Eds). *Testimony: Crises of Witnessing in Literature, Psychoanalysis and History.* pp. 57-74.New York: Routledge.

Laub, D. & Lee, S. (2003). Thanatos and Massive Psychic Trauma: The Impact of the Death Instinct on Knowing, Remembering and Forgetting, *Journal of the American Psychoanalytic Association*, 51, 433-463.

Mamdani, M. (2002). Amnesty or Impunity? A Preliminary Critique of the Report of the Truth and Reconciliation Commission of South Africa (TRC), *Diacritics*, 32 (3-4), 33-59.

Maykuth, A. (1998, Oct 28) In Regret, A Policeman Seeks Amnesty—And Absolution. *Philly articles.* http://articles.philly.com/1998-10-28/news/ 25763490_1_harold-snyman-amnesty-reconciliation-commission

Minow, M. (1998). *Between Vengeance and Forgiveness: Facing History after Genocide and Mass Violence.* Massachusetts: Beacon Press.

Proeve, M. & Tudor, S. (2010). *Remorse: Psychological and Jurisprudential Perspectives.* London: Ashgate.

Reid, F. (Producer) Hoffman, D. & Reid, F. (Director). (2000). Long Night's Journey into Day, [Motion picture] United States: Iris Films.

Rogers, J. (2011). Nostalgia for a Reconciled Future—scenes of catharsis and apology in Israel and Australia, *Griffith Law Review*, 20 (2), 252-270.

Rogers, J. (2010). Torture: A Modicum of Recognition, *Law &Critique*, 32, 233-245.

Rogers, J. (2014). *The jouissance of the torturer as the enjoyment of the unacceptable in Zero Dark Thirty*. Portal, (in press).

Rowan, B. (2009, Aug 11). Husband of Shankill bomb victim tells of letter to Sinn Fein president Gerry Adams, Retrieved from BelfastTelegraph.co.uk.

Scarry, E. (1985). *Body in Pain: the making and unmaking of the world*, New York: Oxford.

Truth and Reconciliation Commission, Amnesty Hearing, Jeffrey, T Benzien, 14th July 1997, Cape Town, South Africa

Truth and Reconciliation Commission, Amnesty Hearing, Eric Taylor, 2nd March 1998, Port Elizabeth, South Africa Promotion of National Unity and Reconciliation Act, No 34 of 1995.

Wüstenberg, R. K. (2009). *The Political Dimension of Reconciliation: A theological analysis of ways of dealing with guilt during the transition to democracy in South Africa and (East) Germany*. (trans) Lundell, R. Michigan: William B. Eerdman's Publishing Company.

Zizek, S. (2002). *Welcome to the Desert of the Real*. London: Verso.

Chapter 3
Towards the Poetic Justice of Reparative Citizenship

AJ Barnard-Naudé

University of Cape Town

> *"[T]he literary imagination is an essential part of both the theory and practice of citizenship" (Nussbaum, 1995, p. 52).*
> *"When all is said and done, the fact remains that what is at issue in all of this is 'poetry'"*
> *(Nancy, 2006, p. 13).*

Introduction: The Irreparable

Much has been written about the successes and especially the failures of South Africa's Truth and Reconciliation (TRC) model and the reconciliatory project in general. Of late, the discourse has moved to an increased emphasis on symbolic and especially material reparation and it has, generally speaking, linked reconciliation to reparation, positing the one as a condition of the other (Doxtader & Villa-Vicenzio, 2004; Langa, 2006, p. 359). This shift in the discourse was primarily occasioned by a growing sense of frustration with the many broken promises of reparation in the aftermath of the TRC's report—a frustration that, like Freud's repressed, doesn't fail to return (De Wet, 2012).

Moreover, the ANC in government, while clearly albeit paradoxically tasked as an agent of reparation, has as yet failed dismally to bring about large scale reparation through structural interventions in the economy, leaving liberal market policies to address South Africa's enormous wealth gap (Terreblanche, 2002), marked so starkly by sudden and uncontrolled eruptions, onto the scene of politics, of the dispossessed, the poor and the disenfranchised. These are the unenviable heirs of the apartheid economy. Indeed, a peculiar liberalism (harnessed to an abarrent notion of formal equality, on the one hand, and precious little more than lip service to substantive social and economic equality, on the other) seems to harbour the preferred instruments of the ruling hegemony's amnesic toolkit—a toolkit that has resulted in atrophy and paralysis which, in turn, has of late produced the cloak of denialism with which this hegemony attempts to cover up South Africa's post-apartheid disasters as if to render them invisible. There are stark indications that gaping holes in this cloak are beginning to show. Recent incidents in South Africa, most prominently the massacre at Lonmin's Marikana mine, underscores that the Emperor's robes are now undoubtedly coming apart at the seams (Jika, Ledwaba, Mosamo, & Saba, 2013, p. 2-5).

Against this background, the state of the lack of reparation in South Africa raises anew the question of what is to be done and of what remains possible. In this contribution I want to take seriously, as a point of departure, the 2003 statement by former President Thabo Mbeki that reparation is a responsibility for all of us, that everyone in South Africa is interpellated by the question of reparation (Doxtader & Villa-Vicenzio, 2004, p. 26-28). This is not to dismiss government's ongoing and irreducible responsibility for reparation, but rather to consider the South African people's responsibility alongside that of government. If we are all responsible for reparation, then it seems to me that it would be important to consider the modality in which such a responsibility can be assumed and here I argue that this modality involves a departure from the "business as usual" approach that seems to be the order of the day—an approach in which we are subtly but powerfully encouraged to think of each other exclusively in terms of utilitarian considerations; an approach in which the Kantian 'dignity' of 'everyone' as proclaimed and legally guaranteed by the post-apartheid Constitution, indeed becomes, as critics of dignity have warned, an empty signifier. Against this approach, I will suggest, following the work of Giorgio Agamben, that the alternative mode of being (which is constitutively a being-with) in which the responsibility for reparation can be assumed, relates to a certain becoming: a becoming aware again of and affirming once again this 'dignity', which Agamben describes as man's poetic status on Earth.

From the outset, it needs to be underscored that I share Mark Sanders' reading of the question of reparation as constituting an aporia: whilst reparation is called for and affirmed as urgently necessary, reparation remains strictly impossible (Sanders, 2007, p. 116). As Sanders argues, an aporia calls for decisions, decisions that are, moreover replete with what Derrida has called the "ghost of the undecidable" (Derrida, 1990, p. 963). Whatever such decisions on reparation may entail, whatever actions are to be taken in the name of reparation, they cannot, precisely because they arise from or through the structure of an aporia, escape the givenness of the irreparable. The irreparable is, to follow Agamben (2005), what is given and what remains—the world broken as it is. Yet, as Derrida (1986, p. 133) argues, the aporia "provokes a leap of memory and a displacement of thinking" which leads to a new thinking of the disjunction, new decisions, decisions of a different nature.

Moreover, as Sanders indicates, if reparation is a relation to the irreparable, then all reparations are "symbolic" (including those made by use of the "symbol" of money) (Sanders, 2007, p. 119). In turn, this means that reparation cannot do what it promises, namely the literal or direct repair of that which has been broken. In this aspect, reparation presents as thoroughly un- or non-economic in that it does not admit of something like equivalent exchange. At best, reparation can be viewed as involving acts and gestures of which the wager is that it provides the possibility of making the breach as it exists irreparably, less unbearable. Obviously, we cannot go back in time, we cannot undo the wrong or the suffering, we cannot give back a severed limb, a dead loved one or unscar a child. While we can provide shelter to the homeless, we cannot undo the trauma suffered as a result of a forced removal.

Facing the aporia of reparation, however, does not mean that reparation (and the responsibility before it) is foreclosed, that nothing can be done to "pour oil on wounds", as Archbishop Tutu once put it (Du Bois & Du Bois-Pedain, 2008, p. 198). As Van Riessen has argued, Agamben's acknowledgement of the irreparable does not lead to an abandonment of "the possibility of redemption" (Van Riessen, 2010, p. 91). Approaching the world from the point of view of the irreparable, allows for the perspective of seeing it not just in terms of its "being thus" but also in terms of its "unfulfilled promises". What would be at stake for reparation, then, would be the redemption of "what is not" (yet), the redemption of what remains possible. This would entail coming to terms with the irreparable in a reparative way, that is, in a way that will make it possible to endure and inhabit the irreparable differently.

I must confess that I do not know what, exactly and practically, a reparative approach to the irreparable would entail in relational situations in South Africa that are as manifold as they are complex. But I want to suggest that they require a change in the quality or character of action, that they require work that proceeds from an acknowledgement of suffering but that they certainly cannot end in mere acknowledgement as a nod of the head to the one who has suffered untold injustice. Sanders has drawn attention to the fact that reparation involves "a setting forth, a making" (as in "making good") and has argued that restoration undertaken in the name of reparation unites responsibility with the kind of making and remaking that is involved in the production of intellectual and artistic work (Sanders, 2007, p. 132). I want to argue here that we will be better equipped to imagine what is required of us to "make" reparation when we become aware (again) of and orientated to the disposition or mode of being that would attune us to a creative engagement with the irreparable—an engagement that would allow us to search for something new, to begin again by challenging the stagnant and dominant given of the irreparable through imagining what, in the face of the unfulfilled promises, needs to be done and can be done; to imagine what "making good" on the unfulfilled promises would entail.

As regards the processual character that such a making would entail, Van Marle (2010, p. 350-353) has explicitly invoked the notion of "becoming" in the general legal and political discourse around the South African transition and the understanding of the term "post-apartheid" in that discourse. Relying on the work of Deleuze and Guattari, Van Marle argues that the post-apartheid question would involve a "double movement" in politics "one in which an identity (stability) is asserted, but in the same move, one in which a becoming, a ceaseless challenge is asserted" (Van Marle, 2010, p. 351). As Van Marle argues, at stake here is what Antjie Krog calls the "kind of self I should grow into in order to live a caring, useful and informed life—a 'good life'—within my country in southern Africa" (Krog, 2009, p. 95).

It is my contention in this chapter, relying on the work of Agamben, Nancy and Nussbaum that a reparative approach to the irreparable would entail a process of becoming-human (again) and that such a becoming human involves the adoption of a certain poetic attitude towards the world from which a conception of politics as creative potentiality (and a "poetic" engagement with the political question of reparation) would ensue. I refer to this political stance harboured in an ontology of the poetic, this being-member or inhabiting of the polis poetically, as reparative citizenship. This is an articulation of citizenship that would face the aporia of repairing the irreparable. It is an articulation of citizenship that would in fact adopt the aporia of reparation as a face. Reparative citizenship as the face of this aporia can only be a product of man's poetic status, because it is constitutively reliant on the uniquely human potentiality to create, make or give oneself a world, precisely in the face or in full view of the irreparable.

Man's Poetic status

In her celebrated book, Country of my skull, Antjie Krog (1998) describes the involvement of her fellow South African poet, Adam Small, in the heated arguments about the justifiability of South Africa's Truth and Reconciliation Commission at the time of its inception. Krog, accounting the appearance of

Small before the government panel that was tasked with the appointment of the Commission's staff, writes as follows: "Considering the enormous task ahead, it is clear that Adam Small's ambivalent rambling is not appreciated by the panel" (Krog, 1998, p. 18). She goes on to quote Small's address to the commission: "'I am a man of two hearts and not of this world. This truth Commission thing is useless—it wastes hard-earned money to listen to a bunch of crooks. Only literature can perform the miracle of reconciliation'" (Krog, 1998, p. 18) Krog continues: "After three quarters of an hour in this vein, Fink Haysom [from the panel] asks 'But you are so critical—do you want to serve on this commission?' [Small answers:] 'If there is space on the Commission for an independent, critical, stubborn, sometimes naughty voice—then I will be there with my heart—but I will always remain critical'" (Krog, 1998, p. 18). Years after accounting this anecdote, Krog would write at the conclusion of the third instalment of her reflections on and experiences and accounts of the South African transformation process, in a book entitled Begging to be black, that "once again, poetry has taught me how to live a lived life" (Krog, 2009, p. 274).

It is clear from the above that both Small and Krog think of literature as transformative. For Small, literature performs miracles and the description of reconciliation as a "miracle" implies that the mode of being that would be implicated in the possibility of reconciliation would be exceptional and extraordinary. Similarly for Krog, poetry is what transforms mere existence into a "lived life". In this section I explore Agamben's description of man's "poetic status", motivated by a reading of Small and Krog as alluding in their statements to access to such a "poetic status" as the condition of an experience of the transformative processes that are indicated when we invoke terms such as "reconciliation" or, more pertinently for my purposes, "reparation".

Agamben's articulation of man's unique poetic status and its possible meanings and implications are primarily articulated in his book, The man without content (1999a, p. 68). One of the challenges as regards the "readability" of Agamben's argument in this book is that it relies, to a great extent, on familiarity with Heidegger's earlier essays on poetry and specifically the discussion of Hölderlin's question, "What are poets for in a destitute time?" (Heidegger, 1971, p. 87-140), the "destitute time" here referring not only to the flight of the gods from the Earth without the possibility of their return, but also to the absence of what Heidegger calls the "divine radiance" that would have given ground to the world (Heidegger, 1971, p. 89). The "destitute time" is the age of the night of the world in which "the abyss of the world must be experienced and endured" (Heidegger,

1971, p. 90). Agamben's name for this abyssal world is, of course, the irreparable and he relates humanity's destitute time explicitly to the subjection, in modernity, of his poetic status to his practical status, the status that primarily involves her in the maintenance of a strictly biological notion of life.

Heidegger argues that the return of the shine of divine radiance in "everything that is" is the precondition of any abode to which a god could return (Heidegger, 1971, p. 90). I read the references to a god and to the divine here as Heidegger's way of articulating a non-technological / artful relation to Being, thus the aspect of Being that first has to do, precisely, with the literary, namely the creative (and thus godly) potentiality of our human existence. Read with Heidegger (1971, p. 90), the inference can be drawn that it is only through a revivification (if not a resuscitation) of man's poetic status that the destitute time of abyssal life / the irreparable can creatively be endured although never overcome.

In order to understand better what Agamben means with his reference to man's unique poetic status (suppressed to the point of loss in the destitute time), we need to know a little bit more about his understanding of life in general and human life in particular. As Claire Colebrook (2008, p. 109) points out, for Agamben the difference between animals and humans is not biological per se. The difference is rather between biological life and poetic life. Whereas biological life "lives only to maintain itself", poetic life belongs to the potentiality of human life to give itself a world, that is, "a life that does not just circle around and maintain itself," but rather "a life that creates and brings forth what is not itself", a life that brings forth an end which is not yet given (Colebrook, 2008, p. 109).

Agamben's notion of human life as poetic life or potentiality challenges the notion of life as simply willing to maintain itself as what it is. Through this challenge he asserts "a supposedly lost higher sense of life as that which creates from itself in order to be more than itself: divine, poetic life—the life of man" (Colebrook, 2008, p. 109). What we are dealing with here is thus in the first and last place not a conception of human life as directed towards a telos that posits the future return of some metaphysical and transcendental god from some unknown, external, mystical non-space or non-time, but rather the re-awakening of the divine in man through a re-awakening of his poetic status as his creative potentiality. Put differently, what is at stake is an understanding of the human being not simply "as a being alongside the animal" (Colebrook, 2008, p. 109), but rather as the being that emerges from animality through poetic speech and the work of art.

For Agamben, it is the work of art that should disclose the potentiality of human life, but in modernity we are precluded from recognising art as disclosive of potentiality, because the work of art has come to be understood in terms of praxis—a mere "object created by a will" (Colebrook, 2008, p. 108). In the modern age, poiesis (or man's productive capacity) has come to be understood in terms of, or as dominated by, praxis. But it should be clarified that here praxis is no longer understood in its frail, unpredictable, nascent and innovative Greek sense—in the sense that Hannah Arendt used and celebrated it as authentic political action (Arendt, 1958, 175-247). Rather, for Agamben praxis refers to the rise of the determinist will to power. In the modern age, he argues, praxis becomes, in essence, the "manifestation of a will that produces a concrete effect" (Agamben, 1999a, p. 68). Agamben writes that the original distinction between praxis as the manifestation of a will "that finds its immediate expression in an act" and poiesis, as a mode of "truth as unveiling" completely disappears with the rise of Western metaphysical thought (Agamben, 1999a, p. 69).

This disappearance is accompanied by the rise to central value of the activity of work. Praxis now becomes the name of the manifestation of the will producing a concrete effect overwhelmingly calculated at the maintenance of a merely biological form of life. Praxis simply becomes work: "Today this pro-ductive doing, in the form of work, determines everywhere the status of man on earth, understood from the point of view of praxis, that is, of production of material life" (Agamben, 1999a, p. 59). Under these circumstances, poiesis becomes eclipsed because it does not fit within the scheme and priorities of work as the maintenance and sustenance of that which relates to the material condition of life as consumption.

Jean-Luc Nancy indicates that poiesis, in contradistinction, "produces something not with a view to another thing or a use, but with a view to its very production, that is, its exposition" (Nancy, 2006, p. 191). With the term "exposition" Nancy is alluding to the opening up of a non- or un-economic space or world—a world in which the activity of making is good for its own sake, precisely because such a making is a "making good" of life in that it discloses or ex-poses to human beings that they are more than (and can bring forth more than) the material production and economic exchanges on which their biological life depends. The age of praxis, however, affects the work of art in this age in such a way that it increasingly itself acquires the character of the industrial product standing ready to be consumed (Colebrook, 2008, p. 109-110). Agamben is very close to Heidegger on technology here when he describes this character of the product as a "mere being-available" (Agamben, 1999a, p. 66). As Colebrook (2008, p. 108) puts it: "Art today either is mere potential for enjoyment or is valuable only insofar as it is the product of an irreducible will; there is no sense of the (once essentially human) power to produce art as other than mere life, as the opening of a world other than the human as it already is, but nevertheless of human making". Below, I turn to the particular engagement with time on which "the opening of a world other than the human as it already is", would depend.

The Time of Poetry and the Time of Law

Agamben opposes this mere availability of the work of art for aesthetic enjoyment to what he calls the obscured "energetic" character of the work of art, its "being-at-work" (Agamben, 1999a, p. 65-66). The remainder of The man without content is devoted to the thinking of a return to the time of the origin of the work of art in order to rediscover man's poetic status. This course is motivated by Agamben's conviction (inspired by the Greek heritage on art) that it is only in the work of art, the poetic, that man truly experiences his being-in-the-world (Agamben, 1999a, p. 101). For Agamben this origin or essence of the work of art, its energetic character, is closely connected to what he calls the "rhythm" of the work of art: "rhythm is not structure […] but is instead […] the principle of *presence* that opens and maintains the work of art in its original space. As such it is neither calculable nor rational; yet it is also not irrational" (Agamben, 1999a, p. 98 (emphasis provided)). Rhythm must be understood not as the linear flow of time, but as introducing a split or interruption (one could also say a hesitation) in the flow of chronological time, rhythm as "the presence of an atemporal dimension in time" (Agamben, 1999a, p. 99). Rhythm, thus, as the arrest of time: "we perceive a stop in time, as though we were suddenly thrown into a more original time. There is a stop, an interruption in the incessant flow of instants […] and this interruption, this stop, is precisely what gives and reveals the particular status, the mode of presence proper to the work of art" (Agamben, 1999a, p. 99).

This does not mean that rhythm can be outside of time. But if we are to have an experience of a world that is not yet given, if we are to interrupt the irreparable, then we have to start from rhythm "which opens up for man the space of his world, and only by starting from it can he experience freedom and alienation, historical consciousness and loss in time, truth and error" (Agamben, 1999a, p. 100). Nancy describes this atemporal temporal dimension of the work of art with reference to what he calls the "present of poetry". For Nancy "the present of presence is not in time but ahead of time, before it. [...] It is pure time, time shielded from temporality: the space in which pure time opens out and is unexposed" (Nancy, 2006, p. 192). "Poetry [...] is technique productive of presence. Presence is not a quality or a property of the thing. It is the act through which the thing is brought forth: prae-est ... [T]he present in time is nothing; it is pure time, the pure present of time" (Nancy, 2006, p. 191-192).

Both Agamben and Nancy describe the time of the work of art in terms of presence, but it is crucial to note that this is not a presence in time as the givenness of time, presence simply as that which is the "incessant flow of instants". It is, rather, a description of presence in terms of an activity or a being-at-work, or to follow Nancy, a pro-duction of presence. Poetry depends on a bringing into being, the creation of a presence (and a present) that is not (yet) given.

I want to suggest that the time of reparative citizenship as rooted in man's poetic status depends upon creative acts of "presencing" the aporia or abnormality of repairing the irreparable, of not coming to terms with it, but rather of being interminably confronted with the difficulty that it engages us in. Reparative citizenship will understand that the "now" of the post-apartheid is not equal to presence, that presence as the time of reparation depends on an appreciation of the precariousness of the now. It will understand that the post-apartheid now as irreparable stands in urgent need of a "technique productive of presence" that would bring forth, give birth, to a future that will live up to the promise of "never again".

In its focus on a non-rectilinear relationship between past and future, reparative citizenship is necessarily an inter-generational concept—a concept that requires us to imagine a future generation to which we will stand accountable not simply for the Apartheid past that lies behind us, but also for the post-apartheid as it becomes a past in the "now" of the irreparable. Reparative citizenship, then, does not belong to the time of the mere being available, rather it has to be brought into existence—presenced. As such, it involves a coming to terms with the past (the irreparable) by way of the imagining, in the present, of a future that remains radically, but urgently, to come. It thus cannot merely be given or "in" existence, conceived as a "now" in terms of a rectilinear concept of time. It is a bringing forth from the future, rather than a challenging forth of what is already given as standing in reserve from the past (Heidegger, 1977, p. 14). As such, reparative citizenship will understand that "politics finds its place neither in the romanticism of the past nor in the yearning for a utopian future but, rather, in a profound presentness, in the realization that within the present lies the possibility/potentiality of change and transformation. Radical change must begin with the time of the present and in this world" (Salzani, 2012, p. 224).

In this respect, there is a crucial dimension of the rise of praxis that Agamben neglects in his discussion but that is a dimension which Heidegger before him had realized as an essential characteristic of the technological mode of revealing that Heidegger called the enframing. With reference to a line from Rilke where man is described as being "before the world" (Heidegger, 1977, p. 108), Heidegger reasons that "[t]o put something before ourselves is to represent it for ourselves: Nature is brought before man by the positioning that belongs to representation (Heidegger, 1977, p. 110). This implies that "where Nature is not satisfactory to man's representation, he reframes or redisposes it" (Heidegger, 1977, p. 110). Heidegger thus recognises that this willing has, as he puts it, "the character of command" (Heidegger, 1977, p. 110).

The time of the rise of the will that has in it the character of command is the time of the enframing—the time in which law becomes the supreme medium by way of which man commands the challenging forth of the enframing. This is the linear time of capitalist utilitarianism and exchange coupled with a thoroughly bureaucratic version of law—a faceless form of law that has become the handmaiden of utilitarian means-end administration, a form of law that Arendt (amongst many others) did not even recognise as law (Klabbers, 2007, p. 10-11). For the Arendt of On Revolution thought of law as "what relates". Indeed, she goes as far as saying that "without *human* law the space between men would be a desert, or rather there would be no in-between space at all" (Arendt, 1965, p. 302 (emphasis provided)).

Rhythm in the authentic experience of the work of art, then, gives us to think the possibility of a world that truly relates, that is, relates in a post-apartheid way and a law that is not yet given or, as Rose refers to it, a "poetics of law" that would permit us to rediscover politics as the "recognition of our failures of full mutual recognition, of the law which has induced our proud and deadly dualisms" (Rose, 1996, p. 76). If it is true, as Small contends in his statement above, that reconciliation, and by my extension, reparation, is a miracle that only literature can perform, then reconciliation and reparation involves a mode of being-together that do not or, at least, do not primarily, proceed from the force of law as command, but are, rather questions of "differential force" (Derrida, 1990, p. 929), of what Derrida calls a counter-law, an a priori counter-law which is the condition of possibility of law itself, an "axiom of impossibility that confounds law's sense, order and reason" (Derrida, 1980, p. 57).

In earlier work (Barnard-Naudé, 2012), I have argued that the name of this force, this counter-law, is poetry, if this word is strictly understood in terms of its Greek heritage as poiesis—the generic name of all art (Nancy, 2006, p. 191), which originally included the art of law-making. Agamben's argument that man's ontological status, that is, his status as a unique being amongst beings, is a poetic status, implies then that it is to be considered in terms of or as this counter-law (Barnard-Naudé, 2012, p. 468) which is nevertheless the condition, as Derrida argues, of the law as such. Below, I argue that the poetic as this counter-law, invites us to inhabit the political reparatively, which is to say, transformatively.

Poetic Justice, Politics and Poetry's Resistance

Viewed in this light, poiesis could be considered to be the name for the time and space in which questions of the argumentative (law and politics) and the poetic overlap and resonate; where the poetic stands the chance of "transforming" or "abnormalizing" the argumentative. Jacques Rancière has remarked that "[p]olitical invention operates in acts that are at once argumentative and poetic, shows of strength that open again and again, as often as necessary, worlds in which such acts of community are acts of community. This is why the 'poetic' is not opposed here to argument" (Rancière, 1999, p. 59). This is where the notion of "poetic justice" becomes helpful as a phrase that articulates the coming together or the "community" of the convergence between the poetic and the argumentative. Small and Krog's observations above clearly link the poetic or the "literary" to the question of transition as an ethical, political and legal—thus argumentative—project. As such these statements are both argumentative and poetic in the sense described by Rancière and thus open up a space in which the confrontation of the argumentative with the poetic could lead to something that is productive and transformative in ethics, law and politics.

The poetic justice of reparative citizenship would recognize that it is only by way of a revival of our uniquely human poetic status that we access the realm of sense (the realm of the spectator) in which light it is possible to imagine a bringing forth (into Being) of a political practice of reparation. Reparative citizenship is thus and can only be strictly a work of art in Agamben's sense of that phrase. Moreover, from our exploration of the time of the work of art, we have seen that reparative citizenship as poetic is always a work in progress—a presencing—in the face of the givenness of the now.

As such it is a kind of hesitation and a difficulty, a "sense that is always still to be made" (Nancy, 2006, p. 4).

Moreover still, reparative citizenship depends on a notion of politics not simply as a means that would produce given ends, but rather as a creative realm—a realm in which potentiality can be seized to produce and maintain something more than mere life, that is, a "fuller life" (Colebrook, 2008, p. 108), thus, a becoming-human of life through "creating and bringing forth an end that is not yet given" (Colebrook, 2008, p. 110).

In what follows, I draw heavily on Martha Nussbaum's celebrated plea for the literary imagination in public discourse as articulated in her book, *Poetic Justice* (1995) in order to claim that such a bringing forth of reparation through actions harboured in reparative citizenship requires acts of the imagination. Although Nussbaum's focus is explicitly the existential and political importance of the genre of the novel, I believe that her argument can be appropriately expanded to cover a truth about poetry as art in general or in the generic sense. I find support for this belief in Nussbaum's own (at least partial) reliance in Poetic Justice on poetry (that of Walt Whitman in particular (Nussbaum, 1995, p. 79))—I also believe that without unduly stretching the interpretation, her argument for the literary or "metaphoric" imagination in political life, resonates with Valéry's celebrated definition of poetry: "The poem: a prolonged hesitation between sound and sense" (Agamben, 1999b, p. 109). The metaphoric imagination would involve a hesitation in which the sound of political speech would not simply precipitate an instinctual or visceral reaction, but rather a response that would be informed by consideration and reflective judgment.

The successful case for the connection between Nussbaum's argument for the literary imagination in politics and Valéry's description of the poem as a hesitation between sound and sense, also depends on the understanding, first articulated by Hannah Arendt (1995, p. 208) and later developed by Nancy (1997), that sense is profoundly a matter of the public or political sphere as the realm of the space of appearance, of the creation of a world, of witnessing; the realm, then, of the spectator. For as Arendt writes: "Nothing and nobody exists in this world whose very being does not presuppose a spectator" (Arendt 1971, p. 19). For Nancy, we accede to such a dawning of sense, only poetically, that is, artistically (Nancy, 2006, p. 3).

In *Poetic Justice* (1995) Nussbaum opposes the literary imagination to political utilitarianism. She points out that one of the key characteristics of utilitarianism is that it does not leave room for the space of appearance, for the separation that makes all relation possible and therefore for the Agambenian idea of man as world-creating. To quote Nussbaum (in turn quoting Sen and Williams): "Essentially, utilitarianism sees persons as locations of their respective utilities—as the sites at which such activities as desiring and having pleasure and pain take place. Once note has been taken of the person's utility, utilitarianism has no further direct interest in any information about him [...] Persons do not count as individuals in this any more than individual petrol tanks do in the analysis of the national consumption of petroleum" (Nussbaum, 1995, p. 14-15).

As Nussbaum points out, from the utilitarian point of view, this means that the qualitative distinctions and differences between persons and the boundaries between them, will not count as salient (Nussbaum, 1995, p. 20-21). Ultimately, the picture of humanity that utilitarianism paints is one that "effaces personal separateness as well as qualitative difference" (Nussbaum, 1995, p. 21). It sees persons as "mere containers or sites of satisfaction" (Nussbaum, 1995, p. 28).

Against this version of human science, Nussbaum pleads for the literary imagination which, by contrast, "sees the boundaries between one person and another as among the world's most salient facts" (Nussbaum, 1995, p. 28). It is important to point out that she explicitly does not reject economic science and does not see her project as antiscientific (Nussbaum, 1995, p. 11). Rather, she argues in favour of the literary as an essential part of economic science's quest for a "more complicated and philosophically adequate set of foundations" (Nussbaum, 1995, p. 11).

Thus, Nussbaum defends the emotions that are foregrounded in the literary imagination as an essential part of social rationality. And, perhaps more explicitly than Agamben, she argues that the ends that man produces through his poetic status or through what Nussbaum refers to as "fancy", are ends that serve no end beyond themselves, they are "good and delightful for themselves alone" (Nussbaum, 1995, p. 42). And it is this poetic stance towards the world that in turn allows us to see the complexity, worth and importance of things and human beings outside ourselves. It is, in other words, the literary imagination that allows us to see the Other as Other and to engage the Other as Other. For Nussbaum, it is literature that represents to the spectator-reader the "complex cast of mind" that "is essential in order to take the full measure of the adversity and suffering of others, and that this appraisal is necessary for full social rationality" (Nussbaum, 1995, p. 66).

Whilst I am here largely in agreement with Nussbaum, I would characterise her emphasis on the literary in somewhat different terms. I do this in order to show that her arguments can be read specifically as a resistance or Derridean "dangerous supplement" to the utilitarian enframing of late capitalist public discourse. My fear is that if this resistance is not repeatedly emphasised, Nussbaum's argument could be appropriated in the service of the kind of "aestheticisation of politics" that worried Walter Benjamin and continues to worry the contemporary influential philosopher, Slavoj Zizek (2012, p. 31), an aestheticisation of politics that ultimately amounts to the fascist adornment of power. This is a view to which Benjamin (2009, p. 228)—in the afterword to his famous essay, The work of art in the age of mechanical reproduction—refers to as "the kind of aestheticization of politics that Fascism pursues" (Benjamin, 2009, p. 259). Benjamin sees Fascism as the political movement that depends ultimately on the aestheticisation of political life; without changing the ownership structure, it consists in giving the masses a voice, but not giving them their due (Benjamin, 2009, p. 257).

The resistance that I would claim for Nussbaum's defence of the literary imagination is that which Jean-Luc Nancy identifies specifically as poetry's resistance, a resistance that belongs to it, that is as old as it. This constitutive resistance that belongs to poetry is exemplary in Western philosophy's most celebrated work, the Republic in which poetry is from the outset in trouble, precisely because it sets itself against and is perceived as a danger for the rule of the instrumental totalitarian reason of rational discourse in the ideal city state. It is for this reason that it is exiled from the Republic in Book X, only to resist this exile by returning, like Marlee's ghost, in the guise of the myth of Er at the end of the work (Plato, 1993, p. 371-379).

Nancy's explanation of the twofold nature of poetry's resistance can perhaps explain to us why poetry always comes back to so-called "rational" discourse in this haunting, subversive way. The first resistance Nancy identifies in poetry is what he calls its resistance to "exhausted discourse" (Nancy, 2006, p. 16). Exhausted discourse is tired discourse, discourse that has run out of breath, that has reached its limit: banal discourse. It is most often accompanied by thoughtlessness, marked by what Arendt has called the repetition of "truths" that have become trivial and empty (Arendt, 1958, p. 5). It is characterised by attempts to finalise and still all contestation, dissent and dissonance in language, the attempt to silence and finally solidify meaning.

An excellent example of exhausted discourse is that of Apartheid at the end of the eighties when no amount of discursive ruses in defence of its necessity, no more obscene pleas of its benignness, of its "good neighbourliness", could breathe life into its already decaying body. This exhausted discourse marked, extraordinarily, the return of poetry when Nelson Mandela inaugurated the new South Africa with Ingrid Jonker's poem, Die kind wat doodgeskiet is deur soldate by Nyanga (The child that was shot dead by soldiers at Nyanga), a poem which, when it was written, itself marked a profound resistance to the political hegemony of Apartheid, a resistance, moreover, from within the language of Apartheid discourse—Afrikaans.

Poetry's resistance to exhausted discourse is closely associated with the second iteration of its resistance, which is its insistence on "that which, in or within language, announces or keeps more than language" (Nancy, 2006, p. 17). For Nancy, this "more than language" "is not any 'superlanguage' or 'overlanguage' but the articulation that precedes language 'in' itself (and that might equally be termed 'affection,' 'praxis,' or 'ethos') […] I would go as far as to say, […] that it insists in the 'unconscious' and as the 'unconscious' that language is" (Nancy, 2006, p. 18). Essentially Nancy is writing here about the fact that language is never simply instrumental or cybernetic, not simply a means of conveying information or news, that language constitutively has an affective dimension harboured within it which reaches beyond its use value. It is this resistance of poetry that makes all literature and all arguments for literature possible in the first place. In the end, then, Nancy's argument is that poetry's mode is constitutively a mode of resistance to the technologico-utilitarian mode of Being that Heidegger called the Gestell (the Enframing).

Here I want to return to Hölderlin's question "what are poets for in a destitute time?". Heidegger tells us that "to be a poet in a destitute time means: to attend, singing, to the trace of the fugitive gods" (Heidegger, 1971, p. 92). And what does it mean to attend, singing, to the trace of the fugitive gods? What are the fugitive gods if they are not the flight of justice from our world? What is the destitute time if not the time of injustice? As Žižek has asked: "Couldn't the entire history of humanity be seen as a growing normalisation of injustice, entailing the nameless and faceless suffering of millions?" (Žižek, 2009, p. 152). What is the destitute time if not the time of what Nussbaum so beautifully describes as the time of the blindness of the economic mind of equivalent exchange? "[T]he economic mind is blind: blind to the qualitative richness of the perceptible world; to the separateness of its people, to the inner depths, their hopes and loves and fears; blind to what it is like to live a human life and to try to endow it with a human meaning. Blind, above all to the fact that human life is something mysterious and extremely complicated, something that demands to be approached with faculties of minds and resources of language that are suited to the expression of that complexity" (Nussbaum, 1995, p. 27).

What, then, are poets for in a destitute time if not for the return of Justice? What are poets for in a destitute time if not for poetry? The poet attends to the trace of justice that is left in our world and in her attending (which is also to say in her presencing) she prepares the space, holds open the possibility and hopes for the perhaps of justice. This is poetry's resistance, its quarrel, its ethico-political protest—it always says "perhaps for justice" (Derrida, 1990, p. 971).

Reparative Citizenship as a Praxis of Poesis

In the context of South Africa, which is after all what most concerns us here, Krog (2012) has argued that in this country "each creative work makes a political point". Quoting Nobel prize winner Horace Engdahl, she writes that "one is either part of […] 'the great dialogue of literature about the improvement of humanity', or suggesting that one doesn't particularly care for it." Krog movingly pleads for contemporary power in South Africa to listen, once more, to its poets, that is to say to its artists. And the reasons she provides are compelling: "[L]iterature inflects the *anguish of reality* in a way that theoretical discussions of the same issues cannot achieve, making possible a kind of understanding not accessible by other means" (Krog, 2012 (emphasis provided)). It provides a "visionary vocabulary", its continuous presencing of the world "creates reflexivity and nuanced knowing" (Krog, 2012).

Let me turn now to post-apartheid citizenship as reparative citizenship, that is, as an active being-member of the polis. I claim that the success of South Africa's reparative efforts crucially depends on an understanding of post-apartheid citizenship as civic friendship but have insisted that it is better rendered in South Africa as reparative citizenship and furthermore, that reparative citizenship is not possible without the literary imagination or what I would call a poetic stance towards the world. Reparative citizenship is the phrase I use to describe what is needed for the South African demos to move towards an Aristotelian or Arendtian version of civic friendship. Reparative citizenship is indeed a need in this sense, for I believe that without it the ideal of civic friendship cannot be approximated.

In a lecture delivered at the University of Stellenbosch law faculty in 2006 the former Chief Justice, Pius Langa, explicitly invoked the work of art as the medium through which reconciliation (and by extension, reparation) could come to be, by asserting that "[a]ll South Africans, beneficiaries, victims and perpetrators, must work together to *create* a climate of reconciliation. There are many ways to foster that climate: through public dialogue, art and music" (Langa, 2006, p. 359 (emphasis provided)). By situating public dialogue within the series, Langa emphasizes the potentiality of political speech as itself disclosive—a work of art—and here comes close to Agamben's argument that it is through the fact of speech (the saying) that the subject is in existence as such, that is, as pure potentiality and as such capable of the creation of a free, open, not already actualised space (Colebrook, 2008, p. 114-117).

In the same lecture, Langa stated unequivocally that the processes implicated in transitional justice (reconciliation and forgiveness) is "beyond the power of the law. We cannot legislate reconciliation and we cannot order forgiveness" (Langa, 2006, p. 358). But he added that reconciliation requires material reparation, what he called "an improvement of socio-economic conditions" a levelling of the socio-economic playing field (Langa, 2006, p. 359). This is the case because where socio-economic conditions are such that they can barely maintain bare life, potentiality is lost in advance. Where there is nothing more than bare life, there is no potentiality, no language and no creative speech, only the expression of desperate material need. (Agamben illustrates this with the example of the silent Muselmann who is neither simply deprived of humanity nor fully human, marked by "the absence of saying as such" and thus non-existent, evacuated potentiality (Colebrook, 2008, p. 115)).

In invoking Langa's emphasis on "material" reparation as the improvement of socio-economic conditions I want to emphasize that I am not arguing that the plea for becoming aware again of our poetic status amounts to an argument that we should all become poets, but rather that proceeding from an awareness of our poetic status can give us to imagine our responsibility for "material" reparation in ways that would direct it away from yet again reducing the Other to a unit of material utility to whom we, in this instance, owe a debt. The direction in which the becoming aware again of our poetic status would point is the direction of engaging the Other from the point of view of her own uniquely human potentiality. Such an engagement would pivot on engaging the Other from the point of view of her potentiality as a friend who is not, as Aristotle would have it, another self, but is, rather, an Other the realisation of whose potentiality is a condition of the realization of my potentiality. In this respect, Agamben argues that friendship is an awareness of the pure fact of my existence simultaneously with yours. As Agamben puts it: "The friend is not another I, but an otherness immanent in self-ness, a becoming other of the self" (Agamben, 2004, p. 6).

It was Arendt who, in modern political theory, resuscitated and defended a "politics of friendship" relying heavily on but ultimately taking its leave from the work of Aristotle. Arendt's theory of civic friendship offers an account of politics that is both post-individualist and post-utilitarian. In fact, Arendt's theory of civic friendship invokes an understanding of citizenship as a radically "horizontal allegiance to friends". Reparative citizenship starts here, for Arendt sees in this understanding of political life the possibility of "words that are not empty and deeds that are not brutal" (Stortz, 1994, p. 417). In other words, As Martha Stortz comments on Arendt's concept of civic friendship: "Civic friendship of all sorts emphasises the interdependence of citizens in public life. It articulates a horizontal understanding of citizenship, which prizes the relationship to another citizen and places that relationship at the centre of civic life" (Stortz, 1994, p. 414).

But it still needs emphasis that the form of citizenship envisioned here is not at all about allegiance to the self and the same. At its heart, Arendt's understanding of civic friendship turns on the underlying notion of plurality — that is, difference — because it is plurality in Arendt that is constitutive of the political. And plurality conditions us in the sense that our very individuality only takes shape through our recognition that we share the world with others.

In a very real sense, then, there can be no authentic politics without the literary imagination, for, as Nussbaum shows, it is the literary imagination that makes us alive to the fact of alterity, to difference, the plight of the Other. It is a poetic stance towards the world that reveals others to us in their singularity and reveals us to them in ours. Civic friendship as reparative citizenship is a way of signifying that there can be no healing for the body politic without reparation, without this recognition, empathy, compassion that the poetic stance can attune us to see. It is a way of being-in-the-world that allows one not just to hear the voice of the Other but to respond to her voice / call. In this sense, it is not just a being-in-the-world as passive spectator or onlooker. It is also a being-involved, a being that demands outcry and resistance in the face of the injustices that crude utilitarian economic calculations perpetrate and perpetuate.

What I think former Chief Justice Langa brings to the table in this creation of reparative citizenship involves Karl Jaspers' notion of metaphysical guilt. Jaspers writes: "metaphysical guilt is the lack of absolute solidarity with the human being as such—an indelible claim beyond morally meaningful duty. This solidarity is violated by my presence at a wrong or a crime. It is not enough that I cautiously risk my life to prevent it; if it happens, and I was there, and if I survive where the other is killed, I know from a voice within myself: I am guilty of being still alive" (Jaspers, 2000, p. 65). This means, obviously, that for Jaspers we are all guilty and therefore responsible, even though some are more guilty and therefore more responsible than others.

From this point of view, reparative citizenship requires also the duty to speak out creatively against ongoing injustices perpetrated in the material or economic sphere. Sanders invokes in this context Émile Zola's famous "J'accuse!" letter concerning the Dreyfuss affair in France and makes two observations: first, that the duty to speak arises from the desire or will not to be complicit in injustice: "The duty to speak out is linked with a will or desire not to be an accomplice. Responsibility unites with a will not to be complicit in injustice. It thus emerges from a sense of complicity — [...] the actively assumed complicity of one whose silence could allow crime to go undiscovered" (Sanders, 2002, p. 4).

Reparative citizenship as a way of being-politically-in-the-world thus also acknowledges and supports the need for peace-driven, dialogical processes of healing, while emphasizing the crucial importance of reparation in the face of the irreparable.

The question remains, in conclusion, where reparative citizenship, grounded as it is in the metaphorical imagination, leaves the role of government. To this question, I will give Nussbaum's answer: "Government cannot investigate the life story of every citizen in the way [literature] does; it can, however, know that each citizen has a complex history of this sort, and it can remain aware that the norm in principle would be to acknowledge the separateness, freedom, and qualitative difference of each in the manner of [literature] [...] [G]overnments, wherever they are, should attend to citizens in all their concreteness and variety, responding in a sensitive way to historical and personal contingencies" (Nussbaum, 1995, p. 44-45). Or as Krog puts it: "Because a government hears only its own voice, it knows it hears only its own voice, yet it likes to harbour the illusion that it is hearing the voice of the people, and it demands that the people too should harbour this illusion. That is why a cabinet should read literature. Neither the state which it controls, nor the good plans to turn the country around, would help in the absence of a visionary vocabulary (produced best by writers and poets) to create what Martha Nussbaum described as an inspired emphatic social cohesion" (Krog, 2012).

Conclusion

I started this chapter with a reference to the troubles that are plaguing the South African body politic. I do not know whether poetry can achieve the reconciliation and reparation that this country so desperately longs for. But I am convinced that, to the extent that poetry educates what Nussbaum calls the "capacity for humanity" (Nussbaum1995, p. 121) it is a crucial aid in the pursuit of restorative justice through reparative citizenship. Nancy remarks that poetry is the "praxis ... of difficulty itself" (Nancy, 2006, p. 5). "It sits there" he says, "and refuses to go away, even when we challenge it, cast suspicion on it or detest it" (Nancy, 2006, p. 15). Poetry's justice, therefore, is not the easy full and finite justice of law, but rather, the difficult justice that Derrida identifies—the justice that is always still to be done and still to come (Derrida 1990). Towards the pursuit of this justice I have relied in this piece on Agamben's hope for the restoration/presencing of man's poetic status through which the opening of a world other than the irreparable world as it is given, becomes possible. What is fundamentally at stake then is a change of perspective: "What restores the human being as 'a potential being', or, to be more precise, what restores the poetic status of man in the world, the potentiality that we are, is not the world, which confronts us in its unfathomable givenness, but a perspective which opens us to the transformation of the world that is presented to us precisely as given and immutable into a space in which the possibility of the world being otherwise than it is, indeed, the possibility of another world, can be brought to presence" (Šumič, 2011, p. 142).

Such a change of perspective would proceed from an acute awareness of the urgency of justice precipitated by the abyssal precariousness of what is given by the post-apartheid now. It would be harboured in a willingness to become otherwise through a process of action-as-risk, participation-as-discomfort, intervention-as-dissent—the justice of difficulty, of difficult becoming and becoming difficult. It is poetry's justice then—a poetic justice without which reparation is destined to remain but an evasive impossibility. With which, it bears the true potentiality of becoming and bringing into being something reparative.

References

Agamben, G. (1999a). *The man without content* (Giorgia Albert, Trans.). Stanford: Stanford University Press.

Agamben, G. (1999b). *The end of the poem: studies in poetics* (Daniel Heller-Roazen, Trans.) Stanford: Stanford University Press

Agamben, G. (2004). "Friendship". *Contretemps*, 5, 2-7.

Agamben, G. (2005). *The coming community* (Michael Hardt, Trans.). Minneapolis: University of Minnesota Press

Arendt, H. (1958). *The human condition*. Chicago: University of Chicago Press.

Arendt, H. (1965). *On Revolution*. London: Penguin.

Arendt, H. (1971). *The life of the mind*. Florida: Harcourt.

Barnard-Naudé, A.J. (2012). "A law of impurity or a principle of contamination": poetry's resistance. *Stellenbosch law review*, 3, 462-475.

Benjamin, W. (2009). *One-way street and other writings* (J Underwood, Trans.). London: Penguin.

Colebrook, C. (2008). Agamben: Aesthetics, Potentiality, and Life. *South Atlantic Quarterly*, 107(1), 107-120. doi: 10.1215/00382876-2007-058

Derrida, J. (1980). The law of genre. *Critical Enquiry*, 7(1), 55-81. Retrieved from http://www.jstor.org/stable/1343176

Derrida, J (1989). *Memoires for Paul de Man: Revised edition*. New York: Columbia University Press.

Derrida, J (1990). Force of law: the "mystical foundation of authority." *Cardozo Law Review*, 11, 920-1045. Retrieved from http://cardozolawreview.com

Derrida, J. (1994). *Specters of Marx: the state of the debt, the work of mourning, & the new international* (Peggy Kamuf, Trans.). New York: Routledge.

Du Bois, F., & Du Bois-Pedain, A. (2008). *Justice and reconciliation in post-Apartheid South Africa*. Cambridge: Cambridge University Press.

De Wet, P. (2012, November 16). *Reparations still on the back foot. The Mail & Guardian*. Retrieved from http://www.mg.co.za

Doxtader, E., & Villa-Vicenzio, C. (2004) *To repair the irreparable: reparation and reconstruction in South Africa*. Claremont: New Africa Books.

Heidegger, M. (1971). *Poetry, language, thought* (Albert Hofstadter, Trans.). New York: HarperCollins.

Heidegger, M. (1977). *The question concerning technology and other essays* (William Lovitt, Trans.). New York: Harper & Row.

Jaspers, K. (2000). *The question of German guilt* (E.B. Ashton, Trans.). New York: Fordham University Press.

Jika, T., Ledwaba, L., Mosamo, S., Saba, A. (2013). *We are going to kill each other today: the Marikana story*. Cape Town: Tafelberg.

Klabbers, J. (2007). Possible islands of predictability: the legal thought of Hannah Arendt. Leiden *Journal of International Law*, 20, 1-23. doi:10.1017/S092215650600 389X

Krog, A. (1998). *Country of my skull*. Cape Town: Random House Struik.

Krog, A. (2009). *Begging to be black*. Cape Town: Random House Struik.

Krog, A. (2012, September 26). *Should power listen to poetry?* The Guardian. Retrieved from http://www.guardian.co.uk

Langa, P. (2006). Transformative constitutionalism. *Stellenbosch Law Review*, 3, 351-360. Retrieved from http://www.journals.co.za/ej/ejour_ju_slr.html

Nancy, J-L. (1997). *The sense of the world*. Minnesota: University of Minnesota Press.

Nancy, J-L. (2006). *Multiple arts: the muses II*. Stanford: Stanford University Press.

Nussbaum, M.C. (1995). *Poetic justice: the literary imagination and public life*. Boston: Beacon Press.

Plato. (1993). *Republic* (Robin Waterfield, Trans.). Oxford: Oxford University Press.

Rancière, J. (1999). *Dis-agreement and philosophy* (Julie Rose, Trans.). Minneapolis: University of Minnesota Press.

Rose, G. (1996). *Mourning becomes the law: philosophy and representation*. Cambridge: Cambridge University Press.

Salzani, C. (2012). Quodlibet: Giorgio Agamben's Anti-Utopia. *Utopian Studies*, 23(1), 212-237.

Sanders, M. (2002). *Complicities: The Intellectual and Apartheid*. Durham and London: Duke University Press.

Sanders, M. (2007). *Ambiguities of witnessing: law and literature in the time of a truth commission*. Stanford: Stanford University Press.

Stortz, M. (1994). Beyond justice: friendship in the city. *Word & World*, XIV(4), 409-418. Retrieved from http://wordandworld.luthersem.edu/content/pdfs/14-4_City/14-4_Stortz.pdf

Šumič, J. (2011). Giorgio Agamben's godless saints: saving what was not. *Angelaki: journal of the theoretical humanities*, 16(3), 137-147.

Terreblanche, S.J. (2002). *A history of inequality in South Africa, 1652-2002*. Scottsville: University of Natal Press.

Van Marle, K. (2010). Reflections on post-apartheid being and becoming in the aftermath of amnesty: Du Toit v Minister of Safety and Security. *Constitutional Court Review*, 3, 347-367. Retrieved from http://web.up.ac.za/research/2011/Faculties/Law/REGR/Researcher/26700.html

Van Riessen, R. Community and its other: Remarks on Giorgio Agamben's The Coming Community from a Levinasian point of view. *Zeitschrift für Dialektische Theologie*, 5, 79-98.

Žižek, S. (2009). *Violence: six sideways reflections*. London: Profile Books.

Žižek, S. (2012). *Less than nothing: Hegel and the shadow of dialectical materialism*. London: Verso.

Chapter 4
"Moving Beyond Violence:" What We Learn from Two Former Combatants about the Transition from Aggression to Recognition

Jessica Benjamin

Psychoanalyst and Clinical Professor, New York University Postdoctoral Program in Psychotherapy and Psychoanalysis

Introduction

In the summer of 2009 while participating in a conference on relational psychoanalysis I was approached by a British-Israeli Psychotherapist, Irris Singer, with the request to comment on a film she was currently putting together on the stories of two founding members of the organization Combatants for Peace in Israel-Palestine. This film, with the working title "Moving Beyond Violence," was meant to explore how the two men stepped into a framework of rejecting violence as a means of solving the conflicts or dealing with the enemy, indeed how they came to redefine the entire relation between the two sides as one of cooperating for peace rather than enmity. Bassam Aramin, a Palestinian who had spent time in prison for acts committed as a teenager resisting the Occupation and Itamar Shapira, an Israeli who grew up in a Zionist military household but came (along with his brothers) to reject the kind of actions he had taken in the Israeli military, present their stories through interviews with Irris Singer.

Singer asked them not only to describe how they reached the unconventional and radical conclusions of standing for peace while surrounded by violence, but also to describe their childhoods and families. Her initial purpose was to demonstrate for educational purposes the developmental history of attachment (Bowlby, 1969) social and personal, that enable individuals to transgress against the conventional rationalizations of violence in their own societies and take a step into a different peace-oriented world view. The tragic events that occurred during the period of filming as well as the deeply meaningful self-reflective processes that Singer, a psychoanalytic therapist, was able to stimulate in her interviews led to a much broader narrative with wider implications. These in turn necessitated going beyond the paradigm of attachment. Perhaps what would be useful was a psychological paradigm of recognition that could conceptualize what it means to transform one's view of a previously repudiated other and step into the space of dialogue—a space where both subjects are equally dignified and ethically obligated to respect the other.

The version of intersubjective psychoanalytic theory I had developed, which offered a paradigm based on the idea of recognition (Benjamin, 1988, 1998, 2004), seemed to Singer and her colleague Graham Lucas appropriate to conceptualize and give meaning to the story. Singer and Lucas worked with my commentary on the film and adopted my use of the concept of the "moral third," (Benjamin 2004, 2009) which is a particular version of a more general idea. The general idea of the third has multiple usages, and has lately been finding currency in psychoanalytic thought. The term appeared as a useful way to refer to the space or position that holds opposites in tension, that transcends the binaries of good and bad, victim and perpetrator, that are based on psychological splitting.

Translated into practice, we can think of the third as a space of dialogue in which clashing views of reality, antagonistic claims and aims can be negotiated. The effort to create a space that can contain such antagonism in the context of violence and enmity is part of the story of the film, or let us say the background against which we see the subjects struggling with both their own vulnerability and that of the ones who they may be responsible for injuring. This paper will touch on some themes in relation to the stories of these two men who renounced war and use them to illustrate the opening of dialogue in terms of the ethical space of the third, or what I call the Moral Third.

The Idea of the Third

I (Benjamin, 2004) have used the term third generally to designate a position that originates in the experience of thirdness—the experience of a co-created space of shared rhythms, attunement and collaboration, of human cooperation, that begins with early relations between infants and caregivers. It is thus seen as a psychological position founded in the infant's capacity for attachment and mutual recognition and developed with the mother or mothering one. But more significant for our purposes, it is on the basis of this rhythmic, primary third that a differentiating third evolves that includes the capacity for a different kind of recognition: to see from the other's perspective, perhaps through the other's eyes; and, as well, to hold in mind more than one reality or self state. The moral third, a term I use more specifically, denotes a position that recognizes the equal value and dignity of the other, the meaning of the golden rule, the validity of the other's viewpoint, the possibility of dialogue. It is the position that transcends the duality of doer and done-to, the inevitability of kill or be killed, power and submission (Benjamin, 2004). In theorizing about the third we understand that moving out of the alternatives Doer and Done-To means giving up the contest for who can best legitimate their actions by claiming victim status and instead recognize the suffering on all sides as deserving recognition. This recognition is concretized in the idea of the witness (Gerson 2009, Ullman 2006)—an embodiment of the moral third.

Implicit in positing the need for such recognition of suffering by a larger witnessing world that cares (Gerson, 2009) is the principle that the Other, all others, deserve to be seen as equivalent and worthy centers of being. The absence of this caring, acknowledging world—a function played by those personally known or globally identified witness—and the ensuing sense of abandonment has been noted in many studies of trauma (Laub & Auerhahn 1993; Levi, 1988; Gerson, 2009; Herman, 1992) In the larger sense, the moral third is the lawful principle or principles that sustain the possibility of such dignity and recognition. Equally important, the concept of the moral third contains within it the notion of rupture and repair (Tronick, 1999), bridging the gap between what should be and what is, between recognition and breakdown. That is, it contains within it the notion that recognition will break down but that the renewal or restoration of recognition remains at least a theoretical possibility.

This notion of repair or restoration relates to another important aspect of the concept, that of acknowledging violations of expectancy, which I base on the perspective of infancy research (Beebe and Lachmann, 2002). From the beginning of life, patterns of expectation are built up between child and caretaker (Sander, 2002), but expectations are also inevitably violated or disappointed and it is the acknowledgement of the violation that affirms our sense of right and wrong—in other words, of what is moral. Moral in this usage refers not to moralizing judgments, not to oppositions between good and bad, but more specifically to those affirmation of rightness, fittedness, that serve to create the sense of lawfulness. The lived experience of the moral third is that of being able to depend on a lawful world, that is, a world in which, to which, you can safely be attached to others because ruptures are repaired through acknowledgment (Benjamin, 2009; 2013; Tronick, 1989). Thus it fosters connection between self and other; and likewise it is a condition for a sense of agency, as one's ability to affect others requires this relationship to expectancy/violations of expectancy. In other words, the early experience that the other can be relied upon to act in a way that makes one feel safe means that one's need for a secure social attachment is mirrored and met; the pattern of predictable responses that recognize one's actions and intentions then affords a person the possibility of acting on her own behalf. This notion is exemplified by the child who, when something goes wrong or is caused pain, can count on their elders doing their best to acknowledge and remedy the hurt, the mistake, the failure, the lack.

Based on this general, developmental idea of the moral third we then extrapolate that the acknowledgement of things gone wrong, expectations violated, and the consequent pain and suffering, is a crucial and indispensable part of developing the belief in a lawful world. Conversely, lack of acknowledgment engenders a lack of such belief and indeed often a failure to be able to represent the idea of the third and access it as a psychological position in relation to others.

When we move from the level of the individual to the global and social, this means that acknowledging and witnessing of suffering and violence affirms the sense that the world can in some way be counted on to make sense, to be lawful, even when bad things happen. Clearly, the demand for some form of justice relates to this notion of acknowledging violation, recognizing wrong that has been done. When for any number of reasons wrongdoing and suffering are not acknowledged, when those who should witness instead turn away, when denial and dissociation cover up the wrongdoing and the pain associated with it, the sense of a meaningful lawful world also breaks. This loss of meaning may become pervasive and undermine most functions associated with the third, even those not directly involved with ethical issues—for instance the ability to take account of an other's feelings and point of view. This very tendency of breakdowns in lawfulness to undermine the third is part of what makes it difficult to define where isolated experiences leave off and general psychological damage and despair related to loss of thirdness begin. This leaves open many questions as to how to define and delineate terms, but this seems to me an unavoidable part of the process of developing complex concepts such as the third. With this caveat in mind, I use the term moral third to refer to this whole constellation of witnessing and recognizing, of repairing breakdowns and acknowledging violations, of maintaining the existence of the lawful world— as well as the overarching ability to contain oppositions that underpins those functions.

This brings us to the matter of what occurs in loss of the third, what happens when recognition fails and violations must be survived in the absence of acknowledgment (Gerson, 2009). Denial and dissociation are both the result of that absence, and they in turn perpetuate and pass it on. They result in individual and widespread social refusal to acknowledge violations and often to even recognize the humanity of those who suffer. Dissociation opposes acknowledgement and is a crucial obstacle to any effort to de-escalate violence or recover in its aftermath. Dissociation (Howell, 2005), that which psychologically separates us from feeling or recognizing the pain and suffering of others, escaping into rationalization and denial of the reality (Cohen, 2001), is inversely related to our developed capacity for thirdness in the form of emotional identification and connection with the other's experience. In this sense there is a complex intertwining of the capacity to bear pain, accept the reality of life as it is, witness and relate to others suffering, and by the same token the mental space that allows dialogue, thirdness, awareness of the injuries committed in our name. Where do we enter this complex circle of functions that lift dissociation, foster acknowledgment of suffering, recognition of the other, and acting in the framework of the third to recreate lawfulness and respect for the other? This is in part the value of the stories we see in "Moving Beyond Violence," that we can try to see how this kind of personal, moral development occurs; what are its preconditions, what paths does this development take? How is it linked to the all important matter of feeling connected to other human beings?

Ultimately denial is not as self-serving as it appears, even if this is not immediately apparent, because it is so dependent on forms of disconnection. There is a feeling of personal helplessness associated with abdicating moral responsibility, the sense of being passive bystanders in the face of violence (Staub, 2006). From the standpoint of certain philosophies, and this is notably true for the *ubuntu* perspective, those who are not directly involved as perpetrators are affected by shutting off their connection to the suffering and violent injury that they experience second hand because it affects their attachment to the larger social world. This position was articulated at Engaging the Other (Cape Town, 2010) in statements by Antje Krog and the Archbishop Desmond Tutu explicitly reflecting on the *ubuntu* philosophy.

But the experience of violence first hand, which is reflected upon in this film, can become a crisis that affords some individuals an opportunity to re-establish connection and reconsider their relationship to a way that allows us to feel more human and connected to the world at large, perhaps even more able to take action on behalf of ourselves and others? It is thus illuminating for those thinking about violence and collective trauma to witness the experience portrayed in "Moving Beyond Violence".

Narratives of Violence and Transformation

Notably, Itamar's narrative in the film begins with his presenting the iconic Yad Va Shem museum of the Jewish Holocaust, which he claims has become a kind of sacred site in a nationalist religion, formalizing the relation to victimhood and suffering. We see him walking near the young armed soldiers outside the building, as a symbolic example of how formalizing the relations of doer and done to becomes the basis for dissociation of how one has moved from a victim to a perpetrator position. As he walks he describes how this state religion that one is indoctrinated or inculcated into as a child becomes the basis for one's social belonging and military participation. A monstrous horror that in turn becomes the basis for denial of being in the position of perpetrator and refusal to engage with the Other. How does a person become liberated from the entanglements of such a legacy of suffering and horror so as not to justify inflicting suffering oneself? Itamar tries with Singer's help to reflect upon and analyze this process.

The story of this disentangling Itamar will tell in the film begins with the ringing of the phone. A cell phone that belongs to a stranger, the "other," the enemy. We watch him describe this in a way that seems matter of fact, his speech slow and ruminative, yet his body movements uneasy and anxious. He is part of a group (an Israeli military squad in the Occupied territory), he tells us, assigned one night to set up a roadblock and stop everyone passing out of a village. But a jeep of Palestinian security police fails to stop soon enough, and whether they planned to stop, did not think they had to stop, Itamar and his companions fire at the jeep, the men in the jeep fire at them. Unclear who starts firing, but Itamar's group fire until the jeep stops and all its passengers are silenced, dead. One officer fell out of the jeep onto the road where he lay wounded. Itamar describes how his superior commander "confirmed the kill"—delivered the coup de grace—and then how he remained all night, watching the body lying in the road. And next to the body of this man was his cell phone, ringing and ringing. "Someone is trying to reach him, perhaps his wife, his child, his mother…" Itamar thought. A phone ringing said that this man had a life, loved ones, someone waiting for him, and so was also human—this ringing opened a crack in his consciousness, and eventually, after much struggle, this crack became an opening he could step through.

Itamar wrapped this memory of killing carefully, placing it consciously into his memory bank and then waited for a long time, numb and uncertain, wondering when he might feel. When would he realize what it meant to have killed another human being—and what does it mean that the other whom we disdain, deplore, even try to destroy is from another point of view a human being just like me. His story chronicles that journey through numbness, a less drastic symptom than some of the form of dissociation that occurs after trauma, into a place of confrontation, self-reflection and realization about people he had been surrounded by throughout his whole life but never noticed or recognized.

For instance, he begins to think about his co-worker on his grandfather's farm, the Palestinian man who came from Gaza, departing in the wee hours of the morning, traveling hours as he passes through the checkpoints, working all day and then returning home for a few brief hours at night, trying to support his large family. The man describes his family depending on one donated sack of flour in hard times. He begins to picture the intense hardship of this man's life compared to his own family, to wonder, What if he had been sent to invade this man's village, enter his house, arrest someone in his family? Itamar also finds himself troubled by thoughts about having blood on his hands. He thinks, what if I had a daughter and she brought home a young man to marry whom I knew had killed? Then he realizes, I have killed. He sees a film where two enemies out of many remain at the end, fighting to the death, and he thinks: Why bother fighting now, after such killing your life is already ruined? Again, he realizes, this may be a thought about himself. Obviously, having been raised with a defining narrative of how his own people were slaughtered by the millions, it takes enormous strength to confront the idea that he has now become a murderer...but as he paces outside Yad Ve Shem he considers that the Palestinian children must look at him (and by extension the other soldiers of the Occupation) and see a Nazi.

And he wonders about how would he hold his own daughter, how would he hold his lover knowing that he has the stain of this blood on his hands. As the film evolves he develops the thought that being the person who performs the killing is a way of being sacrificed, being turned into a murderer by your own social system, becoming compromised and stained in a way that he rejects. His rejection relates to the moral third, that he himself does not want to be part of an immoral lawless system, and is thus an effort to protect his own internal goodness. While he does not entirely renounce violence, he rejects the surrender of his moral agency to the imperatives of the collective; it should be his own decision whether and how to defend himself or others.

Itamar's gradual awakening from the fog of killing illustrates how the attainment of the third position requires that a person transgress against the conventional response to a socially shared threatening situation (war, occupation, terror), which is deeply understandable, certainly not to be judged or condemned from a position of righteousness—yet it is also one of accepting a terrible choice we must try to visualize. The conventional but ultimately destructive solution can be felt as horror when we cease to numb ourselves, because it involves the terrible choice between killing and dying. Recognizing that he does not want to be placed in this exigency, forced into this choice by a power he submits to, is a crucial part of Itamar's awakening to a position of the moral third.

As I suggested earlier, there is a resonance between Itamar's story and the psychoanalytic insight that conventional acceptance of terrible choices results from and perpetuates what we call dissociation. Dissociation involves form of splitting off some knowledge or felt experience—placing it outside the zone where we would otherwise have to act on and think about what we realize. Relational psychoanalysis emphasizes how we cut ourselves off from the knowledge and sensation of pain—"the escape when there is no escape"—and that this dissociation actually perpetuates suffering in many other forms (Bromberg, 1998, 2006; Ogden, 2006). Reconnecting with the pain that we have tried to escape, deny, refused to know—lifting dissociation—is the first step in reconnecting with our humanity and that of the other. That first step usually involves a connection with others, which enables us to restore the position of the witness, inside or outside ourselves, who sees the suffering (Ullman, 2006).

Bassam's story illustrates this process of connection. It begins with a prison sentence, at the age of 17, for engaging as many youth in Palestine did in the first Intifada of the 1990's, acts of resistance to the Israeli occupation. He was sentenced to jail for seven years, not even a grown man when he entered prison. One day a guard, Shimon, said to him "You seem very quiet, you don't seem like a terrorist." Bassam replied, "I am not a terrorist, I am a freedom fighter—YOU are the terrorists, settling on my land." Shimon replied, "No, we let you live here, but you don't let us live in peace." Bassam, understanding that each believed in his own rightness, proposed that they begin a dialogue, learn about each other's point of view, and see who convinces the other. "If you convince me I will declare it to the whole world, and likewise with you if I convince you." Bassam read and studied, he tried to understand the history of Palestine and Israel, so he could ask the right questions. In the end, it was Shimon who was convinced that he was the occupier—but Bassam even as he appeared to "win" the argument was converted to a different way of looking at the struggle between himself and his jailor in a whole other way. Shimon became his friend, not his enemy, a human being rather than simply an oppressor and occupier.

He said "I used to look at the Jews as the other; I saw a Jew, a Zionist, an Israeli, the enemy. …all the same; women, children, settlers, citizens, soldiers… all the same. We have to kill them all… I used to believe in the total extermination of the other side." How does a young man, angry and full of memories of being humiliated, chased or slapped in the streets by occupying soldiers go through such a profound change? Being listened to and having the chance to argue with the enemy as an equal, a chance to defend his own thinking and perceptions, gave Bassam a new set of tools.

For Shimon, who remained friends with Bassam for many years (until Shimon's death), this connection brought him to accept the realization that he was the opposite of what he had believed, that he was an occupier not a victim. It allowed him to hold a position that others in his community found incomprehensible. What kind of recognition and connection did Bassam give Shimon that made this transformation possible? How do we think about the spark in Shimon that made him, a settler, notice the special emanation that came from Bassam rather than merely dismissing him as the Other? In the end we see that this process is a mutual, one in which each person's move to recognize the Other as more than a cut-out encouraged the other person.

Perhaps Shimon was also moved by seeing how his action changed Bassam, how through his agency another was transformed. As he gradually felt his humanity to be recognized by his captor, he began in turn to recognize his captor as human, and this meant that he could become curious about him, his motivations, his history. He could begin to think, to formulate questions and answers about his enemies. During his time in prison he studied the history of the Jews, and so came to a deep understanding of the suffering and fears of the Jews, the horrors they had experienced. At some point, when the prison showed the film Schindler's List, which made a deep impression and moved him to tears, he felt the horror of the dehumanization in the genocide and began to struggle with this intimate knowledge of his enemy. In the moment he hid his tears from his comrades, as he could not yet find a way to embody and express safely what he was coming to know. But later, he would have the confidence and ability to lead others into this understanding, to show them that their enemy had also suffered violence in the conflict between the two peoples.

Bassam had found through his prison experience, as did many other Palestinians imprisoned for resistance who later joined the Combatants for Peace, a new way to think about the oppositions between the two sides in which a possible third position replaced the extremes of annihilate or be annihilated. The process of dialogue in which each person's reality is respected, appeared to him as a more powerful way of pursuing freedom and at the same time working for peace. Recognizing the humanity of the other, the weakness and suffering that was not so different from his own, allowed him as a grown man to find a strength and resilience that helped him go beyond the boyhood position of angry, helpless victimhood, into dialogue and even cooperation. He developed a position of agency rather than helplessness in relation to the social trauma he suffered.

Recognition, Identification and Empathy for Suffering

As we follow the development of such threads of recognition between people we are invited to reflect on the process by which recognition begins with a thin strand and grows into a thick and complexly woven cord of conviction, strong enough that it serves for people to pull themselves out of the violence and destruction of their past. When this recognition process attains that level of conviction, it supports individuals or groups moving into a place of action on behalf of peace and social healing. This process of attaining conviction, which occurred so powerfully in Bassam's process with Shimon, may be understood as a function, the process of building what we are calling the third, the virtual position that allows us to step out of the relation of doer and done-to, perpetrator and victim (Benjamin, 2004). This position of the third, the one that allows a person even in the midst of struggle to step outside the victim-perpetrator opposition, may be thought of in terms of going from the oppositional principle "My way or the Highway," to the Third Way such that the idea of having to eradicate the threatening Other is recognized as the source of the very problem it is intended to solve. Thus Bassam, in the most affecting act of self-assertion imaginable, repudiates violence as a solution, seeing in it the cause of the very suffering that is so agonizing. As have so many of the Bereaved Parents, another group of Palestinians and Israelis in which he participated, he came to realize the only existential act of freedom that feels lawful in an internal sense, that is, producing a sense of internal cohesion and power rather than chaos and fragmentation, is the rejection of violence.

The actual psychological process of making a shift from enmity to identification is stirring, often rupturing a person's whole world view, a shattering that requires them to rebuild from scratch their life, their sense of right and wrong, that is, their narrative of group identity and history. Even if less dramatic, such a shift always has profound ramifications for our interactions with all people, including those nominally on "our side."

What Bassam's story about his dialogue with Shimon illustrates is how a third position grows from the process of dialogue between two different, opposing voices that initially seem as though they can only cancel each other out. A process that embodies that principle in vivo, in an actual interaction between opposing groups or different voices. So the shift we make when we come into the arena of the third is not only that we may have different perceptions, a different idea of how to treat an enemy or opponent but in terms of the pattern of interaction—from the reactive position that is typical of hyperaroused states associated with trauma where the perception narrows to pure self-defense and flight-fight response to a wider pattern of social engagement (Ogden, 2006). In empathic witnessing (Orange, 2011) such as we practice in psychotherapy, our identifications rely not merely on narrative understanding but on the attunement and responsiveness of the rhythmic third (Aron, 2006; Benjamin 2009) and serve to modulate the distance and differentiation that conflict introduces.

As the film continues we have the opportunity to follow the stories of Itamar and Bassam. But as I said earlier, something shattering and unexpected happened not long after Singer began filming: Bassam's daughter Abir was shot. A soldier inside a tank parked outside his 9 year old daughter's school shot a bullet into her brain as she, with her older sister, was about to walk home. There was no combat in the area, no apparent reason for the shooting, and its motivation (was there a deliberate attempt to provoke Bassam) has never been revealed. But her violent death bears us into acute grief and loss, out of abstractions about conflict. We watch as Bassam and his wife Salwa struggle with this incredible loss amidst the support of friends and family. We see Bassam bearing his grief, talking with his younger daughter about why he doesn't cry about Abir in front of her, forswearing revenge. In live scenes from Israeli television news we see how Israeli members of Combatants for Peace gather at the hospital. In particular two parents who had lost their daughter in a bus bombing some years before, Bassam's friend Rami Elkhanan and his wife Nurit Peled, extend their support.

Bassam's Palestinian friends and family at first don't understand why the enemy is there, in the hospital, trying to join them: "What do they want here?" Even in this moment Bassam exerts his leadership, explains that the Israeli friends are suffering too. Later his wife Salwa describes how she, in her grief, felt utter despair and exasperation with all this peace activity, "I don't want this job," she protests. However, what changes her position is the support she receives from the members of the enemy side who have experience with the loss of children to violence and persist in offering her help and friendship. The motivation to repair the injury and loss, to create a different world for her children by calling for an end to killing, is stronger than the feeling of wanting to withdraw.

An important theme thus emerges—not only Bassam's renunciation of violence and unwillingness to taint his call for justice with personal retaliation and vengeance—but his ability to identify with the suffering of those who feel responsible for injury and want to repair it. He has attained an understanding of how the causing of pain is a source of suffering for the one who causes it. Earlier in the film we see him describe how terrible he feels when his mother walks through the snow to visit him in prison, when his father breaks down upon seeing him after months where Bassam was shipped to an unknown location and held in solitary. Bassam describes the shift in his identification as well when he is tormented by the non-stop crying of his first baby, his son, and asks his father if he caused him such pain, to which his father laughingly replies, "You always caused me suffering." Bassam's embodiment of the victim's understanding of the perpetrators suffering and guilt—mediated by his sense of guilt for his parents' suffering when they saw him be imprisoned and punished by the occupiers—shows us an interesting turn in the identification with a witnessing third position.

The intersubjective perspective on the third would show how Bassam's ability to hold the dual positions—knowing that he can be a person who causes suffering as well as a person who suffers—contributed to his sense of agency. Using the categories of Kleinian psychoanalysis, we could say that his ability to tolerate his own potential for destructiveness rather than splitting it off and projecting it onto the other was in part made possible by the way his parents both acknowledged that he caused them suffering while demonstrating their forgiving acceptance, thus allowing him to make reparation to them.

The ability to bear the pain of knowing they can hurt the ones they love—albeit in very different ways—is an essential part of each man's process and is intrinsically associated with taking up a third position in which different parts of self and different identities can be held in tension. In following Itamar's story, we see a similar story of suffering and reparation. Itamar's mother in fact describes how frightening was the position that Itamar and his brothers put her and her husband in, as members of their community were infuriated by their transgressive refusal to serve the military occupation. The ability to recognize that he felt cut off from other human beings by the thought "I have blood on my hands" at the same time separated Itamar from his parents, represented a challenge to his father, a former pilot, whom he describes as essentially dissociated from the damage any of his military actions did to other human beings. In order to bear this knowledge and confront his parents, Itamar has to bear the pain of knowing that he is hurting those he loves and that they in turn are leaving him alone with his sense of guilt and responsibility, which they cannot fully understand.

In our discussion of the film at the Engaging the Other conference in 2012 we had a striking moment of disagreement around this presentation of

Itamar's mother, as I expressed an awareness of feeling annoyance, almost an irrational outrage, at her response to the death threats against Itamar's brother after he initiated the "Pilot's letter," a public declaration of military pilots that they would no longer engage in missions in the Occupied Territories. The mother describes how the father returned home white and shaking after hearing their own next door neighbor carrying on in the local market about how he didn't know who it was, but he would like to put a bullet through the man who wrote that letter. Almost as soon as she describes this frightening moment, she shifts into another state (dissociates) and declares proudly smiling how amazing her husband is, how liberally he accepted his sons decisions to rebel. While some group members rushed to defend the mother, I asked the group to instead help me hold and analyze my reaction, to see the anger as a transference to the mother and reflect on its meaning—a way of using the enactment of transference to expose otherwise dissociated experience that relational analysis emphasizes (Stern, 2010). The anger seemed to be caused by my identification as a protective mother of sons, which for me, as a non-Israeli who is not subject to their conventions or their fears of being attacked, gave rise to the fantasy of confronting the neighbor with his shameful aggression. As a psychoanalyst, I could understand that the mother was trying to relieve her own fear by dissociating, by switching to a soothing image of a good protective and powerful Dad/husband. But as I was not an abstract witness, as I felt drawn in to suffer the fear and pain with her, I must have also felt left alone by her sudden dissociation and withdrawal from those feelings; and consequently I found myself plunged into my own defensive position of outrage and counterattack. In effect, her switch into denial triggered in me the reactivity of the outraged victim who feels she is left unprotected, without acknowledgment, causing a fight-flight reaction that is actually another kind of dissociation (Howell, 2005).

It is crucially important to realize that even when we are committed to witnessing and conscious of the moral third as a potential, it is easy to lose ourselves in dissociation from pain, to have reactions we can't understand until they are expressed. To feel shame about this, or fall into despair, does not allow us to repair the connection we have thus lost. It requires for most of us constant effort to acknowledge the truth of our own suffering and not merely that of others, for the feedback loop of violation, non-acknowledgment, dissociation becomes an internal process in which we separate ourselves from pain of self and other. To overcome denial or indifference and replace them with empathy is, then, not a one-time act but rather follows this loop logic, and is itself a process of breakdown and restoration of recognition. But insofar as we consciously move along the process, we are simultaneously creating a third position that holds or contains all the moments in this movement.

The third position likewise lies beyond strife about which side is right or wrong. This conscious resistance to descent into moralizing has been exhibited in so many arguments about the Israeli-Palestinian conflict. Part of the mad indignation displayed is actually a response to the fact that there is has been a history of victimization on both sides that cannot be escaped by outrage and moral indictments. The witnessing position that seeks to grasp "What does it mean to feel this suffering, cause this suffering, see this suffering?" lies beyond facile or bitter judgments and insists instead on feeling, on the painful embodiment of this third position (Ullmann, 2006). In relational psychoanalysis this requires finding another self state, in which by accepting the connection to the other there is a bridge between pain and meaning.

Acknowledging Multiple Identifications

As I found in the experience of "The Acknowledgment Project," a series of dialogue meetings I helped to organize some years ago between Israeli and Palestinian mental health workers, these kinds of reactivity, taking up one-sided positions against opposite sides, are incredibly common in relation to violent conflict. But I also noted that eventually there developed an identification with the group as a whole, holding the chorus of opposing or different voices, in dialogue, a multiplicity of self states. This ability to hold multiple identifications and states within the self, or identify with the other alongside the self, allowing them to relativize, modify, each other in content, is one that the relational analyst Philip Bromberg (1998) referred to as "standing in the spaces". The capacity evolved based on an attachment to the group as a whole, a separate identity than the national and group identities each individual already held, whose process contained enough acknowledgment and sense of lawfulness to allow this safety of attachment—although it often ruptured and had to be restored.

Thus in situations marked by the challenge of seeing the "enemy" other's experience such as Itamar described, the capacity to hold multiple positions and identifications becomes part of the capacity to uphold lawfulness. Staying aware of the other's humanity while in the grip of fear, where each side sees the other as not merely as someone negating but actually potentially destroying one's identity and world, even one's life, requires the not only a different sense of You as human, but a different sense of Me as complex. I have to see myself as containing different parts, good and bad, violent and peaceful, have to have an emotionally integrated sense of the Third as a position holding the multiplicity not only of me and you but the many parts of me. So, for instance, in my role as relational analyst I could notice how my identification with Itamar's mother broke down and was countered by my other maternal identifications, yet I could restore my sense of compassion for her suffering and fear by committing to repair, through analysis, by engaging a group process in which we identified with multiple positions, including her fear and efforts to escape it by turning back to restore her ideal object, her now frightened husband in his other inflated incarnations.

No doubt my reaction, and those of many others, reflect despair and repugnance at precisely the way in which such fears have been used to bolster triumphalist or aggressive actions on the part of former victims—the way in which the history of victimization has led to the justification rather than moral repudiation of occupation and oppression of an entire people. This inflated triumphalism leads those observing to lose their grasp of the underlying fear that drives those violations. Yet, when we observe the acts of sadism, revenge, power-driven destruction it does call for an analysis that recognizes the fact that perpetrators feel pleasure in inflicting injury, that those in power enjoy their triumph. It is certainly undeniable that torturers express enjoyment, that military victors express triumph over their enemies' humiliation, that people who understand themselves as righteous patriots express satisfaction in repaying the enemy whose resistance they experience as a challenge to their own power and superiority. All these ugly manifestations of entitlement to power have been virulent in the United States especially since the beginning of the retaliatory response to the September 11th attack on the World Trade Center.

The origins of genocide, oppression, and mass transports of lust in violent transgression have been studied and much could be said about them; but the collapse from such inflated states into deflated, frightened and vulnerable states is also well known and documented. I want to be clear that I am only focusing on this latter transition and how to use it to create new relationships based on lawfulness, empathy and recognition of the other. There is no question that some perpetrators, especially those who initiated and organized violent crimes, who most benefited from their exploitation of power, never deflate. Further, my remarks here do not address what it takes to change the political power relations of oppression. But the majority of human beings seem to be capable of being both victims and perpetrators. The issue addressed by the film and in this paper is how to create a vision that goes beyond punitive retaliation and reversal, which perpetuates splitting and dissociation, and denies this duality of our nature. This is the question Bassam asked himself, how will we liberate ourselves without in turn becoming like our oppressors who were once themselves victims.

In fact, there is a psychoanalytic understanding based on the view of the duality of doer and done-to in each psyche. In this view, perpetrators' assertions of superiority and pleasure in defensive triumph (in Kleinian language, the manic defense), can be seen as efforts to repel identification with helpless vulnerability, mortality, the human condition; and then, as inability to bear the shame of having committed crimes against other humans. This shame and attendant horror in fact cause trauma and severe illness in soldiers who return from war. Although far easier to grasp than evil itself, it is far less common to recognize the pain suffered by perpetrators who awaken from the dissociated state of the manic defense to realize their actual condition. We might consider the psychohistorical distance traveled from Aeschylus's early play The Persians where the enemy's humiliation is a source of rejoicing for the Greeks to the Bacchi where the mother awakens from the blood thirsty ecstasy induced by Dionysus to realize it is her own son's dismembered head she is holding. This agony turns into horrific irony the chorus' final chant, "the greatest pleasure is to hold a knife to the enemy's throat and we want it forever." And yet, in displaying the Persians weeping like despised women or children, a display over which the Greeks apparently made merry, they also enacted the very vulnerability that was split off and dissociated from themselves.

The awakening from horror in fantasy, to its very reality, comes when the split off identification with the agonized other suddenly perhaps forcibly comes back into the self. It is a transformation that can occur when the victims assert their human dignity and force a breakthrough of dissociation. While this is often only possible by actually defeating or depriving perpetrators of their power and thus often requires not merely the witnessing but the active intervention of other world powers, that is a necessary but not sufficient condition. The confronting of perpetrators with their actions in a way that transforms the relations of kill or be killed into a more lawful system is not guaranteed by such power interventions; it needs a moral dimension of bringing truth and witnessing to bear on crimes in which the victims can represent their demand for justice rather than retaliation. While there are many writings on and arguments over the success of transitional justice, and many of them rightly hinge on the role of economic power, I am limiting this discussion to the psychological. The process by which victims change the terms and create the third is has been discussed by Grand (2002) and beautifully documented by Gobodo-Madikizela (2003) in the story of former security chief de Kook who after his imprisonment for crimes against black resisters to Apartheid comes to the realization of his guilt and his identification with the victims and their surviving wives and mothers. The move Gobodo-Madikizela describes from helpless victimhood to moral agency in embracing the moral third and re-establishing the lawful community is one of the most powerful statements ever made on behalf of moral strength and conviction upholding the third in the service of non-violent social transformation. It shows the capacity required to grasp the full meaning of the dictum that we are all human. This comprehension was embodied in the action of the Gazan psychiatrist Eyad el Sarraj, my collaborator and the inspiration for the Acknowledgment Project, who was able to say to one of the Israeli soldiers with bayonets who were abusing a helpless victim in his presence, "Let me see your face, I want to know it is a human being who is doing this."

Gobodo-Madikizela (2003) is very clear in her observation of the impact of the victim's forgiveness in restoring the sense of humanity to the perpetrator, as when she describes the effect of the mother of a slain young woman, Gin Foure forgiving the murderers who were involved in armed resistance to apartheid. These young men explained that Gin had given them back their humanity, their sense of the right to belong to the world of human beings who are not criminal outcasts, sinners. She shows us how the mothers of the informant who turned the boys in the Gugeletu 7 over to be killed by the police are able to forgive by saying, we are all sinners.

I have been trying to show what it is that makes the principle "I am human because you are human; we can only be human when we recognize each other as human" a foundational principle of the relational entity I call "the moral third"—not a banal slogan but a representation of a complex psychological process within and between individuals. The idea of the moral third is an attempt to conceptualize a transformational process that enables the step out of a socially accepted narrative that justifies violence based on one's own victimhood and thus causes further violence. I have been using the film "Moving Beyond Violence" to elaborate the idea of the moral third as a basis for ethical action as well as a psychological position that is healing of the trauma caused by violence. I have tried to show how the action of respecting others, connecting to others suffering and needs, meeting aggression with non-violence and conflict with negotiation can actually strengthen the part of the self that holds oppositions and tensions without collapsing into states of disorganization and fear of threat, without splitting off the knowledge of one's own damage or ability to be aggressive and damage others. Ultimately this reinforces the capacity for social attachment or social engagement that play a role in living with trauma differently.

I have also tried to show how the concept of the third can be used to signify the actual incarnation and expression in human interaction of a stance that helps us to preserve agency, maintain empathy and compassion for others' pain, and hold onto the idea of multiple positions and realities in human conflict. At the same time, the third can be seen specifically as a moral principle which transcends and takes us out of the binary, the either-or, in which only one person is human, worthy of respect, deserving of living rather than dying (Benjamin, 2016).

References

Aron, L. (1996). *A Meeting of Minds: Mutuality in Psychoanalysis*. Hillsdale, NJ: Analytic Press.

Aron, L. (2006). Analytic impasse and the third. *Int. J. Psycho-Anal*, 87, 344-368.

Aron, L (2002). *Infancy Research and Adult Treatment*. Hillsdale, NJ: Analytic Press.

Benjamin, J. (1988). *The Bonds of Love: Psychoanalysis, Feminism, and the Problem of Domination* New York: Pantheon.

Benjamin, J. (1998). *Shadow of the Other: Intersubjectivity and Gender in Psychoanalysis*. New York/London: Routledge.

Benjamin, J. (2004). Beyond doer and done to: An intersubjective view of thirdness. *Psychoanalytic Quarterly,* 63, 5-46.

Benjamin, J. (2010). Mutual acknowledgment? Obstacles and possibilities for acknowledgment in the face of asymmetry and injury. In Heuer, G (ed.) *Sacral Revolutions: Reflections on the work of Andrew Samuels* (51-58). London: Routledge.

Benjamin, J. (2009). A relational psychoanalysis perspective on the necessity of acknowledging failure in order to restore the facilitating and containing features of the intersubjective relationship (the shared third). *Int. J. Psychoanal*, 90, 441-45.

Benjamin, J. (2009). Psychoanalytic controversies: Response to Sedlak. *Int. J. Psychoanal*, 90, 457-462.

Benjamin, J. (forthcoming, 2016). Beyond doer and done to: Recognition theory and intersubjectivity. London: Routledge.

Bowlby, J. (1969). *Attachment and loss: Vol. 1*. Attachment. New York: BasicBooks.

Benjamin, J. (1973). *Attachment and loss: Vol. 2*. Separation: Anxiety and anger. New York: Basic Books.

Bromberg, P. B. (1998). *Standing in the Spaces*. Hillsdale, NJ: The Analytic Press.

Bromberg, P.B (2006) Awakening the dreamer: *Clinical journeys*. Mawah NJ: The Analytic Press.

Cohen, S. (2001). *States of Denial: Knowing about Atrocities and Suffering*. London: Polity Press.

Ferenczi, S. (1933). Confusion of tongues between adults and the child. In *Final Contributions to the Problems and Methods of Psychoanalysis* (156-167). London: Karnac, 1980.

Fonagy, P., Gergely, G., Jurist, E. & Target, M. (2002). *Affect regulation, mentalization and the development of the self.* New York/London: Other Books.

Gerson, S. (2009). When the third is dead: memory, mourning and witnessing in the aftermath of the holocaust. *International Journal of Psychoanalysis,* 90, 1341-1357.

Gobodo-Madikizela, P. (2003). *A Human Being Died that Night: A South African Story of Forgiveness.* Boston: Houghton Mifflin.

Grand, S. (2002). *The Reproduction of Evil.* The Analytic Press: Hillsdale, NJ.

Hegel, G. W. F. (1807). *Phenomenologie des Geistes.* Hamburg, Germany: Felix Meiner, 1952.

Howell, E. (2005). *The Dissociative Mind.* New York and London: Routledge.

Laub D.& Auerhahn, N.C. (1993). Knowing and not knowing massive psychic trauma: forms of traumatic memory. *International Journal of Psycho-Analysis,* 74, 287-302.

Levi, P. (1988). *The Drowned and the Saved.* New York: Random House.

Ogden, P., Pain, C., Minton, K. & Fisher, J. (2006). *Trauma and the Body.* New York: Norton.

Orange, D. (2011). *The Suffering Stranger.* London: Routledge.

Sander, L. (2002). Thinking differently: Principles of process in living systems and the specificity of being known. *Psychoanalytic Dialogues,* 12(1), 11-42.

Schore, A. N. (2003). *Affect Regulation and the Repair of the Self.* New York: Norton.

Stern, D. B. (2010). *Partners in Thought; Working with Unformulated Experience, Dissociation and Enactment.* New York: Routledge.

Tronick, E. (1989). Emotions and emotional communication in infants. *American Psychologist,* 44, 112-119.

Ullman, C. (2006). Bearing Witness: Across the Barriers in Society and in the Clinic. *Psychoanal. Dial.,* 16, 181-198.

Chapter 5
Unsettling Empathy:
Intercultural Dialogue in the Aftermath of Historical and Cultural Trauma

Björn Krondorfer

Northern Arizona University

Introduction

In my work as facilitator of intercultural encounters, I often straddle the line between different understandings of trauma as they variously apply to the repairing of broken relations between social groups in conflict. I am not trained to treat traumatized individuals medically or therapeutically, but I am working with dialogical models in group settings in which we address the long-term effects of endured wounding and culpable wrongdoing. We particularly pay attention to the eroding power of injurious and traumatic memory on social relations, with the goal to open pathways for improved communicative patterns and restorative visions. In this sense, the theoretical frames of historical and cultural trauma are relevant for both my conceptual comprehension and my practice of group facilitation.

In this chapter, I will describe and reflect upon my work with intercultural groups in conflict. Embedded within an awareness of the power of historical trauma and set within the dynamics of reconciliatory processes, I will argue for the value of unsettling empathy. I understand unsettling empathy to refer to a posture that needs to be learned and practiced by people who, because of identifying with "large-group identities" (Volkan, 2013), have come to distrust each other based on historical and present antagonisms.

I am calling unsettling empathy a *posture* because it best articulates what I have observed it to be. Unsettling empathy is not just a pedagogical tool in reconciliatory processes or a didactic element of dialogue, although it can be those things as well. I would also hesitate to call it a skill or a method, although unsettling empathy can be learned. Instead, I think of it as a kind of practiced awareness, as a relational commitment to caring responsiveness. The posture of unsettling empathy is a deliberate ethical stance which, ideally and over time, might become something akin to habitus—an acquired disposition and sensibility that eventually informs, guides, and structures one's attitude toward life.

Trauma Discourse

The current ubiquity of the usage of "trauma" in academic writing, public discourse, and the media requires a few words of clarification. This brief exercise is helpful on two accounts: For one, it helps to distinguish medical and psychological definitions of trauma from investigations that speak of historical and cultural trauma; second, it helps to differentiate between traumatic experiences with respect to severity, duration, and agency.

Trauma definitions generally agree on two elements: Trauma is caused by a severe violation of integrity (often described as a shattering of self and the world), and it has a lingering, long-term impact. But beyond this general agreement, descriptive and theoretical investigations differ significantly. For example, does the violation of integrity only concern the physical and psychological wounding of the individual (as medical and a majority of therapeutic models suggest), or does it equally apply to social groups and communities in the form of transmitted injurious memories and sustained malicious discrimination (as historical and cultural theories argue)? Is traumatization a uniform and universal reaction to violence-induced rupture (akin to a biologically innate regulatory mechanism), or is it a culture-dependent response? In the case of the latter, theorists in the humanities and social science argue that trauma gets crystallized through existing cultural frames that give the severity of an assault its specific meaning.

What, then, determines the gravity of the harm experienced: individual or social factors? In the mental health field, on the one hand, the authoritative tool to diagnose disorder (the DSM) remains focused on the psychobiological timelessness of trauma's destructive impact, independent of the individual's ethnic or cultural background. Theorists of cultural trauma, on the other hand, emphasize that it is the social environment that largely determines whether an event is experienced as traumatic. Disparity of theoretical perspective can also be observed between those that see trauma as the result of a single, forceful event (like the medically defined sudden, blunt, radical impact on the body) and those that look at trauma as the result of an insidious web of abiding social injustices, such as colonialism, apartheid, or racism (see Craps, 2013).

Despite differences, there are multiple overlaps among the definitional fields. For example, historical and psychological trauma theories can find common ground on the question of whether secondary traumatization is possible—for example, through witnessing someone else's trauma.[1] As to the possibility of transmission of trauma across generations, some psychoanalysts and therapists have joined historical and cultural theorists in affirming that the effects of trauma can transcend individual life-spans and continue on as subterranean anxieties and pathologies in subsequent generations. Such continuities can be traced *intergenerationally* (traumatic patterns and memories transmitted *within* a family system) as well as *trans*generationally (traumatic patterns and memories transmitted *across* unified social identities, independent of personal family histories).[2]

Finally, there is the issue of agency. Agency, here, refers to the situational and social position that people inhabit vis-à-vis trauma-inducing events. This is particularly relevant in terms of treating people and communities suffering from post-traumatic stress disorder (PTSD). It is known that extraordinary violence does not only threaten, disrupt, and shatter the integrity of victims, but that it also disintegrates people who are actively participating in violent events (such as soldiers in war). Even the culpable wrongdoer—the person inflicting severe harm—can suffer from PTSD in a post-violent or post-genocidal situation. Thus, ironically, the whole spectrum of agency vis-à-vis world-rupturing and self-shattering violence—victims, witnesses, bystanders, accomplices, perpetrators—may require therapeutic treatment or rely on broad support systems for their social reintegration.

While medical and mental health professionals (and also clergy) are, to a large extent, required to treat everyone equally and independent of their agency, historical and cultural trauma theorists pay attention to the ethical and political dimensions of the long-lasting social impact of traumatized communities. Those theorists remind us not only of the staying power of trauma but also of the danger of the ubiquitous use of trauma terminology. In the case of the latter, undifferentiated trauma-talk may lead to a facile equation of all traumatized people, thus erasing the ethical difference

---

[1]   The current *Diagnostic and Statistical Manual of Mental Disorders* (DSM) recognizes that exposure to trauma can come about direct experience to self or witnessing such harm to others: "The person has been exposed to a traumatic event ... [when] the person experienced, witnessed, or was confronted with an event or events that involved actual or threatened death or serious injury, or a threat to the physical integrity of self or others" (DSM-IV-TR, p. 467). On witnessing, see Felman & Laub (1992); for critical views, see Weissman (2004) and Craps (2013).

[2]   For a good discussion of inter- and transgenerational transfer of memory and associated terms such as "postgeneration," see Hirsch (2012, pp. 1-36); she also speaks of "familial postmemory" (a memory that, in my nomenclature, is passed on *inter*generationally) and "affiliative postmemory" (passed on *trans*generationally) (p. 36).

between *harm inflicted* and *harm endured*. They also remind us that the contemporary fixation on trauma in Western academic circles and public parlance may lead to treating someone else's wound as a public spectacle at a non-threatening distance. Such voyeuristic consumption turns trauma into a "sentimental political discourse" (Craps, 2013, p. 125), which prevents an effective call to political action to get articulated. To mitigate such ethical dilemmas, a critical trauma theory would need to negotiate the right balance between fostering (individual) healing and pursuing (communal) justice. It is a quandary that requires sustained transnational discussions about the value of retributive justice versus restorative justice, especially in transitional societies (e.g. Amstutz, 2005).

Intercultural Memory Work

I have elsewhere described my facilitation of groups that have been or continue to be in conflict with each other as "intercultural memory work" (Krondorfer, 2013b). In situations of communal conflicts that stretch over generations, memory work is particularly important, but also particularly difficult, since memory motivates us to act in particular ways in the present. Unchallenged, memory can serve to fortify our communal borders, defend our social group identities, make us cling to stories of suffering and victimization, or make us hold on to tales of a heroic past.[3] In contrast to simply *having* memories that get reiterated in families and communities, *memory work* is the attempt to actively engage troublesome memories. It moves us toward a place where we are no longer prisoners of the past but freed to relate anew to people like us and people not like us.

In intercultural memory work, various facets of traumatic content characterize the interactions of and between the participants. Groups I have facilitated over the years include encounters between third-generation American Jews and their non-Jewish German counterparts, seminars for Christian clergy and Jewish educators/rabbis at sites of atrocities (e.g. the Nazi concentration camp of Buchenwald), artistic cooperation with visual and performance artists (Krondorfer, 2013a), racial reconciliation retreats for U.S. undergraduate students, or trilateral trust-building workshops for Israelis, Palestinians, and Germans.

The particular goals for each of these groups differ, but the guiding paradigms for facilitation remain the same. They include:

---

[3]   National/communal hero and victimhood narratives are "nostalgic constructions . . . clinging to idealized images of the past" (Gobodo-Madikizela 2012, p. 255).

- engaging in alternative forms of communication that require risk-taking, vulnerability, honesty
- practicing careful listening, straightforward responding, and empathic imagining
- attending to the impact of family biographies, of communal memories, and of national histories

These seminars, workshops, and retreats meet within a circumscribed, condensed timeframe. A meeting could be as short as two days or as long as four uninterrupted weeks; they can also be offered as a series of weekend seminars spread over several months. Whether these encounters take place in retreat centers or include travel components, the framework remains that of a protective space conducive to personal and social exploration. In this space, participants are encouraged to challenge their perceptions of themselves and others through affective and cognitive levels of communication, including creative, body-centered, and nonverbal components. Though the work is deeply interpersonal, the focus is always on the dynamics of the whole group, a process I have called "reconciliatory" (Krondorfer, 2012) and described elsewhere as "cultural therapy" (Krondorfer, 1992, pp. 72, 91).

Although the concept of historical trauma informs strongly the intercultural memory work I am engaged in, other forms of trauma also come into play. Sometimes, the traumatic or traumatizing experiences are severe and direct, at other times hidden and subtle. They reach from individually endured severe harm (victims of torture; victims of rape) to the psychological effects of secondary witnessing;[4] from cultural memories of genocide to personal exposure to paralysis in damaged families; from repetitions of politicized communal trauma narratives to unacknowledged losses passed on intergenerationally; from the postmemories[5] imprinted by family members to the felt-memory of continuous threats to one's physical and emotional integrity.

At times, we have participants in our groups who are traumatized without them being aware of it. The lack of individual awareness is often rooted in a lack of communal language because social and political circumstances are such that any acknowledgment of damage to one's own soul and body is communally spurned as aggrandizing self-pity. This is particularly true for individuals and groups that are in the throes of current conflicts and for whom any trauma-talk seems like an emotional luxury they cannot afford. It

---

[4] On secondary witnessing, see Felman & Laub (1992) and Apel (2002).
[5] On postmemory and witnessing, see Hirsch (2012).

is therefore important to distinguish between historical trauma and cultural trauma in intercultural conflict settings. To put the difference succinctly:

- in settings where *historical trauma* is the primary source of contentious social relations due to differing memories, there is generally a stronger willingness to use trauma as a paradigmatic model for restorative efforts. The temporal distance to the past serves as a buffer that allows the conflicting parties to interact with greater emotional and political freedom of social exploration

- in settings where ongoing unresolved conflicts determine large-group identities, there is a less-developed ability to understand the situation through trauma. People who live in such volatile situations rely, instead, on political modes of communication to voice their grievances and seek for solutions. It is the latter setting where we speak of *cultural trauma*. Trauma in this setting is akin to a diagnostic (and sometimes external) comprehension of the severity of threats and harm to integrity, independent of whether the affected individual actors or communal bodies acknowledge it as such.

Further below, I will illustrate the difference between these two settings (historical trauma/cultural trauma) by describing two particularly remarkable occasions from my intercultural work. But before getting to these specific cases, I need to address yet another set of terms so as to fully flesh out the conceptual framework within which I operate.

Dialogue, Reconciliation, Empathy

At first sight, the call for dialogue seems antithetical to trauma discourse. Since trauma is a severely destructive, disruptive, and disorienting force, any restorative effort would seem to work best if done in a safe space, where caretakers can pay undivided attention to repairing the physical, mental, and emotional integrity of the survivor, and survivors can learn to mobilize their own resources for healing and reintegration. Bringing in other agents would only cause detrimental emotional reactions (like anger, guilt, self-blame, etc.) or trigger retraumatizing flashes that would delay the process of restoring trust in oneself and the world.

Though such safety is crucial in the medical and psychological treatment of traumatized individuals, it does not equally apply to historical and cultural trauma settings. Here, dialogical principles can become part of the restorative efforts. As a matter of fact, Cathy Caruth, one of the early pioneers who expanded trauma theory to cultural, literary, and ethical investigations, claims that trauma does not only root us in our historical situatedness but also calls us to acknowledge the ways in which historical trauma links individuals and cultures. "[T]he notion of trauma . . . is aimed not at eliminating history but at resituating it in our understanding," she writes in *Unclaimed Experience*. "[H]istory, like trauma, is never simply one's own." Rather, "history is precisely the way we are implicated in each other's trauma" (Caruth, 1996, pp. 11, 24). In other words, communicating across cultural divides about the effects of trauma not only crystallizes the perception of our boundedness to our respective histories, it also reaches beyond the one-sidedness of parochial history-retelling in order to seek ways of cross-cultural understanding. Applied to working through historical and cultural trauma, we can say then that the realization of being "implicated in each other's trauma" calls for dialogical engagement.

Once we allow for the insight that dialogue is not antithetical to working with mixed groups in the presence of traumatic content, we need to think about the nature of dialogue we wish to pursue. In my own work, I want dialogical encounters to be deliberate about going

- beyond the surface of friendly conversation
- beyond the limitation of a culture's master narrative
- beyond the comfort zones of rehearsed opinions
- beyond loyalties that communities impose on our large-group identities

Of course, the three "guiding paradigms for facilitation" identified above also contribute to successful dialogue. I call such dialogical encounters "reconciliatory processes."

When I speak of reconciliation, I am not speaking of forgiveness or repentance. I would not even summon the words healing or compassion without further qualification. I understand reconciliation to be a process that is open-ended. Reconciliatory efforts are not measured by the attainment of a pre-determined end but by the transformative power of the path we walk. A reconciliatory process is not so much a result as it is a mode of working through injuries, discrimination, social injustice, wrongdoing, guilt, and traumatic memories. Importantly, it needs to include the multiple dimensions of suffering and accountability, or what I have called above the dual dimension of "endured wounding" and "culpable wrongdoing." To engage in reconciliatory efforts requires parties with different experiences and grievances to be fully present to each other. The intent is to go beyond merely describing how each party perceives reality and, instead, to adjust and revise each other's perception of one's being-in-the-world in pursuit of (re)establishing trust. Reconciliatory processes, to use Caruth's words, require us to get implicated in each other's histories and traumas.

The posture of unsettling empathy plays a crucial role in these processes. For an encounter to be transformative, one must go beyond a discourse of politeness and, at times, even beyond a discourse of civility, as long as safety for and respect of each participant is guaranteed. I would also say that compassionate listening alone is not sufficient, if by that we mean a method in which each group in turn can air their grievances while the other group listens attentively without interrupting or contradicting the narrated experience. Compassionate listening works well as an initial step in bringing groups with antagonistic histories together, but it falls short of actually working through the tensions that divide them. Compassion by itself can too easily be mistaken as the kind of civil discourse that uses polite forms of rhetoric to mask underlying tensions. In *Trauma and Recovery*, Judith Herman reminds us that "remembering and telling the truth about terrible events are *prerequisites* both for the restoration of the social order and for the healing of individual victims" (1992, p. 1; emphasis added). As a "prerequisite," truth-telling is an important component, but it is only an initial step in the process of recovery.

Compared to compassion, the posture of unsettling empathy signals that our dialogical engagement may cost us something. It requires risks. It requires the risk of vulnerability, of courage, of being shaken in one's foundation and assumptions about the world and the Other. Having worked for the last three decades with people impacted by the upheavals in Europe in the 1930s and 1940s (Holocaust, Second World War, dictatorships, occupation, massive population transfers, etc.), I am aware of how long it can take before affected communities and their descendants are able to start dialogic exchanges. Effective reconciliatory processes begin where it matters, and where it matters, it might hurt, and where it hurts, it leads (when carefully managed) to transformation.

By suggesting the importance of unsettling empathy, I gesture consciously toward Dominick LaCapra's concept of "empathic unsettlement," which is central to his theory on trauma and narrative. According to LaCapra, it is not sufficient to respond to historical trauma merely through the lens of "objective reconstructions of the past" (2002, p. 41), as many historians do. Equally problematic would be to appropriate historical trauma through a "vicarious" and "unchecked identification" (p. 40) by secondary witnesses. While the first (objective) response errs on the side of neglecting the subjectively experienced traumatic impact, the second (vicarious) response errs on the side of a well-intended, but ultimately facile "surrogate victimhood" (p. 40). Empathic unsettlement, according to LaCapra, avoids these traps by responding to trauma without seeking closure, for it recognizes "unsettling possibility" (p. 41) contained in traumatizing events—for both victims and perpetrators.

My own guiding assumptions about reconciliatory processes share several affinities with LaCapra's ideas. LaCapra, like Cathy Caruth, points to the *dialogical* value of responding to trauma, walking a fine line between cognitive levels (objective history) and affective levels (empathic responses) of comprehension. This "dialogic exchange with the past" (LaCapra, 2002, p. 41) requires a self-reflective awareness of the "subject position" (p. 40) of anyone trying to comprehend the past. When entering into a responsive relationship with traumatic history, we need to know who we are, where we come from, and how we are identified with large-group identities. It matters whether I am German, Israeli, or South African, or whether I am a direct descendant or a professional historian, and so forth. Rather than declaring an amorphous "we are all humans" approach, intercultural memory work depends on the willingness and ability of participants to clarify their agency (or "subject position") vis-à-vis the historical trauma that defines contentious social relations.

A final affinity with LaCapra is his insistence that empathic unsettlement is a response that seeks no closure but accepts unsettling possibilities, which parallels my assertion that reconciliatory processes must be open-ended (Krondorfer, 2013b).

Roger Simon et al. also refer to the notion of unsettlement when speaking of the need for a critical pedagogical practice of remembrance that "initiate[s] a continual unsettling" (Simon, Rosenberg and Eppert, 2000, p. 6). I therefore should briefly explain why I speak—in reversal of LaCapra's wording—of "unsettling empathy." I do so because I wish to be attentive to the actual dynamics of empathy in intercultural group settings. I want to point to an active practice of a particular kind of empathy that triggers the "unsettling" (rather than using "empathic" as a modifier for a noun/concept). The posture of unsettling empathy is less a theoretical concept analyzing trauma in relation to another problem (like historiography or representation) than it is an ethical practice that can be learned and acquired. It must be actively in*corpo*rated (referring here also to its embodied dimension, given the Lat. root *corpus*) within a protective space.

The protective environment that needs to be provided has been variously referred to as third space, liminal space, transitional space, or intermediary space. Importantly, it is an intentional space created outside of ordinary rules that individuals and communities impose on themselves. It is conducive to holding high social tensions while creatively exploring what Caruth might call a "resituating [of] our understanding," or Simon et al. would call a "reworking [of our] notions of community, identity, embodiment, and relationships" (2002, p. 6). In a similar vein, Pumla Gobodo-Madikizela—with respect to apartheid's historical trauma—speaks of the necessity for dialogical engagement with "unsettling testimony" within a frame of "making public spaces intimate" (2012, p. 262; also 2008). Her spatial metaphor mirrors what I consider essential when working with groups in conflict: the necessity to express and reveal the intimate wounds of historical and cultural trauma in spaces that surpass the purely intersubjective in order to include a "public" domain, insofar as it is essential to bring large-group identities to the table. "At the core of what unfolds in these encounters," Gobodo-Madikizela writes, "is a *reciprocal mutual engagement*" (2012, p. 262; emphasis in original).

The posture of unsettling empathy has yet another advantage over a less differentiated notion of compassion. A compassionate attitude has the tendency to erase some of the objective differences of agency vis-à-vis traumatic history. In the name of a common humanity, compassion too quickly glosses over the ethical difference between harm inflicted and harm endured, presenting all sides as victims of circumstances they could not control. Unsettling empathy, on the other hand, calls us into the presence of objective differences without negating the vitality of human interaction. For example, when a secondary witness, who is a descendant of a perpetrator society, cannot fully acknowledge the extent of pain inflicted (note: not endured!) and, hence, fails to address the issue of vicarious accountability, the injustices and abuses of the past remain ignored, with the result of potentially stalling dialogic engagement in the present. When, on the other hand, a secondary witness who is a descendant of a victimized community identifies vicariously with his or her family's trauma to the extent that it disallows the full humanity of the Other to emerge, then dialogic engagement is equally blocked. The posture of unsettling empathy, however, allows for the inclusion of both a critical perspective on power asymmetries (regarding historical and cultural trauma) as well as compassion with the Other despite historical injustices and contentious memories. Unsettling empathy blends the critical/political dimension with the affective/interpersonal dimension of working through historical and cultural trauma, and as such it is a vital element in reconciliatory processes.

Let me summarize the central features of unsettling empathy:

- Unsettling empathy costs something, whereas compassion can too easily be mistaken as the kind of civil discourse that uses polite forms of rhetoric to mask underlying tensions
- Unsettling empathy requires the risk of vulnerability, of courage, of being shaken in one's foundation and assumptions about the world and the other
- Unsettling empathy calls us into the presence of objective differences without negating the vitality of human interaction, whereas compassion may tempt us to erase some of the objective differences in the name of a common humanity
- Unsettling empathy allows for the inclusion of both a critical perspective on power asymmetries as well as the compassionate stance toward the Other despite historical injustices
- Unsettling empathy describes a posture that blends the critical/political with the affective/interpersonal

We are now ready to look at two select examples of intercultural conflict situations, where the posture of unsettling empathy can be observed. The first focuses on a setting that falls into historical trauma. Here, we will get a glimpse at how "memory work" can be intensively personal while simultaneously calling upon large-group responses to trauma. In this example, we will encounter the presence of a haunted past that becomes temporarily embodied in a returning "ghost." The second example foregrounds cultural trauma. Here we will walk with the participants the fine line between collective narratives and the immediacy of political uncertainty.

Haunting Presence of a Ghost: A Case of Historical Trauma

In the fall of 2011, a group of German and Israeli educators, therapists, teachers, and community organizers invited me to conduct a three-day seminar in Germany on the effects of the Holocaust and the Second World War. The group—which ranged in age from mid-twenties to seventies—had already worked together for some time on peace-related activities. But the repercussions of disruptive and traumatic memories kept obstructing their present-day relations. They hoped that this seminar on "Restorative Forgetting/Necessary Remembering" would allow each side to explore the complexity of memory's abyss.

I often bring a material object to my workshops, representing in a symbolically dense, polyvalent, and evocative form the main theme(s) to be tackled. For this meeting, I brought a simple cardboard container, painted pitch-black inside and outside. During the next four days, this black box accompanied our work. Often placed in the middle of our circle, it initiated and guided discussions and interactive exercises. It was our memory box—and, as memory goes, it contained as much of what was remembered than was forgotten. It functioned as storage and archive, as advocate for the forgotten and uncomfortable companion for what needed to be remembered, as retainer of familial remembrances and a black hole into which memory disappeared.

Because the participants of this German-Israeli encounter showed an extraordinary ability to take personal risks and to respond to each other with honesty without breaking the trust that had been built up over time, I knew they were ready to confront directly the ghosts of the past. In the evening of the last day, I proposed to enter with them hitherto uncharted territory. When we met after dinner, the November darkness had already descended around us, hushing the sounds ascending from the small town at whose edge the retreat center was located.

During the seminar's previous sessions, some of the German participants, who were born during the war years, talked about their conflicting emotions toward their fathers and about their wish that these fathers should be present in this mixed Israeli-German encounter. There was a sense of anger about their parent generation not confronting the past sufficiently and, instead, delegating it to subsequent generations. They also bemoaned their fathers' lack of courage to expose themselves to the presence of Jews/Israelis. Their fathers, they surmised, might have benefited from such an encounter—a subtle wish, as I understood it, to redeem the fathers and a desire to break through the unyielding silence that encased so many post-war German families whose fathers had been implicated in National Socialism.

The fathers of these particular German participants had been identified with the Nazi regime to various degrees. It included, for example, one participant's step-father who, until his death in the 1960s, remained an unrepentant Nazi. As an accused war-criminal he had escaped the clutches of justice and kept sheltering Nazis on-the-run for many years after the war. These fathers remained invisible figures in the midst of our Israeli-German encounter, absent and present at the same time. Despite their uncanny presence, they remained elusive. Without flesh-and-blood, without name and identity, we could not get hold of them.

Now, on this last evening, I suggested that we need to visit them, or better, for them to visit us. After making sure that there was consensus for moving into a dimension I had not dared entering previously, we placed the black box in the wide open circle. The task was simple: let us invite one of these German fathers into our midst. Nervousness and incredulity spread: how should this be done? We unfurled a blanket next to the black box, and then asked for a German participant to step forward. A woman, who had experienced the war as a child in the Eastern German provinces, volunteered. When she was comfortably resting on the blanket, we dimmed the lights and opened the top of the box—symbolically representing the opening of buried memories or of a grave. I slowly guided the woman into letting go of her own self and to imaginatively take on the figure that she felt might emerge from the black box.

She took time to transition into her role. She closed her eyes; her body eventually began to squirm, wriggle, and twist. She seemed to resist a presence that was taking over her being. When she finally opened her eyes and looked around in the circle, she was no longer play-acting. Rather, she appeared to be—for the lack of a better term—possessed: a ghostly presence had taken hold of her. If a ghost is "something lost or invisible or seemingly not there [but that] makes itself known or apparent to us," as Avery Gordon writes in *Ghostly Matters: Haunting and the Sociological Imagination* (1997, p. 63), then we were visited by the ghost of one of the German fathers. The woman volunteer had become a German soldier returning from the grave. It was not her own father, though, and the ghost remained nameless throughout the evening. She/he stared into space and asked: "What do you want from me? Why did you call me?" Slowly, the group began to verbally interact with the ghost.

The specific questions and answers do not really matter here, and I am not sure they really mattered during the session itself. The eerie presence of a resurrected soldier-father filled the room, putting everyone under a spell. Questions were asked, but many remained unanswered. The ghost reluctantly offered fragmented bits of information but stubbornly refused to provide specifics. He had returned from the grave with his silence intact. This frustrated and infuriated the group. Hypnotized by the ghost's unsettling aggressiveness, we were in the presence of a dead man teasing and threatening us by hinting at a secret and violent past.

When he unexpectedly led us to an execution site, putting bullets into his victims, we almost preferred his previous silence rather than having to imagine this scene. In a matter-of-fact style, almost catatonically, the soldier-father told of "things" that just needed to get done. He showed no emotional remorse. The group prodded but failed to elicit any small gesture of sorrow or any recognition of culpability. Now that a door had opened to a scene at the killing fields, how could any meaning emerge from this? The group grew impatient.

As is always the case when reporting about the dynamics of such group sessions, words cannot adequately describe what transpired during that evening. Time stood still (we were in the presence of the ghost for more than an hour). It seemed the group had been transposed to a historical trauma that felt in the imagination so real that it took on an aura of reality. We came close to what religious language knows as spirit possession.

In the context of my reflections on historical trauma and unsettling empathy, I want to share just a few observations that characterized the German and Israeli interactions with the ghost.

First, the German group was split in half regarding its attitude toward the ghost. One half was angry at his refusal to speak and his unrepentant attitude; the other half was supportive, gently prodding the ghost to show signs of insight and regret. Both sides, it seemed, acted on the two primary impulses that descendants of perpetrator generations have at their disposal when responding to culpable wrongdoing: on the one hand, taking a firm and angry stance toward their parents' generational silence about the past (which is also an angry reaction to being burdened with the atrocious legacy of their fathers and their nation); on the other hand, adopting a soft and sympathizing stance toward their parents' shameful silence, perhaps hoping to find points of connection. The ghostly father, however, remained as immune to his "children's" angry rejections as to their tenuously therapeutic gesture of inclusion—which made his appearance so hypnotically powerful and threatening.

Second, the Israeli group remained mostly silent throughout the whole sequence/séance. A few dared to ask him questions but largely left the inquiry to the Germans. The Israelis felt the need to put distance to the ghost, reducing their engagement with him to a minimum, and skeptically observing the Germans efforts to interacting with him. The longer the German interaction lasted, the more anxious and threatened the Israelis became. For them, it was time to bring the session to an end.

But how do you return a ghost? How do you exorcise "die Geister, die ich rief"?[6] This leads me to my third observation: Unexpectedly, the father-ghost refused to go back into the box. His resistance was strengthened by those in the German group who also did not want him to leave yet because they were still trying to reach out to him. My suggestion to relieve the German woman from her ghostly possession was simply ignored. Those Germans that sought some entry into the entombed emotional state of the ghostly father protested

---

[6]   Translated as "the spirits that I called," this line from Goethe's *Der Zauberlehrling* (1797; *The Sorcerer's Apprentice*) is frequently used when someone is summoned to help who then cannot be controlled.

my attempt to end the session. They felt that I was interrupting their psychopolitical efforts of understanding the mentality and soul of the perpetrator generation.

The ghost himself, now that he was among us, had begun to enjoy himself. He seemed to get a certain pleasure from the fact that he was emotionally attended to without having to change. He yielded power as a bearer of terrifying secrets (which he hinted at sparingly) and held sway over us by revealing little about himself. I reminded the group several more times that we had already exceeded the allotted time for the evening, but each attempt to bringing the session to a closure was unsuccessful. I eventually had to physically recapture the space that the ghost inhabited, assertively asking for a moratorium on further questions. I put my hands on the ghost's shoulders, gently but firmly making him/her to lie down on the blanket. Slowly, the woman's body relaxed. She sighed. Finally, we were able to close the lid of the black box.

Fourth, the issue about putting the ghost back into the box remained contentious in subsequent discussions. The one half of the German group that had wanted to extend the session voiced frustration, because they felt I had deliberately ignored a critical moment. They argued that we missed out on a chance to approach Germany's legacy not with the usual confrontational attitude but with a more nuanced view of their fathers' mentality. They felt that their valiant efforts to moving toward a platform of shared grief were prematurely interrupted. The other German half, however, felt that it made no sense to keep investing so much energy and effort into the ghost. In their view, he was as irredeemable as the history he represented. It was time to stop the ghost from spreading anymore of his poison. They felt more than ready to have the ghost disappear.

The Israelis had yet another response. For them, the ghostly presence had become unbearable. Had the situation continued any time longer, they confessed later, they would have left the room. For them, what was threatening was not only the appearance of the ghost itself but also the German group's seemingly tireless efforts to engage him. They viscerally began to understand how frustratingly difficult it is for a perpetrator society to work through the past. But they also wondered whether, by trying so hard to understand the ghostly father, Germans began to err on the side of sympathetic identification rather than historical and moral judgment. They felt like uninvited guest witnessing a family feud, like eavesdropping on an intense moment of cultural intimacy. It frightened them, and yet they were grateful for it.[7]

When we finally asked the German woman who had volunteered to "channel" the ghost, she started crying. Although she could not put words to her tears at the time, she later communicated in emails that these were tears of grief for her father and his generation.

The ghost session contained many of the elements I introduced conceptually above, but here I limit myself to some reflections on the power of unsettling empathy. Clearly, the ghost had managed to unsettle just about everyone that evening, though not for the same reasons. For some, the dialogical and emphatic engagement with the ghost unsettled them because they tried but failed to understand the perpetrator's mentality; for others, it was the secondary witnessing of a re-imagined and re-enacted scene of harm inflicted (and, by extension, harm endured) that was deeply disturbing; for yet others, a posture of unsettling empathy allowed them to share a fragile moment of cultural intimacy.

The posture of unsettling empathy also led to particular investments into present relationships. For example, those Germans who had reproached the ghostly father with anger quickly grasped the Israeli sense of threat, for both groups were ready to end the session. But those frustrated about the too early disappearance of the ghost had lost touch with the emotional state of the Israelis. Deeply absorbed in their own history and in their attempts to find an empathic (though not exonerating) understanding of their fathers' generation, they were too busy with their own *Vergangenheitsbewältigung* (coming to terms with the past) to notice the upheaval of their Israeli peers. They were surprised to hear how frightened the Israelis had been.

These fluctuating layers of unsettling empathy demonstrate that memory is multidirectional and that such multidirectionality must be valued in intercultural encounters. The many attitudes toward memory and remembrance do not cancel each other out but enrich each other in a "shared moral and political project" (Rothberg, 2009, p. 132).

Lest I be misunderstood, I want to make clear that I do not advocate inviting the ghosts of the past on a regular basis. In fact, I would rather caution about such an approach in intercultural groups that work through historical trauma. In exceptional circumstances, one might dare making a haunted, invisible past known in some embodied form, but one needs to

---

[7] The next day, we put the Israeli group into the center of our attention. A young Israeli man volunteered to impersonate his grandmother, a Holocaust survivor. He too seemed possessed by a returning spirit, so much so that she seemed literally present in our midst, channeled through her grandson's body.

know one's limits. Certainly, the intellectual criticism about bringing ghosts back from the past relates both to the problem of vicarious identification[8] as well as to the ethical conundrum of trying to redeem and rehabilitate the memory of former perpetrators. Calling on ghosts, however, does not inevitably lead to attempts at reconciliatory exoneration or at healing a genocidal past. To the contrary, it may be conducive to pursuing justice. "Ghosts are about a possibility of justice," argues legal scholar Christiane Wilke, "They are reminders of a need for justice and can point to the impossibility of justice within the constraints of the law" (2010, p. 77)

The ghostly appearance may demonstrate how complex and difficult intercultural memory work can be. Questions of large-group identity and family loyalty are raised, and one's sense of belonging may become unsettled in the face of the Other. Intercultural meetings bring up defensiveness, fears of betrayal, and a desire to withdraw into protected and familiar mental territory. But when they work well, they compel us to reconsider our assumptions and renders us vulnerable in the presence of the Other, which is an indispensable seed for any personal and social transformation to happen. To return to troubled times is not meant to re-inscribe what is already known historically but to change and transform contemporary relations. The goal is not to fortify entrenched communal identities, but to soften these borders, move into territory of unsettling empathy, and risk a transformed understanding of each other.

Walking a Fine Line: A Case of Cultural Trauma

In the fall of 2013, I conducted a trilateral, four-day seminar for Israelis, Palestinians and Germans, who have been engaged in peace-building initiatives in the Middle East. The seminar—bearing the title "Between Trauma and Politics"—was billed as a mentor-training program. It offered participants a chance to explore and reflect upon the multidirectional ways that traumatic memories impel and impede open communication and social trust between these three national groups.

The fine line we needed to walk in this seminar was between dialogic engagement with historical trauma and being attentive to the urgency of the political situation. We negotiated the variously triangulated bonds between Palestinians, Israelis, and Germans.[9] Both individual and large-group

---

8   On vicarious witnessing, see Zeitlin (1998); see also Weissman (2004).

9   The idea of triangulation stems from psychology, where it is used to diagnose and treat family systems that are marred by dysfunctional communication shifting between three

identities crossed and overlapped at the axis of historical and cultural trauma. Indeed, the participants of this meeting were strongly individuated people as well as representatives of larger social identities: grandchildren of Holocaust survivors, children of Nazi war criminals, Palestinians living under the occupation in the West Banks, Israelis having served in the military, etc. Furthermore, the participants brought a number of generational and age perspectives to the table, stretching across a whole spectrum of unresolved past and present tensions. Deeply personal experiences that were marred by traumatic content blended with collective narratives of suffering and guilt. Since the Israeli and Palestinian participants came from living situations marked by acute anguish, discrimination, violence, death, and mutual recriminations, the dialogic exchange was volatile and fragile.

I suggest that we need to understand settings that straddle the line between historical trauma and unresolved political conflicts through the lens of cultural trauma. As mentioned above, describing a particular situation as cultural trauma does not dependent on whether it is recognized as such by the affected individuals or communities. People in politically explosive situations may speak about the suffering they endure—for example as result of unjust treatment by a superior power, or as the inevitable price one pays for resistance—but the use of the term "trauma" is hardly pervasive in these settings or is carefully sidestepped. Claiming traumatization for oneself might actually erode social solidarity, since it could be perceived as undue self-pride in one's injuries over against the commonweal, or as an excuse for not fully participating in the defense of one's people/nation.

Our trilateral meeting included participants who had been in Israeli prison for years, who witnessed neighbors being fatally shot, who served in the Israeli army, who were involved in the militant Palestinian resistance, who survived rocket attacks launched from Gaza, or who, on the other side of the border, were faced with the war-wounded in understaffed Gaza hospitals. Previous trilateral meetings also included Israelis who had lost friends to suicide bombings and Palestinians who had been tortured.

When we asked the group during our four-day meeting to recall and share individual stories of traumatizing or near-traumatic experiences, several Palestinian men looked quizzically at first. But they did tell us about their

---

parties. Depending on who is talking to who defines the nature and strength of bonds (of loyalty) between people caught in a triangle. When applied to trilateral encounters, "triangulation" helps to reveal the psychopolitical dynamics between Israelis/Palestinians/Germans: alliances between them shift depending on whether issues of historical trauma (such as the Holocaust), cultural trauma (such as ongoing Mid-East conflict), individual traumas (such as torture), or generationally transmitted traumas (such as Naqba, Shoah, expulsion) are foregrounded.

experiences: about being struck by a rubber bullet that is still lodged in the neck, threatening to paralyze him any time; about being arrested at age 14 and spending the next ten-years in an Israeli prison; about witnessing the incineration of a whole family when a rocket hit an apartment building in Gaza. They hastened to add that they never thought about these experiences as traumatic. "It's just how it is; everyone is exposed to it."

In cultural trauma settings, wounds are still fresh and fear is ever-present, with little hope for any immediate improvement. In these settings, one frequently meets people who have been exposed to recent traumatizing incidents that fall squarely into the medical and therapeutic definition of trauma. There is immediacy of trauma that historical trauma settings do not have to deal with to the same degree. At the same time, cultural trauma also refers to "chronic psychic suffering" (Craps, 2013, p. 26) due to the ongoing nature of a conflict. The root cause of such chronic conditions is not a sudden, blunt force threatening to disintegrate a person (like a car accident or rape), but collective structural violence (like slavery or apartheid). Hence, another fine line that needs to be attended to in cultural trauma settings is to work with people who may recover from recent medical trauma or suffer from untreated mental trauma while also being attuned to the trauma-inducing structures that are long-term and chronic.

Communities living under the daily stress of politically volatile and violent environments tend, as a psychic defense, to tell nostalgic tales of innocent suffering or heroic tales of resistance (see also Gobodo-Madikizela, 2012). To move away from these tales toward an understanding of cultural trauma requires an active framing of such events. "Disorganization, displacement, or incoherence in culture," writes Piotr Sztompka, are the conditions that lead to "cultural trauma" (2000, p. 453); but those conditions need to be framed by social actors before they get recognized as trauma. "The condition of cultural disorientation, accompanied by social concern and expressed by intensified emotional, intellectual, organizational activism, provides a necessary background for the cultural trauma to appear" (p. 456).

At the 2013 trilateral meeting, we could observe how such emotional and intellectual awareness coalesced around the recognition of cultural trauma. I want to illustrate this briefly with respect to the Palestinian participants, who, each in their own way, had the ability to act and think in non-linear ways, that is to say, in ways that were not predetermined by loyalty to a particular political agenda. The readiness to try out new communicative patterns became obvious early on in the seminar when a Palestinian man did not only recall his years in Israeli prison, but also explained why he had been arrested. As a teenager, he had plotted to grab a weapon from an Israeli soldier in the occupied territories by stabbing him with a knife. In other words, he took the risk of revealing a part of himself related to accountability, and he did so in the presence of Israelis and fellow Palestinians. He abandoned the frame of a national master narrative, in which Palestinian suffering is almost always couched in terms of innocence. He admitted to be part of a wider system of violence, locked into a fatal cat-and-mouse game between an occupying army and an occupied population.

Recalling stories about one's own suffering and listening to stories of the suffering of others are important steps on dialogic engagement. What is missing in such compassionate listening exercises, however, is the possibility of gaining insight into the complicity of one's own community. In our seminar on "Between Trauma and Politics," we went, hence, a step further and asked each group to think about obstacles in their own community. We wanted each group (Israeli, Palestinian, German) to think about their own issues that impede intercultural understanding, and to name three such obstacles, none of which could explicitly or implicitly blame anyone but oneself. This is, admittedly, a difficult task in volatile situations of prevailing power asymmetries. And yet, in this seminar each group was able to name three such obstacles. To everyone's surprise, one of the internal obstacles the Palestinian group identified on a note card read, "National Aspirations." Both the Israelis and Germans had assumed that "national aspirations" were a non-negotiable corner stone of the Palestinian large-group identity.

In a later session, we invited the Palestinians to unfold the meaning of this obstacle for us. We asked them to sit together in the center of our circle, allowing the German and Israeli participants to eavesdrop on their conversation. It quickly became a lively debate among the Palestinians, especially since not everyone had agreed to pick "National Aspirations" as an example of an internal impediment to peace. When listening to their discussion, it occurred to the outside observer that it veered around two separate issues, namely "national identity" and "political aspirations." When made aware of this, the Palestinians agreed. In a next step, we wrote these two phrases on separate cards and placed them apart in the room. I then invited the Palestinians to create a group sculpture for each phrase by using their bodies. Improvising spontaneously, they represented "National Identity" as a close circle of interlocked bodies, arms around each other shoulders, and backs turned to the outside world. It was an image of internal unity and solidarity. The sculptural representation of "Political Aspirations," however, showed a very different image. Every Palestinian quickly scattered in the room, and there was absolutely no contact and connection between them.

The Palestinians themselves seemed most surprised by the striking difference of their improvised sculptures. They were equally surprised that they had taking the risk to show these sculptures in the presence of Israelis/Jews and Germans. It unsettled them. It caused a profound moment of cultural disorientation—the very condition that sociologist Sztompka theorized as essential for the active framing of a cultural trauma. A shift from "disorientation towards cultural trauma," he argues, manifests itself when "tensions and clashes are perceived and experienced as problems, as something troubling or painful that demands healing" (2000, p. 455). It was as if we just witnessed a resituating of understanding of history and a reframing of grievances by an oppressed group. The sculpture "National Identity" anchored the Palestinians in a tight-knit circle of communal support; but "Political Aspirations" split them apart, literally displacing them and leaving them in a state of political incoherence.

Revealing an internal tension in the social body of one's own community in the presence of those with whom one lives in enmity is part of the posture of unsettling empathy. It requires risk-taking. It unsettles what one perceives as reality as it also unsettles what others expect of you.

Unsettling empathy, as I tried to demonstrate with these examples, is different from a mere act of compassion. Compassionate listening may just confirm what one already anticipates: to listen to the other's master narrative of national suffering (and Palestinians and Israelis have mastered the art of telling such stories to each other in mutual indignation). Unsettling empathy, however, leaves people shaken up in their assumptions about themselves and others, and this is precisely what is needed for transformation to occur.

Outlook

There are no miracles in reconciliatory processes. There are likewise no magic bullets in dialogic engagement with the past in the presence of those perceived as Others. When, a few years ago, I facilitated a weeklong seminar in Beit Jalah, West Banks, no one could claim that it brought peace to the Middle East. Yet, evidence of transformative change does not lie in miracles. Rather, it reveals itself in small signs, such as the exchange of a brief gesture between a Palestinian young man from Ramallah, who had been angry and spouting politicized phrases for much of the time, and an orthodox young woman from the suburbs of Tel Aviv, who never had met Palestinians before on a personal level. As these two young people were standing in line for lunch, they exchanged a friendly poke with their elbows and smiled at each other. If success were measured by standards of grand political solutions alone, such dialogical exchange would be disappointing. And yet, such a gesture captures the effectiveness of creating dialogical frames in intractable situations: the little poke with the elbow (with no further words exchanged) was all that these two people were able to muster at that time. Amidst cultivated mistrust and political hatred it signaled the possibility of a different symbolic order.

We have to seek out opportunities where we can cultivate different symbolic orders and practice caring responsiveness. Unsettling empathy is part of our responsiveness toward each other. To the degree that injustices, trauma, and injuries are unequally distributed, the posture of unsettling empathy may, at times, make firmer moral and political demands on people who find themselves in a privileged position or who are beneficiaries of past and present injustices. Yet, unsettling empathy can never function as a one-way exchange. We must proceed in mutual recognition of our shared responsiveness to each other. It is mutual responsiveness that leads to transformation.

References

Amstutz, M. (2005). *The Healing of nations: The promise and limits of political forgiveness*. Lanham: Rowman & Littelfield.

Apel, D. (2002). *Memory effects: The Holocaust and the art of secondary witnessing*. New Brunswick: Rutgers University Press.

Caruth, C. (1996). *Unclaimed experience: Trauma, narrative, and history*. Baltimore: Johns Hopkins University Press.

Craps, S. (2103). *Postcolonial witnessing: Trauma out of bounds*. New York: Palgrave Macmillan.

Felman, S., & Laub, D. (1992). *Testimony: Crises of witnessing in literature, psychoanalysis, and history*. New York: Routledge.

Gobodo-Madikizela, P. (2008). Transforming trauma in the aftermath of gross human rights abuses: Making public spaces intimate. In A. Nadler, J. Fisher & T. Malloy (Eds.), *Social psychology of intergroup reconciliation: From violent conflict to peaceful co-existence* (pp. 57-76). London: Oxford.

Gobodo-Madikizela, P. (2012). Remembering the past: Nostalgia, traumatic memory, and the legacy of apartheid. Peace and Conflict: *Journal of Peace Psychology*, 18(3), 252-267.

Gordon, A. (1997). *Ghostly matters: Haunting and the sociological imagination*. Minneapolis: University of Minnesota Press.

Herman, J. L. (1992). *Trauma and recovery: The aftermath of violence—from domestic abuse to political terror*. New York: Basic.

Hirsch, M. (2012). *The generation of postmemory: Writing and visual culture after the Holocaust*. New York: Columbia University.

Krondorfer, B. (1995). *Remembrance and reconciliation: Encounters between young Jews and Germans*. New Haven: Yale University Press.

Krondorfer, B. (2012). The art of dialogue: Jewish-Christian relations in a post-Shoah world. *CrossCurrents*, 62 (3) (September), 301-317.

Krondorfer, B. (2013a). From pulp to palimpsest: Witnessing and re-imagining through the arts." In M. Goldenberg & A. Shapiro (Eds.), *Different horrors, same hell: Gender and the Holocaust* (pp. 132-162). Seattle: University of Washington Press.

Krondorfer, B. (2013b). Interkulturelle Erinnerungsarbeit als offener Prozess. In H-F. Rathenow, B. Wenzel & N. Weber (Eds.), *Handbuch Nationalsozialismus und Holocaust: Historisch-politisches Lernen in Schule, außerschulischer Bildung und Lehrerbildung* (pp. 481-497). Schwalbach: Wochenschau Verlag.

LaCapra, D. (2002). *Writing history, writing trauma.* Baltimore: Johns Hopkins University Press.

Simon, R., Rosenberg, S., & Eppert, C. (Eds.) (2000). *Between hope and despair: Pedagogy and the remembrance of historical trauma.* Lanham: Rowman & Littlefield.

Rothberg, M. (2009). *Multidirectional memory: Remembering the Holocaust in an age of decolonization.* Stanford: Stanford University Press.

Sztompka, P. (2000). Cultural trauma: The other face of social change. *European Journal of Social Theory*, 3 (4), 449-466.

Volkan, V. (2013). *Enemies on the couch: A psychopolitical journey through war and peace.* Durhan: Pitchstone.

Weissman, G. (2004). *Fantasies of witnessing: Postwar efforts to experience the Holocaust.* Ithaca: Cornell University Press.

Wilke, C. (2010). Enter ghost: Haunted courts and haunting judgments in transitional justice. *Law Critique*, 21, 73-92.

Zeitlin, F. (1998). The vicarious witness: Belated memory and authorial presence in recent Holocaust literature. *History & Memory*, 10 (2) (Fall), 5-4

Chapter 6
Interrupting Cycles of Repetition: Creating Spaces for Dialogue, Facing and Mourning the Past

Pumla Gobodo-Madikizela

University of the Free State

Introduction

This chapter explores how a psychoanalytic framework might deepen understanding of some aspects of the work of the South African Truth and Reconciliation Commission that facilitated moments of transformation in the relationship between victims and perpetrators. The aim of the chapter is twofold. First, I will argue that the Truth and Reconciliation Commission (TRC) was a unique dialogic space that enabled the emergence of new subjectivities in the encounter between victims and perpetrators. Second, I will use the TRC context as a frame of reference for psychoanalytic reflection on the complex dynamics of what I refer to as the empathy-remorse-forgiveness cycle and its relationship to mourning and working through the past. A key element to be discussed is the aspect of concern and care for "the other" that is linked to this transformative cycle in the dialogue between victim and perpetrator. The overall goal of the chapter is the re-envisioning of psychoanalysis in a way that responds to social issues that affect the contemporary world. The discussion contributes to a growing body of work that aims to employ psychoanalysis outside its traditional clinical context to deepen understanding of processes of transformation and change in social context after systematic oppression and political violence.

My discussion of the TRC in the following pages is in no way meant to ignore the problems South Africa faces today—crowd violence that often leads to brutal killings, xenophobic violence, unspeakable forms of rape, and reports of violence committed by the police against civilians. Some may attribute the violence in South Africa to the "failures" of the TRC, and may say that South Africa has not lived up to the dazzling image of change and transformation that the TRC promised. Yet I believe that the answer to the question "What is going on here?" is more complex than these views would suggest. One area of concern is the abuse of power by government officials, accompanied by patronage and corruption, rather than actions that would contribute to the development of communities in order to break the cycles of poverty and humiliation. The issues of mourning I will discuss here do not address the deeper issues of the daily humiliation faced by the majority of Black people, who live at the margins of South African society. Some of the most destructive acts of violence to the human soul are the subtle, systematic acts that undermine the dignity and sense of worth of individuals, the insidious acts of violence that destroy their psychological and spiritual integrity. Brown (2008) refers to the "insidious trauma" that results from ongoing depravity, humiliation, and degradation, rather than from spectacular and extraordinary violence. The problem in South Africa cannot be explained solely as the result of unmourned trauma transmitted from the parents' generation. The post-apartheid generation is living through its own traumas of a life of humiliation. The work of the TRC is perhaps what needs to happen *again* in South Africa, while at the same time addressing these problems of humiliation.

The Birth of an Idea: The Truth and Reconciliation Commission

In February 1991, a year after Nelson Mandela's release from prison, the ANC began releasing prisoners being held in its various detention camps. Reports about some of the grave maltreatment suffered by detainees at the hands of the ANC soon emerged in the press. Later that year, the ANC set up a commission of inquiry to investigate these allegations. Heated debates raged within the ANC about how to respond to these damning reports of abuse committed by its members in violation of a code of conduct adopted in June 1985 (see Sachs, 2009; Ellis, 1994). It was in the context of these debates that the idea was put forward to extend investigations of gross human rights violations to atrocities committed by state functionaries under the new regime. According to the commission that investigated these crimes, most of the witnesses who testified about the severe ill-treatment they had suffered in the detention camps sought mainly "simple justice: a recognition that they have been wronged and assistance to rebuild their lives" (Report of the Skweyiya Commission, 1992). When the TRC was established to investigate gross human rights violations, the need for such recognition was one of the central principles guiding its work. Thus, the public element of the TRC and the issue of accountability were key features of its work, features distinguishing it from the dozen other truth commissions convened in other parts of the globe. As a "victim-centered" space, the TRC made the trauma of victims visible, allowing them to break their silence. Perhaps more important, as a public process "performed" on the national stage, the TRC served a narrative function that went beyond the individual victims' testimonies.

The Truth and Reconciliation Commission as Emotional Container

The Truth and Reconciliation Commission was established through an act of Parliament, the Promotion of National Unity and Reconciliation Act of 1995. This was the culmination of a series of debates within the ANC during the negotiation process following Nelson Mandela's release. At the heart of these debates was the question of how to deal with human rights abuses committed in the past under the apartheid regime, and whether to prosecute perpetrators of these crimes or grant them blanket amnesty. There was consensus among the negotiators that prosecutions would undermine the already fragile peaceful transition to democracy. Violence by extremist groups both left and right was already evident: bombings by right-wing organizations and armed attacks on civilians by the Pan-African Liberation Army. Moreover, the outgoing apartheid government, the National Party, wanted assurance that those who carried out its policies of human rights abuses would not be prosecuted. As one of two main parties in the negotiations, the National Party refused to support the transition to democracy and the holding of all-race elections without the constitutional guarantee of amnesty for security police, members of the South African Defence Force, and other perpetrators of gross human rights violations who were part of the apartheid machinery of violence. The negotiating political parties agreed to establish a mechanism for granting amnesty under specific conditions. Those conditions included the requirement that applicants testify in public about the crimes they committed, fully disclosing the nature of the crimes and those who ordered them. The rationale for the provision of amnesty was outlined in the post-amble of the Interim Constitution of 1993 in the section "National Unity and Reconciliation": past violations of human rights should be "addressed on the basis that there is a need for understanding but not for vengeance, a need for reparation but not for retaliation, a need for *ubuntu* but not for victimisation. In order to advance such reconciliation and reconstruction, amnesty shall be granted in respect of acts, omissions and offenses associated with political objectives and committed in the course of the conflicts of the past."

It is worth noting that the reference to the need for understanding and for *ubuntu* suggests a particular orientation to the work of the TRC, one that is specific to the South African cultural context. The concept of *ubuntu* is an ethic based on the understanding that one's subjectivity is inextricably intertwined with that of others in one's community. From the perspective of *ubuntu*, all people are valued as part of the human community and worthy of being so recognized. This entails not blind acceptance of others, no matter what they do, but rather an orientation of openness to others and a reciprocal caring that fosters a sense of solidarity. *Ubuntu* is often associated with the concept of self "I am because we are,"[1] which stands in contrast to the Cartesian "I think, therefore I am." While recognizing the role of the individual, *ubuntu* values a sense of solidarity with others—the individual always in relation—rather than individual autonomy.

It seems to me, however, that the meaning of *ubuntu* is best captured in the isiXhosa[2] expression *Umntu ngumntu ngabanye abantu*. Literally translated, this means, "A person is a person through being witnessed by, and engaging in reciprocal witnessing of other persons," or "A person becomes a human being through the multiplicity of relationships with others." The meaning conveyed by the expression is twofold. First, subjectivity depends on being witnessed; the richness of subjectivity flows from interconnected-ness with the wider community, and from the reciprocal caring and complementarity of human relationships. Second, the phrase conveys the kind of reciprocity that calls on people to be ethical subjects. Mutual recognition is fundamental to being a fellow human being, a relational subject in the context of community. A person with *ubuntu* "is open and available to others, is affirming to others. . . . My humanity caught up, is inextricably bound up, in yours" (Tutu, 1999, p. 31).

Evoking the ethic of *ubuntu* in the post-amble of the Interim Constitution at the beginning of the transition to democracy conveyed a central message in the work of the TRC. The message pointed toward the building of a society in which people could come together and be fellow human beings sharing in the vision of a more humane society, one inspired by an ethic of *ubuntu*. In this vision, the pursuit of reconciliation was a moral imperative, because in South Africa victims and perpetrators live in the same country. After the genocide of the Tutsi in Rwanda, similar processes were established, including the National Reconciliation Commission and the gacaca "courts," a traditional process of dealing with conflict between people and within communities. In the majority of cases in Rwanda, after the genocide survivors continued to live as neighbors with perpetrators or, in cases where the latter are serving long prison sentences, with their families. In South Africa, the Promotion of National Unity and Reconciliation Act was passed in 1995, after the country's first democratic elections. The TRC was formally

---

[1]   This expression, "I am because we are" has become parlance for *ubuntu*. Yet it is impossible to translate the expression in any African language, certainly not in any of the ten of the eleven official languages in South Africa.
[2]   IsiXhosa is the African language mainly spoken in the Western Cape and Eastern Cape regions of South Africa.

established under the leadership of Archbishop Desmond Tutu in December 1995.

Tutu was an important presence and central figure in the "holding community" and facilitative environment of the TRC, what Prager (2008) refers to as the "redressive community" in which "lovingness and protectiveness can become reactivated" (p. 415). The TRC provided this Winnicottian "holding" function, by virtue of its public nature and the diverse and trusted group of South Africans that presided over it.

Concern about victims was central in debates about the TRC, and the negotiating parties clearly recognised the significance of public testimony as an important step in the restoration of victims' dignity. This public aspect of the TRC was unique among truth commissions at the time, most notably the Chilean truth commission on which the TRC was loosely modeled.

An Exchange of Identifications: Making Public Spaces Intimate

The complex field of relational encounters and the possibilities unfolding at public hearings of the TRC extended far beyond the actual stage of TRC hearings.[3] It encompassed the wider audience "present" as witnesses to what was happening on the national stage through the live broadcast of the testimonies, and through the weekly televised programs that re-presented the trauma testimonies. Elsewhere I have used the metaphor "making public spaces intimate" (Gobodo-Madikizela, 2008b; c) to describe how the internal and external overlapping of a matrix of emotions and memories in the TRC fostered the emergence of new forms of subjectivity extending to a much wider terrain than the audience actually present at the hearings. The power of this broader relational context in the wider social milieu paved the way for a range of identifications and reciprocal influences that are difficult to imagine in prosecutorial responses to historical trauma (e.g., the Nuremberg trials in the aftermath of the Holocaust). The TRC approach was unique in that by adopting an invitational stance—rather than an adversarial one—perpetrators were asked to "give full disclosure" of the crimes they committed in exchange for amnesty. Without the threat of punishment, and with the

---

[3]   For a poignant example of the impact of the trauma testimonies beyond the halls where the hearings were held, see the story of the (White) South African artist Judith Mason and her artwork titled "The Blue Dress" (discussed in Gobodo-Madikizela, Fish, and Shefer 2014). Mason was moved to tears by the testimony she heard over the radio while working in her studio about a black woman activist who was murdered because she refused to succumb to torture. This story, which was related to the TRC by the perpetrators responsible for the murder, inspired Mason's artwork.

promise of amnesty for truth telling, perpetrators were inspired to admit guilt rather than disown it. Thus, it was possible to face and, for some at least, to feel their guilt. This is an important distinction, because one can simply "face up" to what one has done, acknowledging it at an intellectual level, without taking responsibility for the horrific deeds committed, and instead externalizing blame. It is as if the person were saying, "I give you what you want, full disclosure. Here is the list of evil deeds in which I participated under orders." I will revisit the points I make here in my discussion of splitting as a characteristic of the paranoid-schizoid position.

In contrast, feeling the burden of guilt goes beyond acknowledgment to recognize that one's actions have caused injury and led to a rupture in one's human community, and that by the very fact of one's participation in those acts, one excluded oneself from the realm of humanity. It is this recognition of alienation from the bonds of human community, and a deep sense of guilt about it—a feeling of brokenness at one's inner core of humanness—that makes remorse possible. Perpetrators' subject position of guilt for the crimes they committed—rather than the position of innocence "until proven guilty"—is the context within which a new perpetrator subjectivity unfolds, one that seeks integration of the uncomfortable reality within the self at a deeper internal level. Remorse can be a painful affect (Gobodo-Madikizela, 2002; 2003), because it involves facing the past and its uncomfortable and internally unsettling truths. Remorse is also an important moment of recognition of the self in relation to the other, a crucial step in the mourning process.

Remorse: The "Royal Road" to Forgiveness

Most scholars discussing forgiveness from a psychoanalytic perspective recognize the crucial relationship between remorse and forgiveness. While most of this literature on forgiveness identifies mourning as a central element in forgiveness (see, e.g., Akhtar, 2002; Horwitz, 2005; Alford, 2013), the link between mourning and remorse has not always been explicit. "Probably the most significant psychoanalytic contribution to forgiveness is to see it as one possible outcome of grief and mourning over loss" (Alford, 2013, p. 320). Similarly, Horwitz (2005) refers to mourning as one of the "antecedents of the capacity to forgive" (p. 494). Horwitz makes no mention of remorse in his elaboration of the role of mourning in forgiveness. Alford engages in a profound discussion of forgiveness by linking it to Winnicottian transitional experience. He mentions remorse without necessarily linking it to mourning.

A possible reason for the paucity of psychoanalytic research on remorse and its relationship to forgiveness is that psychoanalytic discussions of forgiveness are mainly of the kind that occurs either as self-forgiveness or between patient and analyst (Doyle, 1999; Lansky, 2007; Benjamin, 2004; Horwitz, 2005; Person, 2007). Very rarely is forgiveness discussed in the literature as a response to gross human rights violations, between victims of historical trauma and perpetrators of mass atrocity, the kind I am concerned with here.

Mourning is associated with the "working through" of loss, which requires acknowledging and taking in the loss and confronting the negative aspects of the subject's experience, as well as the subject's self- and object representations. At the core of the inability to mourn is splitting, an intrapsychic mechanism by which contradictory thoughts, feelings, or aspects of the self (and the other) are kept apart. The Kleinian concept of "making reparations" is useful in explaining how the inability to mourn can be resolved. "Making reparations" is also a fitting expression for the unconscious internal dialogue that unfolds when perpetrators of gross human rights violations break away from the splitting that perpetuates states of denial. In their own process of mourning, perpetrators reflect on their deeds and the destruction they have caused the victim. They express acknowledgment based on a clear sense of appreciation and understanding of what the victim has gone through because of their actions. This enables perpetrators genuinely to confront their guilt. Remorse emerges in this reparative state of mind.

In her discussion of shame and guilt, Klein (1975) argues that the grievances we harbor against our parents for the wrongs they have committed, and for having frustrated us with their denial of those wrongs, give rise to feelings of hate and revenge against them. These feelings are internalized, and they become internal representations of the problematic relationship with our parents. At the same time, these feelings of hate and revenge lead to guilt and despair for the injury that they have caused the parents we love. Klein then argues that the process of undoing this labyrinth of conflicting emotions requires making reparations to the internal objects: "by playing at the same time the parts of loving parents and loving children . . . we make good the injuries which we did in phantasy, and for which we still unconsciously feel very guilty" (pp. 312–313). The capacity for making reparations in the internal object world, integrating the split-off "good" and "bad" of experience into a reasonably coherent whole is the basis on which mourning is established.

Splitting is more than simply rendering separate the disparate parts of self and other. It is holding on to, and identifying with, one aspect of the narrative. In the context of gross human rights violations, a victim's hatred is sustained because the external reality offers nothing else—the other is evil because he or she represents the evil system. In Kleinian terms, splitting is characterized as the paranoid-schizoid position. The notion of "position" is a useful one, as it suggests the possibility of movement toward transformation and perhaps transcendence. The "opposite side" of the paranoid-schizoid position is the depressive position, and, accordingly, the depressive position points to the resolution and working through of splitting. This is when the reparative process of mourning unfolds.

Following Klein, Durham (2000) has argued that the capacity for making reparations in the internal object world is the basis on which empathy for others is established. I consider empathy central in both remorse and forgiveness. Both involve a "working through" of the depressive position. The perpetrator must own his destructiveness and come to terms with the loss of a lifelong identity as an agent of destructive laws in a repressive state. Remorse, a phenomenon imbued with the capacity to hold the ambivalence of both the good and the bad of the subject, is a sign of mourning, a working through of the depressive position and movement away from paranoid-schizoid splitting. In the context of victim-perpetrator dialogue, then, and if the victim is sufficiently open to an awareness of the good—or "good-enough"—that is emerging in the perpetrator through expression of remorse, the dialogue can lead to internalization of the perpetrator as a good object, which is a foundation of the victim's own work of mourning. The work of "repair" in these dialogues therefore entails a reciprocal, mutually facilitative process that leads to the acceptance of loss and a coming to terms with it. The intersubjective collaboration that evolves in this context expands the victim and perpetrator's awareness of each other. Benjamin (2004) describes this as "a relation in which each person experiences the other as a 'like subject,' another mind who can be 'felt with,' yet has a distinct, separate center of feeling and perception" (p. 5).

The perpetrator's remorse conveys genuine concern; no longer is the victim seen as a dehumanised object to be destroyed. For the victim, mourning involves the "working through of one's anger, and putting the offense into the context of an integrated view of the whole person of the offender" (Horwitz 2005, p. 485). What Horwitz suggests here is that the underlying process that inspires forgiving involves reflection and developing an understanding of the other, as well as gaining some degree of insight into what motivated one to engage in the painful and cruel action. Horwitz wants to draw our attention to the intrapsychic dynamic at work in the process of forgiving and, in particular, to the pivotal turn to unconscious perspective-taking, which leads to an integrated view of the other. Within this frame of reflective engagement with the past and coming to terms with it, we find the essence of a stance similar to the empathic mode of observation, which Kohut (1977) says is essential for understanding a patient's inner life in a way that can influence change. This is an example of how a psychoanalytic framework can deepen understanding of aspects of the TRC that facilitated change in the relationship between victim and perpetrator, such as the emergence of remorse and forgiveness. My application of psychoanalytic theory also includes moments of empathic failure, or resistance to change in the TRC. These are questions rarely ever explored in contexts outside the consulting room, such as the social or even the literary context.

Examining the psychoanalytic dynamics of phenomena like forgiveness using literary texts instead of clinical vignettes is a common practice among psychoanalysts and scholars who apply psychoanalytic theory to their research. For instance, Shakespearean plays feature prominently in psychoanalytic journals as subjects of psychoanalytic investigation; Lansky's illustration (2001) of the relationship between shame and forgiveness in *The Tempest* is an excellent example. Engaging both literary texts and real-life stories as a frame of reference for psychoanalytic reflection on the complex dynamics of human action in social contexts can bring us closer to ways in which we might broaden our understanding of the construction of meaning, and strengthen and enliven psychoanalytic debates about the conditions that facilitate positive change after violence.

In presenting the TRC as a context for examining the psychoanalytic dimensions of remorse and forgiveness, my aim is twofold. First, the discussion contributes to a growing body of work that aims to employ psychoanalysis outside its traditional clinical context to deepen understanding of processes of transformation and change in social context in the aftermath of political conflict. For example, in June 2015, the opening plenary session of the American Psychoanalytic Association (APsaA) meeting in San Francisco addressed the problem of psychoanalysts' blind spots with regard to racism, and the silencing of issues of race within APsaA. With the establishment of the South African Psychoanalysis Initiative (SAPI), now IPA-accredited, and the South African Psychoanalytical Association (SAPA), similar introspective reflections and discussions about a "socially relevant psychoanalysis" are now under way in South Africa. As a response to the issues raised in these debates about the need for a socially relevant psychoanalysis, conferences organized by SAPI have addressed topics such as race, embodiment, trauma, and remorse and forgiveness. Raphael-Leff (2014) describes the 2013 SAPI conference titled "Trauma, Remorse, and Forgiveness" as "a heady mixture of new discovery and troubled self-examination in the context of a slowly recovering traumatised society" (p. 118). Here I use a psychoanalytic lens to highlight real-life experiences that might yield insight into what "coming to terms with the past" means, and how change and transformation in a social context might be facilitated.

Intergenerational mistrust, hatred, and resentment born out of violence—both the physical kind and the kind that results from decades of humiliation, carried across generations—create boundaries between self and others in relationships both in the external world and in the world of internal objects. My second aim is to explore how dialogue can facilitate the emergence of unexpected moments that might create connections instead of deepening and widening these boundaries. These connections open up new relational experiences that can help heal historical ruptures. Connection with others is fundamental in the theory of intersubjectivity (Stolorow & Atwood, 1996), and experience and subjectivity are shaped by these relationships of interaction with others.

Jordan (2001) and her colleagues at the Wellesley Stone Center have observed that the need and proclivity for "connection" is central to human development. They are correct in arguing for the primacy of interconnected-ness, a concept of development of self in interaction with others. Debunking the "separate self" model of human development, Jordan notes that Freud (1920) once wrote that "protection against stimuli is an almost more important function for the living organism than reception of stimuli" (p. 27). "Yet," she writes, "from a relational perspective, a 'boundary' could be conceived of as a place of meeting and exchange with the surrounding milieu rather than as a place of protection from it" (Jordan, 2001, p. 93).

Jordan provides a crucial counterposition to a bias that has dominated the field of psychoanalysis for too long, and I suggest (though with some reservations) that the reconception of "boundary" as "a place of meeting and exchange" recognises certain ethical potentialities and draws attention to Martin Buber's notion of the "vital reciprocity" of human relationships (Agassi, 1999, p. 84). I would certainly agree with Abram (1997) that "the boundaries of a living body are open and indeterminate; more like membranes than barriers, they define a surface of metamorphosis and exchange" (p. 46).

The intersubjective epistemological model has broadened the notion of the intrapscyhic realm beyond its individualistic confines. Going beyond this idea of the "internal unconscious/intrapsychic" as a concept that refers exclusively to what is happening inside the mind of the subject, contemporary psychoanalytic thought now views the development of the self as occurring in relation to the other. The subtleties of the dynamic at play in the dialogic interaction between victim and perpetrator are shaped by the reciprocal influence and mutual awareness that develops in the intersubjective field created by the victim-perpetrator dyad. Thus, the resonance that unfolds in this interactive process, the capacity to enter into the other's feeling state, and the intrapsychic transformation that evolves profoundly influence the emergence of remorse and forgiveness.

What of Arendt's canonical argument (1998) about acts of "radical evil" that are neither forgivable nor punishable? This is a question posed by Young-Bruehl (2009), a psychoanalyst and Arendt's biographer. In her reflection on insights from Tutu (1999), and from my analysis (Gobodo-Madikizela, 2003) of interviews with both the apartheid government's most notorious perpetrator, Eugene de Kock, and families of his victims who expressed forgiveness for him after meeting him following his testimony before the TRC, Young-Bruehl concludes that the potential to forgive cannot be radically destroyed. She explains her departure from the Arendtian canonical stance as follows:

> When Arendt said of radically evil deeds that all we know about them is that 'we can neither punish nor forgive such offenses and that they thus transcend the realm of human affairs . . .,' she, who had the most profound understanding of the nature of human power and its distinction from violence, was, I think, underestimating the potentialities of human power, which includes the power to forgive. A person *always* has the power to forgive, acting in relationship with the one forgiven . . . (p. 122).

"Acting in relationship"—the intersubjective encounter—makes possible the moments of acknowledgment, recognition, and validation of victims. Arendt's insights about "the unforgivable" were developed at a time when the transformative possibilities that have come to be associated with the TRC, where victims/survivors could confront perpetrators and demand answers, and perpetrators in turn could experience remorse—was unthinkable. Debates in the twentieth century about dealing with the past were dominated by responses to the Holocaust. By the end of the twentieth century, the work of the TRC had introduced new language that opened new avenues of inquiry.

On Witnessing, TRC Testimonies and their Transformative Possibilities

In cases of political trauma, where the trauma has a collective or shared aspect, individual trauma testimonies transcend the individual—they extend beyond the personal to the collective and cultural. Exposure to psychologically traumatic events leads to a profound disruption in the capacity to organize aspects of one's experience into a narrative. Narrative and storytelling are important means by which individuals and communities make sense of their experiences. Traumatic events are too painful to be integrated into the overall landscape of one's life. They cannot be contained within the normal linguistic and narrative structures. Instead of assimilation into narrative memory, traumatic experiences often take on a timelessness (Langer 1993), living on, being relived and acted out in various ways that reflect fragmented temporality, or "time out of synchrony . . . [where] the present is without end," to appropriate Blanchot's phrase (1992, p. 44).

In their testimonies, survivors who suffered under apartheid want to lay to rest the memory of the pain and abuse of the past, not in order to forget, but rather to heal their own brokenness and that of their community, to reclaim the dignity of the living and the dignity and respect of loved ones who suffered dehumanization in life and in death. In this sense, then, the testimonies are not just to get the listeners' "affirmation and validation," as I have suggested elsewhere (Gobodo-Madikizela 2012, p. 253). Felman and Laub (1992) have applied a similar interpretation in their discussion of testimonies. They suggest that the testimonies are deployed "essentially in order to *address* another, to impress upon a listener, to *appeal* to a community" (p. 204). This formulation of the purpose of trauma testimonies gives power to the listener as the one to bestow recognition on survivors and their suffering. This, too, happens. Viewed as assertion of agency and assertion of the dignity of one's community, however, trauma testimonies seek a response from the witness, but in order to wrest away from perpetrators and from the dominant culture the fiat power to destroy. It is part of ridding oneself and the collective memory of one's community of the subject position of the dehumanized other.

Although Holocaust testimonies still occupy center stage in the literature on testimony, scholarly debates on testimony cover a range of historical traumas globally (in Latin America, American slavery, and in stories of "the stolen generation" in Australia). Since publication of works by Felman and Laub (1992), Langer (1993), and Caruth (1995; 1996), and especially since 9/11, discussions on trauma testimonies in the United States have gained great prominence. Some of the insight gleaned from this literature is, however, not generalizable to other contexts. Laub, for example, in his discussion of the relationship between trauma testimonies and the listener, describes the role of the listener: "The listener, therefore, is a party to the creation of knowledge *de novo*. The testimony to the trauma thus includes its hearer, who is, so to speak, the blank screen on which the event comes to be inscribed for the first time" (Felman & Laub, 1992, p. 57).

The notion that a listener—or "secondary witness" (LaCapra, 2001, p. 97)— participates as a "blank screen," requires critical examination. In countries like South Africa and Rwanda, where victims, perpetrators, and beneficiaries of oppressive regimes are present in the audience as "secondary witnesses," victim testimonies confront not only perpetrators with their guilt, but also stir up the conscience of beneficiaries about their complicity. In the case of beneficiaries of oppressive regimes, victims' testimonies cannot be regarded as falling on a "blank screen," because beneficiaries know about the traumas suffered by victims under the repressive regimes in which they, as beneficiaries, led a life of privilege.

LaCapra's reflections on secondary witnessing (2009), and the distinction he makes between identification, empathy or compassion, and "empathic unsettlement," raise important questions regarding the unavoidably problematic nature of witnessing and also indicate the limits of understanding the experience of an other: "I would argue that there may well, perhaps even should, be a form of empathic unsettlement in the commentator who addresses the traumatic experiences of others . . ." (p. 65).

LaCapra (2004) distinguishes two forms of impact of traumatic testimonies on the listener. In the first, the listener is vicariously affected by the trauma testimony. The problem with vicarious traumatic impact, argues LaCapra, is that the listener identifies so strongly with the witness that he or she takes on the role of "surrogate victim," and that this blurs the line between the trauma of the witness and the secondary witness's vicarious experience of this trauma. The other way the secondary witness may be affected is the "virtual" experience of trauma, in which the secondary witness puts him- or herself in the victim's shoes "while respecting the difference between self and other" (p. 125). LaCapra then refers to this "virtual" experience of trauma as "empathic unsettlement," which he considers the desirable kind of empathy because it recognizes "that one cannot take the victim's place" (p. 125). It is respectful of the other and "does not mean identification . . . appropriation or incorporation" (LaCapra, 2009, p. 66).

On the one hand, Laub's concept of the "blank screen" (Felman & Laub, 1992, p. 57) suggests a blank slate on which the story of the victim's trauma becomes inscribed on the listener without the listener's agency. On the other hand, LaCapra's "empathic unsettlement" suggests that the listener responds empathically to the victim's trauma testimony while at the same time engaging reflectively with his or her response in order to distinguish between the witness's trauma and the listener's virtual traumatic experience. Yet there is something in both Laub's and LaCapra's formulations that falls short of an adequate explanatory framework for the transformative possibilities witnessed at TRC public hearings. The "empathic unsettlement" that emerges goes beyond the notion of "virtual" experience, a term that is problematic because it suggests an event that manifests only in the brain, rather than through shifts in the intrapsychic and intersubjective relational realms. It is a response that, to borrow a phrase from Stern (1985), arises from affective attunement with the other.

Empathy and Caring-For: Victims' Responsibility to the Perpetrators

Kohut (1984) defined empathy as "the capacity to think and feel oneself into the inner life of another person" (p. 82). Other definitions of empathy are aligned with this view of empathic responsiveness (e.g., Stern's "affect attunement"). Neuroscientific insights on empathy have largely dealt with the biological roots of this resonant connection in the worlds of self, objects, and others. Yet an aspect of empathy that has received scant scholarly attention is the component of care for the other that sometimes emerges in the context of empathic responsiveness. Caring goes beyond "mirroring" or feeling into the mental state of an other. It arises from the moment-by-moment negotiation of the intersubjective relationship between actors, as well as from introspection and ongoing mutual reflection, and it involves making sense of the intersubjective experience of empathic resonance. In this desire-to-care-for-the-other aspect of empathy, the empathic response of the victim is imbued with a quality of wishing to "rescue" the remorseful perpetrator, as if to affirm his identity as a member of the human community (instead of a "monster" or "evil one"). This desire to rescue the perpetrator, I argue, constitutes the fundamental moment, a pivotal point in the intersubjective context in which forgiving feelings emerge.

The word *forgiveness*, I argue further, is the wrong word for describing what unfolds in these victim-perpetrator encounters. Forgiveness seems to suggest a fixed position, or a coming to an end—"I offer you forgiveness so that I can have closure and move on." There is a subtext here that seems to signify an act of leaving something *behind*, moving on without looking back. This is evocative of the notion of "letting go" in the stages theory of forgiveness advocated by Enright and North (1998). The notion of "letting go" has also been used in psychoanalytic explications of forgiveness. Horwitz (2005), for example, associates letting go with the process of mourning. However, if we consider the movement toward a forgiving attitude as inspired by mourning, then forgiveness should be seen as a transition from the paranoid-schizoid position and a working through of the depressive position. Accordingly, a characteristic of the latter is the integration of disparate aspects of one's self- and object representations. These aspects must be owned as part of the self, the loss that brought about the rupture must be mourned, and the transition to forgiveness must be worked through. Something else *grows in the place of* whatever it was that prevented connection to the other—anger, resentment, desire for revenge, etc. "Letting go" does not capture this subtlety.

Perhaps we might think of what takes place in victim-perpetrator encounters as "the emergence of the unexpected." A certain degree of caring for the other evolves from being witnesses to each other's pain—the "witnessing dance" (Gobodo-Madikizela, 2008c) that brings survivor and perpetrator into step with each other, into the spiral movement of a new intersubjective context that edges them toward the center of possibility, and then upward toward the apex of transformation. The new intersubjective context that emerges allows for integration and containment, rather than "letting go." Acknowledgment that bears responsibility, that conveys compassion and care, and that is prepared to enter the pain of the other: this is what is crucial for this transformative process.

The development of the capacity for empathy is deeply embedded in early childhood development, and Fonagy and Target (1996; 1997) refer to this developmental process as mentalization, the capacity to reflect on one's mental state and that of others. Mentalization might also be considered the capacity to *engage imaginatively* with the mental state of an other. While I would hesitate to reduce empathy to an imaginative act, there does seem to be something in considering the part that the human capacity for imagination plays in the desire to understand the experience of others. More extraordinary is the idea that the imagination is necessary even to recognize the existence, the human beingness, of the other. This is what seems to be suggested by Benjamin's conceptualization (1990; 1999; 2004) of "mutual recognition" as the core of intersubjectivity through which "the subject gradually becomes able to recognize the other person's subjectivity" (Benjamin, 1990, p. 33). The idea of a "gradual" process that leads to recognition is suggestive of an ongoing dialogue with self and with the other (as well as with internal "others") in a way that allows one to continually test, through multiple levels of reflective engagement, one's perceptions of the other. The process occurs both internally and externally, through language and other, more subtle forms of nonverbal dialogue.

Linda and Peter Biehl's work with the killers of their daughter, Amy Biehl, illustrates the idea of expression of care beyond empathic resonance. Amy Biehl was a Stanford University student on a Fulbright scholarship in South Africa. She was stabbed to death when, as part of her work with a nonprofit organization, she visited a Black township in Cape Town with a group of colleagues from the nonprofit. Her killers' remorseful submission to the TRC led the Biehls to support their amnesty application. When the TRC granted amnesty to the men, Peter and Linda Biehl arranged skills training for them and offered them positions in the Amy Biehl Foundation, which they had established in their daughter's memory. "I have no hatred in my heart," Linda said in an interview I conducted with her and her husband. "All I am concerned about is how these young men can reenter their community and rebuild their lives" (interview, June 2000).

This kind of response presents a paradox. Yet it is this stance of *hearing* the perpetrator's desire—expressed through remorse—for readmission into the world of shared moral humanity, and a caring-enough, that helps sustain the perpetrator's remorse and prevents disintegration and a regression to the paranoid-schizoid position. I am beginning to think about this act or "gesture" of reparation on the part of victims as a "position" that goes beyond forgiveness, and that serves two possible functions. First, it seeks to "restore" the survival of the lost loved one who was murdered by the perpetrator. Second, by showing the kind of caring and containment that can help prevent disintegration in the perpetrator, the victim creates a new relational experience with him, which reconstitutes the memory of the loss as a positive narrative.

The "caring-for" element in empathy is the result of a deeper level of imagination and understanding of the other's experience. This deeper level of imagination takes "feeling into" the mental state of the other to another level, and asks the question, What should I do about it? Thus, rather than empathy considered simply as "resonance," the notion of "empathic repair" (Gobodo-Madikizela 2008a) might usefully be applied to capture the transformation and potential for healing that emerge from dialogic encounters between survivors and perpetrators. The perpetrator's transformation stands as a symbol of the victim's capacity (and, more generally, of the human capacity) for imagination and understanding, and of the power of empathic care that is inherent—always a potentiality (Young-Bruehl 2009)—in dialogic encounters between victims and perpetrators. The transformative possibilities may also be seen as pointing to the more general horizon of an ethics of care and responsibility for the other in the context of "dealing with the past."

For Kearney (1993), "imagination is indispensable to ethics," a claim resting on what he regards as imagination's "*empathic* powers of receptivity to the other" (p. 224).

> While the role of imagination in understanding pertains to its productive and projective powers, its role in sensible intuition expresses its ability *to remain open to what is given from beyond itself.* . . . Imagination is ethical to the extent that it suffers the other to be other while suffering with the other as other (p. 225).

One might hesitate to impute to empathy and the imaginative capacity too many ethical potentialities (and, at best, that is what they are: potentialities). Regardless of the breadth of one's conceptualization of empathy, however, what might one reasonably expect empathy to "do" at minimum? Edith Stein's phenomenological analysis of empathy (1964) provides a possible point of entry:

> We could proceed from the complete, concrete phenomenon before us in our experiential world, the phenomenon of the psycho-physical individual. . . . This individual is not given as a physical body, but as a sensitive, living body belonging to an 'I,' an 'I' that senses, thinks, feels, and wills. The living body of this 'I' not only fits into my phenomenal world but is itself the centre of orientation of such a phenomenal world. It faces this world and communicates with me (p. 6).

Stein is pointing here to the importance of a deeper level of recognition, one that goes beyond acknowledgment (which may at times simply recognize the other as a mere object). Reciprocal recognition of the other's humanity, acknowledging the reality of each other's pain and suffering, whatever its source, is the kind of empathy that creates pathways to caring for the other as a fellow human being—remorse cannot be evil. The words of Cynthia Ngewu, whose son Christopher Piet was lured, along with six other young men from the Gugulethu Township, into a death trap by a Black police collaborator (they came to be known as the Gugulethu Seven), illustrate this point. In response to a question I asked her when I facilitated a public dialogue in Cape Town on the sidelines of TRC hearings, she explained her position on reconciliation: "This thing called reconciliation—if I am understanding it correctly—if it means that this man who killed Christopher has a chance to become human again, so that I, so that all of us... so that our humanity can be restored, then I agree with it. I support it" (November 1996).

This brings me to the point I made earlier about forgiveness being the wrong word. Cynthia Ngewu and other mothers of the Gugulethu Seven victims met with their sons' killer, Thapelo Mbelo, at his request. The women expressed strong emotions, including anger at Mbelo and disdain for his actions, calling him a wolf in a sheep's clothing. Yet when Mbelo addressed the women as he would his own mother, referring to them as "my parents," and using language imbued with cultural nuance, this gave his expression of remorse resonance and meaning for the mothers of the victims.[4] By addressing the mothers in this way, Mbelo was drawing on the relational bonds in the African cultural context, and reclaiming his own sense of belonging within a wider community. The women's words of forgiveness, with one of them referring to Mbelo as "my son," seemed like a gesture of acceptance of Mbelo back into the community fold.

Winnicott (2005), one of the first psychoanalysts to introduce "the third" or potential space, offers us language to reflect on the deeper significance of the "cultural layer" in the language used in this dialogue between the remorse of the perpetrator and the forgiveness of the victims' mothers. Winnicott explains that human experience cannot be defined solely in terms of the polar realities of the internal and external worlds. There is an "intermediate area of *experiencing*," a potential space "to which inner reality and external life both contribute" (p. 3). Cultural experience is linked to this "intermediate" space, which is the location of "the inherited tradition"; this is "the common pool of humanity, into which individuals and groups of people may contribute, and from which we may all draw *if we have somewhere to put what we find*" (p. 133).

Engaging in dialogue about the past is a multifaceted terrain. In considering encounters between survivors and perpetrators of gross human rights violations, what is perhaps necessary is shifting the lens from a focus on forgiveness and reconciliation (concepts that imply a goal) to "experience" – complicated, enigmatic, muddy, elusive, and unpredictable – because I think that much of what happens in these encounters remains implicit, and the word forgiveness falls short of adequately capturing this complexity.

---

[4]　For an extensive discussion of this encounter see Gobodo-Madikizela (2008b).

Conclusion

Expressions of remorse and forgiving emerge from reciprocal recognition in the context of dialogue about historical pasts between victims and perpetrators. Remorse *performs* a range of other responses to historical trauma that are crucial in the process of mourning and working through the past (its traumatic as well as its guilt- and shame-inducing aspects), including accountability, admission of complicity, and acknowledgement (of the pain of the "other," and of the guilt and shame for having caused the pain). The disruptive feelings of historical trauma, such as a sense of injustice, humiliation, and a diminished sense of identity at individual and collective levels, tend to persist across generations. However, as discussed in this chapter, historical trauma also points to the possibility of interrupting these cycles of repetition, when, through honest dialogue, the authenticity and legitimacy of another's pain is acknowledged, and when compassion emerges unexpectedly, opening the door for new relational experiences to unfold.

Creating space for dialogue that might lead to interrupting transgenerational transmission of trauma may be easier to achieve in interpersonal or familial contexts than at the wider collective level of a society affected by massive collective trauma and systematic oppression. The stories of remorse, forgiveness and even reconciliation that came out of the South African TRC's report illustrate this point. Despite the important example of the historical moment of the TRC, the transformative possibilities that emerged, and the global model of "transitional justice" that the TRC came to represent, a question that remains urgent is how to deal with the deep feelings of injustice that continue to persist among the younger generation almost 25 years after the fall of apartheid? The urgency of this question pertains in almost all countries with a history of mass trauma and violence where victims, perpetrators and beneficiaries of oppressive regimes continue to live as compatriots after the end of protracted wars or internal political conflict. In Australia, for example, scholars like Judy Atkinson and Rosanne Kennedy have discussed the intergenerational repercussions of historical trauma of the "stolen generation" at length in several studies. Kennedy in this volume (see Chapter 10), sums up the challenge faced by young Aboriginal people in contemporary Australia with the metaphor "the poetics of survival." Similarly, Jaco Barnard Naudé (this volume, Chapter 3), explores what it might mean to repair "the irreparable" in post-apartheid South Africa. He concludes that what is required is action that "proceeds from an acknowledgement of suffering" that goes beyond a simple "nod of the head to the one who has suffered untold injustice." The kind of action that is needed, he suggests, is one that begins with a "reparative citizenship … that *would bring forth, give birth, to a future that will live up to the promise of 'never again'*" (italics added).

Creating spaces for dialogue matters; the encounters between former enemies provide points of identification, entryways into the experience of others. This might open up the possibility for engaging in the kind of action that Barnard Naudé calls for in his chapter, action that reaches out beyond mere acknowledgement of the wrongs of the past, and toward a new vision of a reparative citizenship.

References

Abram, D. (1997). *The spell of the sensuous: Perception and language in a more-than-human world.* New York: Vintage Books.

Agassi, J. B. (1999). *Martin Buber on psychology and psychotherapy: Essays, letters, and dialogue.* Syracuse, NY: Syracuse University Press.

Akhtar, S. (2002). Forgiveness: Origins, Dynamics, Psychopathology, and Technical Relevance. *Psychoanalytic Quarterly, 71,* 175–212.

Alford, C. F. (2013). Forgiveness as Transitional Experience: A Winnicottian Approach. *International Journal of Applied Psychoanalytic Studies, 10,* 319–333.

Arendt, H. (1998). *The Human Condition.* 2nd ed. Chicago: Chicago University Press.

Benjamin, J. (1990). An Outline of Intersubjectivity: The Development of Recognition. *Psychoanalytic Psychology, 7,* 33–46.

Benjamin, J. (1999). Recognition and destruction: Afterword. In Mitchell, S. & Aron, L. (Eds.), *Relational Psychoanalysis: The Emergence of a Tradition.* Hillsdale, NJ: The Analytic Press.

Benjamin, J. (2004). Beyond doer and done to: Recognition and the intersubjective third. *Psychoanalytic Quarterly, 73,* 5–46.

Blanchot, M. (1992). *The Infinite Conversation* (trans. Susan Hanson). Minneapolis: University of Minnesota Press.

Brown, L. (2008). *Cultural Competence in Trauma Therapy: Beyond the Flashback.* Washington, DC: American Psychological Association.

Caruth, C. (1995). *Trauma: Explorations in memory.* Baltimore: John Hopkins University Press.

Caruth, C. (1996). *Unclaimed experience: Trauma, narrative, and history.* Baltimore, MD: Johns Hopkins University Press.

Doyle, G. (1999). Forgiveness as an intrapsychic process. *Psychotherapy: Theory, Research, Practice, Training, 36,* 190-198.

Durham, M.S. (2000). *The therapist's encounters with revenge and forgiveness.* Philadelphia: Jessica Kingsley.

Ellis, S. (1994). Mbokodo: Security in ANC Camps, 1961-1990. *African Affairs, 93,* 279-298.

Enright, R. D., & North, J. (1998). *Exploring forgiveness.* Madison, WI: University of Wisconsin Press.

Felman, S., & Laub, D. (1992). *Testimony: Crises of witnessing in literature, psychoanalysis, and history.* New York, NY: Routledge.

Freud, S. (1920). *Beyond the pleasure principle.* Standard Edition 17:1–64.

Gobodo-Madikizela, P. (2008a). Transforming trauma in the aftermath of gross human rights abuses: Making public spaces intimate. In A. Nadler, J. Fisher, & T. Malloy (Eds.), *Social psychology of inter-group reconciliation: From violent conflict to peaceful co-existence,* (pp. 57–76). London: Oxford.

Gobodo-Madikizela, P. (2008b). Trauma, Forgiveness and the Witnessing dance: Making public spaces intimate. *Journal of Analytical Psychology, 53,* 169-188.

Gobodo-Madikizela, P. (2008c) Empathic Repair after Mass Trauma: When Vengeance is Arrested. *European Journal of Social Theory, 11* (3), 331-350.

Gobodo-Madikizela, P. (2011). Intersubjectivity and Embodiment: Exploring the Role of the Maternal in the Language of Forgiveness and Reconciliation. *Signs: Journal of Women in Culture and Society, 36*(3), 541–551.

Gobodo-Madikizela, P., Fish, J., & Shefer, T. (2014). Gendered Violence: Continuities and Transformation in the Aftermath of Conflict in Africa. *Signs: Journal of Women in Culture and Society, 40*(1), 1 – 21.

Horwitz, L. (2005). The capacity to forgive: Intrapsychic and developmental perspectives. *Journal of the American Psychoanalytic Association, 53,* 485-511.

Jordan, J.V. (2001). A relational-cultural model: Healing through mutual empathy. *Bulletin of the Menninger Clinic 65,* 92–103.

Kearney, R. (1993). Poetics of imagination: From Husserl to Lyotard. London & New York: Routledge.

Klein, M. (1975). Love, Guilt and Reparation: And Other Works 1921-1945. London: Simon and Schuster.

Kohut, H. (1977). *The Restoration of the Self.* Chicago: University of Chicago Press.

Kohut, H. (1984). *How Does Analysis Cure?* Chicago: University of Chicago Press.

Lansky, M. R. (2001). Hidden Shame, Working Through, and the Problem of Forgiveness in the *Tempest. Journal of the American Psychoanalytic Association, 49,* 1005-1033.

Lansky, M. R. (2007). Unbearable shame, splitting, and forgiveness in the resolution of vengefulness. *Journal of the American Psychoanalytic Association, 55,* 571-593.

LaCapra, D. (2001). *Writing History, Writing Trauma.* Baltimore: John Hopkins University Press.

LaCapra, D. (2004). *Representing history, representing trauma.* Ithaca, NY: Cornell University Press.

LaCapra, Dominick. (2009). *History and its limits: Human, animal, violence.* Ithaca & London: Cornell University Press.

Langer, L. L. 1993. *Holocaust Testimonies: The Ruins of Memory.* New Haven, CT: Yale University Press.

Person, E. S. (2007). Forgiveness and its Limits: A Psychological and Psychoanalytic Perspective. *The Psychoanalytic Review, 94,* 389-408.

Prager, J. (2008). Healing from History Psychoanalytic Considerations on Traumatic Pasts and Social Repair. *European Journal of Social Theory* 11(3): 405–419.

Raphael-Leff, J. (2014). Trauma, Reconciliation, Embodiment: An account of the 9th and 10th SAPI Conferences [Franschhoek, February, 2013; February 2014]: Forum. *Psycho-analytic Psychotherapy in South Africa: Psychoanalytic Psychotherapy in Contemporary South Africa, 22,* 118-125.

Sachs, A. (2009). *The Strange Alchemy of Life and Law.* Oxford University Press.

Skweyiya Commission (1992). Report of the Commission of Enquiry into Complaints by Former African National Congress Prisoners and Detainees. Retrieved from http://www.anc.org.za/ancdocs/misc/skweyiya.html

Stein, E. (1964). *On the problem of empathy* (trans. W. Stein). The Hague: Nijhoff.

Stern, D. N. (1985). *The Interpersonal World of the Infant.* New York: Basic Books.

Stern, D. N. (2004). *The present moment in psychotherapy and everyday life.* New York: Norton.

Stolorow, R. D., & Atwood, G. E. (1996). The Intersubjective Perspective. *Psychoanalytic Review, 83*, 181-194.

Tutu, D. (1999). *No Future without Forgiveness.* New York/London: Doubleday.

Winnicott, D. W. (2005). *Playing and Reality.* London, Routledge.

Young-Bruehl, E. (2009). *Why Arendt Matters.* New Haven: Yale University Press.

Chapter 7
Memoryscapes, Spatial Legacies of Conflict, and the Culture of Historical Reconciliation in 'Post-Conflict' Belfast

Graham Dawson

University of Brighton

Introduction

The reproduction of historical trauma and associated memories of the conflicted past are closely entwined with the spaces and sites where violence took place. In critical analysis of 'post-conflict' cultures, there is now a growing interest in these spatial manifestations and legacies of the past and their implications for work concerned with transforming the aftermath of violence, breaking cycles of trauma, and promoting reconciliation. In this chapter these issues are explored in relation to post-conflict spaces shaped by the conflict known as 'the Troubles' in and over Northern Ireland since 1969 and the peace-building initiative begun in 1993-94, focusing specifically upon the 'post-conflict' city of Belfast. Since the paramilitary ceasefires of 1994, the re-imagining and regeneration of Belfast has involved official strategies and a range of initiatives engaging with the spatial consequences of the city's history of sectarian violence and armed political conflict. This activity is integral to the task of 'deal[ing] with the legacy of the past' in a context where members of the 'divided communities' of Ulster loyalism and Irish Republicanism 'carry different experiences and understandings of the past in their minds' (and in their bodies), account for the conflict in contested narratives of memory that attribute responsibility and blame to other parties, lay claims to victimhood inflicted by their enemies, and pursue historical justice for the wrongs they have sustained (Consultative Group on the Past, 2009, pp. 16, 24).

Reconciliation, defined as 'the process of addressing conflictual and fractured relationships' after conflict (Hamber & Kelly, 2005, p. 7), is always historical in the sense that 'acknowledging and dealing with the past' is one of its fundamental aspects. However, the process of reconciliation has a complex temporality, being necessarily both 'backward– and forward–

looking'. It is directed towards 'developing a shared vision of an interdependent and fair society' to be achieved in the future, but this requires breaking down 'the culture of suspicion, fear, mistrust and violence' bequeathed by past conflict, so as to enable 'engag[ement] with others who are different from us' and with whom we must work to bring about 'substantial social, economic and political change' (Hamber & Kelly, 2005, p. 38). This work of future-oriented conflict transformation takes place within post-conflict spaces where legacies of the traumatic past continue to exert a hold and make themselves felt. How are we to understand the intertwining of these spatial and temporal dimensions of conflict transformation in a city such as Belfast?

In recent debates in heritage studies and cultural geography, a number of new concepts have been proposed to inform analysis of this kind. One of the most suggestive is Tumarkin's (2005) concept of 'traumascapes'. This refers to 'a distinctive category of place [...] marked by traumatic legacies of violence, suffering and loss' where 'the past is never quite over' (pp. 12-13). Here, an analysis of temporal disturbance, associated with the psychic and physical experience of '[t]raumatised people [who] have to live with the past that refuses to go away', is transferred to particular geographical spaces 'where events are experienced and re-experienced across time' (p. 12). Tumarkin writes:

> Full of visual and sensory triggers, capable of eliciting a whole palette of emotions, traumascapes catalyse and shape remembering and reliving of traumatic events. It is through these places that the past, whether buried or laid bare for all to see, continues to inhabit and refashion the present (12) [...] At traumascapes [...] neither the past nor the present is disposable or infinitely malleable (p. 14).

Tumarkin's 'traumascape' evokes a sense of something residual or reproduced from the past in embodied geographical form; a quality of place that 'elicits' emotional responses from those who go there. Yet she also suggests that traumascapes are produced by cultural practices—of witnessing, mourning, memorializing and so on—undertaken by individuals, social groups and organizations that may have diverse interests in a site, and different or even conflicting responses to it. This question of agency in the production of place–based significance and affect—whether it is seen as a property of the space itself, or located in those who encounter or inhabit it—remains ambiguous.

The problem reappears in a related concept developed to think the relationship between memory, space and affect, that of 'memoryscape'. Rowlands and de Jong (2008), for example, use this term to refer to spaces and sites—such as 'memorials, neighbourhoods, city centres'—that are inscribed with 'old' meanings and memories, but may be 'reworked' or reinscribed, becoming 'palimpsest memoryscapes that are both real and imaginary' (p. 133). Such 'reinscription of new memories in established places' is associated by Rowlands and de Jong with their concept of 'heritage [that] heals' (p. 133). This refers to heritage sites (and practices) which, they suggest, offer 'recognition [of loss, suffering and injustice] and a space from where to work through memory and achieve reconciliation' (pp. 131-132). In this way, 'heritage may provide a technology for healing' (p. 133), enabling 'a reworking of past traumatic experiences [... that] is particularly needed in post-conflict societies' (p. 131). In a memoryscape, a dialectic of hurting and healing maps onto the temporal interaction of past and present, figuring a place where the painful and damaging affective legacies of conflict in the past become subject to post-conflict transformative processes of recognition, reparation and reconciliation.

Such concepts of traumascape and memoryscape are valuable in focusing analytical attention on the infusion of affect, emotion and memory within post-conflict spaces. Yet they tend to collapse together elements that ought to be distinguished analytically when considering the relation between space and subjectivity and the mediating role of cultural representations and practices. Such conceptual distinctions are crucial to understanding the complexity of post-conflict geographies and their significance for conflict transformation and historical reconciliation, for four main reasons. Firstly, sites of violence that are marked by memorial cultures ought to be distinguished from those whose marking is less visible or indeed invisible. Not all places where traumatic violence has occurred are memoryscapes inscribed with tangible meanings of the past. Some are invisible and subject to material erasure and redevelopment, and to silencing and forgetting within cultural practices; yet they may remain significant in the psychic and somatic experience and living memory of victims and perpetrators, witnesses and the bereaved. Secondly, interpretive differences and conflicts may occur between plural cultural landscapes that construct alternative or competing versions of the same place and its past. These require analysis. Thirdly, sites of violence are not necessarily transformable into 'healing heritage', as concepts of traumascape and memoryscape may be taken to imply. Finally, analytical tools are needed for consideration not only of those sites that principally concern Tumarkin, where spectacular violence manifests in a singular event such as a massacre, a bombing or a siege, having an intense and overt affective impact and giving rise to various kinds of memory-work and the negotiation or contestation of significance. In other post-conflict spaces, everyday life continues without overt signification of the conflicted past;

strategies are deployed to transform sites of violence by re-integrating them into the spaces of everyday ordinariness rather than marking them as special (Switzer & McDowell, 2009, p. 343); and psychic or affective legacies are reproduced and lived in often intangible ways, over longer temporal spans and across generations. In the case of Northern Ireland, memoryscapes marking sites of spectacular violence, such as the Bloody Sunday shootings and the Enniskillen bomb, exist in close proximity to less visible sites like many of those derived from the war in rural border areas (Dawson, 2007, pp. 214-217, 229), and Republican and loyalist memoryscapes produce selective and antagonistic versions of the past. Belfast is the location not of one but thousands of violent incidents, in the course of a war that lasted for thirty years and was itself the latest episode in a longer history of violent political conflict which has produced multiple traumatic legacies.

A useful, threefold conceptual schema that enables distinctions of this kind to be made is proposed by the anthropologists, Stewart and Strathern (2003, cited in Dawson, 2005, p. 155). They use the term 'place' to refer to a specific and 'identifiable' material environment and its constituent spaces and sites, as shaped socially and historically by human activity. A 'cultural landscape' occurs when a place is represented and made meaningful by social groups in specific ways, as signifiers and affective associations become attached to it through 'creative and imaginative' cultural practices. These may inscribe or mark the place *in situ* but may also be produced, circulated and received at other cultural locations where meanings of that place are constructed. The 'inner landscape of the mind' refers to the subjective sense of both place and cultural landscape that is internalized within the psyche (and, it should be added, 'felt' within the body) as a result of lived experience informed by cultural knowledge. Using Stewart and Strathern's schema, I have argued in previous work that traumatic experiences of political violence give rise to 'psychic "sites of trauma" [...] within the internal landscape', that are derived from—and complexly related to—the material sites of violence within social environments, together with the meanings and memorial markers that constitute cultural landscapes of violence, horror and mourning (Dawson, 2005, p. 156). The term memoryscape is best reserved to signify a particular type of cultural landscape where cultural practices and forms of representation overtly mark the history of a place and construct the significance of its past for the present.

In what follows, I utilize a framework derived from Stewart and Strathern's threefold schema to investigate places that became sites and spaces of Troubles-related violence in Belfast, the cultural landscapes and memoryscapes that construct the meaning of places and their pasts, and their subjective significances and affective resonances within psychic geographies during both the time of conflict and that of post-conflict transformation. This analysis will provide the basis for exploration of the traumatic spatial legacies of the Troubles in the 'post-conflict' city, and the tensions and contradictions that must be negotiated in strategies for 'dealing with the past' and 'historical reconciliation' in these spaces.

Belfast: City of Conflict and the 'Post–conflict' City

Throughout its history, Belfast has been a city deeply divided by the segregation of its population. Two 'ethno-sectarian' groups, one Irish nationalist or Republican and largely Catholic, the other British Unionist or loyalist and largely Protestant, inhabit an urban space consisting of a patchwork of predominantly 'single identity' enclaves or areas (Shirlow and Murtagh, 2006, pp. 57, 60). The boundaries or 'interfaces' between them have been, in Shirlow and Murtagh's words, 'rigidified by violence' (p. 66) in the course of a conflicted history of British colonial rule and the industrial and commercial development of the city, as well as political conflict over national belonging and the form of the State. A.C. Hepburn has argued that: 'Rioting, the fear of it, and the bitter memories associated with it, have been the main determinant of community relations in the city' (quoted in Dawson, 2007, p. 12). During the nineteenth century, interface tensions stemming from Catholic rural migration and settlement in the growing city, regularly erupted in violence including major outbreaks of inter-communal rioting, and by 1914 'the frontier zone between the main Protestant and Catholic enclaves' in north and west Belfast was being described as 'the seismic area of the city' (Bardon, 1992, p. 306). These same locations saw anti-Catholic pogroms by the police and loyalist paramilitaries during the war over Irish independence and partition 1919-22, in the 1930s, and in August 1969 when a repetition of this historic pattern of violence, in an attack by police and loyalists across the 'Orange–Green line' separating the Shankill area of West Belfast from the nationalist Falls, sparked the recent conflict (Dawson, 2007; Farrell, 1980).

During the first years of conflict, spatial division was consolidated by large population movements out of 'mixed' as well as interface areas into the relative safety of more homogeneous communities, such that by 1972, 70% of Catholics and 72% of Protestants lived in streets which were almost exclusively segregated (Jarman, 1993). This historical process of segregation was given material form within the physical organization of the city through the construction by the State, under pressure from local communities, of some forty-one so-called 'peace-line' barriers ranging from back-garden fences of brick or barbed wire to the 30-foot high concrete and steel wall that runs for one and a half miles along Cupar Way on the Shankill/Falls interface (Jarman, 2005). Erected by the British Army as a short-term measure to separate the conflicting parties, the Cupar Way peace-line was extended westwards after a further wave of rioting and house-burning in 1971. As the peace-line became permanent, its consequence, predicted by the Republican Clubs movement in 1977, was to 'irrevocably split the city into two sectarian ghettoes' (Conspiracy, 1977), to the benefit of the State's conflict management strategy and to the detriment of effective, sustainable cross-community activism on common socio-economic problems by the working-class communities on either side of the divide.

The launch of the Provisional Irish Republican Army's (PIRA) bombing campaign targeting commercial properties in 1970 caused widespread destruction in the city centre, while the intensification of counter-insurgency measures by the State led to a militarization of space through the construction of a 'ring of steel' (security gates with checkpoints across forty-one streets), a range of other security measures, and the high-profile presence of the Army and police monitoring everyone entering the controlled zone (Jarman, 1993). Militarization spread across the city, especially into Republican enclaves, through the construction of heavily fortified Army and police barracks, a system of barriers and checkpoints that augmented the peace-lines, visible technologies of surveillance, and routine Army patrolling. Sustained over more than thirty years, the violence of the armed conflict transformed the spatial co-ordinates of social life. In the city centre, '[t]he places of the everyday—a hardware shop, newspaper offices, bars, a post office, an amusement arcade, a restaurant, a car park and public streets—[...] became sites of violent death' (Switzer & McDowell, 2009, 339). Nearly 1,700 people, 66 per cent of whom were civilians, died in Belfast between 1966 and 2006. Over 1,200 of these lost their lives in the enclaves of North and West Belfast (McKittrick et al, 2007, pp. 1559-1560), and one third of all Troubles-related deaths in the city occurred within 250 meters of an interface boundary (Shirlow & Murtagh, 2006, p. 72).

Perceptions of Belfast as a place transformed by war into a battlefield or fortress were articulated in metaphors drawn from the cultural landscapes of other well-known conflict zones such as the Berlin Wall and the Western Front (Switzer & McDowell, 2009, p. 339). Local knowledge of specific locations associated with violence circulated in a culture of fear that shaped patterns of movement around the city according to an imaginative landscape whereby safe zones became demarcated from zones imbued with otherness and threat, 'the spaces of fear' (Mapping the spaces, n.d. 2003?). Internalized in psychic landscapes, this splitting of the cityscape produced 'mental maps' imbued with affective as well as cognitive significance (Shirlow & Murtagh, 2006, p. 70). In the memoryscapes of the Republican and loyalist enclaves, plaques, monuments and murals memorializing the dead—whether paramilitary fighters or martyred victims—became integrated into broader commemorative cultures centred on symbolic political events from the historic past, such as the 1690 Battle of the Boyne for loyalists and the 1916 Easter Rising for Republicans. Articulating antagonistic histories of violence inflicted and suffered, these competing memoryscapes embedded 'social recognition of [traumatic] psychic realities' (Dawson, 2007, p. 74) into the places of everyday life, whilst also coalescing with geographical assertions of political identity through the marking of local territory as well as national belonging, in the form of flags, murals, painted kerbstones and lamp-posts (Jarman, 1993). In these interface zones, 'grief and mourning, as well as politics, have been split in two, polarized across the axis of violence' (Dawson, 2007, p. 3).

Launching the Irish peace process in December 1993 with their Joint Declaration on Peace, the Prime Minister of the United Kingdom of Great Britain and Northern Ireland, and the Prime Minister of the Republic of Ireland, pledged to work together to 'remove the causes of conflict, to overcome the legacy of history, and to heal the divisions which have resulted' (Dawson, 2007, p. 21). Since the Declaration, political negotiations have delivered the paramilitary ceasefires of 1994; the Belfast 'Good Friday' Agreement of 1998—this established the basis for an agreed political settlement including institutions to enable devolved, 'power-sharing' government and equality of citizenship underpinned by human rights legislation; the so-called 'decommissioning' of the IRA's military arsenal in 2005, accompanied by 'demilitarization' by the British State; and in 2007, democratic elections to the new Northern Ireland Assembly and the establishment of a governing Executive led jointly by a Unionist First Minister and a nationalist Deputy First Minister. While political violence continues, the armed conflict has largely been brought to an end, and a basis created for working towards new political and social relationships in what the devolved, power-sharing government has called a 'shared future'.

It is in this context that the transformation of Belfast and debates about its future as a 'post-conflict' city have developed. Three main strategies have guided the 'slow transition from "troubled" city to a less violent city' (Shirlow, 2006, p. 105). Firstly, a significant reduction in the scale and intensity of political violence, due to the ceasefires and the gradual implementation of decommissioning and demilitarization established by the Agreement, have made Belfast a broadly safer city. These measures have eradicated the architecture and technologies of military occupation and promoted the closing of British Army barracks and return of these occupied spaces to 'peace-time' use, an ongoing programme that is continuing twenty years into the peace process. Secondly, a strategy of economic 'normalization', driven by public policy to attract large-scale inward investment by the private sector, focusing on business development, tourism and place promotion of the city's 'brand' within global markets, has transformed the city centre and harbour–side areas through the construction of prestigious new buildings like the Waterfront Hall and the Hilton Hotel; the opening-up of riverside walkways; the regeneration of the old, largely derelict commercial district and parts of the old shipyard; a proliferation of new bars, clubs and restaurants in what has become the 'Cathedral Quarter'; the construction of shopping malls and other retail sites; and the marketing of a Belfast cultural heritage. Thirdly, a strategy led by Belfast City Corporation in alliance with a range of social and economic organizations. working within the wider political framework established by the Office of the First Minister and Deputy First Minister (OFMDFM) and, since 2007, the Northern Ireland Executive, has sought to re-imagine post-conflict Belfast as a 'shared city', and to introduce policies aimed at the transformation of the ethno-sectarian divided space that is the legacy of its conflicted history into the 'safe and shared space' of the future (OFMDFM, 2005, 21). In order 'to establish, over time, a shared society defined by a culture of tolerance [...] equity and diversity' (OFMDFM, 2005, 10), this strategy envisages 'reclaim[ing] the public realm for people who are living and working in, or as visitors to, Northern Ireland', by freeing it from 'displays of sectarian, racist or any other form of aggression', threat and intimidation (OFMDFM, 2005, 21-22), and replacing symbols that endorse ethno-sectarian identities and belongings with others that elaborate 'a shared heritage' (Shirlow, 2006, 106; Graham & Nash, 2006).

This transition towards the peaceful, shared city is fraught with a number of significant tensions and contradictions centred on the projection of a future-oriented 'post-conflict' image and experience in relation to the city's engagement with unresolved legacies of its troubled past and (unfinished) history of violence. Driving these contradictions are the dynamics of what Murtagh and Keaveney (2006, 188) describe as a 'twin-speed economy'. This, they argue, has produced 'an increasingly bifurcated place' characterized by a 'new socio-economic cleavage'; between the 'modern, outward-looking and progressive' Belfast of the redeveloped central area, and another Belfast 'stratified by poverty, ethno-religious segregation and fear [...] spatially fixed in the sink estates' in the city's enclaves (pp. 187-188). The contradictions driving this new post-conflict bifurcation constitute the terrain on which the significance of the conflicted past is negotiated between the various organizations and groups with an interest in the future of the city. Hegemonic leadership of the transition by capital and the policy-making elite encounters contradictory needs and interests articulated by grass-roots community organizations which continue to grapple with unresolved legacies of conflict that are acknowledged in politicized memory cultures and reproduced through the workings of a 'logic of spatial separation' (Shirlow, 2006, p. 105) in interface areas. These contradictions give rise to competing approaches to the question of historical reconciliation, to be explored next in each of Murtagh and Keaveney's contrasting zones in turn.

'New Belfast': Heritage, Development, and the Erasure of the Conflicted Past

In the zone characterized by Murtagh and Keaveney as 'modern' and 'progressive', the 'New Belfast' of the redeveloped city centre where visitors are attracted to spend time and money, public commemoration of the Troubles is absent or ephemeral, and there are no permanent memorial markers on any of the sites of Troubles-related killing. As Switzer and McDowell (2009) argue, the erasure of 'site[s] of death and trauma' from the cultural landscape of the city centre is a result of material reconstruction of these places, most commonly due to practices of 'rectification' that restore a damaged site and often return it to its original use 'without reference to what has occurred there' (p. 345); and in some cases, to practices of 'obliteration', which 'involves not just removing the immediate signs of traumatic events but effectively effacing the evidence from existence' through demolition and redevelopment (pp. 343, 345). These processes usually occurred in the immediate aftermath of the violent event—a reminder that normalization predates the peace process—but have continued in the context of the redevelopment of the post-conflict city centre. The creation of a memoryscape dedicated to commemoration of the Troubles has no place in these strategies. On the contrary, they have led directly to further obliteration of previously rectified sites. One example is the Oxford Street bus station, a location of the IRA's 'Bloody Friday' bomb attacks in 1972, which was returned to use thereafter but demolished in 1996 to establish the footprint for the Waterfront and Hilton development (345). A memoryscape has been constructed on this site, drawing its motifs from earlier layers of history—the use of this space as a cattle market, its role in the industrial and maritime economy, the associated forms of social and working life—that are less charged by affect within the living memory of the city's current residents. The creation of this heritage memoryscape is the mechanism whereby 'the violent aspect of the site's history has effectively been erased' and rendered 'invisible in the urban landscape of present-day Belfast' (Switzer & McDowell, 2009, p. 346), overlaid by another historical narrative made present in its place.

The origins of this strategy lie in 1987, whilst the conflict was ongoing but violence in the city centre had been largely eradicated, in a plan 'to transform completely the environmental quality of a vital part of the City, and by this means to help transform perceptions of Belfast at an international level' (quoted in Neill, 2006, p. 109). In 1989 the British Government established the Laganside Corporation, a regeneration agency with a remit to develop several sites spanning both sides of the River Lagan (and later extended to include the 'Cathedral Quarter'). Until its dissolution in 2007, the Corporation secured some £900 million of investment for the construction of hotel and housing accommodation, business and entertainment facilities, and 'distinctive and memorable public places' (Laganside Corporation website). An important aspect of this strategy was its role in the regeneration of tourism, once a significant sector of the city's economy but badly damaged by the Troubles. Laganside pioneered the construction of a city heritage linking the 'New Belfast' to a version of its past centred on images of economic prosperity and civic pride, through the restoration of historic buildings such as the Custom House and St George's Market, and the creation of 'art trails' featuring a range of public art-works, some of which 'reflect Belfast's great industrial history while others celebrate its changing face' (Laganside Corporation website).

While often interpreted as an expression of nostalgia for the lost past, 'the construction of heritage is a means for the definition of the contemporary, which it reveals in a fantastic or fetishised form' (Brett, 1996, p. 8). This fantastic refraction of history is closely linked in mainstream heritage practice to the celebration of what is taken to be the positive inheritance from the past, inculcating pride in a social group by establishing allegiance with its forebears and inviting identification with their achievements. The attraction of heritage in this mode lies in its capacity to affirm for its consumers a subjective sense of their own identities (both individual and collective) as essentially positive, virtuous and firmly rooted in the past. The narratives and images encountered at conventional heritage sites tend to avoid or sanitize the complexities of power, conflict and suffering that would unsettle or disrupt such identifications; and thus are relatively undemanding on their audience, and ripe for commodified consumption. Driven by an alliance between private enterprise in the culture industries and public policy initiatives promoting capital investment and a particular agenda for 'moving the city forwards into the twenty-first century', heritage development in post-conflict Belfast has tended towards commodified constructions of 'the past' (Neill 2006), the erasure of the city's recent (and unfinished) history of violent conflict, and what Brett (1996, p. 2) terms '"deproblematised" story-telling'.

This strategy has come to further fruition in the development of the city's new Titanic Quarter situated on Queen's Island, the former shipyard area, and its centrepiece, Titanic Belfast, which is now established as one of the city's foremost visitor attractions. This development has transformed the infamous ocean liner *RMS Titanic*—built between 1909-11 in Belfast's Harland and Wolff shipyard and sunk after its collision with an iceberg in the North Atlantic with the loss of 1,490 lives on its maiden voyage in 1912 (Bardon 1992, p. 438)—as the city's emblematic, visitor-friendly and unificatory heritage symbol. Launched in 1999 in the wake of James Cameron's (1997) film which stimulated increasing popular interest in the already mythic story of the Titanic, this initiative brought together Laganside, the Northern Ireland Tourism Board and Belfast City Council with the aim of 'bringing the legacy of the Titanic home' (Neill 2006, pp. 114-15). Historically a source of embarrassment and shame in Belfast (Titanic town, 2012; Neill, 2006, p. 114), the project reclaimed the Titanic for the city by focusing on the engineering achievement represented in its construction. In 2002 Tom Hartley, Chair of the Councils' Tourism and Promotion of Belfast Sub-committee, placed the commemoration of the ninetieth anniversary of its sinking at the centre of the city's new cultural tourism strategy:

> For far too long, Belfast has been content to ignore the positive aspects of its history—a history which has a vibrant and vital role to play in its development as a tourist destination. The story of the Titanic highlights this: for too many years, Belfast shied away from her, almost in shame, while other cities around the world have made capital out of her. But Titanic belonged, and still belongs, to Belfast [...] What happened to RMS Titanic was a disaster of historic proportions, and it is right that we remember and commemorate the tragedy that befell her and the 1,500 souls who lost their lives. However, the creativity and ingenuity that brought Titanic to life was an achievement equally as great, and we are wholly justified in acclaiming that achievement (Titanic tourism, 2002).

Detaching the city from the disaster—a stance captured later by the marketing slogan, 'It was fine when it left Belfast'—enables the transformation of a shameful legacy into a 'positive' heritage; and of deathly destruction into life-giving creativity and ingenuity.

The 'biggest property development scheme ever undertaken in Northern Ireland' (Neill, 2006, p. 114), the Titanic Quarter is a thirty-year project still under construction on a 185-acre site that was formerly part of the Harland and Wolff shipyard. First established in the 1850s, by the 1890s the shipyard had grown into 'the most important single employer of male labour in Ulster' and 'headed the list for the largest number of vessels built by any shipyard in the United Kingdom', at the height of Britain's imperial power (Bardon, 1992, pp. 334-338, 340). Confronted in 2004 by the threat of terminal decline in its shipbuilding and repair business, the shipyard owners sold part of its leasehold to a subsidiary established by a Dublin-based development company. In 2005 Titanic Quarter Ltd launched an ambitious plan to 'provide Belfast with a new urban quarter' comprising a 'futuristic mix of residential, commercial, tourism, education and retail space', which, it is claimed, 'is redefining what it means to work, live, play and stay in central Belfast. We can help you build your future among the inspiring legacy of Belfast's maritime and industrial past' (Titanic Quarter website, 2014).

The centre-piece of the development is the £97 million Titanic Signature Building, home of Titanic Belfast, situated beside 'the atmospheric places where Titanic was designed, built and launched'. These sites of 'world significant' marine and industrial heritage preserved from the former shipyard include the Thompson dry dock, once the largest in the world; the twin slipways of Queen's Yard with their adjacent waterways; and the famous gantry cranes, Goliath and Samson, Belfast landmarks since their construction in 1969 and 1974 respectively (Titanic Quarter website, 2014). The striking architectural form of the building 'conjures up a mass of maritime metaphors', from 'ships prows ploughing their way through the North Atlantic swell', to the five-star logo of the White Star Line, and the iceberg itself (Civic Arts, 2011). Titanic Belfast and associated sites was one of five 'signature projects' identified by the Northern Ireland Tourist Board (2003) as national priorities for investment with the capacity to attract significant numbers of international visitors to Northern Ireland. In its first Programme for Government after taking office in 2007, the new Northern Ireland Executive invested £60 million of public money (Northern Ireland Audit Office, 2011) and established an independent charitable organization, the Titanic Foundation, to run the visitor attraction and to 'develop and promote Queen's Island as an authentic maritime heritage destination and shared space for Belfast and Northern Ireland' (Titanic Foundation website).

Titanic Belfast was opened by the First Minister, Peter Robinson, and the Deputy First Minister, Martin McGuinness, on 31 March 2012 to coincide with the centenary, not of the ship's launching, but of its maiden voyage and sinking. Its centre of attraction, the 'Titanic Experience' exhibition, offers a technologically sophisticated sensory journey into 'the past', telling a story that principally concerns the development of the shipping industry and the work of shipbuilding within the Harland and Wolff yard, the construction of the Titanic, its fitting-out and interior design, launch, and maiden voyage. The galleries at the core of the exhibition evoke 'the sights, sounds, smells and stories of the shipyard and its most famous creation' (Titanic Stories website), while the sinking is addressed more cursorily. It concludes with an exploration of cultural representations and myth-making about the disaster, and a final gallery about the discovery and exploration of the wreck site. The centenary was marked by extensive coverage in the global media, and in Northern Ireland by a Festival with 120 events (Northern Ireland Executive, 2012). The extent of initial interest in the memoryscape constructed by Titanic Belfast is suggested by figures indicating that, during its first year, it was visited by over 700,000 people from 128 countries and contributed £43 million to the economy (Titanic Foundation website), with, according to its CEO, 'new emerging markets of China, India and Australia [...] showing significant interest in us as a product' (Addley and McDonald, 2012). Anecdotal evidence indicates that local visitors are also attracted, and when I visited in May 2012, considerable numbers of school children in organized parties were in evidence. With an extensive outreach programme involving schools across the city, Titanic Belfast is clearly engaged in a process of cross-generational heritage construction and transmission.

However, there are also indications of local alienation from the attraction. John Keenan, owner of the Union Jack Shop on the nearby Newtownards Road in the loyalist Ballymacarrett area of East Belfast, suggested that the local community has been 'badly left behind' by the Titanic commemoration: 'Obviously in this part of Belfast, if you go back in your family history there's someone who worked in the shipyards back then. But all the pensioners who live on this road, they are not going to trek over to see a Titanic museum. The tourist buses go about here, they slow down at the murals, click click click click click, but they don't stop. So how is that helping East Belfast?' (quoted in Addley and McDonald, 2012). Keenan's criticism points to a nexus of contradictions generated by the Titanic heritage project: between the needs of local communities and the transformation brought about by city planners and developers; between generations—the older people of Ballymacarrett and the children whose presence has been orchestrated through institutional links and funding programmes; and between the past of the shipyard and surrounding area, and its present circumstances and planned future. As Neill (2006, p. 114) puts it, the post-conflict transformation envisaged for the Titanic Quarter implied the 'decommissioning of the [ship]yard as Protestant space', which it has been throughout its previous history. At its origins in the 1860s, only 7.5 per cent of the shipbuilding workforce at Harland and Wolff were Catholics—a situation that had barely improved by 1911, the year RMS Titanic was launched when Catholics constituted 24 per cent of the city's population and the yard's largely Protestant labour force of skilled shipwrights and engineers and unskilled manual workers were staunchly loyalist and organized in Orange lodges (Farrell, 1980, p. 16; Bardon & Burnett, 1996, pp. 77-78). In 1970, only 400 Catholics were employed at Harland and Wolff out of a workforce totalling ten thousand (Bardon, 1992, p. 641). The maintenance of the shipyard as a Protestant space was secured through restrictive employment practices but also by violence, with the expulsion of Catholic workers a recurring theme of history at moments of heightened political tension in the city, including 1912 when 2,000 Catholics were driven out during city-wide rioting in loyalist protest against the Home Rule Bill, and 1970 when the entire Catholic workforce was expelled in the context of fierce sectarian rioting across the city and a loyalist attack on the Short Strand enclave in East Belfast, which drew the newly formed Provisional IRA into its first major armed engagement (Bardon & Burnett, 1996, pp. 61-62, 75; Farrell, 1980, pp. 28, 139, 173; Bew and Gillespie, 1993, p. 28).

There is no trace of this history of sectarian division and violence in the Titanic Experience. Only the first of its nine galleries, 'Boomtown Belfast', considers the labour-force that built the ships and touches on differences between Catholic and Protestant workers in displays on living in the city and working in the shipyard and docks. However, the historical account presented here is a superficial simplification that emphasises working-class commonalities and is uninterested in analysing the significance of the political and sectarian divide within the shipyard or the wider city. In order to secure its signification of Belfast's pride in the construction of the Titanic, Titanic Belfast explicitly avoids fundamental realities of the shipyard experience, as if 'decommissioning the [ship]yard as Protestant space' requires the suppression of all reference to its history as such. This representational strategy is consistent with the Titanic Foundation's obligations regarding the development of Queen's Island as a 'shared space' accessible to all city-dwellers and visitors; this goes hand-in-hand with a shared heritage whose 'fantastic and fetishised' form (Brett, 1996, p. 8) requires the erasure of all signs of sectarian division and violence from the memoryscape of the former shipyard.

Interface Memoryscapes, Spaces of Fear, and 'Post Conflict' Subjectivities

In contrast to the 'modern', future-oriented New Belfast a very different relation between past and present exists in Murtagh and Keaveney's (2006) second zone of the twin-speed, 'post-conflict' city. Twenty years into the peace process, 'the majority of persons from a Catholic or Protestant community live in places that are at least 81 per cent Catholic or Protestant', and access not only to housing but also to education, employment, and all kinds of urban facilities and services, as well as opportunities for social mixing, are structured by 'ethno-sectarianized space' (Shirlow & Murtagh, 2006, p. 71). For much of the city's population, belonging and identity is still constituted in relation to largely segregated local areas and enclaves; some, like loyalist Ballymacarrett and the nationalist Short Strand, half a mile away from Laganside and the Titanic Quarter; others, including the Falls and Shankill, as well as the outer-city estates of North and West Belfast, at some geographical remove. These are the living spaces of many of the local children who are taken on educational visits to Belfast Titanic and involved in its outreach work; and of the older generations who have lived through the conflict and remember its impact in family histories.

Whereas the memory of conflict has been largely erased from public space in the modernizing central region of the city, post-conflict memory-scapes engaged with the Troubles have continued to flourish in the ethno-sectarian areas and enclaves, 'establish[ing] powerful symbols representing and commemorating significant aspects of the past that has been lived here, and testifying to its compelling hold on present-day life' (Dawson, 2007, p. 1). These Troubles memoryscapes function to reproduce the political and affective lines-in-the-sand of the ongoing memory wars that continue to be fought out in 'post-conflict' times over the responsibility for, and effects of, the violence since 1966. They also establish necessary loci of continuing engagement with the unresolved traumatic legacies of the past, establishing sites of mourning and of struggle, where the dead may be honoured within their 'own' community and the persistent psychic as well as political affects of the conflict acknowledged (Dawson, 2007). Both these aspects, and their intertwining in a particular discourse of victimhood, can be seen in the case of the Bayardo memorial, erected by the Bayardo Somme Association on

Easter Sunday 2008 (Belfast Forum website; CAIN, 2009)—less than a year after the restoration of devolved government in May 2007—at a prominent location on the junction of the Shankill Road and Argyle Street in the Middle Shankill area of West Belfast. A brick and steel structure the size and shape of the gable-end of a house, the memorial marks the site of the Bayardo Bar destroyed in a gun and bomb attack by the PIRA thirty-two years earlier. It comprises the photographs and names of the five civilians who died, photographs of the bar before and after the attack, and a memorial stone with their names and the dedication to what is described as a 'forgotten atrocity': 'In memory of five innocent Protestants slaughtered here by a Republican murder gang on 13th August 1975'. A notice attached to the memorial (CAIN, 2009) identifies 'this spot' as the site where 'five Protestants were killed and up to sixty injured' by 'homicidal' Republicans in the course of their 'vicious campaign of genocide [...] against [...] you and I, the Protestant people'. The political significance of the Bayardo Bar memorial, established by this language, lies in its challenge both to the justificatory discourse of the PIRA which avows that the actions of its Volunteers were 'non-sectarian' and directed not at Protestants *per se* but at British State forces and the loyalist paramilitary groups, and to pro-Agreement claims that theirs is now 'a message of peace'. At the same time, for the family and friends of those (including a 17-year-old girl) who lost their lives in August 1975, the Bayardo memorial functions (in the words of the attached notice) as a 'place [...] that hold[s ...] the bitter sweet memory of loved ones and how those loved ones met their premature end', and ensures that the affective legacy of hurt and loss is not 'forgotten' by a society too eager to put the past behind. As part of the wider memoryscape, it bears witness, within the spaces of everyday life along the Shankill Road, to a past that has not gone away but requires acknowledgement and redress for unresolved questions of truth and justice, the so-called 'legacy issues' that have now become central to the complex and uneven process of 'coming to terms with the past' in Northern Ireland.

In interface areas of the still-divided city, twenty-five of which existed in 2005 (Shirlow & Murtagh, 2006, p. 64), the unfinished business of the past makes itself felt not only in memoryscapes but also through the reproduction of traumatic spatial legacies of the Troubles. Interface areas have continued to be experienced as 'spaces of fear' (Shirlow) plagued by routine sectarian violence—the bombardment of houses across the peace line, regular rioting, and dangers associated with moving out of 'sanctuary space' (Shirlow & Murtagh, 2006, 58)—that has increased since the paramilitary ceasefires of 1994. The prevalence of such violence has created a 'dynamic of fearfulness

[...] associated with perceptions of threat and the twin forces of resentment and incomprehension' (Shirlow & Murtagh 2006, p. 71). In one significant manifestation of this dynamic, the desire of interface communities for security in their lives has led to grass-roots campaigns for further peace-line barriers to be built; Jarman (2005) found that over half of the forty-one barriers he identified in the city had been either extended or newly built since 1994. The reproduction of fear within the city continues to be driven by rioting. Controversial parades provide annual flashpoints of violent confrontation, like the 12th July march by the Orange Order past the nationalist Ardoyne area of North Belfast that is opposed as triumphalist and inflammatory by local residents' groups, and triggered days of serious rioting again in summer 2013 after it was banned by Northern Ireland's Parades Commission (Harte, 2013). Fierce rioting involving gunfire broke out in summer 2011 on the Ballymacarrett and Short Strand interface in East Belfast, only eight months before the opening of Titanic Belfast just half a mile away (Bowcott, 2011). Further rioting on this interface occurred between January and March 2013 in the context of sustained loyalist protest right across Northern Ireland against the decision by Belfast City Council to limit the number of days when the Union Jack will be flown on City Hall, which itself became the scene of violent confrontation between protesters and police at the heart of the city centre (CAIN, 2013).

Over fourty years after the construction of the first peace-line, the polarization of identities remains deeply inscribed into the spaces of everyday life and the subjectivities of those who inhabit them. Mental maps that encode and reproduce the traumatic past and psychic defences against it are a legacy of fear that is inherited by children in the form of 'sectarianized spatial practices' (Mapping the spaces, n.d. 2003?), acquired and lived out in the course of everyday social interactions. The 'Mapping the Spaces of Fear' project (n.d. 2003?), points to the 'complex body of information about the relative dangers of particular spaces' that working-class children draw on 'to negotiate their daily life choices' and 'manage their own behaviour'. One interviewee, a Catholic woman in her early forties, vividly illustrates this point:

> My youngest daughter is 9 and she goes to school on the Falls Road (Catholic area) and her name is Maebh (Catholic name) and I have never, ever once said that she had to take her school uniform off, or explained it, but she *always knew* that if she was going to Connswater Shopping Centre (located in a Protestant district) with me she couldn't say her name was Maebh, and she had to put a coat over her to cover her school uniform. (Parentheses are editorial insertions in the original; italics are mine.)

What this 9-year-old girl, one of the 'cease-fire generation' born since 1994 (Leonard & McKnight, 2011, p. 572), has 'always known' is the vulnerability that follows from her own visibility whenever outside sanctuary space the consequent need to practise identity-masking.

Such knowledges are learned through children's largely segregated school and street cultures. Leonard and McKnight (2010, 31) found that nearly one quarter of her sample of school students from across the city 'felt unsafe' wearing uniforms whilst travelling to and from school, an affect linked in many cases to 'perceived or actual sectarian abuse/attack'. The young people shared common understandings of the 'invisible barriers [...] utilised to mark off Catholic from Protestant areas (Leonard & McKnight, 2011, p. 579). These local knowledges become internalized in modes of 'self-regulation', reinforced by peer-group judgements and the 'censure' of behaviours considered naive (Mapping the spaces). So deep are these internalizations that the divided landscape itself appears 'normal and natural' to the extent that, for some young people, the peace-line walls overshadowing their streets have become invisible within the interior landscape, unnoticed 'because they had always been there'. This normalizing of spatial division is accompanied by a lack of curiosity about 'those living on the other side of the wall' (Leonard & McKnight, 2011, p. 579). Those on 'the other side', of course, do feature in the mental maps of young people in the form of the threatening other who may be encountered outside sanctuary space.

Since 2007, a debate opened up by the community organization, Belfast Interface Project, together with the Northern Ireland Community Relations Council, has begun to consider how 'the removal of all interface barriers across the city of Belfast over time' might be undertaken, without disregarding 'the perceptions of safety and security of the people living near to [them]' (Community Relations Council, 2008, p. 9). In May 2013 the Office of the First Minister and Deputy First Minister proposed working towards the dismantling of all Northern Ireland's peace-line walls by 2023 in order to promote integration across the ethno-sectarian divide in accordance with the 'shared future' agenda (OFMDFM, 2013). This aspiration involves transformation not only of the city's physical space but also of the interior landscapes that have developed in response. Research (Byrne, Gormley Heenan & Robinson, 2012) into the attitudes and feelings held by interface residents about the peace-line walls discovered high levels of persistent anxiety, with 69 per cent wanting the walls maintained to give continuing protection from feared violence, and for Protestants especially, from a perceived threat to their culture and identity. Yet the study also detected considerable ambivalence, with 58 per cent simultaneously stating their desire to see the walls come down.

Expressions of hope associated with this possibility were qualified by 'a sizeable degree of pessimism about what the future physical landscape might look like' and the likelihood of positive change ever occurring (Byrne et al., 2012, p. 24). Leonard and McKnight (2010, p. 29) found that one third of her school-student sample considered Belfast to be an 'unsafe city' due to sectarian violence and rioting, especially when orchestrated by paramilitary organizations. this signifies that the time of conflict is by no means seen as 'over'. Among the young people involved in Leonard and McKnight's (2011) research, nearly half believed that the Troubles had not yet fully ended and a further 45 per cent were unsure, while for Protestants in particular, the periodic resurgence of gun and bomb attacks by paramilitary groups leads to increasing levels of insecurity and anxiety about the possible return of 'a big war again' (Leonard & McKnight, 2011, p. 575). For some, the 'stories told by older generations' (Leonard & McKnight, 2011, p. 579)—a transmission of popular memory encoding common sense about recurring cycles of violence within the city—endorse the rationality of these fears and the consequent logic of continuing separation.

Initiatives concerned with 'historical reconciliation' in the context of the spatial politics of Belfast must also negotiate such contradictions in considering ways in which antagonistic narratives of the conflict, that are reproduced within the polarized memoryscapes and subjectivities of the interface areas, might be transformed. One approach, adopted here as in the city centre, advocates replacing any potentially divisive commemoration with symbols of 'shared heritage'. The Arts Council of Northern Ireland's 'Re-imaging Communities' programme, for example, aims to utilize public art in challenging racism and sectarianism, and has promoted the removal of murals with militaristic themes and their replacement with less controversial images; George Best and CS Lewis as well as the Titanic have all featured in East Belfast (Troubled walls, 2013). An antithetical approach seeks to open the conflicted history of the interfaces to engagement and dialogue with 'dark tourists' (Sharpley and Stone, 2009) who are fascinated precisely by 'the "dangerous" parts of the city' and want 'to hear the history of the violence' (Holland, 1994), constituting audiences for stories by members of the communities on either side of the peace-line, passed on by tour guides, who may themselves be ex-combatants or former prisoners (Reynolds, 2001; McKittrick, 2004). Responding to the protests of 2013, the Northern Ireland Assembly established all-party talks chaired by the former US Presidential envoy to Northern Ireland, Richard Haass, that led to the Stormont House Agreement of 2014, seeking consensus on how to tackle divisive parades, flag-flying and other expressions of identity. Developing ways, through local negotiation of the kind pioneered in Derry/Londonderry, to acknowledge and allow space for the different cultural symbols and commemorative traditions of the other, whilst removing their potential for inflammatory provocation, is now widely understood to be central to reducing divisiveness and building new relationships.

The careful negotiation of difference through dialogue also lies at the heart of cross-community history-making that engages people from local communities in collaborative work with others across the divide. One pioneering example of this is the Bridging Oral History Project, established in 2009-10 as a cross-community collaboration between the Dúchas Oral History Archive, a Republican project based at the Falls Community Council, and the Lower Castlereagh Community Group in loyalist Ballymacarrett, East Belfast, under the auspices of the Belfast Conflict Resolution Consortium (Moloney, 2013). Drawing on the expertise developed in 'single identity' local history and archiving projects in nationalist communities, the Bridging Project took participants from both groups into the space of the other where they worked together, first to hear and discuss interviews from the Dúchas Archive, and subsequently to record a number of oral history interviews with loyalists. Moloney (2013) notes that anxieties amongst the Republican participants on their initial visit to Ballymacarrett—due to 'the geography of this part of the city [being] unfamiliar', recent tensions on the Short Strand interface, and uncertainty about how their stories would be received—was alleviated by actually meeting the loyalists, who demonstrated 'particular interest in hearing the stories of IRA activists'. A reciprocal visit brought loyalists to the Falls Road, and 'The Voices from the Yard' project was initiated, focusing on the loyalists' stories of the shipyard but exploring conflicting interpretations across the two communities: 'There was explicit acknowledgement that the issue of discrimination in the shipyard could raise tensions. However, what was also acknowledged was the respect for the broader history of the shipyard within the loyalist community as well as the Catholic experience' (Moloney, 2013). Disagreements and differences were 'openly and respectfully discussed and where possible resolved'. In this way, the Bridging Project made a small beginning in opening up the more complex and difficult history of the shipyard concealed by the memoryscape of the Titanic Quarter.

'The Voices from the Yard' project broke down after five months due to a number of factors, including complex power dynamics and questions of trust within the group and pressures brought to bear upon it by both cross-community and intra-community politics. Renegotiation of the collaboration led to a new project on loyalism in the 1970s. These stories were presented for discussion at community events in each location, a number of the interviews were deposited at the Dúchas Archive, and in March 2011 the East Belfast Oral History Archive was launched by the First Minister, Peter Robinson. Moloney (2013) argues that, despite its difficulties and limitations, by bringing together members of politically opposed communities in the negotiation of a new, practical cooperative relationship, the project developed participants' confidence in their own agency and power to effect change within their marginalized communities; created opportunities for breaking conflict-created divisions and silences; and enabled critical reflection and dialogue, leading to new understandings of the past, present and future that recognize and include the historical experience of the 'other'.

I have suggested in this chapter that the task of historical reconciliation after conflict has a spatial dimension, and argued for a complex and nuanced understanding of post-conflict spaces as these intersect with histories and memories of the violent past. The concept of memoryscape becomes a more precise analytical tool to the extent that it is deployed in relation to other categories, enabling the reproduction and transformation of the physical existence of places to be distinguished from continuities and changes, firstly, in the cultural and affective significance of those places, and secondly, in the internalized landscapes of subjectivity. Such distinctions allow identification of the different speeds and temporalities of change, as well as different relations between past and present, at work in each of these dimensions of post-conflict geography. 'Trauma', a term signifying the affective consequences and repercussions of past violence reproduced in the present, together with the psychic defences that are mobilized to contain and manage its effects, is a property of the interior world of subjectivity. It is also a shaping factor in the making of cultural landscapes, narratives and memories, that construct knowledges and interpretations of places, their significance and history. In order not to be trapped in the conflicted past, social groups and individuals within post-conflict societies need to evolve shared understandings of its hold upon them, in spatial as well as temporal terms, and of the resulting ambivalences and contradictions that complicate a sense of the future.

Subjectivities in 'post-conflict' Belfast are decisively influenced by the reproduction and internalization of local spatial knowledges as these intersect in various ways with the affective residues of past violence and with templates of memory warning of the return of conflict from the past. These psychic legacies of the past, both conscious and unconscious, are negotiated in a complex and ambivalent relationship with desires for a future society freed of violence and fear. Strategies designed to promote the transition to a 'shared city' have not sufficiently engaged with historically-formed subjectivities and identities, or attended to the complexities of their 'attachments to the past' (Dawson 2007, p. 5), and to the spaces where such attachments are embodied. The production of new spaces and cultural landscapes in the city centre and Queen's Island, based on rectification and obliteration of the sites of conflict and the suppression of all traces of conflict within memoryscapes designed to figure a common heritage, remakes the present and transforms the relation between present and past on the template of a particular version of the desirable, shared future. This hinders the necessary creative engagement with these legacies.

An alternative is figured in the dialogical encounters across the spaces of fear as negotiated in grassroots history-making within the Bridging Project, and in the 'animated exchanges'—about the removal of the peace walls, and about their own 'core role [...] in facilitating future cooperation [...] across the divide'—stimulated amongst her young participants by Leonard and McKnight's (2011) research. Both cases involve, simultaneously, 'dual processes of accepting and challenging' the historical and geographical divisions, and their subjective correlates, which 'characterise [...] daily spatial lives in interface localities' (Leonard & McKnight, 2011, p. 580). Through the exercise of agency that originates from below, starts from where people find themselves placed now, and is willing to allow difference and conflicting histories to exist, 'new shared space' may be created in the city; in which 'boundaries [become ...] more permeable [...] leaving space for identities to change and evolve' (Komarova, 2008).

References

Addley, E. & McDonald, H. (2012, 24 March). Will the new Titanic centre do for Belfast what the Guggenheim did for Bilbao? *Guardian*.

Bardon, J. (1992). *A History of Ulster*. Belfast: Blackstaff.

Bardon, J. & Burnett, D. (1996). *Belfast: A pocket history*. Belfast: Blackstaff.

Belfast Forum. (2008). Retrieved 15 February, 2014, from http://www.belfastforum.co.uk /index.php/topic,10796.msg196571.html#msg196571

Bew, P. & Gillespie, G. (1993). *Northern Ireland. A chronology of the Troubles 1968-1993*. Dublin: Gill and Macmillan.

Bowcott, O. (2011, 22 June). Belfast riots: a setback for area barely reshaped by peace process. *Guardian*.

Brett, D. (1996). *The construction of heritage*. Cork: Cork University Press.

Byrne, J., Gormley Heenan, C., & Robinson, G. (2012). *Attitudes to peace walls. Research report to the Office of the First Minister and Deputy First Minister*. June. University of Ulster. Retrieved 4 February, 2014, from www.ark.ac.uk/peacewalls2012/

CAIN. (2009). Photograph M693P1/8 (Monument 693, eight photographs). Retrieved 4 February, 2014, from http://cain. ulst.ac.uk/cgi-bin/AHRC/photos.pl?id=1102&mon =693

CAIN. (2013). A background note on the protests and violence related to the Union Flag at Belfast City Hall, December 2012-January 2013. Retrieved 20 February, 2014, from http://cain.ulst.ac.uk/issues/ identity/flag-2012.htm

Civic Arts. (2011). Titanic Belfast. Civic Arts website. Retrieved 4 February, 2014, from http://www.civicarts.com/titanic-signature-project.php

Community Relations Council. (2008). *Towards sustainable security: Interface barriers and the legacy of segregation in Belfast.* Belfast: Community Relations Council.

Conspiracy. (1977, 13 March). A conspiracy to split city—candidate. *Sunday News*.

Consultative Group on the Past. (2009). *Report of the Consultative Group on the Past.* Belfast: Consultative Group on the Past.

Dawson, G. (2005). Trauma, place and the politics of memory: Bloody Sunday, Derry, 1972-2004. *History Workshop Journal, 59,* 151-178.

Dawson, G. (2007). *Making peace with the past? Memory, trauma and the Irish Troubles.* Manchester: Manchester University Press.

Farrell, M. (1980). *Northern Ireland: The Orange State.* London: Pluto.

Graham, B., & Nash, C. (2006). A shared future: territoriality, pluralism and public policy in Northern Ireland. *Political Geography, 25* (3), 253-278.

Hamber, B. and Kelly, G. (2005). *A place for reconciliation? Conflict and locality in Northern Ireland.* Belfast: Democratic Dialogue.

Harte, A. (2013, 5 August). Ardoyne, north Belfast: Eye of the storm. *BBC News*. Retrieved 20 February, 2014, from http:// www.bbc.co.uk/news/uk-northern-ireland-23554868

Holland, J. (1994, 6 September). Guided tours of Belfast's lion's den. *Irish Echo*.

Jarman, N. (1993). Intersecting Belfast. In B. Bender (Ed.), *Landscape: Politics and Perspectives.* Oxford: Berg. 107-137.

Jarman, N. (2005). *Mapping interface barriers.* BIP Interface Mapping Project. Belfast: Institute for Conflict Research. August. Retrieved 15 February, 2014, from http://cain.ulst.ac.uk/issues/segregat/docs/ jarman0805.pdf

Komarova, M. (2008). *Shared space in Belfast and the limits of 'A Shared Future'.* Divided Cities/Contested States Working Paper No. 3. School of Sociology, Social Policy and Social Work, Queen's University Belfast. No page numbers. 28pp.

Laganside Corporation website. Retrieved 4 February, 2014, from http:// www.laganside.com

Leonard, M. & McKnight, M. (2010) Teenagers' perceptions of Belfast as a divided and/ or shared city. *Shared Space: A Research Journal on Peace, Conflict and Community Relations in Northern Ireland, 10,* 23-37.

Leonard, M. & McKnight, M. (2011). Bringing down the walls: young people's perspectives on peace-walls in Belfast. *International Journal of Sociology and Social Policy, 31* (9/10), 569-582. doi: 10.1108/01443331111164151.

Mapping the spaces. (n.d 2003?). *Mapping the spaces of fear: Socio-spatial causes and effects of violence in Northern Ireland. Summary of findings.* Centre for Spatial Territorial Analysis and Research, Queen's University: Belfast. No page numbers.

McKittrick, D. (2004, 30 August). A coach tour with a twist: your guide to Belfast was an IRA leader who spent 16 years in jail. *Guardian*.

McKittrick, D., Kelters, S., Feeney, B., Thornton, C., & McVea, D. (2007). *Lost lives. The stories of the men, women and children who died as a result of the Northern Ireland troubles*. Edinburgh: Mainstream Publishing.

Moloney, M. (2013). *Reaching out from the archive: the role of community oral history archives in conflict transformation in Northern Ireland*. Unpublished PhD thesis, University of Ulster.

Murtagh, B. & Keaveney, K. (2006). Policy and conflict transformation in the ethnocratic city. *Space and Polity,* Special Issue: Belfast: The 'post-conflict' city', *10* (2), 187-202.

Neill, W.J.V. (2006). Return to Titanic and lost in the Maze: The search for representation in 'post-conflict' Belfast. *Space and Polity,* Special Issue: Belfast: The 'post-conflict' city, *10* (2), 109-120.

Northern Ireland Audit Office. (2011). *Northern Ireland Tourist Board: Review of the Signature Projects*. 13 December 2011. Northern Ireland Audit Office: Belfast. <http://www.niauditoffice.gov.uk/a-to-z.htm/report_nitb_rev_sig_pro>. Retrieved 4 February, 2014.

Northern Ireland Executive. (2012, 29 February). News release: Spectacular line-up for Titanic Belfast Festival. Retrieved 4 February, 2014, from http://www.northernireland.gov.uk/news-deti-290212-spectacular-line-up

Northern Ireland Tourist Board. (2003). *Tourism in Northern Ireland: A strategic framework for action 2004-2007.* Retrieved 4 February, 2014, from http://www.discovernorthernireland.com/A-Strategic-Framework-for-Action-2004-2007-A248.

Office of the First Minister and Deputy First Minister (OFMDFM). (2005). *A shared future: Policy and strategic framework for good relations in Northern Ireland*. Belfast: OFMDFM.

Office of the First Minister and Deputy First Minister (OFMDFM). (2013). *Together building a united community*. Belfast: OFMDFM. May. Retrieved 15 February, 2014, from http://www.ofmdfmni.gov. uk/together-building-a-united-community

Reynolds, P. (2001, 2 September). Moving into the past lane. Tour the Troubles—by taxi! *Sunday Life.*

Rowlands, M. & De Jong, F. (2008). Postconflict heritage. *Journal of Material Cultures, 13* (2), 131-134. doi: 10.1177/1359183508090894.

Sharpley, R. & Stone, P. R. (Eds.). (2009). *The darker side of travel. The theory and practice of dark tourism*. Bristol: Channel View Publications.

Shirlow, P. (2006). Belfast: The 'post-conflict' city. *Space and Polity,* Special Issue: Belfast: The 'post-conflict' city, *10* (2), 100-107.

Shirlow, P. & Murtagh, B. (2006). *Belfast: Segregation, violence and the city*. London: Pluto.

Switzer, C. & McDowell, S. (2009). Redrawing cognitive maps of conflict: Lost spaces and forgetting in the centre of Belfast. *Memory Studies, 2* (3), 337-353.

Titanic Foundation website. Retrieved 12 February, 2014, from http://www.titanic-foundation.org/TitanicBelfast

Titanic Quarter website. Retrieved 4 February, 2014, from http://www.titanic-quarter.com

Titanic Stories website. Retrieved 4 February, 2014, from http://www.the-titanic.com/Titanic-Today/Attractions/Titanic-Belfast.aspx

Titanic tourism. (2002, 14 June). Titanic tourism takes off. *Irish Independent.* Special supplement in association with Belfast City Council.

Titanic town. (2012, 15 April). *Titanic town.* Radio broadcast, BBC Radio 4. Retrieved 12 February, 2014, from Box of Broadcasts website, http://bobnational.net/record/96081

Troubled walls. (2013, 17 October). *Troubled walls.* Radio broadcast, BBC Radio 4.

Tumarkin, M. (2005). *Traumascapes. The power and fate of places transformed by tragedy.* Carlton, Victoria: Melbourne University Press.

Chapter 8
The Anglo-Boer War (1899 – 1902) and Its Traumatic Consequences

André Wessels

University of the Free State

Introduction

Growing up in a 'typical' Afrikaner home in the 1960s and 1970s, the Great Trek of the 1830s and the Anglo-Boer War of 1899 to 1902 formed—from an early age—part of one's historical frame of reference; something which was strengthened by the stories told by a paternal grandmother (who passed away in 1980 at the age of 98). She lived through the latter conflict between Boer and Briton as one of the (relatively few) Boer civilians who were able to evade capture by the British forces and consequently did not suffer in the camps, but rather in the veld, where survival was sometimes dependent on food provided by local black inhabitants. This 'typical' Afrikaner home was not a house in the platteland (rural) in an Afrikaner-dominated town, but a flat (apartment) in Durban, in Natal (now KwaZulu-Natal), a province then often referred to as "the last outpost of the British Empire". There were books in the flat: Afrikaans, and English, Dutch and German; many books, as well as many more books in the Durban Municipal Library in the imposing (British) Durban city hall complex.

To the inquiring and critical mind it soon became clear that the Anglo-Boer War (like the rest of the history of South Africa, and all history) is not simplistic. There are seldom clear-cut good people and bad people. To understand many political, social and even economic developments, one often has to study the wars and other forms of conflict that have shaped our societies. What starts as a hobby, can develop into a vocation. What starts as a fascination with military campaigns and battles, strategy and tactics, can lead one to asking questions about the consequences of the decisions taken by ambitious politicians, and vain military commanders. When elephants fight, it is the grass that suffers. Thus, one can end up doing research on the traumatic and other consequences of a war between staunch imperialists and proud nationalists; a war of which the after-effects still resonate with us today.

Fast-track to some twenty years after South Africa became a true democracy in 1994. When one looks around South Africa today (2014), one unfortunately sees many people who are angry, or disillusioned, or bitter; or all these things, and more. There are people who suffer from historical amnesia: they do not know who they are, where they come from, where exactly they are (historically speaking) today, or where they are heading. There are also many traumatised people around us—people either traumatised by events of the past (for example, the humiliation and hardships they suffered under apartheid), or by recent events, such as crime, or the Marikana massacre near Rustenburg (16 August 2012) when miners were killed in police action. One meets people who yearn for the so-called 'good old days' of the past and others who want to refight the battles of the past—including those between the British and the Afrikaners/Boers of long ago.

Notwithstanding a Truth and Reconciliation Commission, reconciliation is still a problem in South Africa. Why? Why all the bitterness, the hostility, the unresolved trauma? In an effort to understand these challenges, it is imperative that one should understand the history of twentieth-century South Africa. Of course the root causes go back much further in history, but in this chapter there is space to go back only as far as the Anglo-Boer War of 1899 to 1902—a war that set in motion a train of events which, in due course, had profound implications for inter-group relations in South Africa. It goes without saying, that the above-mentioned questions, as well as an understanding of the historical context of the challenges South Africans are facing today, are of paramount importance if we are to find truth, reconciliation, and healing.

From 11 October 1899 to 31 May 1902, the Anglo-Boer War raged in what is today South Africa. This bitter conflict may be regarded as the first liberation struggle of the twentieth century, with the Afrikaners being the first African freedom fighters. Thus far, it is the most extensive and destructive war that has been fought in southern Africa. In this chapter, it will be shown how the military conflict between the world's only superpower on the cusp of the twentieth century (i.e. the British Empire) and two small Afrikaner/Boer republics (i.e. the Zuid-Afrikaansche Republiek/Transvaal and the Oranje-Vrijstaat/Orange Free State) wreaked havoc on the civilian population in the war zone, and what trans-generational trauma it caused. What started as a white man's war and a so-called 'gentleman's war', soon degenerated into a conflict that—at least to some extent—displayed the characteristics of both a civil war and a total war, affecting the lives of all the inhabitants (i.e. white, black, brown and Asian) in the region.

Thus, proceeding from the assumption that a basic prerequisite for breaking intergenerational cycles of repetition is knowledge of history (one's 'own' history, but also the history of 'the other'), it is the purpose of this chapter to focus on what can be regarded as the most important conflict in the history of what is today, South Africa, namely the Anglo-Boer War of 1899 to 1902; and more specifically, to indicate what the profound "collateral damage" and concomitant consequences of this war were. The issues that will be addressed in this chapter link up with the work that has thus far been done by scholars such as Spies (1977), Nasson (2010), Pretorius (2001), Kessler (2012), and van Heyningen (2013).

In this chapter the connections between the past and present regarding the trauma caused by the Anglo-Boer War (and in particular the camp system) will be highlighted—something that is not often addressed in the scholarship on the war of 1899 to 1902, albeit that the author has done some work in this regard in the past. But, in an effort to understand the terrible collateral damage done by a particular conflict, the basic military events should always be understood, and consequently a brief overview of the events in the South African war zone in 1899 to 1902 will be provided. In the following section, the traumatic consequences and legacy of the Anglo-Boer War will be analysed.

The Course of the War: A Brief Overview

The causes of the Anglo-Boer War can be summarised as the culmination of a very long struggle between British imperialism and Afrikaner nationalism. The finer details of the course of the war are not relevant to the purposes of this study. Suffice it to say that there were false expectations on both sides regarding the duration of the conflict; many British and Boers indeed believed that the war would be over by Christmas 1899 (Wessels, 2000, pp. 83-84). If a closer look is taken at the Boer and British strategies and how these strategies were implemented during the first three (semi-) conventional phases of the struggle, it becomes clear that both sides made serious mistakes. The British and the Boers underestimated each other: the British were not well-prepared for the war; the Boers did not exploit either their initial advantages or their initial tactical successes, and the first British commander-in-chief in South Africa, General Sir Redvers Buller, made serious errors. He was then removed from his command and replaced by Lord Roberts of Kandahar, who succeeded in defeating a large Boer force at Paardeberg (27 February 1900) and who captured the Boer capital cities:

Bloemfontein on 13 March 1900, and Pretoria on 5 June 1900 (Amery (Ed.), 1902-1906; Breytenbach, 1969-1983).

By then, however, the character of the war had changed; as a matter of fact, already from March 1900 onwards (i.e. when the Boers changed their (semi-) conventional strategy to that of guerrilla warfare). The British Army in South Africa took several drastic measures in a desperate effort to counter the new Boer onslaught. This included: the scorched-earth policy and concomitant camp system; the building of some 8 000 blockhouses across the length and breadth of the war zone; mobile drives against the Boer commandos; and the employment of as many as 140 000 black and brown (as well as a few Asian) local inhabitants (either in a combatant or non-combatant capacity), as well as more than 5 500 Afrikaners who had surrendered and then joined the British forces (Grundlingh, 2006).

The consequences of the British counter-guerrilla strategy included the 'collateral damage' it inflicted on the country and its inhabitants. The British scorched-earth policy, for example, led to the destruction of approximately 30 000 Boer farmsteads, and the houses of tens of thousands of black labourers, as well as approximately 40 towns and villages were partially or totally destroyed. The fact that more than half of the total (only 219 000 strong) Afrikaner population of the Transvaal and Orange Free State, and more than a 100 000 black civilians, were left destitute, and that in due course the British authorities established internment camps (a term preferred to the emotionally-charged term 'concentration camps') where these civilians were housed—most of the time in unsanitary conditions, and without sufficient food or medical facilities—speaks for itself. The result was a humanitarian disaster, which led to the death of at least 28 000 white civilians (80% of them children, aged sixteen years and younger), and at least 23 000 (but probably many more) black civilians (once again, most of them young people and children). The trauma was incalculable (Pretorius (Ed.), 2001; Kessler, 1999). However, it has to be clearly understood that there was no intention on the side of the British authorities to let either white or black civilians die in the camps. Thus, to make a clear distinction between the Nazi concentration/extermination camps of the Second World War and the camp system established by the British in South Africa, this author prefers the term 'internment camp(s)' when referring to the camps in South Africa, 1900-1902.

The Anglo-Boer War was the 226th of 230 wars, campaigns and punitive expeditions in which the British Army took part in the 64 years of Queen Victoria's reign from 1837 to 1901 (Farwell, 1973, pp. 364-371). Although both sides initially saw the Anglo-Boer War as a 'gentleman's war', as well as a white man's war, the conflict was from the start neither the one nor the other. Lord Kitchener of Khartoum, who succeeded Lord Roberts as the British commander-in-chief in South Africa at midnight on 28-29 November 1900, had to bring the war to a conclusion as soon as possible, but the Boers frustrated his efforts, and consequently his measures became very harsh—albeit, that from a military point of view, he had no other option. Eventually he was ruthlessly successful (from a military point of view), but his actions caused much trauma (Wessels (Ed.), 2006). However, it should be kept in mind that had the Boers realised by mid-1900 that they could no longer win the war, had accepted the fact, and had surrendered to the British forces, their women and children would have been spared much suffering.

During the Anglo-Boer War, the distinction between soldiers and civilians, combatants and non-combatants, in due course became blurred. Civilian casualties (collateral damage), including deaths in internment camps, henceforth had military significance. For example, news about the plight of loved ones in camps caused burghers serving in commando units to think seriously about their role in the continuation of the struggle. On another level, the idea that military conflict could be coupled with respect for the enemy, gradually faded away. In this sense, the Anglo-Boer War was—albeit on a small scale—a precursor to the destructive total wars of the twentieth century.

Boer civilians were not sent to internment camps primarily for what they did, but for what they were (Giliomee, 2003, p. 354). Although the British justifiably regarded the Boer farmsteads and Boer civilians as legitimate military targets, and although the Afrikaner was correct in arguing that the British waged war against civilians, it has to be understood that there were no intentional attempts on the part of the British to exterminate Boer civilians in the camps—as happened during the Second World War to the Jews in the Nazi extermination camps. However, it is true that when the camps were first erected, as well as in the course of 1901, administration was sometimes very poor and that this, and negligence, with regard to the provision of food and medical services, for example, led to the deaths of many women and children. Thus, it is understandable that during the war the camps were already known among Afrikaners as 'murder camps' and 'hell camps'. If conditions in the white internment camps were bad, they were, generally speaking, worse in the black internment camps. In fact, one could regard the lack of planning and the limited supplies these camps received as criminal neglect on the part of the British authorities (Kessler, 1999; Kessler, 2012).

Through the ages, it has always been innocent civilians who have suffered most during wars—and innocent civilians continue to bear the brunt of present-day conflicts. In the South African context, however, the Anglo-Boer War is prominent as a conflict in which civilians had intentionally been targeted by a military strategy. Since then, numerous examples can be found in history, and for this reason, this war in South Africa, more than any other local conflict, had an incredibly negative effect on the white and black civilian population in the war zone.

However, it was not only the internment camps that impacted negatively on inter-group relations in South Africa and led to trauma. Relations were also strained by other traumatic events during the war, such as the baKgatla attack at Derdepoort on 25 November 1899; the murder of Abraham Esau (the coloured man who was tortured at Calvinia by the invading Boer commando and who was killed on 5 February 1901); the Boer attack at Leliefontein on 27 January 1902; and the Zulu attack on the commando of Field-Cornet Jan Potgieter at Holkrans (Mthashana) on 6 May 1902 (Nasson, 1991; Laband, 2000, pp. 123-124; Botha, 1969).

By the end of 1901, the British forces' counter-guerrilla strategy of directed severity began to yield results; however, in the western Transvaal and in the northern and north-eastern Orange Free State, the Boer commandos (under the command of General Koos de la Rey and General Christiaan de Wet respectively) pursued the guerrilla war relentlessly and with relative success. No wonder, therefore, that the British forces' counter-guerrilla operations in the western Transvaal and in the northern and north-eastern Free State were more comprehensive (and more forceful) than in other parts of the war zone. But by May 1902, the Boers' situation was hopeless. Lord Kitchener had forced the Boers on commando into a position where most of them had given up hope. Consequently, on the conclusion of negotiations between Boer delegates at Vereeniging, the British conditions for surrender were accepted (by 54 votes to six) on 31 May 1902 (Kestell, & Van Velden, 1912).

The fact that the war had ended with the loss of Boer republican independence, left most of the bittereinders (bitter-enders, die-hards) and their families filled with dismay. As time passed, most Afrikaners accepted the outcome of the peace negotiations. However, some bittereinders' unhappiness with the conditions of surrender led to their believing that some of the negotiators had sold out the Boers at Vereeniging and Pretoria (Wessels, 1988, pp. 103-105, 109-112).

Like many Germans after the Great (First World) War of 1914 to 1918, some Afrikaners believed, albeit erroneously, that they were not actually defeated militarily in the war, and could therefore have continued their struggle. Like the Germans who after 1918 believed that they had been stabbed in the back by the Weimar politicians who negotiated for peace and had surrendered (see the Dolchstoss-im-Rücken lie that was propagated by Adolf Hitler and his Nazi followers), some Afrikaners believed (erroneously), on conclusion of the Anglo-Boer War, that they could have continued to pursue the guerrilla war against the British with success, but had been betrayed by people, such as General Louis Botha and General Jan Smuts—both of them prominent Transvaal commanding officers (Wessels, 1988, p. 103).

However, there is no evidence that Boer leaders, such as General Louis Botha and General Jan Smuts, had sold out or betrayed the Boers; indeed, in many respects, their carefully considered and diplomatic initiatives during the peace negotiations at Vereeniging and Pretoria, saved the Afrikaner nation from complete destruction. Together with other Boer leaders, Botha and Smuts negotiated exceptionally generous conditions of surrender; for example, those who decided to become British subjects would retain their personal freedom and property; Dutch could still be used as a medium of instruction in the Transvaal and Orange River Colony schools; and the granting of voting rights to black people would be discussed only after responsible government (i.e. self-government) had been instituted (Kestell, & Van Velden, 1912, pp. 133-135). The last-mentioned clause meant in effect, that Afrikaners would decide the political future of black and coloured South Africans, and in practice, once the Transvaal and the Orange River Colony (as the Orange Free State was called under British rule) received self-government, they did not give blacks and coloureds the right to vote. Thus, at the peace negotiations in Pretoria, the political and other interests of black and coloured people were sacrificed to facilitate reconciliation between Boer and Briton. Those traumatised by the Anglo-Boer War, soon became the new traumatisers. This then brings us to the point where the legacy of the war of 1899 to 1902 has to be analysed in more detail.

The Traumatic Consequences and Legacy of War

To most Afrikaners north of the Orange River, the only way that the injustice of the 'peace' of Vereeniging could be reversed, was by regaining the independence of the Boer republics (and much later, the establishment of a Republic of South Africa). The Afrikaners who suffered most during the war were indeed those who lived in the Transvaal and the Orange Free State, and more specifically, the inhabitants of farms and towns whose houses had been partially or entirely destroyed by the British forces.

However, the Anglo-Boer War left almost all the race groups discontented in the country that from 1910 onwards was known as South Africa. Afrikanerdom was left divided (the bittereinders versus the hands-uppers and, especially, the joiners), while the bittereinders in particular, were embittered and humiliated. Coloureds, and especially black people, were frustrated because the end of the war did not yield the expected political and other privileges.

Although the British authorities had created the impression during the war that they would give equal political and social rights to black people in exchange for their support against the Boers, some of them did not really intend to do so (Walshe, 1969) while others—as has already been pointed out—were prepared, in the interest of reconciliation with the Afrikaners, to sacrifice the blacks' right to vote. Thus, black people were more suspicious of whites than ever and would soon seek their political salvation in an organisation such as the South African Native National Congress (SANNC), which was established on 8 January 1912 (with Sol T. Plaatje, who had been besieged by the British at Mafeking, as one of the founder members) and which was known from 1923 as the African National Congress (ANC) (Odendaal, 1984, pp. 270-277). As time passed, the black resistance movement (primarily working against white domination) would come into conflict with the conservative white resistance movement (initially fighting against British domination), and an important Leitmotiv in the political history of twentieth-century South Africa would thus emerge, namely that of black nationalism versus Afrikaner nationalism; sometimes also manifesting itself in the binary opposition of black expectations versus white fears.

Many Afrikaner leaders intended consolidating Afrikaner power and therefore desired to heal the rift in Afrikaner ranks. Not everyone was prepared to co-operate with English-speaking South Africans, while co-operation with other race groups was not even on the cards. There were indeed attempts to uplift the Afrikaner in a material sense (Van Rensburg, 1967), but otherwise there were no co-ordinated initiatives to come to terms with the trauma caused by the war of 1899 to 1902. In due course, this contributed towards the development of an aggressive Afrikaner nationalism, with separate development (apartheid) as one of its most important manifestations.

During the Anglo-Boer War, the British humanitarian Emily Hobhouse launched the world's first (informal) 'truth and reconciliation commission' when she compiled the book *The Brunt of the War and Where it Fell* (published in the second half of 1902), consisting of, inter alia, letters (and excerpts from letters) in which Boer women related their experiences during the war. Hobhouse also tried to offer traumatised camp and other victims of British collateral damage the opportunity to provide an account of their narratives of loss, suffering and despair, so that they could rid themselves in this way of the trauma of the then recent past. The Women's Memorial in Bloemfontein, adjacent to the world's largest Anglo-Boer War museum, was unveiled on 16 December 1913 in honour of the white Boer civilians who suffered during the Anglo-Boer War. Hopefully this Memorial will in due course be embraced by all South Africa's cultural groups as a symbol of mutual suffering and trauma.

Since Hobhouse's work was, in a large measure, a one-person action, she could reach only a very limited number of (white) persons, and the therapeutic value of her work, viewed as a whole, was therefore also limited. There were also never any formal attempts at reconciliation between Boer and Briton. And, of course, black and coloured people were totally left in the cold to deal with their own trauma. For this reason, most of the war trauma was transferred to the next white and black generation. The Afrikaners who suffered in the internment camps, stored the negative experiences in their memories. The trauma was internalised, and for many years, some Afrikaners harboured great resentment, bitterness, frustrations and fear. In some cases only many years later, even in a succeeding generation, these traumatic experiences once again gained prominence, and sometimes manifested themselves in one or other political view, for example in the apartheid policy. As time passed, the Afrikaner developed a terrible fear of foreign (non-Afrikaner) domination.

The South African government's decision to declare war against Germany in 1914, i.e. at the start of the First World War, and invade German South-West Africa (today Namibia), was an important reason why some Afrikaners rebelled and took up arms, in the hope that they would be able to regain their republican independence. On the whole, the rebellion was not well organised, and the government forces were able to suppress it fairly quickly. Nevertheless, it left many Afrikaners bitter and traumatised.

In May 1924, Emily Hobhouse put the finishing touches to a second book that offered white civilian victims of the Anglo-Boer War the opportunity to 'be heard'. In *War Without Glamour or Women's War Experiences, Written By Themselves 1899-1902* (London, 1927), Hobhouse included approximately 30 statements that were written during or just after the war by Boer women. She held the view that the voices of the generals and the politicians had indeed been heard, but that the voices of the wronged civilians had not yet received a hearing. This book strikingly illustrates the terrible effects (collateral damage) of war on civilians. Unfortunately, nothing was—once again—done to alleviate the plight of black, coloured and Asian South Africans. As a matter of fact, in the years following unification in 1910, the plight of black South Africans worsened, as the policy of segregation (a precursor to post-1948 apartheid) was implemented.

In May 1948, the 'right-wing' National Party of Dr D.F. Malan defeated General Jan Smuts's United Party at the ballot box and introduced a new era in the history of South Africa. In contrast to the rest of the world, where the emphasis was increasingly placed on equal treatment and justice for all races (owing to the Second World War, and especially Nazi racism), the National Party implemented a policy that accentuated racial differences and segregation.

From 1948 to 1954, under the leadership of Malan, and after that under the leadership of Adv. J.G. Strijdom and Dr H.F. Verwoerd, the National Party government passed various apartheid laws and implemented measures to transform South Africa into a country where racism was institutionalised. Thus, in due course, apartheid systematically dehumanised and traumatised many millions of people.

In the years from South Africa's becoming a Union (1910) up to the founding of the Republic (1961), the Anglo-Boer War, and in particular the suffering associated with the white internment camps, formed an important part of many Afrikaners' historical (and political) frame of reference. Since most inhabitants of the internment camps never resolved their trauma successfully, this psychological collateral damage was transferred to their children. In the minds of many Afrikaners, there was the idea that what the Afrikaner had to go through during the Anglo-Boer War, should never again happen to 'us'.

The excessive emphasis on the protection of their own interests meant that the next logical step, namely, to prevent universal oppression and suffering, was never taken by the Afrikaner. The Afrikaners had not learnt from their history and they, who had been humiliated and oppressed earlier, and who had suffered an immense amount of collateral damage and concomitant trauma during the war of 1899 to 1902, became the new oppressors (of black, coloured and Asian people) from 1948 onwards under the banner of separate development (apartheid). In this way, the traumatised from the era of the Anglo-Boer War (and their descendants) became the new traumatisers, thus causing a new wave of collateral damage, to the detriment of mutual relationships in South Africa, and to the disadvantage of the 'non-white' inhabitants of the country. This is probably the greatest tragedy in the history of the Afrikaner people—and in the history of South Africa.

The traumatisation of the largest part of South African society continued after South Africa became a republic on 31 May 1961 (i.e. exactly 59 years after the end of the Anglo-Boer War), and at the same time, there was an ever-increasing sense of alienation among the races. South Africa's relations with the outside world were also gradually affected, an aspect that led to increasing isolation in sport, the imposition of a mandatory United Nations arms embargo in November 1977, and economic pressure. This, in turn, led to the emergence of a siege and laager mentality in a large sector of the Afrikaner community (Giliomee, 2003, pp. 578-589).

On the home front, the violence that erupted in the black 'township' of Soweto, and elsewhere, in 1976, had a negative effect on South Africa's position internationally. The 1980s were characterised, inter alia, by black-on-black violence (which left about 30 000 people dead), police brutality, and an increase in operations by the ANC's military wing, uMkhonto weSizwe (MK)—all of which were contributing factors in the traumatisation of South African society. By the late 1980s, South Africa seemed on the verge of total anarchy; then came the year 1990, which brought various dramatic political changes, for example: the unbanning of several organisations (including the ANC), the release of political prisoners (in particular Dr Nelson Mandela), and the start of negotiations between the National Party government and other political organisations. These events led to the first truly democratic election in 1994, with the accompanying dramatic political transformation. In addition, the establishment of a formal Truth and Reconciliation Commission (TRC), which, like Emily Hobhouse's informal discussions with Boer women almost a century earlier, offered the marginalised victims of conflict the opportunity to voice their suffering, so that their trauma would hopefully be resolved and perhaps healed (Jeffery, 1999).

Concluding Perspectives

In the light of the terrible slaughter that took place during the First World War of 1914 to 1918, the nature, scope and meaning of the Anglo-Boer War of 1899 to 1902 were relegated to the background in Britain. However, for the Afrikaner nation it was the most extensive conflict in which they had been involved in their entire history, and this war guided Afrikaner thinking for a large part of the twentieth century. Moreover, the history of the Afrikaner nation cannot be fully understood if we do not consider the significance of the Anglo-Boer War. Together with the Great Trek of the 1830s, the Anglo-Boer War was indeed the most epoch-making event in the history of the Afrikaner.

The consequences of the internment camps probably tower above all the other after-effects of the war. Unlike the razed farmhouses that could be rebuilt, those who died in the camps could not then be restored to life. The trauma caused by the British internment camp system would continue to haunt both the Afrikaner and the other inhabitants of South Africa for many years to come. The internment camps of the Anglo-Boer War led to disruption, trauma and alienation. A large section of the Afrikaner people was impoverished, and various Afrikaners who lost everything on their farms sought a new life in towns and cities. In the course of time, some of them became part of the so-called 'poor-white' problem. In the urban areas, fear of the British was soon replaced by fear of domination by black people, inter alia, because the Afrikaners had to compete with black people for employment opportunities. Many of these whites in due course became supporters of the National Party's policy of apartheid (Dubow, 1989).

More than a hundred-and-ten-years after the conclusion of the Anglo-Boer War, we are able to reflect on the immense political and social fallout from this traumatic conflict. These negative consequences include the scorched-earth policy and the internment camps of the Anglo-Boer War; the rebellion of 1914-1915; the years of political Sturm und Drang in the 1920s and 1930s; the political changes of 1939 and (in particular) 1948; the implementation of the policy of apartheid since 1948; the events at Sharpeville and elsewhere in the 1960s; the uprisings in Soweto and elsewhere in 1976; and the violence of the 1980s—violence which spilt over into the 1990s. Not all of these conflicts and their ensuing collateral damage can be directly linked to the Anglo-Boer War, but the war of 1899 to 1902 did cause immense damage, disruption and trauma, and set in motion a train of events which to a large extent determined the course that twentieth-century South African history would take.

Taking everything into consideration, one cannot understand the history of twentieth-century South Africa (including the country's political development) without knowledge of or insight into the traumatic history of the Anglo-Boer War and the consequences it had for the country's white, black, coloured and Asian inhabitants. The war's trauma was internalised by both the white and black victims of the war, and was 'transferred' to next generations. This, in turn, had profound implications for the political, social and economic developments in the country. Indeed, the war left deep spiritual and psychological scars, the powerful effects of which continue to be felt in the third millennium.

The transgenerational traumas of the twentieth century have haunted South Africans for far too long. Traumatic memories with regard to the Anglo-Boer War (and other events) should be used to bind people together across cultures, races, political and other beliefs. It should be kept in mind that all South Africans share a common past, including the history of traumatic events such as the Anglo-Boer War. This war is indeed an integral part of all South Africans' colonial past. If the intergenerational cycles of repetition have thus far not been broken, the time has now come to do exactly this, in the interest of all the people of South Africa. It is up to present-day South Africans to prove that it is possible for the negative consequences of the memory of trauma experienced collectively, to end. For this to happen, South Africans indeed need empathy as an important element in overcoming inter-group prejudice, but also economic empowerment, and education; i.e. knowledge and insight into South Africa's chequered past, including the history of the Anglo-Boer War of 1899 to 1902 and its traumatic consequences. After all: History enables one to forgive, without the need to forget.

References

Amery, L. S. (Ed.). (1902-1906). *The Times history of the war in South Africa 1899-1902*, 1-4. London: Sampson Low, Marston and Company.

Botha, H. J. (1969). Die moord op Derdepoort, 25 November 1899: Nie-blankes in oorlogsdiens. *Militaria*, 1(2), 3-98.

Breytenbach, J. H. (1969-1983). *Die geskiedenis van die Tweede Vryheidsoorlog in Suid-Afrika, 1899-1902*, 1-5. Pretoria: Die Staatsdrukker.

Dubow, S. (1989). *Racial segregation and the origins of apartheid in South Africa.* Basingstoke: Macmillan.

Farwell, B. (1973). *Queen Victoria's little wars*. London: Allen Lane.

Giliomee, H. (2003). *The Afrikaners: Biography of a people*. Cape Town: Tafelberg.

Grundlingh, A. (2006). *The dynamics of treason: Boer collaborators in the South African War of 1899-1902*. Pretoria: Protea Book House.

Grundlingh, A., & Swart, S. (2009). *Radelose rebellie? Dinamika van die 1914-1915 Afrikanerrebellie*. Pretoria: Protea Book House.

Jeffery, A. (1999). *The truth about the Truth Commission*. Johannesburg: South African Institute of Race Relations.

Kessler, S. V. (1999). The black concentration camps of the Anglo-Boer War 1899-1902: Shifting the paradigm from sole martyrdom to mutual suffering. *Historia*, 44(1), 110-147.

Kessler, S. [V.] (2012). *The black concentration camps of the Anglo-Boer War 1899-1902*. Bloemfontein: War Museum of the Boer Republics.

Kestell, J. D., & Van Velden, D. E. (1912). *The peace negotiations between the governments of the South African Republic and the Orange Free State, and the representatives of the British government, which terminated in the peace concluded at Vereeniging on the 31st May, 1902*. London: Richard Clay.

Laband, J. (2000). Zulu's and the war. In J. Gooch (Ed.), *The Boer War: Direction, experience and image* (pp. 107-125). London: Frank Cass.

Nasson, B. (1991). *Abraham Esdu's war: A black South African War in the Cape, 1899-1902*. Cambridge: Cambridge University Press.

Odendaal, A. (1984). *Vukani Bantu! The beginnings of black protest politics in South Africa to 1912*. Cape Town: Philip.

Pretorius, F. (Ed.). (2001). *Scorched earth*. Cape Town: Human & Rousseau.

Scholtz, G. D. (2013). *Die rebellie 1914-1915*. Pretoria: Protea Book House.

Van Rensburg, A. P. J. (1967). Die ekonomiese herstel van die Afrikaner in die Oranjerivier-Kolonie 1902-1907. *Archives Year Book for South African History*, 30(2), 134-340.

Walshe, A. P. (1969). The origins of African political consciousness in South Africa. *The Journal of Modern African Studies*, 7(4), 599.

Wessels, A. (Ed.). (1988). Die oorlogsherinneringe van kommandant Jacob Petrus Neser. *Christiaan de Wet-annale*, 7, 5-131.

Wessels, A. (2000). Afrikaners at war. In J. Gooch (Ed.), *The Boer War: Direction, experience and image* (pp. 73-106). London: Frank Cass.

Wessels, A. (Ed.) (2006). *Lord Kitchener and the war in South Africa 1899-1902*. Stroud: Sutton Publishing Limited.

Wessels, A. (2011). *The Anglo-Boer War 1899-1902: White man's war, black man's war, traumatic war*. Bloemfontein: Sun Media.

Chapter 9
Breaking the Cycles of Repetition? The Cambodian Genocide across Generations in Anlong Veng

Angeliki Kanavou; Kosal Path; Kathleen Doll

Center for the Study of Morality; Political Science; Peace Studies

University of California, Irvine; Brooklyn College; Chapman University

Introduction

After a long day's work interviewing former Khmer Rouge (KR) cadres, our last interviewee, a former female cadre from Cambodia's north, recounted her compelling story. Her life too, she told us, was turned upside down. She had joined the KR at the age of 14 when the US Air force destroyed her village. "We are going to liberate Cambodia," the local cadre told her. She followed her superiors to Phnom Penh on a truck. She had to eat gruel too, she said. She starved and did not finish school. And, never, "ever" did she see anyone being actually killed, she insisted. She was interviewed as a swarm of barely dressed toddlers just surrounded her, while she simultaneously worked on a piece of fabric. Her home, a square wooden structure on four poles, had no electricity or running water. One could describe her as poor even by Cambodian standards. Our translator, fluent in English in his early 20s, was the picture of coming success. He was following world affairs on a daily basis and every morning gave the team the daily briefing. One of many siblings, he used his language skills to fund his education. He offered very little information about his roots and how the Genocide that ravaged his country between 1975 and 1979, or the violent years before, had affected his family. That evening, on our way back to the base he shared: "See, she said she saw no killings…all these stories are made up by the Vietnamese." His reaction puzzled us and lead us later to ask this question: What does it mean for the young to be born into a society where so much socio-political trauma such as in Cambodia during the KR, has occurred? Specifically, what does it mean for the potential well-being of the offspring of former KR to be born to parents with a strong association to a regime responsible for roughly 2.000.000 (Chandler, 1999) deaths of fellow Khmer and Cham Muslim Cambodians?

In Cambodia, despite the Khmer Rouge Tribunal (KRT), the Genocide has either been talked about very little or vehemently denied. Such a trend of unaccountability raises the question: What is the likelihood of a re-emergence of extreme violence in this post-Genocide setting? We will argue that in order to break the cycle of repetition as this volume aims, we have to start by assessing how the past is framed by the different variously affected groups. We want to know if the thinking that led to such destruction and disruption of life, namely blind obedience to authority, evasion of responsibility and limited reflection still exist among cadres and the extent to which these attitudes have been passed on to the younger generation. While "repetition" often implies strictly resurgence of violent patterns, we believe that it should also imply the regeneration of attitudes that embolden the glorification of the past. These attitudes perpetuate intergroup divisions and allow the passing of denial from generation to generation through transferring the blame and the acting out of individual and group trauma.

In this examination, we present findings from survey analysis we conducted in 2011-12 among 157 former KR cadres and 44 second generation individuals from the same community in Anlong Veng, the last KR stronghold. Because of the relative isolation of this community the two groups offer real life (as opposed to laboratory) conditions to study the transmission of patterns of obedience and psychosocial trauma from first to second generation and the long term effects of thought reform as they pertain to associates of a genocidal regime. Other KR communities in more mixed parts of Cambodia may have had more opportunities to interact with different segments of the population and more exposure to the historical record of the KR. In such areas, we suspect the second generation may have grown more critical of their parents as opposed to this relatively homogenous group.

Studying the extent of transmission of political and psychological attributes in this community is important in two critical ways. It will offer points of reference for a more comprehensive study of Cambodia's post-Genocide society and will allow a comparison of first and second generation KR with parallel groups from survivor communities. We hypothesize that the first generation has passed on its attitudes about the past, present and future of the country, as well as patterns of unquestioning obedience to authority and socio-psychological traumatisation to the younger generation. Given the problematic state/society relationship within Cambodia, these patterns can only nurture violent trends. While more research is required to study offspring of genocidaires and survivors across Cambodia and their relative similarity to their parents' outlook, this chapter is a first step towards a better understanding of how the youth of Cambodia relate to the past and the future in a context of denial and very limited dialogue. After a brief overview of the Genocide and its ripple effects, the chapter presents a political psychological profile of the former KR cadres' community in Anlong Veng and discusses the research findings. Ongoing assessment of views about the past will give a picture of how KR cadres and their offspring relate to not only the past and present but to the future as well.

The Cambodian Genocide: Social Experimentation Amidst the Cold War

The Cambodian Genocide is unique in the sense that nearly a quarter of the population of the country perished either through hardship (killing fields) or torture and execution (Hinton, 2005). The breeding ground for the genocidal regime that the KR established was provided by conditions in Cambodia, as well as throughout East Asia, that had been simmering since the early 1950s and throughout the 1970s. The Lon Nol dictatorship (1970-75) polarized the population. The US carpet bombing of Cambodia (1969-73) to disrupt the supply line of the Northern Vietnamese led to 500,000 victims, mostly in the country side (Kiernan). The ensuing climate for chaos was exacerbated by the Cold War rhetoric, the nearby Vietnam War (1959-75), and China's Cultural Revolution (1966-1976). Additionally, the local political and cultural context resulted in rigid hierarchical structures and disproportional revenge norms for ill-doing (Hinton). In these conditions, the cult-like system that Saloth Sar (Pol Pot, 1925-1998) and his immediate entourage nourished took over the whole country.

By all accounts, during the KR Cambodia became a laboratory of pervasive fear. Pol Pot and his "executive" board were facilitated by the political context in which they functioned. The KR leadership drew inspiration from existing norms in Cambodian society such as respect and obedience to hierarchy as well as thought reform practices that were first developed by the Soviets (during the show trials of 1936-38) and then the Chinese (re-education campaigns) (Chandler, 1999; Lifton, 1999: 122-127). The method of imprisonment that dictated thought reform procedures was first introduced to the KR leadership during the 1950s. At the time, Pol Pot and his associates were studying in France. In the early post-war years, the French communist party was closely associated with the Soviet communist party (Chandler, 2008).

The KR demanded blind obedience to the Communist Party of Kampu-chea (Angkar) and disregard for each other's humanity. The KR applied social experimentation and sought to create an agrarian utopia (Chandler 2007; Boyden & Gibbs, 1995). This extent of social experimentation, despite similarities with the Chinese Cultural Revolution, was unique in that Cambodia was sealed from the outside and the majority of the population left the cities. The aim was to forge among the population a new collective and agrarian identity where the individual mattered as long as it served the Angkar (the KR party). The systematic tools of the KR depended upon hundreds of thousands of workers/prisoners in the killing fields as well as the prison system. This system included forced confessions, self-confrontation in the presence of superiors, performance of repetitive tasks, and dehumanization of those outside the Angkar. Constant surveillance and celebration of the spirit of the KR revolution were also vital components. Indoctrination of young cadres was the first step to turning them into in most cases obedient executioners. It continued throughout the regime and in areas where the hard core KR withdrew after their fall in 1979. This indoctrination aimed at what Lifton (1979) called "thought reform." Accordingly, thought reform is the process of "death and rebirth" of the self through focused emotional power with the purpose to achieve total control of the human mind (4). Upon taking power in 1949, the Chinese Communists developed thought reform systematically. They implemented among dissenters and their own ranks a practice of confession about past and present and re-education in hopes of reducing former habits and recasting the person into the mould of an obedient soldier of the revolution.

In the context of thought reform, "enemies" were sought out within one's own "undeveloped consciousness" as well as in those who were not members of the Angkar (the KR party). The crimes varied; they ranged from exhibiting bourgeois attitudes, working slowly, and having doubts for, or hating the revolution, and therefore serving its enemies such as the Vietnamese, the KGB and the CIA. Similar to China and the Soviet Union, the cult of confession that was applied in Cambodia included purging of the inner self (outmost inner thoughts); self-surrender of the individual to his or her environment, and making public one's own individual thoughts to maintain the revolutionary ethos through self and other observation. Eventually, the culmination of the process involved statements that signalled a "born again" self. The cadres in Anlong Veng and elsewhere experienced persisting examinations of their "revolutionary selves" in a continuous basis.

The Anlong Veng District

Following the Vietnamese invasion in 1978, lower KR cadres dispersed themselves throughout the country. Most returned to their villages and eventually were absorbed by the other inhabitants. Those who followed the higher echelons, and often had reason to hide, were more reluctant to reintegrate. Such groups withdrew towards the mountainous regions close to the border with Thailand, such as Pailin and Oddar Meanchey. They subsequently did not integrate with the rest of the country until 1998. Odar Meanchey became home to Pol Pot and his trusted military commander (who eventually turned against him), Chhit Choeun (alias Ta Mok), also known as "the butcher" for his ruthlessness. Reportedly, some 3,500 troops followed Ta Mok towards Anlong Veng. Ta Mok exercised authority over his cadres' lives until he was arrested and died in captivity in 2006 while awaiting trial with genocide charges. Ta Mok would distribute land and even arrange the marriages of several cadres. The District, until recently, was considered as outer periphery and dangerous for travel. More recently, Anlong Veng became a trade hub due to its proximity with Thailand. Ta Mok is still regarded with reverence by many KR cadres, and his home is a destination for unrepentant former KR mourners and tourists alike. The KR cadres who have been living here in relative autonomy since their withdrawal in 1979, are immune from prosecution under a 1994 amnesty law by the Cambodian government. In the 1990s, there were 5,122 KR households with 22,466 former KR and their family members. In 1998 Prime Minister Hun Sen's "win-win" policy of national reconciliation allowed the last Khmer Rouge stronghold in Anlong Veng to enjoy a semi-autonomous control over this region.

Collective Trauma and Memory Transmission in the Cambodian Context

Destruction of the existing infrastructure by the KR impacted the quality of life for generations. The extreme poverty that ensued ensured their ascent to power that until today has allowed retraumatizing conditions to affect the majority of the population. Seeking to define this impact, Chhim (2013) points to the Khmer term baksbat (broken courage) and other terms of distress such as phey-khlach (double fear); bor –veas-cheas-chgnay (wishing that the trauma would go away) as distinct ways in which Cambodians in Cambodia, and those who live as refugees in the United States, describe distress. By definition, trauma implies a psychological breakdown caused by external events. When in trauma, individuals' capacity to respond to these externalities diminishes (Becker, 2004). These externalities within societies that have experienced trauma are eventually morphed into new challenges and continue to trigger negative responses in individuals and groups. For example, socioeconomic challenges of parents such as those experienced in post-Genocide Cambodia, are known to affect the cognitive development and emotional health of children (Najman et al., 2004). Also, studies on the Holocaust and Northern Uganda further illustrate that traumatic events affect individuals in different ways depending on the age they experienced it (Schauer and Elbert, 2010; van IJzendoorn et al. 2003; Keilson, 1979). The age of parental traumatization (the first generation in this study) as well affects how the second generation will manifest trauma symptoms such as PTSD and anxiety (Yehuda, 2005; Solomon, 1998)

Traumatic experiences are unavoidably part of the memory content from generation to generation. Memory transmission between family members discloses that family memories consist of controversial, inconsistent, and incoherent stories. As Weltzer (2010) argues, the purpose of memory transmission is to affirm the very existence of the family. Specifics of a story such as what, where, or how a family member underwent certain experiences are secondary to the function of communicating about the past that confirms the very existence of the family. Individuals in what Weltzer calls memory communities like the community of former KR cadres in Anlong Veng as we discuss later, have "chosen" which aspects to remember. This choice is determined based on what makes sense to them. These stories are not always historically factual. Rather, they contain a strong emotional message but may, nevertheless, refer to historical facts. Also, they offer "emotional frames" that help the listener interpret the past. Pertinent to intergenerational memory transmission is the notion that different generations of people remember what is specific to them (Bartlett, 1932; 1997). Interestingly, members of the same generation will remember the same facts from a story even if it is not actual families remembering, but rather random groups of people.

The young are particularly vulnerable to absorb the "aftershocks" from the environment and their own inventory of experience. This accumulation of experience starts at the beginning of life through emotional learning from parents and continues through socialization at home, school, and the broader society (Bandura, 1989). However, autobiographical development occurs later between the ages of 10-25 and takes the form of what is regarded by each generation as "the normal way of things" (Bartlett 1932; Shore 2008: 20). Young adults tend to have informal social involvement through their active, yet less organized social lives. Thus their reflections on the causes, the effects of the Genocide, and its reverberations that exist today are expected to have been filtered through their parents' Genocide memories, especially considering memory outside the family circle in Cambodia is highly controlled and politicized (Chandler, 2007).

Intergenerational dynamics in post Genocide Cambodia were more recently studied by Field et al (2011, 2013). This study explored the mediating function of role reversing and overprotective parenting between parental trauma symptoms on the child's anxiety and depression. The findings are corroborated in similar situations outside Cambodia. An exploration of Holocaust survivors asserted that even in cases where first generation Holocaust survivors did not manifest symptoms of Post-Traumatic Stress Syndrome (PTSD), second generation survivors were more susceptible to PTSD than second generation non Holocaust survivors from the same community (Baider et al., 2005). This transmission of emotions and experience becomes integrated as part of the second generation expression and functioning in society. It also underlines the role "restorative" education can play to reverse victimization and address traumatization.

The Politics of Post-genocide Memory in Cambodia: Denial and Human Rights Violations

Cambodia's young adults have inherited a sharply divided society, one that consists of survivors and another of perpetrators. Both groups coexist in a political context where human rights violations are an ever present fact of life. Given the politically oriented production of public memory and the limited focus on justice by Cambodian People's Party (CPP), public discourse and historical accounts of events and the genocidal process have been tinged by the CPP rhetoric or what Chandler called "the hegemonic historiography" of the ruling party (Chandler, 2007, 358). A most serious symptom of the genocidal process in Cambodia in particular, was caused by the vast implementation of thought reform practices that the Khmer Rouge (KR) used on the population. Cadres and the silenced population had to deny that events they were experiencing, such as mass murders, were unnecessary and were living in denial. The "Killing Fields" emerged as the ultimate solution for people deemed incapable of becoming appropriately re-educated. Survival was achieved by successfully convincing authorities that capitalistic values had been replaced by community communist doctrine. The culture of unquestioning obedience to authority took on new meaning during the KR.

As a consequence of the widespread denial about the atrocities, many perpetrators and observers seem impassive about testimonies of survivors, observers, and even perpetrators before the Court during the trials of five protagonists of the Genocide. Despite the stark and incriminating evidence the KR left behind, "induced amnesia" had been the official policy of Cambodia's government until June 17, 2013. In a move to undermine his opponent, Cambodia's Prime Minister (since 1985) Hun Sen introduced a law that made it illegal to deny that atrocities were committed by the KR.

In a context of denial, human rights violations can be a predominant challenge for rebuilding the social fabric. These violations range from trafficking to forced evictions. Both the State Department Bureau on Democracy, Human Rights and Labour and Amnesty International, reported that forced evictions among the very poor constitute common practice. Amnesty International included in its report that forced evictions since 2003 have affected 420,000 individuals. In Phnom Penh reportedly ten percent of the population has either been evicted or planned resettlement (http://www.amnesty.org/en/ region/cambodia/report-2012). Forced evictions today strike a chord since during the Genocide forced population transfers were part of the KR social engineering program. Another notable human rights issue concerns freedom of expression. There has been a heavy repression of protesters and challengers of the Hun Sen government. Police have opened fire at relatively quiet protesters regardless of sex or age. Violence against protesters has been perpetrated by either police forces or the so called "Pagoda Boys," a group who promotes an agenda of the current government among the young (Kurtenbach, 2012; Hensengerth, 2008). The "Pagoda Boys" have participated in violence against their protesting peers from the garment industry and have claimed that they will not stop at anything if the rule of the current government is disrupted. Besides human rights violations, other crimes such as domestic violence or street crime numbers are also high. NGOs working on domestic abuse in Cambodia report that 20-25% of women in Cambodia have experienced physical abuse by their partner. From 2000to 2004, Cambodia had an increase in prison population to 112% compared to 50% in San Salvador. The fact that violence continues and takes other forms (domestic and gang violence, petty crimes and crimes against life and corruption) in post-genocide societies constitutes a major challenge for the rebuilding of civil society (Berdal, M & Suhrke, A, 2012).

Population and Method

The research team led by Kosal Path, came to Anlong Veng in 2011 and 12. The team obtained the approval from the district governor of Anlong Veng, Yim Phanna, who himself led the mass defection to the Hun Sen government in 1998. Village chiefs were also contacted to facilitate communicated with local cadres. The first generation respondents, who were willing to respond, joined to take the survey. The second generation was accessed in the only high school of the district and a group of 44 students above 18 was surveyed. A valid starting point to the investigation is the extent of similarity that might exist between the perceptions of a self-identified group of 157 first generation KR cadres and a self-identified group of 44 second generation KR offspring from this community. We were interested to know how the second generation found out about the Genocide, their views of the first generation's involvement, and their predominant emotions when they initially discovered their parents' involvement. Also, we wanted to find out whether any similarity existed in attitudes regarding obedience towards authorities between the first and the second generation group as well as whether the second generation might have adopted the first generation's views about what led to the Genocide. Any such similarities might be indicative of the younger group inheriting elements of the thought reform process that the older generation was subjected to after they willingly or unwillingly joined the KR. The extent to which the second generation group may have adopted this feature might explain the difficulty in observing the emergence of coherent narratives across the perpetrator/survivor divide in post Genocide Cambodia. As we will discuss, in Anlong Veng the narrative of the second generation manifested a rather truncated truth in the sense that their parents' involvement in the Genocide was glossed over by heroism and sacrifice to fight the Vietnamese invaders during the 1980s.

Two versions of the same survey were distributed among 157 former cadres (first generation) and 44 young adults ranging in age. In 1975, the year the KR took power, the first generation had a mean age of 21, with ages ranging from 7 to 44 years old. In their majority they were unmarried. They described their quality of life as "poor" or "average," with 67.5% stating their parents' occupation as farmers and 14.6% as peasants. The second generation were upper high-schoolers between 18-22 years of age (second generation) from the only high school of Anlong Veng. Incidentally, in rural areas such as this, it takes longer for children to finish high-school as they often interrupt to help their farming families. These young adults self-identified as KR offspring.

Data

Memory Transmission in Anlong Veng: Evading the Past

One of the most pertinent question to initiate reflection on the past was phrased as: Is it necessary to think about the past? The inclusion of this survey measure was critical in establishing the foundation upon which the second generation's responses would be analysed. 43.3% of first generation respondents replied "not at all" with another 43.9% responding, to various degrees, that the past should be remembered. These results reveal a split position on the importance of memory among former perpetrators. Perhaps this also revolves around the idea of how things are remembered. Almost 70% of first generation respondents strongly agreed that Cambodians today should not think about the KR period and instead think that "things are different now," and thus desire to focus on something else. This idea among the majority of former KR we sampled, that "things are different now," may refer to the fact that the current government does not outwardly resemble that of the "three year regime" also known as Democratic Kampuchea (DK) the official title of the KR genocidal government.

The initial question for second generation respondents was about the source of their knowledge regarding the KR three year regime. 70% of those surveyed responded that they heard about the KR rule by their parents as opposed to newspapers, seeing a segment of TV, finding out from friends and (or) reading about it at school. This number calls into question the role of the education system to inform the younger generations about what has transpired. Then the question became: How often do you discuss with your family about the KR regime? 76.67% of the second generation respondents replied "sometimes" as opposed to 3.3% for never and often.

Predominant Emotions for a Difficult Past

The majority of respondents reported that they had avoided activities, thoughts and feelings associated with the KR in the past week. Specifically, 66.9% of respondents report that, to varying extents, they avoided thoughts or feelings associated with the KR regime; with 59.2% avoiding, to varying extents, activities that remind them of traumatic or hurtful events. Consciously avoiding thoughts, feelings or activities associated with the KR necessitates a controlled, critical awareness of the stimuli and its influence on their inward state. In recognizing an unresolved past and choosing to avoid it, the majority of former perpetrators also acknowledged a low level of reflection about the atrocities they committed, witnessed or suffered from, as well as a general lack of moral confrontation. Whether attempts at evading the past are a result of a personal shame or due to a negative societal depiction of former perpetrators, the mere need to resort to avoidance techniques hints that remembering is both traumatic and stressful, or would involve an emotional trade-off toward self-condemnation that may be too costly.

Consistent with their perception about the extent of their responsibility in the Genocide, the first generation do not feel ashamed of their participation. While it may be theorized that the cadres also wish to forget the past out of some sense of guilt, shame, or regret, we found that 54.1% of those sampled do not feel ashamed of their involvement in the KR regime, with only 37.5% feeling various degrees of shame ranging from a little to quite a bit. Yet we also discovered that 67.5% of respondents reported that they feel some sense of shame, regret, or resentment about what happened to them and their fellow Cambodians during the KR period. 45.6% of these respondents also reported experiencing a great deal of shame, regret, or resentment. These findings highlight the degree to which KR cadres continue to deny a sense of personal agency or responsibility in the atrocities committed. Furthermore, 50.32% of respondents reported that they joined the KR because they had no choice, 55% joined because to some degree they wanted to overthrow the corrupt Lon Nol regime backed by the US or restore Sangkum Reas niyum (the political organization created by Prince Norodom Sihanouk in 1955 which lasted until 1970). The carpet bombing by the US during this period exacerbated misery in the country side. Additionally, 47. 8% said they believed the KR would bring justice and equality. Any outside observer at the time would have also attested to the need for both in Cambodian society. This agenda, however, was obscured by the means the KR eventually employed.

We then inquired how the second generation felt when they first heard about the parents' association with the KR. They appeared to be split on the question of whether they felt love (for the parents) with 36.6% answering "absolutely do not" and 30% "absolutely do." An additional emotional response gauged was pity. 63.33% of this generation reported pity, ranging from "somewhat do" to "absolutely do," when they found about their parents' association with the KR. These results accentuate the previously asserted first generation perpetrators' denial of personal agency. Moreover, the responses elicited by the second generation elucidate various justifications of why their parents joined the KR. 51.72% of respondents answered that their parents joined the KR because they had no choice. These responses indicate that the young see the older generation as victims and by 40% reasoned their parents wanted to overthrow the Lon Nol regime.

Assigning Blame for the Genocide

We then asked the first generation respondents: Who is to blame when wrong-doing happens? 82.1% of respondents agreed, 48.4% of which strongly agreed, that those in positions of leadership are responsible for the effects of actions exhibited by those under their command, even in cases where they are not aware of a cadre's actions. This extreme degree of responsibility placed on Khmer Rouge leaders may be directly related to the collective predisposition toward unquestioning obedience. By engaging in duties with absolute compliance, former members may have disassociated the consequences of their actions from their own sense of personal agency, again perceiving themselves merely as the means through which their superiors are the primary actors. Yet, 26.1%, over a quarter of those sampled, do blame themselves for what happened, with 37.5% feeling some sense of shame regarding their involvement in the regime. The additional 10% of respondents reporting shame in relation to their involvement with the Khmer Rouge indicates that disgrace was not necessarily predicated on feeling culpable for their offenses.

Further survey research was aimed at discovering when these cadre saw their decision to obey orders to kill or torture as justified and considered right or reasonable. This sense of justification was qualified through different statements as morally, reasonably, or legally justified. Respondents were given a series of potential consequences if they were to refuse their orders, and then rate whether the decision to kill/torture was justified under the given condition.

Consistent with such value prioritization, the cadres' preferred self-descriptive during the years they spent with the KR was that of the soldier. During interviews, soldiering was projected as an alternative to either a revolutionary or a victim. "I saw myself as a soldier who defended our country and our people," one cadre argued. By calling himself a soldier he could avoid associating himself with the revolution. Clearly, his allegiance was then transferred to the government using words such as happiness to describe how he felt for the governmental action to open pagodas in Anlong Veng and openness regarding his attitude towards what the government wanted to do.

The extent of intergenerational memory transmission furthermore raises questions about similarities that may exist between first and second generations as to how the former regard themselves in the context of the Genocide and how the latter see them. 73.9% of the first generation responded that they do not feel responsible for events that happened during the KR regime. This compares to 70% of the second generation that they do not think the first generation is to be blamed. In fact, the second generation perceive the first generation as victims. Similarly, 50.3% of the first generation argued that they had no choice in joining the KR. On their part, 43.3% the second generation responded very much/a lot that their parents had no choice but to join. Consistent with their self-view as victims, 83.4% of the first generation responded that the regime was regretful but now it is time to focus on the future. The second generation offspring agreed by 66.7%.

A Good Citizen is an Obedient Citizen

We then sought the respondents' perceptions as to what constitutes a good citizen. 90.4% of the first generation of the adults very much/a lot agreed that a good citizen complies with the government of Cambodia. And 87.3% very much/a lot agreed that good citizens respect laws and authority. Also, 61.1% of the first generation respondents reported obligation to support the government despite contrary views. For their part, 56.7% of the second generation reported very much/a lot agreeing that good citizens complied with government policies. 66.7% of the second generation poll reported very much/a lot agreeing that good citizens respect the laws. From the survey of adults, 88.5% "very much" agreed that a good citizen will sacrifice their life to defend the national sovereignty. Among the second generation, 63.4% very much/a lot agreed. With regard to national pride, 87.27% of the first generation agreed very much/ a lot of good citizens work to restore national pride. 76.6% of the second generation gave the same response.

With the only channel for dissent ending in execution for a KR cadre or his/her family, many cadres found themselves in a state of pervasive fear. Obedience, therefore, became an internal survival tactic. This concept was supported in our findings, with 81.5% agreeing, 62.4% strongly agreeing, that if they followed their superiors' orders, they and their family would stay out of trouble. When asked if soldiers should commit crimes their superiors order, over half of those sampled, 52.3% of respondents, agreed that they should, with 34.3% of respondents responding that they did not know or did not want to answer. Additionally, 74.5% said that one should have supported the Angkar, and 56.1% that one should not have taken an active part in evaluating and questioning Angkar's policies. Former perpetrators continue to uphold that during the period of DK, whether out of indoctrination, fear, or an inclination to obedience, one should have upheld the Angkar as valid and right. In their responses, former perpetrators seem to suggest the necessity for a separate frame of judgment for perpetrators of the Khmer Rouge, one in which perhaps guilt can only exist in such cases when one is not threatened.

These results reveal not only a disavowal of responsibility when following superior orders, but a general inclination towards complicity in the face of apparent injustice. When respondents were asked if they feel responsible for their actions under the regime only 1.3% of the sample, two respondents, reported "yes" with 76.9% reporting no sense of personal responsibility, and 24.8% choosing not to answer the question. These results reveal that over 30 years after the Khmer Rouge regime's end, the majority of the former KR cadre sampled continue to deny their liability as the primary agent behind their own actions under the regime. This finding supports a general pattern of former KR cadres' denial of their wrong-doing across the country.

For many, personal responsibility and even guilt was nullified once they were given orders from those in positions of authority. Mid and lower-level cadre's knew that they had a choice, but that choice to disobey meant possible execution for themselves or for their family. The result of this end-game decision, whether individuals joined of their own volition or as child recruits, meant that many felt there was no choice to be made, or rather that the choices they made were not their own, but those of their superiors. In their perspective, they were merely the means through which the superiors executed their orders, no more than powerless puppets controlled by omnipotent puppeteers.

This reasoning or justification has only been reinforced since the fall of Democratic Kampuchea as successive governments have focused on bringing only senior leaders to justice. With blame for the atrocities committed during DK placed solely on the regime's leadership, and lower level KR members effectively pardoned, issues of individual or collective responsibility were never raised. Instead nearly all responsibility on behalf of former perpetrators has been deferred to the regime's leadership.

The cadres by 84.1% agreed or strongly agreed, that the best a citizen can do is actively support the government. When in doubt about the government, 76.5% of respondents reported that it is "a lot" or "very much" true that the best thing to do is to stay out of trouble. Support for the government, therefore, may continue to be seen as an alternative to oppression. Yet, despite a high volume of respondents who report feeling a great degree of obligation to respect, support, and compliance the government, 65.6% of respondents reported that it is "a lot" or "very much" true that they would protest, or engage in some form of demonstration of disapproval, if the government violated their basic rights. This notion reveals that while conceptions of right and wrong may be clearly outlined by the regime or state power in office, it has also become part of the collective social consciousness, perhaps as a result of the country's progression toward democracy, and empowerment of the people as conscious actors in the public realm.

Discussion

"'Do I have remorse? No," said Ieng Sary, Pol Pot's brother in law who helped engineer the KR regime. "I have no regrets because this was not my responsibility," Sary added (New York Times, September 18, 1996). Denial is not atypical of genocidaires especially when the historical record is undermined by the official government. Despite a 1979 conviction in absentia of Pol Pot and Ieng Sary himself, it took decades of negotiations between the UN and the Cambodian government for KRT to materialize. Those who carried the agenda of the KR regime were free and often rewarded with land and positions in the army as the cadres we surveyed in Anlong Veng. The implications of this amnesty and denial are just becoming obvious for the collective mind of the young adult generation through their emotional responses and re-interpretations of the past.

Here, we presented findings of a 2011-12 survey researching 157 first generation self-identified former KR cadres and 44 second generation young adults who also self-identified as KR cadres' offspring. Both groups came from the relatively homogeneous, and until 1998 semi-autonomous, Anlong Veng District. In this environment of cadre support systems, the cadres maintained openly their identification through self and other reinforcement. Their narrative involved heroism for having defended Cambodia against real or imagined (through thought reform) enemies, self-victimization and a strong obedience to authority orientation that they (inadvertently or otherwise) passed down to the younger generation. These narratives provide a starting point for us to further examine how the KR mind has evolved in other areas of Cambodia where the cadres have co-existed with survivors. It remains to be seen if, in such areas of increased societal integration, cadres and their offspring manifest guilt for the atrocities of the KR regime. However, given the limited extent of discussions about the Genocide across the country, we suspect that our population may be considered representative of the majority of cadres who live elsewhere in Cambodia as well.

Overall, the cadres of Anlong Veng and the second generation reflect the challenges of preserving the historical record in post-genocide societies. Such guilt can only be inferred indirectly from the population we surveyed here.

During an interview, one cadre argued: "I followed their [KR recruiters'] orders to protect my own family from danger." At the time he joined the KR in 1973, he and the rest of villagers did not know the big picture, he explained. "So, (he remarked), the best way was to follow everyone else," he commented. During the KR hold on power, he claimed that he had lost his capacity to think about the direction of the Angkar and went with the flow. Then again after the defeat of the KR he followed his group of fleeing cadres to the jungle "because [he] had heard that the Vietnamese would cut [his] throat."

There is merit to the idea that to an extent our population was victimized by the pre-KR violence during Lon Nol's rule and the carpet bombing of Cambodia by the US air force. However, there is marked difference with how survivors and their offspring were victimized. Here, we offer a first look into how these affiliates of a genocidal regime and their offspring have processed the past and relate to the present and the future. There has been worldwide far more attention on survivors. Field et al and Bar-On et al (1998) that studied parenting patterns of survivors of the Cambodian Genocide and the Holocaust respectively, pointed out towards over protection and parent/child role-reversing. From a political psychological perspective, our study shows that the second generation in Anlong Veng mirrored the first generation's self-view as victims and has adopted the way in which they relate to the state. The predominant feelings of the younger when they first found out about the involvement of the first generation were pity towards their parents and anger for their difficult experiences. Furthermore, the second generation manifested a similar orientation to the first generation's perceptions of the original reasons that they had joined. Leadership is important for the second generation. However, while respect for leadership is not all surprising in a hierarchical society like Cambodia, its high numerical value among the young also implies the absorption of their parents' attitudes on how to relate to authority.

Also, we found that intergenerational memory of the KR regime within the KR community in Anlong Veng is filtered through the local collective narrative of "KR heroization." Although the children of former KR cadres in Anlong Veng have been exposed to news about the KRT, these news sources are filtered through their family narratives and war traumas. Members of the first generation were either willing or unwilling (through child soldiering) participants in a group of hard core genocidaires and thus exposed to violence for the majority of their lives. Self-heroization and victimization due to poverty and prolonged fighting, has curtailed the cadres' opportunity for self-confrontation and acceptance of any share of blame. Children of former KR cadres born in the 1990s were significantly impacted by their parents' war against the Vietnamese occupation of Cambodia in the 1980s. In their view, their parents were "heroes" fighting against the Vietnamese invaders. Despite the fact that this second generation grew in the relative safety of their closely knit community, they have been re-victimized similarly to their peers, KR or survivors' offspring, elsewhere due to deprivation and limited infrastructure throughout Cambodia.

Our insight into the Anlong Veng KR cadres' frame of mind, challenges the idea that there is one public discourse of the Cambodian Genocide and highlights the need for deeper exposure of the ex-KR community in Anlong Veng (and across Cambodia where former KR reside) to the truth of what happened during the KR regime. As these results reveal, over 30 years after the end of the Genocide, the majority of the former KR cadres sampled continue to deny their liability as the primary agents of the KR lethal record. For many, personal responsibility and even guilt was nullified once they were given orders from those in positions of authority. Mid and lower-level cadres knew that they had the choice to disobey, but such choice meant possible execution for themselves or for their family. The result of this end-game decision indicated that most KR cadres and successive generations, feel that there was/is no choice to be made, or rather that the choices they made were not their own, but those of their superiors.

Traumatic memories for perpetrators as well as survivors and obedient observers constitute a distinct entity in the individual/collective psyche of Cambodians. These memories have intergenerational effects and lead to collective anxieties and alienation. The extent of denial among perpetrators of the Cambodian genocide is pervasive and comes at an enormous social cost. Even outside the realm of genocide studies, studies that offer focused observations on groups of executioners indicate the very extent that families of perpetrators and the whole society(ies) live with painful and shameful memories (Bandura, 1989; Osofsky, Bandura, Zimbardo, 2005).

An expanded curriculum from hourly sessions to entire subjects about the Genocide would serve well the young people in Cambodia and would contribute to the elimination of the consequences that come along with denial. However, teaching about the history of the Genocide started only after 2009 and is confined to a class session during the terminal year of high school. It is mostly attributed to the efforts of organizations like those of the Documentation Center for the Cambodian Genocide (DC CAM) that teachers have underwent the necessary training on how to teach about the Genocide. In Germany, despite occasional denial glitches, Holocaust education has been successful. Yet, in this instance too, once the Holocaust narrative becomes personal and the youth seek to place their ancestors into the picture of events, the following theme emerges; "one's grand-pa is never a Nazi" (Welzer, 2002) or in the Cambodian context, one's ancestor was never a genocidaire.

The results of the Genocide are felt across Cambodia today. The extensive collective trauma of the population is exacerbated by socio-economic injustice (Sonis et al., 2009). Coupled with corruption, such large-scale trauma is only intensified with the post-Genocide realization that civil society is unable to operate. Avoidance on the part of the government to address the past has contributed to the sense that justice is rarely served in Cambodia. What happens in this post genocide society is what sociologist and psychoanalyst Jeffrey Prager calls " a historical cycle of destructiveness" (2008, 2003). Such cycles are exacerbated by silence. Prager and South Africa's Truth and Reconciliation Committee (TRC) psychologist Pumla Gobodo-Madikizela (2012, 2007) raise concerns about silencing as a public attitude. As we see in the case of Anlong Veng, the silencing over the Genocide and self-heroization indicate a rift in Cambodian society not only between KR cadres and survivors but the groups of their offspring as well. While in other societies such as post-Holocaust Germany, South Africa, and Rwanda efforts are made to reverse the cycles of destructiveness, Cambodia's inability to address the past leaves a negative legacy for future generations. The reparation of trust and cultivation of empathy that hold any society together will have to start from within and between communities, as well as within individuals and their microcosms through accurate portrayals of the past.

References

Baider, L., Goldzweig, G., Ever-Hadani, P., & Peretz, T. (2006). Psychological distress and coping in breast cancer patients and healthy women whose parents survived the Holocaust. *Psycho-Oncology*, 15(7), 635-646.

Bandura, A. (1989). Social Cognitive Theory (pp. 1-60). In R. Vasta (Ed.) *Annals of Child Development: Six Theories of Child Development*. Greenwich, CT: JAI Press.

Bartlett, F. C. (1997[1932]). *Remembering: A Study in Experimental and Social Psychology*. Cambridge University Press.

Berdal, M & Suhrke, A. (Eds.), (2012). *The Peace In Between: Post-War Violence and Peace Building*. New York: Routledge.

Bohleber, W. (2011). *Remembrance, trauma and collective memory*, Keynote address" 45th IPA Congress, Berlin.

Chandler, D. (1999). *Voices from S-21: Terror and History in Pol Pot's Secret Prison*. London, England: University of California Press, Ltd.

Chandler, D. (2007). Cambodia Deals with Its Past: Collective Memory, Demonization and Induced Amnesia. *Totalitarian Movements and Political Religions*, 9(2-3), 335-369.

Chhim, S. (2013). Baksbat (Broken Courage): A Trauma Based Cultural Syndrome in Cambodia. *Medical Anthropology: Cross-Cultural Studies in Health and Illness*, 32(2), 160-173).

Field, N., Muong, S. & Sochanvimean, V. (2013). Parental Styles in the Intergenerational Transmission of Trauma Stemming From the Khmer Rouge Regime in Cambodia. *American Journal of OrthoPsychiatry*, 84(3), 483-494.

Balcells, Laia (2013). The Consequences of Victimization on Political Identities: Evidence from Spain. *Politics and Society*, 40(3), 311-347.

Gobodo-Madikizela, P. (2008). Empathetic Repair after Mass Trauma: When Vengeance Is Arrested. *European Journal of Social Theory*, 11(3): 331-35.

Gobodo-Madikizela (2012). Paper presented at the Engaging the Other Conference, University of The Free State, Bloemfontein, South Africa. December 5-8, 2012.

Hensengerth, O. (2008). *Social and Political Fractures after Wars: The Role of Youth Violence in post-1993* Cambodia. Project Working Paper No. 4. Duisburg: Institute for Development and Peace (INEF), 1-52.

Hinton, A. L. (2005). *Why Did They Kill?* Cambodia in the Shadow of Genocide. Berkeley and Los Angeles: University of California Press.

Hinton, A. L. (2009). *Genocide: An Anthropological Reader*. Blackwell Publishing.

Keilson, H. (1992). *Sequential Traumatization in Childhood*. Magnes Press. Jerusalem: The Hebrew University.

Kelman, H. and Hamilton, V.L. (1989). *Crimes of Obedience*. Baltimore: University of Maryland Press.

Kiernan, B. (1993). *The Pol Pot Regime: Race, Power and Genocide in Cambodia under the Khmer Rouge*, 1975-79. New Haven, CT: Yale University Press.

Kurtenbach, S. (2012). Post-War Youth Violence: A Mirror of the Relationship between Youth and Adult Society. *Violence and Security* No. 199. Hamburg: German Institute of Global and Area Studies (CIGA), 1-28.

Lempp, R. (1995). *Delayed and Long-term Effects of Persecution Suffered in Childhood and Youth*. Echoes of the Holocaust, 4(June).

Lifton, R.J. (1989). *Thought Reform and the Psychology of Totalism: A Study of 'Brainwashing' in China*. Chapel Hill: University of North Carolina Press.

Lun Seng Private Notebook. Anlong Veng, Cambodia.

Osofsky, M.J., Bandura, A., Zimbardo, P.G., (2005). The Role of Moral Disengagement in the Execution Process. *Law and Human Behavior*, 29(4), 371-393.

Prager, J. (2008). Healing from History: Psychoanalytic Considerations on Traumatic

Pasts and Social Repair. *European Journal of Social Theory*, 11(3): 405-420.

Prager, J. (2003). Lost Childhood, Lost Generations: The Intergenerational Transmission of Trauma. *Journal of Human Rights*, 2(2), 173-181.

Schauer E. & Elbert T. (2010). The Psychological Impact of Child Soldiering. In Martz, E. (Ed.). *Trauma Rehabilitation After War and Conflict*. New York: Springer.

Shore, B., (2008). "*Memory Narratives*," paper presented at the Communicative Memory Conference, 10-11 December, MARIAL-Center, Emory University, Atlanta, GA.

Solomon, Z., Kotler, M., & Mikulincer, M. (1988). Combat-Related Posttraumatic Stress Disorder Among Second-Generation Holocaust Survivors: Preliminary Findings. *Am. J Psychiatry* 145(7), 865-868.

Van Ijzendoorn, M., Bakermans-Kranenburg, M. & Sagi-Schwarz, A. (2003). Are Children of Holocaust Survivors Less Well-Adapted? A Meta-Analytic Investigation of Secondary Traumatization. *Journal of Traumatic Stress*, 16(5), 439-469.

Weltzer, H. (2010). Re-narrations: How pasts change in conversational remembering. *Memory Studies*, 3(1), 5-17.

Weltzer, Harald (2010). Communicative Memory; History and Development of the Concept of Communicative Memory. In A. Erll & Nünning, (Eds.). *Cultural Memory Studies: An International and Interdisciplinary Handbook*. Berlin: De Gruyter,

Weltzer, Harald (2008). Collateral Damage of History Education: National Socialism and the Holocaust in German Family History, *Social Research*, 75(1), 287-314.

Welzer, H., Sabine Moller, S., Karoline Tschuggnall, K. & Jensen, O. (2002). *Opa war kein Nazi. Nationalsozialismus und Holocaust im Familiengedächtnis*. Frankfurt: Fischer (Tb.)

Yehuda, R., Halligan SL, Grossman, R. (2001). Childhood Trauma and Risk for PTSD: Relationship to Intergenerational Effects of Trauma, Parental PRSD, and Cortisol Excretion. *Developmental Psychopathology*, 13, 733-753.

Chapter 10
Reflections on Post-Apology Australia: From a Poetics of Reparation to a Poetics of Survival

Rosanne Kennedy

Australian National University

Introduction

In the Australia of the 1990s, the idea of reconciliation, backed by government initiatives, enjoyed popular support. Reconciliation was concerned with acknowledging and redressing the wrongs of the past in relation to Australia's treatment of its Indigenous people. In 1991 the Federal government launched the Council for Reconciliation, with the expectation that reconciliation would be achieved by 2001. Perhaps the most iconic event of the reconciliation era was the national inquiry into the Stolen Generations, conducted in the mid-1990s by the Human Rights and Equal Opportunity Commission (HREOC). This inquiry investigated the policies, practices and effects of separating children of mixed Indigenous descent from their families and communities during much of the twentieth century. Its landmark report, *Bringing Them Home*, recommended that the Federal Parliament, State parliaments, and churches offer an apology to the Stolen Generations (HREOC, 1997). Fearing litigation and compensation, John Howard, then Prime Minister, refused to offer a parliamentary apology, and the Stolen Generations and the Australian public had to wait until 2008, when Kevin Rudd, newly elected Prime Minister, made the long-awaited apology.

Although the apology was apparently well-received by Indigenous and non-Indigenous Australians (Moses, 2010), even before it was offered the discourse of reconciliation was being superseded by a discourse of 'crisis' in Aboriginal Australia. In this era of crisis, the Stolen Generations paradigm, characterized by a compassionate politics of testimony and witnessing, has lost much of its moral and political purchase. The reasons for the shift from a discourse of reconciliation to crisis are complex, and here I can only sketch what have been divisive and contested issues (see Altman & Hinkson, 2007; Altman & Hinkson, 2010). This shift, however, provides the context for my consideration of a parallel shift, from an aesthetics of reparation that flourished during the reconciliation era, to an aesthetics of survival which mediates an era of 'crisis ordinariness' (Berlant, 2011).

The waning of the era of reconciliation was hastened by the publication of *Little Children are Sacred,* the Report of the Northern Territory Board of Inquiry into the Protection of Aboriginal Children from Sexual Abuse (Wild & Anderson, 2007). The report, which detailed cases of child sexual abuse in remote Indigenous communities, prompted sensationalizing media accounts on high levels of crime, sexual assault, violence, substance abuse and sub-standard living conditions in central and northern Australia. In response to the report the federal government, at the time led by John Howard, declared a state of national emergency and devised a controversial plan known as the Northern Territory Intervention. Taking a 'muscular humanitarian' approach (Orford, 1999), the government spent millions, bringing in the army, police, bureaucrats and teams of medical personnel to conduct child health checks and to police communities.

Shortly after the intervention, anthropologist Peter Sutton published *The Politics of Suffering* (2009), which intensified public and scholarly debate on issues facing remote Aboriginal communities. He controversially proposed that the negative outcomes Indigenous people were experiencing today could not all be traced back to colonialism; some outcomes stemmed from the internal dynamics of Aboriginal culture (7). Improving health, education and life expectancy would require a change in Indigenous behavior, and particularly in child socialization. He singled out the politics of *Bringing Them Home* as problematic, arguing that while it "vitally raise[d] awareness of a relatively unknown negativity in Australia's past," it also "enhanced victimhood as a basis of positive regard for Indigenous people, and polarizes opinion about the state or other collective historical guilt" (p. 210). He contends that the national project of reconciliation, with its grand symbolic gestures such as apology, divisively entrenches the notion of two separate peoples, Indigenous and non-Indigenous, in one nation (203). Sutton's effort to articulate a "contemporary moment from within that moment" is an example of the present as a "mediated affect", which Lauren Berlant describes as "a temporal genre whose conventions emerge from the personal and public filtering of the situations and events that are happening in an extended now whose very parameters....are also always there for debate" (2011, p. 4). Discussions about the shared historical present are "always profoundly political" and "under constant revision" because they are about "what forces should be considered responsible and what crises [require] urgent attention" (Berlant 2011, p. 4). While Sutton is only one of many contributors to the debate about how the government, anthropologists and the public should respond to Aboriginal disadvantage in the present and prepare for the future, his book has ignited significant debate (see Altman & Hinkson, 2010; Lattas & Morris, 2010).

Like Sutton, Indigenous commentator and anthropologist Marcia Langton (2010) agreed that the conditions in Aboriginal Australia constitute a crisis and require urgent attention. Lamenting "how much worse [Aboriginal] suffering has become in the last forty years," she argues that "an older, gerontocratic view of Aboriginal culture" has occluded "the new reality" that has taken hold in Aboriginal Australia (Langton 2010, pp. 95-96). Radical changes include the growing number of children, many of whom are at risk: children under 14, she reports, constitute 38% of the indigenous population, and are eight times more likely to be subject to care and protection orders than non-Aboriginal children. She contends that there has not been enough attention to alcohol-fuelled violence, nor public debate about Aboriginal customs and their role in contributing to the crisis in the Aboriginal world. She describes what she calls the "the shock of the new" in Aboriginal Australia:

> The overwhelmingly young Aboriginal population, along with the poor outcomes in Aboriginal health, education and employment, demonstrate that the Indigenous Australian population has altered fundamentally from one typical of the former hunter-gather way of life to one that is very poor, marginalized, powerless and sedentarised, much like the billion or so people living in poverty in the developing world. The future for those young Indigenous people…will be one of accelerating poverty and exclusion (112).

The Northern Territory Intervention and the commentary and media reporting brought the 'shock of the new' to the Australian public. While non-indigenous Australians could identify with children who had been wrongfully removed and the suffering of their mothers, articulated by *Bringing Them Home,* and mediated in films such as *Rabbit Proof Fence* (2002), many Australians were shamed by the media reports and images of poverty and extreme violence in remote indigenous communities. The government's heavy-handed intervention created uncertainty and fragmented the public, most of whom thought something needed to be done, but did not agree with the government's militaristic or racially-targeted tactics.

New social and material conditions call for new genres. The shift I have been tracing, from a discourse of reconciliation to one of crisis, has been accompanied in the cultural domain by a shift from a poetics of reparation to a poetics of survival. In this chapter, I identify features of what I call the Stolen Generations paradigm, which conceives of child removal as a traumatic event, and imagines reconciliation as a process of national and personal healing, facilitated by a dialogic model of testimony and witnessing. I explore this paradigm as it is articulated in the genre of the human rights report, in this case, *Bringing Them Home*, and in fiction. Specifically, I read Gail Jones' novel *Sorry* (2007) as an example of a poetics of reparation for the Stolen Generations, which is grounded in a model of trauma, recovery and compassionate witnessing. In contrast to a poetics of reparation, Warwick Thornton's compelling film, *Samson and Delilah* (2009), produced during the Northern Territory Intervention, exemplifies a poetics of survival, and demands a different kind of response from non-Indigenous audiences. *Samson and Delilah* is a rare film which uses cinematic language to convey the unfolding present, on terms neither of melodrama nor sentimentality. It conveys something of "the new reality" of Aboriginal Australia that Langton has described, but nonetheless retains a degree of optimism.

The Stolen Generations Paradigm: Trauma, Testimony and Witnessing

The 1990s was a decade in which the concept of trauma moved out of the clinical domain of psychiatry and into culture more broadly (Farrell 1998, 2). In *The Empire of Trauma*, anthropologists Didier Fassin and Richard Rechtman argue that it has only been within the last twenty-five years that trauma, and with it the figure of the victim, has been legitimated; previously "the victim was tarred as illegitimate" and "trauma was a suspect condition" (2009, 5). Indeed, trauma has become the dominant moral discourse for understanding and interpreting violence in our time. They propose that "trauma…has created a new language of the event" (Fassin & Rechtman 2009, 6), and a new way of understanding the effects of war, colonialism and violent conflict, which has replaced an older language of oppression and liberation struggles. Adopting a Foucauldian approach, they seek "to understand how the contemporary moral economy has been reshaped" by the now "global idea of trauma…which designat[es] an irrefutable reality linked to a feeling of empathy" (6). Their analysis is grounded in ethnographic observations of humanitarian psychiatry, which produces new knowledges, new subjectivities and a "new condition of victimhood" (5). In conflict zones, humanitarian psychiatrists do not simply diagnose and treat, they make moral judgments, and testify and advocate on behalf of victims, thereby engaging in a "politics of trauma" (9). In the Israeli/Palestinian conflict, for instance, "recourse to the concept of trauma…expands the range of victims considerably," (Fassin 2008, 550) and enables people on both sides of the conflict, and potentially the entire population of Israel, to identify as victims of posttraumatic stress, and to appeal to the public for support and empathic understanding. Although based on fieldwork in conflict zones, Fassin and Rechtman's (2009) analysis of trauma discourse helps to explain how Indigenous suffering has been legitimated and become a moral touchstone in the Australian public sphere since the 1990s.

In *Post-Traumatic Culture*, Kirby Farrell (1998) also adopted a Foucauldian approach, but with particular attention to the implications of trauma discourse for literature and film. He argued that people not only suffer trauma; the concept of trauma is used for all kinds of ends (Farrell 1998, 21). Trauma is not only a diagnostic category. Rather, when trauma moves from the clinic into the domain of culture, its explanatory powers come to the fore: "whatever the physical distress...trauma is also psychocultural, because the injury entails interpretation of the injury" (7). He adds that "Cultures not only report but classify traumatic events: a train wreck may be a 'catastrophe' or a 'tragedy' or merely an 'accident'" (16). At stake in this cultural shift is how authoritative institutions and discourses interpret an event or injury. When an event is described as 'traumatic', rather than simply as an 'accident', claims are being made about the deep and ongoing psychological impact on the affected population, including future generations, which raise issues of responsibility and reparation. In the Australian public sphere, the language of trauma has produced new understandings of the long-term psychological and social effects of settler colonialism, with its practices of violence, dispossession, assimilation and child removal, on Indigenous people and communities. This language has changed understandings of the political struggle in which Indigenous people are engaged. Today, in government discourse, the political language of Aboriginal self-determination has been replaced by a bureaucratic language of 'closing the gap' in health and education outcomes between Aboriginal and non-Aboriginal Australians.

In the 1960s and 1970s, the struggle for Aboriginal rights was framed in terms of a national discourse of land rights, sovereignty and self-determination, as well as a transnational discourse of liberation, equality and black power. With the emergence of the reconciliation movement in the 1990s, and especially, the publication of *Bringing Them Home*, the discourse of trauma, suffering and compassion provided a new idiom through which Australians could understand the harmful legacy of settler colonialism. This moral idiom, which can be traced through several key statements of the reconciliation movement in the 1990s, required non-Indigenous Australians to recognize and acknowledge the pain and suffering caused to Indigenous Australians by colonization, dispossession and child removal. For instance, in a widely-quoted speech delivered in Redfern, an Aboriginal neighborhood in Sydney, the Prime Minister at the time, Paul Keating, exhorted white Australians to recognize our role in contributing to Indigenous suffering:

> We took the children from their mothers. We practised discrimination and exclusion. It was our ignorance and our prejudice. And our failure to imagine these things being done to us. With some noble exceptions, we failed to make the most basic human response and enter into their hearts and mind. We failed to ask how would I feel if this were done to me (as quoted in HREOC 1997, 286).

Keating urged his fellow Australians to respond compassionately—to imagine "how would I feel if this were done to me". Compassion—"to feel the pain of another"—became a moral foundation of reconciliation. This understanding of reconciliation as requiring acknowledgement of past wrongs, and recognition of the ongoing effects on Indigenous people and communities in the present, was expressed by Chief Justice Brennan in his opinion in the 1992 Mabo case. It also underpinned HREOC's approach to the national inquiry into the Stolen Generations.

Bringing Them Home used both legal and moral discourses to assess the policies, practices and effects of Indigenous child removal. Applying the 1948 UN genocide convention to the circumstances of Indigenous child removal in Australia, *Bringing Them Home* controversially interpreted forcible child removal as constituting 'genocide' and as a breach of human rights (HREOC 1997, 266-275). Less widely recognized, it interpreted forcible child removal as constituting individual and collective trauma, which had impacts both on Indigenous and non-Indigenous Australians (HREOC 1997, 196). The commissioners recognized that children, their mothers, and their communities were often traumatized by the circumstances and the aftermath of child removal, family separation and cultural dispossession. The report explicitly drew on a psychocultural and, at times, a clinical discourse of trauma to interpret child removal as traumatic: "Separation and institutionalisation can amount to traumas. Almost invariably they were traumatically carried out with force, lies, regimentation and an absence of comfort and affection. All too often they also involved brutality and abuses. Trauma compounded trauma" (HREOC, 1997, 196). Citing evidence from numerous psychiatrists and psychologists, the report linked the intergenerational legacy of trauma to a range of conditions that continued to afflict individuals who had experienced child removal, including high levels of violence, alcohol and drug dependency, family breakdown, self-harm and suicide. In interpreting child removal as a traumatic event, the national inquiry legitimated the physical, emotional and psychological suffering experienced by individuals who had been removed and their mothers and communities. In identifying the legacy of suffering and harm caused by policies and practices of removal, it implicated white Australians, who inherited the task of acknowledging and atoning for the harms of colonialism.

Unlike a truth commission or legal trial, the national inquiry did not aim to identify specific crimes or individual perpetrators. Rather, Sir Ronald Wilson, who chaired the national inquiry, conceptualized it in therapeutic terms, as participating in "healing the nation" and in "prepar[ing] the way for reconciliation." "What this inquiry provides," he stated, "is an option to bring to light the anguish and suffering associated with being a victim of the actions of past governments, and to engage present governments in addressing the issues and suffering which affects peoples today" (as quoted in Devitt 2009, 54). Listening to the stories of survivors of removal was considered to be essential for promoting healing and for the reconciliation process. Rather than using forensic methods of proof that would hold up in court, the national inquiry adopted testimonial methods aimed at promoting healing and reconciliation. Commissioners travelled around the nation to listen to members of the Stolen Generations tell their stories, thereby facilitating the production and reception of testimony. Unlike a truth commission, the testimonial process was not open to the public, and fragments of the testimonies were published anonymously in *Bringing Them Home* to protect the identities of survivors.

In the 1990s, the Australian Stolen Generations inquiry was one of many such efforts that nations were making to respond to histories of violence, colonialism, genocide and dispossession. The testimonial approach had its roots in the 1961 Holocaust trial of Adolf Eichmann in Jerusalem. Historian Annette Wieviorka (2006) contends that whenever testimony is collected and archived today, including in trials and truth and reconciliation commissions, it bears the trace of a paradigm that gained legitimacy in the Eichmann trial (89). The Eichmann trial, and the testimonial methods it initiated, had profound implications for collective memory. Rather than the past being regarded as distant and inaccessible, "... [w]ith the Eichmann trial, the witness became an embodiment of memory, attesting to the past and to the continuing presence of the past" (Wieviorka 2006, 88). As a public record, the historic significance of the Australian inquiry resides, in large part, in the credibility and publicity it granted to Stolen Generations testimony. The testimonies made public those feelings and emotions that were previously experienced as private and individual. *Bringing Them Home* opens by acknowledging that it contains material that 'is so personal and intimate that ordinarily it would not be discussed' in the public sphere (HREOC 1997, 3). This archive of Indigenous testimony brought the Stolen Generations into a 'global archive of suffering' (Sarkar and Walker 2010), and constituted a collective emotional and moral truth that supported a demand for national recognition and justice.

Constituting Australians as a Witnessing Public

Testimony is widely understood not simply as a statement about past events or 'what happened'. It is understood, rhetorically, as an address to an audience, an actual or implied listener, which optimistically hopes for a response. Anthropologist Meg McLagan argues that testimony functions as an "intercultural technology, connecting individuals together from different worlds through the medium of pain, creating solidarity out of difference" (2003, 607). She proposes that "[a]s narratives and images of suffering travel, they have the potential to construct audiences as virtual witnesses, a subject position that implies responsibility for the suffering of others" (608-609). The publication of anonymous testimonies from members of the Stolen Generations served not only to inform the Australian public about the harm done by government policies aimed at eradicating Aboriginal culture; it also made "ethical claims on viewers and cultivate[d] potential actors", and thereby engaged the public in the process (608-609). As Geoffrey Hartman (1995) observes in the context of Holocaust testimonies, however, we have to "enable reception, it isn't simply there" (220). Reception, he explains, "has to do with a specific concept of the communal" (220). During the reconciliation era, the Australian community was taught to become compassionate witnesses to Indigenous suffering (Kennedy 2011a). For instance, Governor General William Deane, who mediated the reception of *Bringing Them Home*, played a key role in enabling reception by hailing Australians as a witnessing public. He cautioned that the legacy of child removal 'cannot be addressed unless the whole community listens with an open heart and mind to the stories of what happened in the past and, having listened and understood, commits itself to reconciliation' (HREOC 1997, 3). Deane's appeal to the public to respond from 'the heart' was crucial for soliciting a compassionate response, and positioning Australians as an 'affective community' for the Stolen Generations (Kennedy 2011a).

Many Australians responded to Deane's solicitation. For instance, the Sorry Books campaign provided Australians with the opportunity to respond compassionately to the Stolen Generations and commit to reconciliation (Kennedy, 2011a). The Sorry Books campaign, organized by Australians for Native Title and Reconciliation, was a grass roots movement which developed in the wake of Howard's refusal to offer an official apology. Sorry

Books, which opened with a pledge in which the signatory committed to reconciliation, circulated in communities around the nation and enabled ordinary Australians to say 'sorry' to the Stolen Generations. Community events were organized in schools, workplaces, churches and community centres at which members of the Stolen Generations told their stories, and the public listened. Novelists have also pursued the work of reconciliation by revisioning the past and mourning Indigenous losses in fictions that revisit frontier violence, dispossession and child removal. Such work has been particularly important in the Australian context, in which federal governments have, since 1996, progressively backed away from what has been called 'symbolic reconciliation' in favour of a 'practical' focus on health, education and housing.

A Poetics of Reparation: Trauma and Compassion in Gail Jones's *Sorry*

Gail Jones's novel, *Sorry*, published in 2007, provides an opportunity to examine the cultural reach of the trauma paradigm as a model for national healing and reconciliation.[1] *Bringing Them Home* positioned white Australians as belated witnesses to the ongoing effects of traumatic practices such as child removal and forced assimilation. By contrast, *Sorry* is told from the perspective of the child of a perpetrator who is both complicit in the injustice and a beneficiary of it. Offered as an act of literary reparation, the novel tells the story of a lonely white Australian child, Perdita, the daughter of eccentric, alienated British migrants. Perdita struggles to remember and atone for her unwitting complicity in a crime that results in the wrongful incarceration of an Indigenous girl, Mary, who has befriended her. Sixteen-year old Mary has come from a convent to help Perdita's family after her chronically depressed mother, Stella, has become incapacitated. Ten-year-old Perdita impulsively stabs her father, Nicholas, when she witnesses him raping Mary. As her father's blood spurts on the girls, Perdita represses the horrifying knowledge of what she has done; Mary confesses and is incarcerated. Perdita spontaneously develops a debilitating stutter, and the events that took Mary and her father from her become literally unspeakable. The novel narrates the story of Perdita's recovery of her memory and her speech under the guidance of a gifted Russian doctor, Dr. Oblov. The novel may be read as an allegory of the inability of white Australians to confront

---

[1]   The following five paragraphs draw on material from Kennedy (2011b).

their own complicity in acts of violence against Indigenous people. Perdita benefits from Mary's sacrifice, but she also inherits—like Australians today—the responsibility of atoning for her father's crime, and her own unwitting crime against Mary.

In *Sorry* complicity is explored in relation to the larger ethical issue of compassion—of recognizing and responding with "appropriate distress" to the suffering of others, both proximate and distant (Jones 2007, 185). The novel is set in and around Broome, a small town populated by Japanese and Malay pearl divers and Aborigines, with a minority of whites, in the remote northwest of Western Australia in the early 1940s. In February, 1942, thousands of Dutch refugees from Indonesia were passing through Broome to Perth, seeking shelter from the Japanese. On March 3, 1942, Japanese pilots based in East Timor attacked Broome, killing scores of Dutch refugees crammed into flying boats on the harbour. This scene, which Perdita witnesses from the safe distance of the beach, forms an important historic context for the novel's exploration of trauma and witnessing. Observing that "war may destroy scale altogether," *Sorry* juxtaposes the intimate gendered and racialized trauma of sexual assault and child removal with the historic, public trauma of WWII, and of the Spanish influenza which kills Dr. Oblov's two sisters when he is a boy.

The point of departure for *Sorry*, never directly stated, is the issue of justice for the Stolen Generations, and John Howard's refusal to apologize.[2] Readers are told that Mary, of mixed descent, is taken from her Aboriginal mother when she is six years old and raised in a convent. Mary later learns that her mother, tortured by grief for the loss of her stolen child, rolls into a campfire and allows herself to be consumed by flames. Mary's removal and her mother's tragic death are only mentioned in passing. The novel approaches the Stolen Generations indirectly, through the broader theme of "damaged childhoods" (see Felman 2002, 43). In *Sorry*, damaged childhoods, racial violence, and trauma are condensed onto the figure of the vulnerable and traumatized child. Perdita, Mary, and Billy, a deaf-mute, all suffer from damaged childhoods. What are the effects of representing white Australian complicity in colonial violence and racist injustice on the model of trauma and recovery?

Trauma discourse has become a favored idiom for exploring experiences of and responses to individual and collective violence and injustice. As a psychocultural trope, trauma conveys the collective cultural and psychological obstacles that prevent British settlers from witnessing

---

[2]   Jones discusses the issue of apology in an afterward to the novel.

indigenous suffering. In *Sorry*, a clinical understanding of trauma and its aftermath provides the narrative frame for Perdita's personal journey of recovery. For instance, Dr Oblov tells Perdita that the aim of the therapy is "that she should one day tell her own story with simplicity and lucidity" (Jones 2007, 174). Perdita does recover her memory, but her mother's refusal to corroborate her story to the police prevents her from securing justice for Mary. The narrative describes Perdita's anguish when she realizes that Mary, who is paying for her crime, is suffering an injustice: "She sobbed uncontrollably for what she believed was her heartless forgetting. She sobbed for her mother's deception and her own self-delusion and . . . for Mary's extraordinary sacrifice" (Jones 2007, 195). Read as an allegory of national contrition for the harms perpetrated against the Stolen Generations, this scene exemplifies a politics of "true feeling", grounded in "a popular belief…that a nation can be built across fields of social difference through channels of affective identification and empathy" (Berlant 2000, 128). "Sentimentality," Berlant argues, "is the means by which mass subaltern pain is advanced in the dominant public sphere, as the true core of national collectivity. It operates when the pain of intimate others burs into the consciousness of classically privileged national subjects, in such a fashion that they feel the pain of flawed or denied citizenship as their pain" (Berlant 2000, 129). Perdita's psychological suffering is her means of atoning for the injustice that Mary experiences. As a narrative of national atonement, the novel values compassion and recognition of the other's pain as a basis for reconciliation.

As in *Bringing Them Home*, in *Sorry* redress for historical injustice is conceived on a model of reconciliation grounded in compassionate recognition and empathic feeling. When Perdita confronts Mary about her sacrifice, Mary responds by insisting on her agency to act: "Deeta, I chose. I chose to help you eh?" (Jones 2007, 203). Perdita later realizes "this was the point at which she should have said 'sorry.'" Perdita deeply regrets her failure to apologize to Mary. Perdita imagines her failure to apologize as a failure of "affective identification and empathy" (Berlant 2000, 128). Reflecting on Mary's incarceration, Perdita thinks she "should have imagined what kind of imprisonment this was, to be closed against the rustle of leaves and the feel of wind and of rain, to be taken from her place, her own place where her mother had died, to be sealed in the forgetfulness of someone else's crime" (Jones 2007, 204). It's not only Mary's lack of freedom that Perdita tasks herself with imagining; it is also Mary's removal from "her place" and, ultimately, from her mother. This scene of regret for an apology not offered can be described as a "fantasy reparation," which involves a "therapeutic conversion of the scene of pain and its eradication to the scene of the political itself" (Berlant 2000, 132). In the context of a public debate about the prime minister's refusal to apologize to the Stolen Generations, the title of the novel, *Sorry*, completes the logic of "fantasy reparation": it connects the scene of suffering conveyed in the narrative to the external scene of the political—and offers itself as an act of reparation for all of those people who had been removed from their families and their place. Fantasy reparation is achieved here through what memory critic Alison Landsberg (2004) calls "prosthetic memory", the ability to imagine oneself, through the vehicle of a film or a cultural text, in the place of the other, without confusing the other's experience as one's own.

A Poetics of Survival: *Samson and Delilah*

Cultural memory scholar Andreas Huyssen (2003) has argued that the paradigm of traumatic memory is focused too exclusively on the past, at the expense of the future. The national inquiry into the Stolen Generations investigated practices of removal from the 1930s to the 1970s. The cultural texts that have brought Stolen Generations into cultural memory, such as *Rabbit Proof Fence* (2002), Baz Lurhmann's melodrama, *Australia* (2008), and *Sorry* (2007), are set in the past, often during the era of World War II. By contrast, the significance of Warwick Thornton's 2009 film, *Samson and Delilah*, is its mode of conveying an unfolding situation in the present. Berlant argues that it is important to theorize the present event as it unfolds; she is concerned with fantasies of "the good life" that have become unsustainable as a result of deteriorating economic, environmental and social conditions (2011, 2). She is interested in how people maintain an attachment to each other, to ideals, to habits, and to the political in such circumstances. Of course, fantasies of "the good life" vary and her archive consists of American and European texts. Nonetheless, there is much in her thinking about attachment that is usefully applied to an Australian film about the precarious conditions of life for young people in an impoverished Indigenous community.

Samson and Delilah, which tells a love story focused on two marginalized teenagers living in a remote community in Central Australia, was released in the wake of the Northern Territory Intervention. While the film brings what *Bringing Them Home* refers to as the "appalling living conditions" of a remote indigenous community onto the big screen, it also tells a personal story, which conveys something of the everyday texture of life, and the challenges that the young characters face simply to survive. Samson, around fourteen years old, loves music and dancing, and would play in his older brother's band if allowed. Excluded, he takes comfort in petrol sniffing, the drug of choice for Indigenous youngsters seeking escape from the pain and monotony of their lives. Delilah, about the same age, is the responsible granddaughter of an elderly artist, who teaches her to paint, but things turn sour for her when her grandmother dies. In a customary ritual following the death of her grandmother, Delilah is severely beaten by a group of Aboriginal women who blame her for the death. She chops off her hair with a carving knife as a sign of her grief. She, like Samson, is left to fend for herself. In one scene, Samson, who lives with his brother, opens the door of the refrigerator, only to find it empty, flies buzzing around. He retreats to a bedroom with a mattress on the floor, soiled clothes piled around, and inhales petrol fumes. Abandoned wheelchairs take the place of a skateboard, as kids take turns racing them. A caravan serves as the clinic, on those days when a visiting nurse comes to the community. The pair head to Alice Springs, the only sizeable town in the region, to try their luck at making a life, but end up living on the fringe. Delilah tries to sell her grandmother's paintings, but without a white intermediary she is unsuccessful. There is little dialogue; in contrast to the testimonial paradigm that characterized *Bringing Them Home*, the story of *Samson and Delilah* is conveyed almost entirely through visual language and the soundtrack. The cinematography, and particularly Thornton's hand-held camera work, images a visually stark and stunning landscape that appears endless.

The narrative merges love story and road trip, but to call it a love story is to defy the usual sexually and verbally explicit expectations of the genre. Love is conveyed only through sly glances, subtle gestures, and primarily through Delilah's actions. In Alice Springs, the pair is subjected to racist slurs, and Delilah is abducted and presumably raped by a group of white youths, who later throw her out of the car. She joins Samson, living under a bridge, and takes up petrol sniffing. Stoned, she is hit by a car, and ends up in hospital. After recovering in hospital, Delilah returns to the bridge under which Sansom lives, to find him sitting cross-legged under a tent-like blanket, sniffing petrol and slowly killing himself. With the help of Samson's brother, the pair return to their community, load up the car, and Delilah takes Samson to her grandmother's country to live remotely in what is known as an "outstation". There she sets up a home in a tin shed to care for him while he withdraws from petrol sniffing.

Susan Ryan-Fazileau views *Samson and Delilah* through the lens of trauma theory. She argues that the film, through its representation of the lives of two teens, invites viewers to "reflect on the legacy of trauma in an

Indigenous community in today's Australia" (2011, 1). To facilitate this reading, she draws on Indigenous researcher Judy Atkinson's understanding of the intergenerational transmission of trauma in Indigenous communities as "chronic, cumulative and ongoing" (Ryan-Fazileau 2011, 1). Trauma was originally produced by colonial dispossession and structural violence, and compounded in later generations through ongoing racism, exclusion, alcohol and drug dependency and violence (Ryan-Fazileau 2011, 2). Atkinson contends that narrating stories of trauma in a community context is an important step in the recovery process, as it enables Indigenous people to gain an understanding of the structural conditions that produce trauma (as cited in Ryan Fazileau). Ryan-Fazileau reads the film as "a trauma story narrated to a caring group-the spectators, who identify with the protagonists thanks to the way the filmmaker presents their plight" (Ryan-Fazileau 2011, 2). While this analysis is compelling, it reads the film through the familiar interpretive frame of trauma and recovery. When and if the protagonists recover, however, the conditions of 'ordinary crisis' - the violence, drug addiction, welfare dependency and the like - will still be present. Recovering from trauma does not extinguish the intensifying conditions of precarity produced by racism, neoliberalism and globalisation, and for Samson and Delilah, exacerbating their already marginal position. In fact, the film's aesthetics, and the almost complete lack of dialogue, suggest an emergent genre of the historical present (Berlant 2011). Taking this into consideration, I suggest that the film can be productively read as initiating a shift from the exceptional logic of trauma, organized often around a spectacular 'event', to what Berlant calls "crisis ordinariness" (2011, 10). This shift is accompanied by another, from a poetics of recovery to a poetics of survival or living on.

Berlant advocates a shift from the language of trauma, which tends to focus on a singular extraordinary or catastrophic event. She proposes, instead, the concept of "crisis ordinariness" as a means of registering the entrenched conditions of precariousness and vulnerability that are present in ordinary life (2011, 10). Crisis ordinariness, which seeks to capture the "intensities of a situation that spreads into modes, habits and genres of being" is a particularly apt term for identifying the precarious conditions of ordinary life for Samson and Delilah in a remote community (Berlant 2011, 82). Whereas *Rabbit-Proof Fence* focused on the theft of the children as a traumatic event in their lives and the lives of their mothers and community, *Samson and Delilah* depicts the perilous conditions of ordinary life in a remote community shaped by decades of structural economic and social inequality and isolation. Even when violent or extreme events occur—when Delilah is abducted, raped and hit by a car—these events are not singled out as 'exceptional', but rather, as 'normal' in her everyday life. Samson's addiction to petrol sniffing is a response to the conditions in which he lives, conditions of disenfranchisement from the social and economic world. In contrast to the genre of melodrama, "whose depictions for the good life now appear to mark archaic expectations about having and building a life" (Berlant 2011, 6), *Samson and Delilah*, unlike *Rabbit Proof Fence* and *The Sapphires* (2012), is relentlessly based in the present. It can be described as a "situation tragedy"—the narrative of an unfolding "situation" the contours of which are not yet clear. In a situation tragedy "the subject's world is fragile beyond repair, one gesture away from losing all access to sustain its fantasies: the situation threatens utter, abject unraveling" (Berlant 2011, 6). It takes the form of a "menacing new realism" (Berlant 2011, 6), which is precisely the aesthetic mode of *Samson and Delilah*.

The film, billed with the slogan "love never judges," was well-received both in Australia and at Cannes Film Festival, where it was selected for Un Certain Regard. Margaret Pomerantz and David Stratton, host of the weekly Australian television show, "At the Movies," give the film a coveted 5 star rating—the only film they both rated "5" in 2009 (Pomerantz & Stratton). Many non-Indigenous audiences experience the film, which depicts extreme poverty, social isolation, repeated violence, racism and the lack of the material goods that many Australians identify with "the good life," as confronting. Audiences have described their reaction in visceral terms, saying the film left them feeling as if they had been punched. Indeed, in describing the affective experience of watching the film, Pomerantz uses precisely that term: "The emotional punch that *Samson and Delilah* delivers is one of those rare things in cinema which doesn't come along very often. And when it does you feel like falling down on your knees in gratitude. And it's not because Thornton has gone for sentimentality. It's the reverse." What impresses Stratton, however, is the film's optimism and hope, in bleak circumstances. He comments that "it's a film that, while you're watching it, you feel that it's a tragedy…. It's a very sad story. But the way it concludes with such optimism, I think it really soars and I think every Australian should see this film." Like William Deane's appeal to Australians in the wake of *Bringing Them Home*, Stratton's review of the film exhorts "all Australians" to see it; through this address, he appeals to viewers as a witnessing public to the lives of Aboriginal teens living in circumstances of extreme poverty, deprivation and social isolation. I want to pursue Stratton's observation about the film's optimism. What kind of future does the film permit us to envision for these two characters? Berlant's concepts of "crisis ordinariness" and "cruel optimism" provide a useful analytic lens for considering the affects and relationships depicted in the film, and for considering how the scene it describes and the affects it produces differ from Stolen Generations melodramas such as *Rabbit Proof Fence* (2002) and *Australia* (2008).

Delilah's attachment to Samson, her love for him and desire to be with him, despite the fact that he thwarts her efforts by stealing petrol from their truck and leaving them stranded, could be described as having the affective structure of "cruel optimism". Berlant introduces the concept of "cruel optimism" to describe the nature of our attachments, and particularly, perverse attachments. "A relation of cruel optimism exists," she proposes, "when something you desire is actually an obstacle to your flourishing" (2011, 1). It is not the "experience of optimism," but rather its "affective structure" that is especially important for explicating the nature of our attachments to fantasies of the "good life". Optimism becomes cruel when "the very pleasures of being inside a relation have become sustaining regardless of the content of the relation" (Berlant 2011, 2). Delilah hopes that Samson will quit petrol sniffing, and she aims to support him. The film brilliantly succeeds in transmitting what Langton (2010) has called "the shock of the new"—the violence, poverty, isolation and monotony in some remote communities—and its effects on children and young people. Delilah attempts to give Samson the care and space to recover by taking him to a remote outstation on her grandmother's land—a move which also enables her to reconnect to her "country" and to her grandmother, and recover a sense of purpose. They will live in a shed, hunt for food, and be self-sustaining. This fresh start is possibly what Stratton has in mind when he refers to the film's optimism. The film leaves open their future, and the question of whether moving to remote country will facilitate their flourishing. It is a risk Delilah is willing to take.

Made shortly after the Northern Territory Intervention was initiated, *Samson and Delilah* introduces a new aesthetic, which conveys the conditions of the unfolding present as experienced by young people growing up in remote Aboriginal Australia. What most Australians know about life in remote Indigenous communities they learn through sensationalist media reports, which inevitably position children and teens as victims of neglect and alcohol-related violence. The Intervention enraged Warwick Thornton, who felt that as an Aboriginal male, he and others like him were under suspicion of being paedophiles. He originally considered referencing it but instead decided not to, as it would date the film. While *Samson and Delilah* does show the teens as subjected to violence both from white and Aboriginal communities, and surviving without adult help, Thornton conveys this reality without sensationalising or sentimentalising it.

The film refuses to render life in this Indigenous community totally intelligible to outsiders; rather, it engages viewers by making us work to make sense of what we see. Nor does it provide the comfort for viewers that comes from compassionate recognition and fantasies of rescue; rather, we have to find another way of engaging and relating to it. On this issue, anthropologist Stewart's (2007) work on "ordinary affects" provides a lead. Referring to herself in the third person, Stewart distances the authorial voice in order to foreground the provisional status of narrative and identity. In her role as an anthropologist of "the ordinary," sensitive to the affects of everyday life, she writes of herself: "She is not so much a subject position or an agent in hot pursuit of something definitive as a point of contact; instead she gazes, imagines, senses, takes on, performs, and asserts not a flat and finished truth but some possibilities (and threats) that have come into view in the effort to become attuned to what a particular scene might offer" (p. 5). Thus, Stewart is able to create the distance that critical thinking requires. I suggest that *Samson and Delilah* offers one such space of affective encounter where we may engage the other not through familiar notions of victimhood and rescue, but through potentialities that are not yet entirely obvious. *Samson and Delilah*, through its menacing realism, denies the possibility of a sentimental response; it doesn't allow us to sustain the fantasy of a nation forged out of pain, across boundaries of difference. Instead, it brings us face to face with entrenched precarity in Australia, and challenges Australian fantasies of a "fair go" for all, and of ourselves as "good" people.

Conclusion

The Stolen Generations paradigm was based on a therapeutic model of testimony and witnessing, reconciliation and recovery, which is conveyed through the narrative structure of cultural texts. For instance, *Rabbit Proof Fence* and *Australia* are film melodramas that brought the Stolen Generations into national and international visibility, travelling on a global vernacular of trauma, suffering and disrupted family bonds. *Rabbit Proof Fence* has a double ending—the diegetic ending tells of two of the girls' triumphant return home, and the non-diegetic ending grimly reports that the practice of child removal continued into the next generation, bringing more grief and loss to the girls who returned. *Australia*, by contrast, optimistically imagines reconciliation as a path to national redemption. Gail Jones' novel, *Sorry*, does not take the form of melodrama, but the novel's narrative trajectory is modeled on a paradigm of trauma as an exceptional event. Compassionate feeling and imaginative identification with the pain of the other is vital to its conception of atoning for past wrongs. These Stolen Generations texts all, to some degree, focus on relations between black and white, and in that sense they can be considered to be within the discursive framework of reconciliation.

Samson and Delilah initiates a shift from a sentimental poetics of reparation grounded in "true feeling" to a poetics of survival. An Aboriginal film which depicts ordinary life in an Aboriginal community, *Samson and Delilah* focuses the viewer's attention on the teens' struggle for survival both within the impoverished community in which they live, and in town, where they experience white racism and violence. The white viewer is peripheral, a positioning that provides the possibility to move away from the presumption of white authority. *Samson and Delilah*, through its visual language and soundtrack, manages to convey what Marcia Langton has identified as the "shock of the new." In contrast to the optimism associated with "going home" and reconciliation, it transmits something of the cruel optimism that stems both from the struggle for survival in conditions of entrenched poverty and disadvantage, and from the deep attachment to ideals of self-determination and sovereignty under ongoing conditions of settler colonial neo-liberalism.

References

Altman, J. C., & Hinkson, M. (Eds.). (2010). *Culture Crisis: Anthropology and Politics in Aboriginal Australia*. Sydney: University of New South Wales Press.

Altman, J. C., & Hinkson, M. (Eds.). (2007). *Coercive Reconciliation: Stabilise, Normalise, Exit Aboriginal Australia*. North Carlton, Vic.: Arena Publications.

Berlant, L. (2011). *Cruel Optimism*. Durham, NC: Duke University Press.

Berlant, L. (2000). The Subject of True Feeling: Privacy, Pain and Politics. *Cultural Studies and Political Theory*, ed. Jodi Dean. Ithaca, NY: Cornell University Press.

Blight, R. (Producer), & Blair, W. (Director) (2012). *The Sapphires* (Motion picture). Australia: Goalpost Pictures.

Devitt, R. (2009). 'Healing the heartbreak'?: the Role of Testimony in the Australian Inquiry into the Separation of Indigenous Children from Their families. *Humanities Research* XV(3), 49-70.

Farrell, K. (1998) *Post-Traumatic Culture: Injury and Interpretation in the Nineties*. Baltimore: Johns Hopkins University Press.

Fassin, D., & Rechtman, R. (2009). *The Empire of Trauma: An Inquiry into the Condition of Victimhood* (R. Gomme, Trans.). Princeton, N.J.: Princeton University Press.

Fassin, D. (2008). The Humanitarian Politics of Testimony: Subjectification through Trauma in the Israeli-Palestinian Conflict. *Cultural Anthropology* 23(3): 531-558.

Felman, S. (2002). *The Juridical Unconscious: Trials and Traumas in the Twentieth Century*. Cambridge, MA: Harvard University Press.

Hartmann, G. (1995). Learning From Survivors: The Yale Testimony Project. *Holocaust and Genocide Studies* 9(2): 192–207.

HREOC. (1997). *Bringing Them Home: Report of the National Inquiry into the Separation of Aboriginal and Torres Strait Islander Children from Their Families.* Retrieved March 25, 2015 from http://www.humanrights.gov.au/publications/bringing-them-home-report-1997

Huyssen, A. (2003). *Present Pasts: Urban Palimpsests and the Politics of Memory.* Palo Alto, CA.: Stanford University Press.

Jones, G. (2007). *Sorry.* North Sydney: N.S.W.: Vintage Books.

Kennedy, R. (2011a). An Australian Archive of Feelings: The Sorry Books Campaign and the Pedagogy of Compassion. *Australian Feminist Studies,* 26(69), 257-279.

Kennedy, R. (2011b). Australian Trials of Trauma: The Stolen Generations in Human Rights, Law, and Literature. *Comparative Literature Studies,* 48(3), 333-355.

Landsberg, A. (2004). *Prosthetic Memory: the Transformation of American Remembrance in the Age of Mass Culture.* New York: Columbia University Press.

Langton, M. (2010). The Shock of the New: A Postcolonial Dilemma for Australianist Anthropology. In J. Altman & M. Hinkson (Eds.), *Culture Crisis: Anthropology and Politics in Aboriginal Australia.* Sydney: University of New South Wales Press.

Lattas, A. and Morris, B. (2010). The Politics of Suffering and the Politics of Anthropology. In J. Altman & M. Hinkson (Eds.), *Culture Crisis: Anthropology and Politics in Aboriginal Australia.* Sydney: University of New South Wales Press.

Lurhmann, Baz. (Director & Producer). (2008). *Australia.* [Motion picture]. Australia: 20th C Fox.

McLagan, M. (2003). Principles, Publicity, and Politics: Notes on Human Rights and Media. *American Anthropologist,* 105 (3): 609-612.

Moses, A. D. (2010). Australian Memory and the Apology to the Stolen Generations of Indigenous People. In A. Assmann & S. Conrad (Eds.), *Memory in a Global Age: Discourses, Practices and Trajectories.* Basingstoke: Palgrave Macmillan.

Noyce, P. (Director & Producer). (2002). *Rabbit-Proof Fence.* [Motion picture]. Australia: Miramax.

Orford, A. (1999). Muscular Humanitarianism: Reading the Narratives of the New Interventionism. *European Journal of International Law,* 10(4): 679-711.

Pomerantz, M. & Stratton, D. (2009). *Sansom and Delilah. At the Movies with Margaret and David.* Retrieved March 25, 2015 from http://www.abc. net.au/atthemovies/txt/s2542612.htm

Ryan-Fazileau, S. (2011). *Samson and Delilah:* Herstory, Trauma and Survival. *Journal of the Association for the Study of Australian Literature (JASAL),* 11.2: 1-11.

Sarkar and Walker, J. (2010). *Documentary Testimonies: Global Archives of Suffering.* New York: Routledge.

Shelper, K. (Producer), & Thornton, W. (Director). (2009). *Samson and Delilah* [Motion picture]. Australia: Madman Entertainment.

Stewart, K. (2008). *Ordinary Affects.* Durham, NC: Duke University Press.

Sutton, P. (2009). *The Politics of Suffering: Indigenous Australia and the End of the Liberal Consensus.* Carlton, Vic.: Melbourne University Press.

Wieviorka, A. (2006). *The Era of the Witness.* Ithaca, NY: Cornell University Press.

Wild, R., & Anderson, P. (2007). *Northern Territory Government Australia: Inquiry into the Protection of Aboriginal Children from Sexual Abuse.* Retrieved March 25, 2015 from http://www.inquirysaac.nt.gov.au/pdf/bipacsa_final_report.pdf.

Chapter 11
Ending the Haunting, Halting Whisperings of the Unspoken: Confronting the Haitian Past in the Literary Works of Agnant, Danticat, and Trouillot

Sarah Davies Cordova

University of Wisconsin-Milwaukee
Senior Research Fellow, University of Johannesburg

There was no way to escape this dread anymore, this pendulum between regret and forgiveness (*The Dew Breaker*, p. 242).

Introduction

A 2010 painting by the Haitian painter Frantz Zéphirin, entitled "il était une fois le 12 janvier" (once upon a time on the 12th of January), foregrounds, before a deep dark blue-black background, two light azure rimmed single lapis eyes that are surrounded by roughly strung pairs of smaller, seemingly blinking eyes that cover the canvas like beads and whose pupils' shades run from blue to purple. The haunting piece captures the fear, the eyes, the looking for dear ones, of the after moments to 4:53 pm when the 2010 January earthquake struck in and around the Haitian capital city as the darkness that envelops Port-au-Prince on any given evening transfixed the peering of the citizenry into staring human twinkling lights. But the speechless painting also represents for me a darkened other "once upon a time" which continues to haunt Haitians still living both at home and dispersed abroad and which after the earthquake, took on a sharpened *vérité* with the return of the deposed dictator Jean-Claude Duvalier, alias Baby Doc as the son of Papa Doc, François Duvalier, both of whom instigated the tonton macoutes' deeds. As the regime's death squads, the tonton macoutes petrified the Haitian public into silencing the disappearances, torture, and mass murders that they perpetrated and that constitute the charges of crimes against humanity that lie in waiting for the Duvaliers and their henchmen. The forced silence that haunted and still contains the era of the Duvalier dictatorship let fall a few whisperings, and it is these barely audible snatches that the women authors, who dialogue here through their novelistic fiction, try to tender and fill in through their writing.

In her February 2012 article in the *Montreal Gazette*, journalist Sue Montgomery reports on the Haitian ruling that Jean-Claude Duvalier (Baby Doc) would not be tried for grave human rights abuses committed under his watch and underlines the disturbing silence that ensued in France, the United States, and the Caribbean, as well as the mildness of Canada's response. The case had been formerly brought against Jean-Claude Duvalier when he travelled back to Port-au-Prince, with his current partner Véronique Roy on January 16th, 2011, almost twenty-five years to the day since his departure on February 7th 1986.[1] Questions abounded as to Duvalier's motivations[2] especially since he immediately took up his old habits with impunity and was seen eating in town, and attending weddings and parties all over Port-au-Prince; and this, even though two days after his return, his passport was confiscated so that he could not leave Haiti and he was placed under house arrest following his arraignment before a Haitian court for his crimes against the people of Haiti which include human rights violations, torture, arbitrary imprisonment, killing of civilians, and embezzlement from state coffers.[3] His return a little more than a year after the 2010 earthquake had appeared timely to some, even if others thought it would re-awaken fears, and reopen scars that run deep as Martine Theodore of Haitian Women of Miami indicated:

> Now that Haiti is in such a terrible situation, some people might see him as some sort of liberator—he embodies an era of relative peace and quiet, though things were not perfect, [....] However, Duvalier's regime brings a lot of fear and emotional aspects to the equation that we may not need right now. (quoted by Daniel, 2011, Jan. 17, *The Miami Herald*, n.p.)

Indeed over the past decade, in the selective memory of some, the Duvalier years have taken on a confounding softer undertone as the infrastructure of Haiti and its cities have lacked upkeep, and the implementation of safety standards and generalised planning in the areas of public works—notably with regards to the enforcement of building codes both before and since the 2010 earthquake—remain marred in bureaucratic stagnation.[4] Theodore adds that "In the past ten years, a sense of nostalgia for the Duvalier-era of cleaner streets and better government services has emerged, even though the bulk of the population is too young to remember Duvalier's bloody rule" (*Miami Herald* 2011, Jan. 17). It is this very deadening silence that allows and enables Haiti's newly elected president, Michel Martelly, to place Duvalieristes in key governmental positions who in turn construct and revise the history of the Duvalier era in nostalgic hues. As Jan J. Dominique, the novelist and daughter of the assassinated radio station director and agronomist Jean Dominique, points out "In Haiti, young people are never taught about what it was like under Duvalier, and those old enough to remember fear speaking out."[5] And with the current political conjuncture, it is once again risky to speak out.[6]

On the eve of Baby Doc's return, Haiti's capital and its other cities, situated along the fault line whose movement brought down the state's figure-head—the presidential palace—and smothered so many in the rubble that the earth's quaking left in its wake, learned the effects of this (geological) mis-alignment, just as several women authors of Haiti were re-membering and working dangerously at enunciating other (socio-political) mis-alignments: those unsaids of their childhood.[7] Three of these authors, Marie-Célie Agnant, Kettly Mars[8] and Evelyne Trouillot spoke out at book fairs in France in 2010 and 2011, alongside other contemporary writers of the diaspora and living in Haiti, and returned to the injunction of their diasporic US-based sister Edwige Danticat, to her anxious cry to "create dangerously." They pushed up against the virtual yet forbidding barriers, insisting on the role of authors and artists in telling, recounting, giving news, gifting responsible stories as Marcel Mauss (1923-24) might have expressed their politics of engagement. Kettly Mars described at the 2011 Paris Book Fair how the adults whispered among themselves and fell silent when children happened on their conversations and, acknowledged that with *Saisons sauvages*, she wants to render visible and public the murmurings of the Papa and Baby Doc eras.[9] Agnant, for her part, is concerned on the one hand about the generalised impunity accorded such persons as Rosalie Bosquet (otherwise known as Madame Max Adolphe) which can be witnessed for example with the library being built and named after her in Mirebalais, Haiti, even though she led the tonton macoutes under Papa Doc after having shot nineteen men whom she pretended were plotting to overthrow the "father of the nation." On the other hand she attests to aching to know what such women, whose names keep coming up, were doing in and amongst the tonton macoutes. At the Paris Salon du livre, talking about the French edition in 2011 of her 2007 novel, *Un alligator nommé Rosa*, Agnant expressed how creating a space with the other in which to take back the silenced is a process, one with which she hopes readers will help her.[10]

Ending the Haunting, Halting Whisperings of the Unspoken

Despite the frequent presence of the Duvaliers, their henchmen and the tonton-macoutes in the stories situated or written during the hereditary dictatorship, it has been rare to find them incorporated as key protagonists except for François Duvalier himself, and even he is rarely portrayed realistically. Generally, they have been characterised by the black clothes they wear, the reprehensibly cruel acts they perform, and their uncanny hovering presence that triggers the silence that allows the fictitious characters—as well as the families of the authors writing out these stories—to remain out of harm's way. However on the pages of Danticat's, Trouillot's and Agnant's novels that give no easy answers, fear of reprisals gives way to a face to face between violators and victims. In Agnant's *Un alligator nommé Rosa*, Antoine Guibert doggedly pursues the murderer of his parents to the south of France where she is bed-ridden and (uneasily) cared for by her adopted daughter, another orphan of the invalid's murderous acts; in Trouillot's (2010) *La mémoire aux abois*, Marie-Ange, the nurse's aide, pieces together her family's tragedy as she is ordered to care for the widow of the dictator who wrought such horrors upon the people of her native land; and in Danticat's (2004) *The Dew Breaker*, the daughter Ka learns from her father after he returns from drowning her carving of him that he had not been a prisoner in the Casernes in Port-au-Prince but the barracks' chief officer—working under his superior Rosalie, the head of the female force known as Fillette Lalo (Fyèt Lalo)—and the assassin of her mother's brother.

Writing from the painful place of addressing the victimizer, each of these women authors restage head on and have their characters relive—some in diegetic memory, others in fictionalised "real time"—the violence perpetuated by the political actants of the 1960s, 70s and 80s without the transpositional ploys, and the more individualised characters that Marie Chauvet felt compelled to use especially in *Amour*, *Colère*, *Folie* which she elaborated in Haïti under the dictatorship in 1968. The characters, deeply scarred by the legacy of the muted, unexplained violence of their childhood, live with its remnants, liminally and madly obsessed by their attempts to reconnect with their own subjectivity. In attempting to understand, the characters go beyond the violence of the interdicts and emerge from the trajectory of their encounters with the demons of their nightmares out in the open, in an allegorical no-man's land, at the edge of life. Where Danticat (and Mars) present stories that place their female protagonists literally in the camp of the perpetrators—as their children, and as their lovers respective-ly—Trouillot and Agnant evoke and stage the necessary fascination of coming eye to eye with the elder woman whether she be the widow of Papa Doc or Rosa Bosquet[11] (the reine-choche—she devil) the head of the VSN and of the parallel female force, the Fillette Lalo, both of whom are at death's door and living in exile in France.

I am struck by the ways in which Agnant and Trouillot have moved forwards in time, away from their earlier foci on the trauma of historical displacements across the Atlantic when they sought to give voices to the echoes of slave-ships and slavery, to speak out and resist the undertow of silencing the past and closing out the future. After Danticat, these women novelists have elected to write *in* the hushed, whispered forbidden and the frightfully fascinating fear that accompanied their childhood during the 1960s and 1970s, a fear still with them, haunting their living memory. Moving beyond regrets and forgiveness, these works seek a conciliatory opening with which to unlock the past. Resisting the amnesia that this certain nostalgia for the Duvalier years encourages, *Un alligator nommé Rosa* and *La mémoire aux abois* follow in the tracks of Edwige Danticat's 2004 *The Dew Breaker* for they place centre page the very characters of Haiti's history—alarmingly powerful men and women of the Duvalier regimes—and, bring them face to face, in their demise, with their nemesis*, in situ* of distributive justice.

Danticat's title—*The Dew Breaker*—alludes to the 'shoukét laroze', the Haitian Kreyol syntagm for torturers who act before the morning dew as Beatrice, the protagonist of the sixth story "The Bridal Seamstress" explains: "We called them shoukèt laroze, [....] They'd break into your house. Mostly it was at night. But often they'd also come before dawn, as the dew was settling on the leaves, and they'd take you away" (p. 131). The title of this collection of nine stories also recalls that of Jacques Roumain's (1944) classic novel: *Gouverneurs de la rosée*, an intergenerational story that seeks to redress long held wrongs, by seeking out the source, a source of water to re-distribute its life-giving sustenance to the divided Fonds-Rouge community of peasants. Ka's father, the dew breaker in Danticat's work, takes once he is in exile in New York the name of Roumain's hero's father, Mr. Bienaimé. *Gouverneurs de la rosée*'s linear pattern counters the puzzle-like structure of the contemporary women's novels that gradually fills in past ellipses—silences, non sequiturs, missing pieces—tremulously at times and with flash floods of recalled instances. These narratives situate the historical personalities, alone in lowly ex-isled positions,[12] or in sickness at death's threshold, and where they can no longer hold anyone in their power, where they are bound back within the limits they crossed with such hubris. The characters finding or sounding them out are counter-positioned to reach towards an afterwards. The fictions portray a conciliation, a coming to terms, a poetics of survival that intimates a release from the stranglehold of feared power holding them and the perpetrators back. Such movement forwards out of ill-living and living-sickness *(mal-vivre/le mal de vivre)* augurs a promissory *habitus* for an ethics of survival, one that patterns learning to live as an evidential form of disobedience.

Such release takes on different contours as triggers from the historical past lived in fictional time, as well as in creative engagements, generate actual and imagined responses. One such release occurred in a set of knee-jerk reprisals to Jean-Claude Duvalier's flight from Haiti in 1986 that Danticat scripts into her chapter "Monkey Tails" in *The Dew Breaker*. At this sudden switch in February 1986, the populace suddenly, fervently, searched out the Volunteers for National Security, the tonton macoutes:

> Overnight our country had completely changed. We had fallen asleep under a dictatorship headed by a pudgy thirty-four-year-old man and his glamorous wife. During the night they'd sneaked away—I had to see the television images before I could believe it—the wife ornately made up, her long brown hair hidden under a white turban, her carefully manicured fingers holding a long cigarette, the husband at the wheel of the family's BMW, driving his wife and himself to the tarmac of an airport named after his dead father, from whom he'd inherited the country at nineteen, to an American airplane that would carry them to permanent exile in France. The presidential couple's reign had ended, his having lasted fifteen years and hers the span of their six-year marriage. Their departure, however, orphaned a large number of loyal militia-men, who had guarded the couple's command with all types of vicious acts. Now the population was going after those militiamen, those macoutes, with the determination of an army in the middle of its biggest battle to date. (*Dew Breaker*, p. 140)

Danticat in particular examines the amorphous liminality between fiction and reality to interrogate through the creative process the validity of clichés and presumptions present in phlegmatic statements like: "atonement, reparation, [is] possible and available for everyone" (*Dew Breaker*, p. 242). In *The Dew Breaker*, Anne, the sister of the preacher who was killed at point blank range in the Casernes prison by Bienaimé, the man who would become her husband and would father Kâ, dithers, probing her maternal trustworthiness when he finally crosses over and exposes his past *modus vivendi* to their daughter, to a member of the next generation. She wishes that the verbatim of his former *modi operandi* would permit her to account for the fear and self-hatred that embody her instinct of survival. Hoping for Kâ's forgiveness, Anne searches for the empathic words to wrap the corporeal rebellion that their daughter represents in an affectionate embrace of regret.[13]

Another such trigger from the historical past is a recurrent scene from the Papa Doc era which appears like a palimpsest in the works of authors and artists alike—men and women like Jan J. Dominique (1984) in *Mémoire d'une amnésique* (p. 66); Danticat (2010) in *Create Dangerously* (pp. 1-5, 150, et passim); Emile Ollivier (1999) in *Mille eaux* (p. 134); Blondel Débrossé (1985) in his play *Conscience criblée* (p. 2) and in *La mémoire aux abois* (pp. 65, 155) as well as *Un alligator nommé Rosa* (p. 75). The writers mark, in these works, one particular execution on November 12th, 1964 at the Port-au-Prince cemetery by a firing squad made up of seven helmeted men in khaki military uniforms, of two young men, Marcel Numa and Louis Drouin, ordered by François Duvalier. It occurred seven years into his fifteen-year term as president, and has remained etched upon human memory maybe because a public holiday was declared; all government offices and schools closed so that everyone—school children alongside army officers—would attend together with the hundreds of people, often peasants, who were bussed in from outside the capital of Port-au-Prince; and probably because the masses assembled were filmed watching as the two men were shot and the recording rebroadcast daily for a week in an eerily sinister emplotment of secondary witnessing.

Exiled in New York, Drouin had belonged to an organisation called Jeune Haïti, and in 1964 he had returned with thirteen others including Numa, his childhood friend, to "engage in a guerrilla war [...] to topple the Duvalier dictatorship" (*Create Dangerously*, p. 2) and "[a]fter months of attempting to capture the men of Jeune Haïti and after imprisoning and murdering hundreds of their relatives, Papa Doc Duvalier wanted to make a spectacle of Numa's and Drouin's deaths" (p. 2). Antoine Guibert, the male nurse and writer who has tracked down Rosa Bosquet, in Agnant's novel, points out the photo amongst the many he has posted around her room, demanding that she explain it:

> Regarde bien, Rosa, une autre photo: deux hommes, [...] la vingtaine. Ils sont beaux, vigoureux, instruits. Ils ont pour nom Numa et Drouin. On les disait généreux. Ils étaient l'avenir de leur pays; aujourd'hui ils n'ont même plus de place dans sa mémoire. Ils sont ligotés à des poteaux dressés face au mur d'un cimetière. Leurs yeux sont clairs, ouverts, ils affrontent la barbarie, et tomberont sous les rafales meurtrières de ta bande de chacals. Ils recevront le coup fatal de ton complice, Franco Néro, spécialiste, paraît-il, des coups de grâce. Allez, Rosa Bosquet, explique afin que je comprenne: au nom de quelle cause ces jeunes ont-ils été assassinés ? Vous aviez, tes accolytes et toi, exigé des écoliers qu'ils assistent à cette exécution. Pour ce crime supplémentaire, tu vas aussi payer, Rosa. Pour le regard franc de ces deux jeunes hommes que vous avez éteint ce jour-là, tu vas devoir payer, Rosa Bosquet! (*alligator*, p. 75-6)

> Look Rosa, another photo: two men [....] about twenty years old. They are handsome, strong, educated. They are called Numa and Drouin. They are said to have been generous. They were their country's future, today they don't even hold a place in its memory. They are tied to posts set up against a cemetery wall. Their eyes are unclouded, open, they confront the barbarity, and will fall under the murderous bursts of gunfire from your band of jackals. They will receive the fatal blow from your accomplice, Franco Nero, a specialist, apparently, of the coup de

grâce. Come on, Rosa, explain so that I can understand: in the name of what cause were these young men murdered? You and your acolytes insisted that school children be present at this execution. For this additional crime, you will pay too, Rosa. For the frank gaze of these two young men that you extinguished that day, you will have to pay, Rosa Bosquet!

The visual iterations of this event effectively bound and tied tongue and body into a silence that nevertheless ends up returning in the words of this multitude of works and in particular this generation of women writers who were barely ten to fourteen-year old girls and among those who could have been forced to watch the public execution, or in Danticat's case not yet born. For many then, whether present—or not even—at the execution, this story haunts and obsesses them. To Danticat, it feels like a creation myth for "aside from its heartrending clash of life and death, homeland and exile, the execution of Marcel Numa and Louis Drouin involves a disobeyed directive from a higher authority and a brutal punishment as a result" (*Create Dangerously*, p. 5) one which she places alongside Adam and Eve's disobedience when they defied "God's order not to eat what must have been the world's most desirable apple" (p. 5).

In this nexus of novels, it is disobedience that is at stake, a tactic in Michel de Certeau's sense rather than a strategy that effectively responds to militarised violence from the perspective of women working at living. Where Numa and Drouin used strategy to undermine the Duvalier regime, Danticat, Agnant and Trouillot tactically seek to uncover the halting whisperings of the Haitian torturous dictatorship and render a gift of nemesis to themselves and to all who live with the haunting silence of the past. Nemesis, the name of the Greek goddess of proportion and retribution, who was instructed by Zeus to take care of the world's harmony by chastising those who would compromise it, is derived from the Greek *neimein*—the gift of what is due. She brings down all immoderate good fortune, checks the presumption that attends it, and is the punisher of extraordinary crimes.[14] Nemesis of antiquity personifies the law establishing equilibrium in the world. Representing distributive justice through the rhythm of destiny, Nemesis recommends discretion as *modus operandi*, and retracts happiness and pride from those who live in excess, and with hubris.

Agnant and Trouillot each incorporate an eminently recognisable historical female personality as the central protagonist of their narratives to stage in their texts the encounter of victim and victimizer. They each also position their victimised characters as disobedient nurses intriguing with messages of death, moving back and forth between angrily wishing for vengeance and seeking proportional justice, until a point is attained—seemingly so improbable at the start—when they tip the scales and reach the victimizer, as if on a par with her. As adults who when they were children either lived with or witnessed the violence perpetrated on their parents, they reset the muted button. Through discourses about (gendered) violence—literal, physical and psychological—they navigate the precarity of public and private spheres of human life. They speak for themselves (and for others who have testified privately) to or alongside the two elderly women who elect to wall themselves in behind an anxious mutism. Of a single mindedness, as grown-ups having lived bound up in the unexplained, the unsayable, and the undecidable, they play out private TRCs, truth and reconciliation commissions of self and other in their tropological encounter with Nemesis.

Each of the two novels reconstructs a female historical figure, contemporaries of each other, as the central protagonist of their respective narratives. Encountering a return of Nemesis' justice, both women are now bed-bound and close to death, living in exile in France, holed up with their own form of self-imposed resentful silence. The yesteryear Commandant Rosalie Bosquet is the main character referred to in Agnant's eponymous title: *Un alligator nommé Rosa*. Described similarly as that "short, stout, bespectacled" superior to the preacher's killer in Danticat's *Dew Breaker* (p. 216) and as the "femme sanglée dans un uniforme sévère, des lunettes noires barrant son visage, un fusil à baïonnette dans les mains" (*alligator*, p. 77; "woman tightly buttoned up in a strict uniform, with dark glasses cutting across her face, a bayonet in her hand"), she has since fled Haiti and settled in Gourdaix, a remote village in the Alpes Maritimes region of the South of France. There Antoine, who witnessed as a ten year old child his parents' brutal murder upon Rosa's orders, and who has tracked her down some forty years later, has just arranged to be hired as her nurse and ghost writer-biographer. In *La mémoire aux abois*, Trouillot's prominent figure is a barely disguised Simone Duvalier, the wife of Papa Doc who fled Haiti in 1986 to settle in Paris. The novel opens some ten years later, with her hospitalisation. She is tended to by Marie-Ange, a young twenty-three year old Haitian woman, who fled Haiti with her mother to Martinique when the latter's husband was shot by the tonton macoutes in 1980, a second traumatic loss for her since her brother Jean-Édouard had been killed for participating in an opposition organisation after the public execution at the cemetery of Port-du-Roi of two anti-government men—Lionnel Dubois and Marc Noisin—in whose initials Louis Drouin and Manuel Numa are readily recognisable as the two who participate in Danticat's creation myth.

Where Rosalie loses the final syllable from her first name in Agnant's text, Simone becomes the widow of Doctor Fabien Doréval, of the dictator Fab Doc—whom she refers to as le Défunt (the Deceased). In keeping with the parodic distancing shifts within semantic fields that characterise the translations from historical reality to historicised diegesis in Trouillot's novel and that seem to help bring the unspeakable to the written page, the protagonist is known as Odile Doréval (golden vale), a name that borrows the 'val' from Duvalier and precedes it with a suffix-like 'doré' (golden) in reference to the dictatorship's ostentation and the family's embezzlement of Haitian state funds.[15] Mme Odile Doréval keeps the titles of first lady, and "gardienne de la revolution", one that her real-life model received after her son, Baby Doc displaced her when he married Michèle Benett.

Odile Doréval has consciously decided to keep silent and to take refuge in her memory in order to keep her thoughts organised, and to ensure that she does not let slip anything in front of the hospital staff so as to prevent them from talking about her and pointing her out with such mutterings as "veuve" (widow) or "dictateur" (dictator). Rendered almost an object by the gaze of the nursing staff, as well as by the binary structure of the four chapters' titles that divide up her life into her various positions and roles, the monologue that constitutes her self-ordering and remembering logically extends her life-long quest for control—of her corporeality as well as of the nation's insatisfaction—and emphasizes from the outset this very retreat into her memories with its third person voice formulation:

> Le moyen de contrôle le plus garanti demeurait finalement le silence. [....] Sa seule issue résidait dans sa capacité de maîtriser toute communication vers l'extérieur. [....] Ils arrêteraient d'essayer de lui tirer les vers du nez ou de la considérer comme la bête curieuse de la maison. Celle que l'on montre du doigt aux parents des autres pensionnaires. [....] Celle autour de laquelle les murmures s'attardent assez longtemps pour que les mots "veuve" et "dictateur" lui arrivent. A partir de maintenant, elle se laisserait faire sans prononcer une parole. Elle se réfugierait dans sa mémoire, mais il lui fallait de l'ordre, une méthode pour que ses pensées ne s'effilochent pas comme ces draps ternes qui lui recouvraient le corps. (*mémoire*, p. 9)

> In the end silence remained the surest means of control [....] Her only way out lay in her capacity to control all outward communication [....]. They would stop trying to worm her secrets out of her or considering her the strange beast of the house. The one who is pointed out to the relatives of the other residents [....] The one around whom the whispers last long enough for the words "widow" and "dictator" to reach her. From now on she would let them care for her without pronouncing a word. She would take refuge in her memory, but she needed order,

a method so that her thoughts did not fray like the drab sheets which covered her body.

The silence that has controlled all discourse within and about Haiti, which Simone Duvalier enforced, returns this time usurped to serve the ends of her simulacrum, Odile who fights the effects of her exilic unrootedness and its concurrent "démémoire" (de- or un-memory).[16]

Answering Chauvet's denunciation of hypocritical silence, and the resultant sinking of Haiti's official history into oblivion, Trouillot's novel calls to mind the switching between the story and the interior monologue which constructs the former's powerful *Amour*. Marie-Ange's first person monologue runs alongside her ward's, for neither of them speak to each other. The young Haitian working in the Parisian hospice speaks in an internal dialogue to her mother who has just died leaving so much unsaid. Yet their personal logs run through their minds day in and day out. As the two women's internally spoken words criss-cross and almost answer each other in the tense alternation and altercations of their memories, these streams of thoughts speak louder than words, and more contentiously than if they had been in dialogue.

Watching the hospice's new resident's face, Marie-Ange never has any doubts about her identity. After all the Dorévalist period's horrors that her mother had lived with and shared with her, how could she forget "[c]e visage qui symbolise pour moi aujourd'hui la somme de toutes les horreurs d'un régime qui a laissé sa marque sur mon pays d'origine?" (*mémoire*, p. 76; "this face which symbolizes for me today the sum of all the horrors of a regime which has left its mark on my country of origin?"). Giving free rein to her thoughts and dreams, and unable to contain her nightmares, she recalls her mother's stories and their years together in Martinique in an imaginary dialogue with her that mirrors the subject roles that Odile goes over in her mind. Their respective internal discourses intersect and work out their disappointments, fears, regrets, reproaches, failings as well as their inherited anxieties as they revisit and weave in the events of the 1960s, 70s and 80s. At times defiant, and at others beaten down, replete with non sequiturs, they contradict each other as they revisit Haiti's recent past from their opposite positions and different generational perspectives. Justifying Doc Fab's and her decisions, as well as their behaviour and actions, Odile's journey back through her life traverses her repeated battles for recognition from being an orphan to ending up as a lonely widow. Where she remembers the creation of "cité Odile" as her consecration, Marie-Ange recalls what she dismisses as insignificant details:

Elle donnait son nom à ce quartier où la misère inhumaine s'installait jambes ouvertes et fesses au vent. Donnait son nom comme une gifle à la désespérance de ces gens qui vivotaient, sans eau potable, sans latrines, dans des taudis poussant comme de la mauvaise herbe sur une terre boueuse. Sans direction ni dignité. Elle osait se montrer fière dans sa robe de soie aux manches longues et son chapeau d'imposture. Première Dame, pseudonyme de l'avilissement endimanché. (*mémoire*, p. 78)

She gave her name to this neighbourhood where inhuman misery established itself with legs spread open and buttocks to the wind. Gave her name like a slap in the face to the desperation of these people who subsisted, without drinking water, without latrines, in hovels sprouting like weeds on muddy ground. Without direction or dignity. She dared to appear in her long-sleeved silk gown and her hat of deception. First Lady, pseudonym for Sunday-best degradation.

Repeatedly, Marie-Ange recalls her mother's stories of loneliness and the self-imposed silence of fear that determined family relationships in response to new governmental decrees determining that meetings of all sorts—public and private—were forbidden.

Gradually she returns to her notes about the Dorévals and assigns them to her computer confessing to finding herself both drawn to the invalid and disgusted by this urge in her:

Avec un mélange de fascination et de ressentiment. De dégoût aussi envers moi-même, car je refrène difficilement les élans qui me poussent mon travail terminé vers le lit, dans cette chambre [....] Ma mémoire s'affole, emmêlée entre souvenirs et réalités, assiégée par tes cauchemars et mes rêves à moi. (*mémoire*, p. 129)

With a mixture of fascination and resentment, Of disgust too towards myself, for I curb with difficulty the momentum which thrusts me, my work finished, towards the bed, in this room [....] My memory panics, muddled between souvenirs and realities, besieged by your nightmares and my own dreams.

In a *dialogue de sourds*—or like sleeptalkers (night-talkers as Danticat designates them in *The Dew Breaker*) who can only talk away their troubles in their sleep—they rewrite history as their own story, with the tactics of their criss-crossed, over-lapping yet silent logs.

Similarly in *Un alligator nommé Rosa*, Antoine is assailed by his memories and his years of research into Rosa Bosquet. He however does not leave her to her silence. He confronts her and determines the course of her writing project for it is his intent to extort a signed affidavit from her after he has constituted her case with her in order to understand how she could be, like the alligator, so pitiless and remorseless in the execution of her victims.

He arranges about the enclosed space of her bedroom the incriminating evidence of his collective archive and testimonials that he has gathered alongside his own embodied knowledge.[17] As he sets up his "end game" he plays testimonial recordings and adds in her notebooks and all that she herself has brought with her from Haïti, before instigating a tête-à-tête trial to push her to confess by using the same evidentiary-seeking methods as she utilised:

> Demain, je viendrais avec le nécessaire pour te photographier, te filmer pendant le repas. Il est des moments qu'il faut immortaliser! On dit que, dans le temps, tu aimais bien photographier tes proies, les voir souffrir ne te suffisait pas, tu collectionnais leurs souffrances également. (*alligator*, p. 72)

> Tomorrow I will come with what I need to photograph you, to film you during the meal. There are moments which must be immortalized! They say that, at the time, you liked to photograph your prey. To see them suffer wasn't enough for you, you also collected their sufferings.

Wishing desperately that she might have been madly inspired to become a celluloid heroine, that she might lie, or that she might try to make him believe that she was not responsible, that it was the men with whom she drank, ate and fornicated that had transformed her into a bloody jackal and forced her into performing such acts, he waits for the moment to confront her with her crime against his father and mother:

> Tu n'aurais jamais cru te retrouver un jour prisonnière de ton passé? Malheur à toi, Rosa! La preuve nous est donnée tous les jours que les victimes peuvent dépasser en cruauté et de milliers de coudées leurs bourreaux d'hier. La malveillance des uns finit-elle par s'imprimer, encre indélébile... parvient-elle à s'inscrire dans les cellules des autres? Malheur à toi, Rosa Bosquet, car ce fameux livre que tu prétends vouloir écrire, ce fameux livre s'écrira, mais il ne sera rien d'autre que les minutes de ton procès! (*alligator*, p. 73)

> You would never have thought that you'd find yourself one day a prisoner of your past? Woe betide you, Rosa! We are given proof every day that the victims can exceed in cruelty and by thousands of cubits their former tormentors. Does the malevolence of some end up by imprinting itself, indelible ink ...does it succeed in inscribing itself in the cells of others? Woe betide you, Rosa Bosquet, for this infamous book that you claim to want to write, this infamous book will be written, but it will be nothing more than the record of your trial.

He has been hired to help her write her memoirs by Laura Bosquet, a fellow orphan, who is caring for Rosa after the latter adopted her and tried to transform her into one of the young girls that as the Commandant, she trained to become the Fiyèt Lalo.

Agnant who lived her own childhood in the shadow of the dictatorship's hubris creates two characters caught up in trauma's web, exacting answers as nemesis' request for what is due from each other and from Rosa, answers to explain the crimes perpetrated against them and others like Numa and Drouin too:

> – C'est vrai, crie-t-il, il n'existe aucun châtiment à la mesure des crimes de Rosa Bosquet! Il n'est de loi que l'on puisse inscrire dans sa chair ! Un seul choix s'impose malgré tout, à moi, à nous, Laura: faire régner notre propre justice, celle de deux être bafoués, deux êtres dont elle a détruit l'existence. La justice ne doit pas être un vain mot ! La justice ne doit pas être un vain mot ! (*alligator*, p. 101)

> – It's true, he cried, there is no punishment that fits the crimes of Rosa Bosquet! There is no law that one can inscribe on her flesh! One single choice imposes itself after all, on me, on us, Laura: making our own justice prevail, that of two jilted beings, two beings whose existence she destroyed. Justice must not be a vain word! Justice must not be a vain word!

With the third person narrator as nemesis repeatedly giving the floor to Antoine's and Laura's interior monologues and dialogues, their enunciations express a form of "refusal", of "protest", or what Certeau (1994) sees as a violent gesture of denial that pushes back against their inexistence (*Prise de parole*, p. 41),[18] and as a form of emancipation from their suffering in silence. Laura asks herself: "Comment guérir de la parole bannie?" (*alligator*, p. 99; "How can one recover from the banished word?") remembering Rosa's threats: "Ne rien dire, tu entends! Apprends à te taire ! Faudra-t-il te couper la langue ?" (p. 99; "Say nothing, do you understand? Learn to be silent! Must your tongue be cut out?"). Antoine's intrusion into her space unlocks the mutism that Rosa Bosquet has imposed upon her, and brings her gradually, in the novel's second part, to face her own contradictory feelings of detestation and recognition, the years she has spent in France unable to leave Rosa, and all that she has kept to herself:

> ...en tant qu'êtres humains, n'avons-nous pas la possibilité de diriger à notre gré notre mémoire, de sélectionner ce qui doit l'encombrer ou non? N'est-ce pas, en réalité, ce qu'elle-même avait toujours fait, s'accommoder, malgré elle ? Trahison infâme de l'âme. [....] "C'était là le prix de la survie, Laura. D'où te serait venue la force de te rebâtir une vie nouvelle?" [....] Cette même voix sans cesse... depuis ce jour où elle avait compris que sa vie et celle de Rosa étaient liées et qu'aucune

terre ne serait assez vaste pour toute la haine qu'elle ressent pour Rosa. (*alligator*, p. 122)

… as human beings, do we not have the possibility of directing our memory as we please, of selecting what should or should not clutter it up? Is it not, in reality, what she herself has always done, compromise despite herself? Infamous betrayal of the soul […] "It was the price of survival, Laura. Where would you have got the strength to rebuild a new life for yourself?" […] This same unceasing voice … from the day when she had understood that her life and Rosa's were bound together and that no land would be vast enough for all the hatred that she felt for Rosa.

Together Antoine and Laura, two orphans of everything, except of their memory (*alligator*, p. 126), wait on each other's time, exchange listening and speaking. Opening up to each other, they share stories long locked away.

As they give cognition to their fears, cowardice, resentment and death wishes, they confront Rosa's self-enforced muteness with her heinous crimes wanting her to ask for forgiveness, to sign her own accusation. Gradually, they reach the point when they come to the decision to institutionalise her in a hospice where she can await her death wheelchair-bound, watching, on the news, similar horrors to those she perpetrated and had broadcast, in places resembling Haiti. In the novel's last chapter, the two orphans turn their back on their alligator and break out of the dead-lock that has paralysed their life. No longer caught in her grip, they depart, leaving her to eat in front of her nemesis: a TV screen distributing haunting testimonial images of the hubris of human militarised violence, like that of a young soldier whose gaze locks on an old woman hanging on to an olive tree next to her burnt-out home.

In *La mémoire aux abois*, Marie-Ange too considers calling a vaudou priest in, using toxic substances, resorting to asphyxia; she wishes her ward would identify herself, face justice and look to her memory until, with Christmas drawing near, the immobile form of her charge seems to interpellate her. She places her hand on her arm calling out to her as she quickly withdraws to the doorway, even expresses a grateful thank you when Marie-Ange still in dialogue with her absent mother wipes the widow's tears brought on by the latter's on-going third person monologic historicising project. Wondering about her gesture of kindness, Marie-Ange's memory gradually escapes the barbed scars imprisoning it in secret wounds ("Sommes-nous prisonniers de notre mémoire ou serait-elle plutôt tributaire de nos blessures secrètes et de nos défaillances? Incapable de s'épandre lorsque nos cicatrices s'accumulent et l'encerclent de barbelés ensanglantés", *mémoire*, p. 177; "Are we prisoners of our memory or would it rather be dependent upon our secret wounds and our failures? Incapable of spreading when our scars accumulate and encircle it with bloodstained barbs") and while she readies herself to bid farewell to her ghosts, she instinctively saves the widow by sounding the alarm: "J'aurais pu la laisser mourir. Simplement. En ne faisant rien. En ne disant rien. Mais tu sais bien, maman, tu avais toujours su que je n'aurais jamais pu la laisser mourir. Il y a déjà tant de morts autour de moi" (*mémoire*, p. 186; "I could have let her die. Quite simply. By doing nothing. By saying nothing. But you know very well, mummy, you always knew, that I could never have let her die. There are already so many dead around me"). Instead of killing her retributively with her own hands, Marie-Ange surveys in her mind's eye as though she were on a reconnaissance flight, many of those killed—anonymous, forgotten who happened to sell some rice to the Thirteen; to be the mother of a militant; or be run over by one of the president's cars—for being alive at the wrong time in the wrong place, as if she were following Nemesis' charge. As the room closes in on both of them, isolating them, pushing out the past, its ghosts, the regrets and the reproaches, she elects to sit and wait by the body that she has just pulled from death's door, giving Odile her due.

None of these works circumscribe a neat conclusion. Rather this nexus of novels dissolves tactically the silence that allowed Papa and Baby Doc, Simone Duvalier and Rosalie Bosquet to perpetrate the crimes that they committed. Between the lines that historical actions and annals stress in bold, channels for long muffled, unheard and muted voices are written in. The novels probe the darkness that contained the hushed fear-filled conversations of the authors' parents' generation in advance of and in ways that account for the possibility of Jean-Claude Duvalier's return to Haïti. Their characters' internal monologues, soliloquies and *dialogues de sourds*—spoken, shouted, held back, inscribed into diaries and files—serve a charge to the reader as tropological figure of Nemesis. With the former instigators and perpetrators of the executions, the rapes, and the torture, who enjoyed their fear-inspiring unjust advantage for so long, now diegetically ex-isled, de-mobilised and im-mobilised, the children of their victims engage in voicing the trauma of the unexplained and of the unspoken that haunts them. By retelling even imperfect composites of traumatic encounters with the Duvalier/Doréval reign of terror, whether to herself as Marie-Ange does, or to Rosa and with Laura in Antoine's case, the private and public versions interconnect to fill in gaps in understanding horrific witnessed scenes left unexplained, under-silence. Coming between disappeared parent(s) and the instigators of the crimes (against humanity), these characters come to a—*con/naissance*[19]—a knowledge and co-birth with the gift that is due. Seeking to find balance,[20] they do not nurse to heal, but to accept a restorative e/motion of *reconnaissance*—a reconnoitering move of redress, feeling its way towards self-knowing and recognition.

A fellow Caribbean writer from the Dominican Republic, Junot Díaz characterises Danticat's work as being about "how one deals with historical silence and amnesia—national, personal, inter-generational" (cited by Jaggi in *The Guardian*, 2004); "her fiction gives voice to unspeakable grief and trauma, genocide and torture" and as the author ascertains herself, *The Dew Breaker* enables one to "look at the human face of the dictatorship. We knew the Tontons Macoutes, went to school with their children. I wanted to explore the aftermath on another generation" (Jaggi, 2004). Robert Antoni adds that "[i]nverting the story [as Danticat does] allows us to enter it as a puzzle with pieces missing, so we have to reconstruct it" (Jaggi, 2004). Each of these dangerous creative works reconstruct the past and etch out a space where the unspoken of the past becomes a conciliation for the self—the protagonists of the respective novels and those hurt by the regime—and structures text as a means to distributive redress, as an evidential form of disobedience that unclenches the powerful's hold over those egregiously treated. Nemeses all, Edwige Danticat, Marie-Célie Agnant and Évelyne Trouillot, women writers each in her own manner, disobey by writing in side by side soliloquies that arch up against one another, that cut across each other, that cull a shared event to sound out a polyphony of counteracting engagements devoid of simplification. Interacting with one another, the constructed multidirectional memories weigh in on the silences of the past to trigger their open circulation. Mnemonic performances on the page, the novels counter the nostalgic Sweet Mickey strains playing on the airwaves and, facing the dread, they drum out the ellipses of selective memories, to plead for a cognisant nemesis.

Notes

I thank the Center for Latin American and Caribbean Studies at the University of Wisconsin-Milwaukee for its travel grant in support of the presentation of this work. I am indebted to Myriam Chancy and Renée Larrier for their generosity in sharing their insights into these works as well as their knowledge of Haitian society; and to Brenda Davies for translating the quotations from the original texts.

1. To further this aleatory situation, Aristide also returned, after what appears as much dithering, on the eve of the second round of the presidential elections (March 21, 2011) which placed Michel Martelly, alias Sweet Micky the popular Kompa pop star, ahead of Mirlande Manigat and therefore as president-elect of the Republic of Haiti. The uncertainty still surrounding Aristide's own departure from the Haitian presidency in 2004–often referred to as a coup-napping–and the banning of his Lavalas party from the 2010-2011 elections raised predictions of violence and reprisals just like those that occurred immediately following the departure of Jean-Claude Duvalier in 1986, as Danticat writes in her chapter "Monkey Tails" in *The Dew Breaker*.

2. As William Booth (2012, Jan. 17) reported in "In Haiti, Former Dictator Baby Doc Duvalier is thriving," *The Washington Post*, Duvalier was giving commencement speeches; and attending memorial services to the victims of the 2010 earthquake alongside President Martelly, former president Prosper Avril and former US president Bill Clinton right up to his fateful heart attack on October 4, 2014.

3. See Bob Corbett's former haiti@lists.webster.edu and current moderator@corbethaiti.org for regularly posts about Haiti. A 7 January 2011 post entitled "Victims of Duvalier Regime" included the following links to lists of victims:
http://haitiforever.com/bbs/mensajes/66.html; and to those of Fort Dimanche: http://www.fordi9.com/page/Victlist/ListA.htm. The extensive legal documentation of Mr. Duvalier's crimes includes: A July 3, 2009 order from the First Court of Public Law of the Federal Court of Switzerland, which notes that the Haitian government had informed it of current criminal proceedings against Mr. Duvalier as late as June 2008; the Decision of the U.S. District Court for the Southern District of Florida, Jean-Juste v. Duvalier, No. 86-0459, dated January 8, 1988, finding Mr. Duvalier liable for over US$500,000,000 for his misappropriation of public monies for his personal use; and an extensive accounting of Mr. Duvalier's misappropriation of public funds conducted for the Haitian government by a U.S. accounting firm between 1986 and 1990, establishing the theft of over US$300,000,000 of public funds. This legal documentation is supplemented by an extensive public record of Mr. Duvalier's human rights violations, including the torture and the disappearance of political dissidents at the Fort Dimanche prison.

4. The September 2013 reports regarding the cosmetic prettification of the Jalousie quarter of Port-au-Prince address the Martelly government's lack of enforcement or compliance with structural building requirements since the 2010 earthquake: "it is in the process of spending over US$6 million on the slum, but not to deal with the double danger–the neighbourhood sits on a secondary faultline and rain run off causes precipitous mudslides–nor to provide the basic services like water and electricity distribution. Instead, the administration is doing what some have called a "make-up job"–painting the houses in a project called "Jalousie en couleurs" (Jalousie in Colour), as a homage–one he would surely have found horrendously ironic–to the Haitian painter Préfète Duffaut (1923-2012) who often filled his paintings with brightly colored hillside houses (see Haiti Grassroots Watch's "The Jalousie Project: Make-up for Misery" in "This week in Haiti, " *Haiti Liberté* 7: 11 (Sept. 25 - Oct. 1, 2013) http://www.haitiliberte.com.

5. Sue Montgomery. "Frustration follows Duvalier ruling" in *The Montreal Gazette* (Feb 3, 2012) http://www.montrealgazette.com/news/Frustration+follows+Duvalier+ruling/6095084/story.html (retrieved Feb. 6, 2012). As a young girl, Jan J. Dominique fled the Duvalier dictatorship with her father Jean Dominique. Since his gunning on April 3, 2000 in front of Radio Inter, the radio station that he directed, she has been fighting with her step mother to bring the assassins to justice. See Jonathan Demme's film *The Agronomist* for details about Jean Léopold Dominique's engagement in Haiti's socio-politics. J. J. Dominique's re-edition in Montréal of *Mémoire d'une amnésique* in 2004, twenty years after the original edition published during Baby Doc's dictatorship in Port-au-Prince, fills in many of the allusive references of the first version.

6. This renewed feeling of the necessity of self muzzling was anxiously expressed during the question period of a session on the Haitian women's recent works, discussed in this article at the 23rd Annual Haitian Studies Association (HSA) conference which was held at the University of the West Indies, Mona campus, Kingston, Jamaica in November 2011.

7. Two novels by women writers were published a few months apart: Trouillot's on January 13, 2010, a day after the earthquake, and Agnant's later in May 2010, in time for the St Malo meeting of Étonnants Voyageurs which transferred to its Britanny setting its Haitian edition of the book fair that had been planned to open in Port-au-Prince on January 13, 2010.

8. Kettly Mars published *Saisons sauvages* also in early 2010. Clearly situating her diegesis during the Duvalier dictatorship, one peopled with characters that might easily be identified with historically recognisable individuals, this author does not, as do Agnant and Trouillot and to a lesser degree Danticat, use well known and recognisable (named) figures such as Papa Doc's wife and Rosalie Bosquet as a protagonist of her story. Instead as Yves Chemla indicates, Mars unlocks the secrecy of intimacy in a story of an atrocious gendered master-slave relationship which holds the two protagonists in an impossible deadlock *(Culture Sud)*. Their complicit liaison reconstructs the past through dangerous (re)readings: diegetic of the two male protagonists' past – the diary of her husband, Daniel Leroy, and the revolutionary past of her lover, the secretary of state for public safety, Raoul Vincent – and intertextual with canonical Haitian literary texts (as John Walsh explained during his presentation at the 2011 HSA meeting in Jamaica) (John Walsh, see previous note) as well as with Danticat's *The Dew Breaker*.

9. Where the feminist movement of the women in Haiti and in the diaspora had experienced a second or double stifling and curtailing as a result of American imperialism and of the Duvalier regimes as Myriam Chancy elaborates in ""No Giraffes in Haiti": Haitian Women and State Terror", the current w/ri(gh)ting out of women's perspectives on such silencing and absence in the literature seems to organise a different discourse around their participatory resistance to the patriarchal and the state's violence perpetuated against those without a voice or a power base, one which is beginning to remedy the "textual ellipsis"–the lacunae–that Marie Chauvet perhaps most evidently bridged with her trilogy and with *Les rapaces* [written between 1971 and 1973] in *Écrire en pays assiégé Haïti Writing under Siege*, eds. Marie-Agnès Sourieau & Kathleen M. Balutansky (p. 308).

10. Marie Célie Agnant's father who was in hiding in the countryside when she was a young girl, was abducted by the tonton-macoutes who followed him to his home when he attempted to visit his family. He was never seen again. She was then adopted and her second father did all he could to help her forget this cruel disappearance. Continually harassed by the coming and going of the dictatorship's henchmen, he decided despite his advanced age to go into exile with her and his family to Quebec, in Canada (*alligator* [2010], pp. 189-90).

11. Rosalie Bosquet Adolphe alias Mme Max Adolphe, as head of the VSN (Volontaires de la Sécurité Nationale otherwise known as tonton macoutes) and of the Fyèt Lalo, a women's militia that she created, led in particular the section known as Mie Jeanne under Papa Doc before leaving her position and Haiti in 1986. During this time, she was responsible, among other murderous actions, for the fire set to rase the Saline quarter (that burnt numerous babies to death) in order to create the Cité Simone, so named after Papa Doc's wife.

12. The formulation of "ex-îlé" (transl. ex-isled) is Joël Des Rosiers (1996), from *Théories caraïbes: Poétique du déracinement*.

13. Simon Baron-Cohen (2011), in *Zero Degrees of Empathy: A New Theory of Human Cruelty*, explains a lack of empathy as a mechanism which has been triggered in childhood by some awful experiences which then subdues or disengages activity in certain parts of the brain. Having empathy for those who lack it becomes a question which these novels address as have those who have been part of the Rwandese gacaca courts and the South African Truth and Reonciliation Commission, and other such instances.

14. These definitions are drawn from the (1989*) Oxford English Dictionary*, 2nd Edition, Oxford: Clarendon Press and the *Trésor de la langue française*, the dictionary of the Académie française. The common noun 'nemesis' was removed from the latter in 2011. In Roman mythology: Nemesis is also Invidia representing indignation before an unjust advantage.

15. Other such transformations include a geo-political nomenclature whereby Haiti becomes 'Quisqueya' one of the names historically associated with the island while the capital shifts differentially from Port-au-Prince to Port-du-Roi, from prince's port to king's port. Other recognizable switches play with figures of speech, moving from metonymic to synecdochal references as when the political group Jeune Haïti becomes les Treize (the Thirteen), or use similar metaphors to denote their role as end places in referencing key sites that are indelibly marked with the imprimatur of the Duvalier era, as is the case with Fort Dimanche turning into Fort Décembre.

16. Antoine calls their island the "pays de la démémoire" (*alligator*, p. 170).

17. Antoine Guibert's memory rests upon having witnessed, forty years, before his parents' assassination at the age of ten and upon the trauma of his ensuing adoption with its concomitant loss of identity as he was renamed which gives him that (generational) remove. As such for the reader, it is not and yet is what Marianne Hirsch calls 'post-memory' for Antoine practices "citation"; looks back as a result of traumatic recall; and bases his memories on others' accounts as he regains his own self and identity ("The generation of Postmemory" *Poetics* 29:1 (Spring 2008), pp. 103-128).

18. Michel de Certeau (1994) in *La prise de parole et autres écrits politiques*, indicates that by taking the floor, the person is stating that s/he is not nothing, s/he exists (p. 41).

19. I borrow this homonymic wordplay of *connaissance* as knowledge and shared or co-birth from Catherine A. F. MacGillivray's preface to her (1998) translation of Hélène Cixous' *Firstdays of the Year*, p. xxi, in which she indicates that she is reiterating Paul Claudel's idea.

20. In understanding mourning, Elizabeth Kubler-Ross' fifth step–acceptance--comes after four stages of grief: denial, anger, bargaining, depression; each of which play a part in the development and process that Agnant's and Trouillot's characters undergo as they face Rosa and Odile respectively.

References

Agnant, M.-C. (2007, 2011). *Un alligator nommé Rosa*. La Roque d'Anthéron: Vents d'ailleurs.

Baron-Cohen, S. (2011). *Zero Degrees of Empathy: A New Theory of Human Cruelty*. UK: Allen Lane Publishing.

Booth, W. (2012, 17 January). In Haiti, former dictator Baby Doc Duvalier is thriving. *The Washington Post*. Retrieved from http://www.washingtonpost.com/world/americas/in-haiti-the-former-dictator-duvalier-thrives/2012/01/13/gIQAaYbM6P_story.html

Débrossé, B. (1985*)*. *Conscience criblée*. Montréal: CIDIHCA.

Certeau, M. de. (1990). *L'invention du quotidien, 1. Arts de faire*. Paris: Gallimard.

Certeau, M. de. (1994*)*. *La prise de parole et autres écrits politiques*. Paris: Seuil.

Chancy, M. (2004). "No Giraffes in Haiti": Haitian Women and State Terror. In M.-A. Sourieau & K. M. Balutansky, Eds., *Écrire en pays assiégé Haïti Writing under Siege* (pp. 303-321). Amsterdam: Rodopi.

Chauvet, M. Vieux. (1968). *Amour, Colère, Folie*. Paris: Gallimard.

Chauvet, M. Vieux. (1986*)*. *Les rapaces*. Port-au-Prince: Deschamps.

Chemla, Y. (2010). Notes de lecture: Kettly Mars, *Saisons sauvages. Cultures Sud: littératures du Sud*. Retrieved from http://www.culturessud.com/contenu,php?id=157

Daniel, T. (2011, January 17). Duvalier's return to Haiti puzzling. *The Miami Herald*. Retrieved March 20, 2011, from http://www.miamiherald.com/2011/01/17/2019547/observers-duvaliers-return-puzzling.html.

Danticat, E. (2010). *Create Dangerously: The Immigrant Artist at Work*. Princeton: Princeton University Press.

Danticat, E. (2004). *The Dew Breaker*. NY: Alfred A. Knopf.

Des Rosiers, J. (1996). *Théories caraïbes, Poétique du déracinement*. Montréal: Éditions Triptyque.

Dominique, J. J. (1984). *Mémoire d'une amnésique*. Port-au-Prince: Eds Deschamps.

Jaggi, M. (2004, November 19). Island memories. *The Guardian*. Retrieved April 19, 2011, from http://www.guardian.co.uk/books/2004/nov/20/featuresreviews.guardianreview9.

Hirsch, M. (Spring 2008). The Generation of Postmemory. *Poetics* 29:1, 103-128.

Kubler-Ross, E. (2005). *On Grief and Grieving: Finding the Meaning of Grief Through the Five Stages of Loss*. N.Y.: Simon & Schuster Ltd.

Laraque, F. (2008, September 1). Haiti: Il n'y a pas de bons duvaliéristes. *Alterpresse*. Retrieved April 19, 2011, from http://elsie-news.over-blog.com/article-33665744.html

MacGillivray, C. A. F. (1998), trans. *Hélène Cixous, Firstdays of the Year*. Minneapolis: University of Minnesota Press.

Mars, K. (2010). *Saisons sauvages*. Paris: Mercure de France.

Mauss, M. (1923-24). Essai sur le don. Forme et raison de l'échange dans les sociétés archaïques. *Année sociologique* 1, 30-186.

Montgomery, S. (2012, February 3). Frustration follows Duvalier ruling. *The Montreal Gazette*. Retrieved February 6, 2012, from http://www.montrealgazette.com/news/Frustra tion+follows+ Duvalier+ruling/ 6095084/story.html

Ollivier, É. (1999). *Mille eaux*. Paris: Gallimard.

Oxford English Dictionary. (1989). 2nd edition. Oxford: Clarendon Press.

Trésor de la langue française. http://atilf.atilf.fr/

Trouillot, É. (2010). *La mémoire aux abois*. Paris: Eds Hoëbeke.

Chapter 12
Intergenerational Jewish Trauma in the Contemporary South African Novel

Ewald Mengel

University of Vienna, Austria

Introduction

Jewish people have been living in South Africa from the beginning of white settlement, but only in the second half of the 19th century, there is a notable rise in numbers (Shain & Mendelsohn, 2008). The Jewish population had its peak in the seventies of the 20th century with roughly 120 000, but, due to emigration, this number has dropped to about 80 000 in the present, most of them living in the areas of Johannesburg (around 60%) and Cape Town (around 20%). Even if the Jewish community in South Africa forms only a relatively small minority of the total population, it can boast quite a few well-known figures, for example, Helen Suzman, Jo Slovo, Ruth First, and Albie Sachs.

A number of Jewish authors have chosen to write about the life of Jewish people within the South African context. Family sagas such as Maya Kriel (2004), *Rings in a Tree*, Joanne Fedler (2005), *The Dreamcloth*, or Patricia Schonstein (2007), *A Quilt of Dreams*, relate the fate of different generations of Jewish immigrants to South Africa. They form part of the great number of trauma novels written after the fall of apartheid. In the South African context, they give the authors the opportunity to thematise collective, transgenerational, and multiple traumatisation: Collective, because not only families but a whole community (the Jews) are concerned; intergenerational, because the traumas of the grandparents and parents are handed down to the children (Volkan, 2009); and multiple, because the protagonists suffer from more than just one trauma: from the holocaust, the collective trauma of their community, which is kept alive in the memories of the survivors, and from the individual traumas they suffer for various reasons in the course of their lifetime in a South Africa that, especially in the time before WW II but also after the war under the apartheid government of the National Party, seems to be sharing a fascist ideology, if not clearly anti-semitic sentiments (Gilbert, 2010).

In the following, I should like to concentrate on Patricia Schonstein's *A Quilt of Dreams* and Joanne Fedler's *The Dreamcloth*, two novels in which "cloth" figures prominently in the novels' titles. From a literary point of view, the "dreamcloth" and the "quilt" are the novels' central symbols. Psychologically speaking, they play the role of transitional objects. According to Winnicott, little children use dolls, teddy bears or 'safety blankets' as substitutes of the mother/child bond. However, the concept signifies more than just a mother Ersatz. As Robert M. Young explains, Winnicott believes that the transitional object is "the fundamental element of culture, the way into the world of play, creativity, including the arts, religion and science" (Young, 1994, pp. 145-146).

In the trauma novel, the transitional objects help the traumatised persons to find their way back into normality. The objects are 'transitional' in a double sense of the word: 1) They are handed on from one generation to the other, and 2) they become important 'markers' that signify the transition from a traumatised state back into normal life. As "linking objects" (Volkan, 2009) they help to mourn the loss of a beloved person. More generally speaking, they play an important role in the coping process which allows the traumatised persons 'to get on' with their lives—if not to thrive in the aftermath of trauma. At the end of these novels, the giving away of the transitional object to somebody else who needs it more than the original owner is a symbol for the beginning of a healing process that seems to be promising a better future. Both novels I have chosen for closer analysis show the survivors' 'taking on' of their traumas, their struggles, and their final success. If trauma cannot be overcome completely, it can at least be "shackled," "handcuffed" in such a way that surviving—sometimes even thriving—in the aftermath becomes possible.

Winnicott's theory of transitional objects is widely known. In the following quotation, he explains this phenomenon with regard to infants:

> It is well known that infants as soon as they are born tend to use fist, fingers, thumbs in stimulation of the oral erotogenic zone, in satisfaction of the instincts at that zone, and also in quiet union. It is also well known that after a few months infants of either sex become fond of playing with dolls, and that most mothers allow their infants some special object and expect them to become, as it were, addicted to such objects. There is a relationship between these two sets of phenomena that are separated by a time interval, and a study of the development from the earlier into the later can be profitable, and can make use of important clinical material that has been somewhat neglected. (p. 1)

Less well-known is the fact that not only dolls, teddy bears or blankets can fulfil this role but any kind of object which has a relevance to the person concerned. In this context, Winnicott's case study of a young boy suffering from separation anxiety becomes interesting. As Winnicott reports, fearing the separation from his mother the boy develops a predilection for strings:

> String can be looked upon as an extension of all other techniques of communication. String joins, just as it also helps in the wrapping up of objects and in the holding of unintegrated material. In this respect string has a symbolic meaning for everyone; an exaggeration of the use of string can easily belong to the beginnings of a sense of insecurity or the idea of a lack of communication. In this particular case it is possible to detect abnormality creeping into the boy's use of string, and it is important to find a way of stating the change which might lead to its use becoming perverted. It would seem possible to arrive at such a statement if one takes into consideration the fact that the function of the string is changing from communication into a denial of separation. As a denial of separation string becomes a thing in itself, something that has dangerous properties and must needs be mastered. In this case the mother seems to have been able to deal with the boy's use of string just before it was too late, when the use of it still contained hope. When hope is absent and string represents a denial of separation, then a much more complex state of affairs has arisen, one that becomes difficult to cure, because of the secondary gains that arise out of the skill that develops whenever an object has to be handled in order to be mastered. (p. 13)

As Winnicott emphasises here, the fixation on a transitional object can easily become perverted, namely when it becomes a "thing in itself" that "must needs be mastered," a kind of fetish that has taken possession of the person's mind. This happens when the borderlines between play and reality collapse, when the transitional object does no longer 'represent' but becomes identical with reality.

In Winnicott's theory, the transition from childhood to adulthood implies playing, symbolising, 're-lating' and 're-cognition'. It is interesting to note here that successful attempts of coping with trauma point into the same direction. In the novels to be analysed, the giving away of the transitional object to someone else who seems to be in greater need of it, signals an important step in the healing process of the traumatised character.

Both novels that I want to analyse make use of cloth as their central symbols. Cloth consists of individual threads or 'strings' woven together with the purpose of forming a texture that 'holds', does not come apart again. It goes without saying that sewing as an activity—which is symbolically very prominent in both novels—has the same purpose. Apart from the mythological intertexts that sewing and weaving create, it is also important in this context that especially women are related to it. Finally, sewing and weaving may be understood as metaphors for narrative construction and novel writing, which adds a metafictional level of self-reflection that contributes to the complexity of these novels. The novelists, 'weavers of words', thus make their contributions to the overcoming of trauma by way of their art.

Joanne Fedler (2005), *The Dreamcloth*

This novel's title is inspired by W.B. Yeats' poem "He Wishes For the Cloths of Heaven", which thematises in Romantic fashion the power of the imagination. Joanne Fedler's *The Dream Cloth* deals with various traumas of a Jewish family, handed on from generation to generation. In the first generation, Maya, a Jewish woman, emigrates from the little village of Kovno in Lithuania to South Africa, following her husband Yankel, although, by doing so, she has to leave her lesbian lover Rochel behind (who later commits suicide). Her marriage is not a happy one: Since she can no longer endure Yankel's insensitive sexual approaches, she sews herself up after having given birth to Issey. In this context, sewing takes on a bitterly ironic meaning. Otherwise meant to hold things together, it here is used to shield off the male approach and to separate the male from the female.

In the second generation, the talented painter Issey suffers from the early death of his mother Maya—who leaves him the dreamcloth (a present of Maya's lover Rochel, the seamstress). He loses his emotionally frigid wife Fran to Rochel's son Asher, who lives in Israel but also turns up in South Africa and who has sworn to take revenge on Maya's family. He takes his life when he feels that he has lost both his wife and his daughter to this stranger.

In the present (1994), Issey's daughter Mia, a gifted poet and journalist, is traumatised by her Jewish heritage, by her job as journalist (which brings her into contact with rape victims of the fights in Bosnia-Herzegowina), by the emotional coldness of her mother Fran and the suicide of her father Issey.

Joanne Fedler's *The Dreamcloth* is framed by a paratext implying that the whole novel itself is a long, extended diary. The headings of the individual parts of the novel and the chapter headings are printed in a font that suggests handwriting, thus underlining the subjectivity and privacy of the narration and the importance of the diary form. For Mia, writing is a form of self-realisation: she writes down her dreams, her inner life, her hidden feelings and thoughts. For her, writing also has to do with the holocaust: Writing keeps the memory alive, puts the Jewish fate on the map and safeguards it against being forgotten:

> There she sat, pen poised at the page's surface, until wick was consumed by candle wax or the sound of footsteps crushed the voice. She watched her hand

move across the page, its letters sometime neatly touching the lines, at other times crossing them, a swelling growing in her breast that never failed to cause her to weep. As long as she put ink to the page, her hidden life was not forgotten, not wiped out in a pogrom, not buried in an unmarked grave, despite the days and hours she had to live outside of the writing. (p. 76)

Mia's writing is aimed at the ghosts of the past: the holocaust and the nightmares of her people which she inherits from her grandparents, her own personal nightmares, caused, for example, by the coldness of her mother and the suicide of her father, and the traumatising sights and testimonies she has to witness as a journalist reporting about the pogroms in Bosnia-Herzegowina in 1994, especially about women who were raped, tortured, or killed.

Most of the novel's story is set in the Johannesburg of 1994, but there are many flashbacks into the past, focussing in the first generation on Maya and her husband Yankel, Maya's lesbian relationship with Rochel, and her unhappy marriage. In the second generation, the story concerns Maya's son Issey, Mia's father and a talented painter, and his wife Fran, Mia's mother. In the third generation, the present, we witness the restless wanderings of Mia, who has inherited Maya's poetic talent but also her father's artistic ability and vulnerability. The structure of this novel, its shuttling between past and present, emphasises the idea that trauma is omnipresent, that it is handed down from the past, and that it is very difficult to get rid of it in the present.

The dreamcloth is the novel's transitional object and its central symbol. The dreamcloth is sewn by Rochel, the seamstress, who gives it as a present to Maya:

From the dark seam between her bosom, she drew out a piece of cloth, no bigger than a small handkerchief, and held it flat in the palm of her hand. Maya did not know where to look first or longest—into her palm or her eyes, for in both she saw tricks of light and sleights of wonder, a glimmer of blue silk, a copper sequin, a moon of filigree lace, a rosebud of buttons, woven cobblestones of amber and jade. Maya was made to think of meadows in starlight and rainbows after thunder, things unseen by her eyes, but suggested by her heart. That cloth whispered stories, its promises made her weak with longing.

"Why, it's a poem!" Maya whispered,

And then as quick as she had shown it, she folded it back into her breast, and put a finger to her mouth, and Maya nodded. Perhaps it was the secret threaded from her palm to Maya's eyes and back to her that changed the world that day when she first beheld such beauty wrought from nothing. For the first time, she wanted to share her poems. (pp. 104f.)

Maya receives the dreamcloth as a parting present from Rochel who has to stay behind when Maya follows her husband Yankel to South Africa. The cloth symbolises Rochel's and Maya's secret love affair, and their wishes and unfulfilled dreams. It appeals directly to the imagination and seems to have the mythical power of transforming reality. On a metafictional level, it stands for the transforming powers of art, for art's power to heal and make whole what is broken under the pressures of everyday life.

When Maya dies from a broken heart after Rochel's suicide, the dreamcloth goes to her son Issey, the talented painter who believes that "art comes from suffering" (p. 183) and is "exhaled pain" (p. 182). Issey often lends it to his daughter Mia who believes that the dreamcloth makes her nightmares go away. When Rochel's son Asher arrives in Johannesburg and gets to know about the dreamcloth, he is very keen on it and finally steals it and takes it with him to Israel. Mia nurses him there in the last days of his life upon his request, and is rewarded by his returning the dreamcloth to her. At the end of the novel, Mia passes it on to her former friend Grace, from whom she had become temporarily estranged but with whom she makes up and becomes friends again at the end of the novel. Obviously, Grace needs the dreamcloth more than she does.

Mia has inherited the artistic sensibility of her grandmother and her father. As a baby she cries a lot, and only when her father recites Tennyson's "Mariana" for her, can she be calmed down. It comes as no surprise that the first word she speaks is "dead", referring to the refrain "I would that I were dead" of Tennyson's famous poem (and not 'Dad', as Issey first wants to believe). Tennyson's poem is about a woman who lives a lonely life in a 'moated grange' waiting in vain for her lover to come and see her. All in all, it is a study of a deranged (traumatised?) female mind for which the baby Mia instinctively feels something like sympathy.

Mia herself is struggling to come to terms with her multiple traumas. When Fran gives birth to her, she not only tears Fran's vulva but brings the whole uterus along with her, thus sealing Fran's infertility. Fran takes a long time to be able to face her baby, falling into post-natal depression. Mia is not her firstborn, but she is the first to survive. A few years before, Fran gave birth to a baby boy who came into the world with a crushed skull and could not live.

There is something special about Mia: A white curl in her otherwise black mane calls up the crushed skull of her baby brother and seems to show where fate has touched her, too, this time however without taking a life. Her name is reminiscent of the name of her grandmother Maya. At the age of seven she already writes stories, and also begins to compose her own poetry.

Rabbi Goldenbaum who has been called in to find out what is wrong with Mia has a theory based on the idea of Jung's collective unconscious:

> "I have a theory about South African Jews. I call it 'Destabilized and Detribal-ized'.—it's my own name for what in layman's terms could be called confused identity. Or multiple identities. Don't forget that our ancestors left Eastern Europe, escaping pogroms and anti-Semitism, scattered into the diaspora, and settled wherever they were allowed to stay. Africa allowed them in. Not all countries were so generous. And here, we hoped to find acceptance. But what happened when we got here? We found that we had little in common with the schwartzes who hate us because we're white and have a work ethic and contribute to the economy. And on the other hand we had little in common culturally with the Afrikaners who hate us because they think we are all communists. Joe Slovo is a Jew, did you know that?"

> Fran and Issey both nodded their heads.

> "Scapegoats in the diaspora, lost from the fold, unable to find our way back again. That's the fate of the Jews in South Africa." (pp. 132f.)

As far as Mia is concerned, she is no longer entirely stuck to South Africa. She travels around the world, and her home is where her friends are. She shares this lot with a number of other South African expatriates who love to come visiting from time to time but who prefer to live in countries such as England, Australia or the USA.

Although Mia can never completely rid herself of her various traumas from which she is suffering, she is capable to get on with her life. This becomes clear at the end of novel when she gives the cloth to her friend Grace who seems to need it more desperately than she does.

> "There's something I want you to have," putting her hand inside her shirt and removing a folded rag.

> She opened it up in the sunlight. It winked, even in old age.

> "It's beautiful," Grace said. "What is it?"

> "A bit of history … that needs a good home."

> Grace took the cloth in her fingers and ran them lightly over the beaded stubble.

> "I inherited it from my dad, he got it from his mother, and she got it from someone who loved her greatly." (p. 348)

Giving away the dreamcloth signals Mia's readiness to tackle her life again, to 'get on with it' in spite of her multiple traumas. She does not become 'fixated' on the transitional object but is able to free herself from it and from all that it symbolically implies, especially the various traumas to which it is related. The novel therefore ends with a strong symbolic gesture that underpins the idea that thriving in the aftermath is possible after all.

Patricia Schonstein (2007), *A Quilt of Dreams*

In Patricia Schonstein's *A Quilt of Dreams*, the arts of quilting and sculpting play a decisive role. In the novel, quilting is conceived of as an art, not only on the realistic level of the story, but also on the discourse level as a metaphor for novel writing as such.

In the present, the story concerns the life of Baby (Reuben) Cohen, of Jewish origin, living in the South African Diaspora. Reuben's life is in a mess—everybody looks down on him, he is a heavy drinker, his marriage is in shambles, and he is suffering from PTSD due to the fact that, as a member of the SADF reserve, he took part in the killing of four youths.

But Reuben has also decided to make some changes in his life. He insists on being called Reuben instead of Baby from now on, he is determined to give up drinking, and he is undergoing psychological treatment. At the end of the novel, he rescues the black girl Vita (who has been shot at) out of the turmoil of violent protestations in the late eighties. He gives her a little toy, a carved wooden bull that was sent on to him and was made by his father—whom he never got to know. This is the event which knits together more tightly the two strands of the plot which are based on two different lifelines: Reuben's, whose family is of Jewish origin and who feel like foreigners in this country although they are whites, and Vita's, whose father and brothers are working for the black resistance movement and who have been suffering from the persecutions of the apartheid regime. Vita herself is on a mission: Since her grandmother has explained to her that all the bad luck of her family (no money and no decent food, father imprisoned, brother disappeared) stems from the fact that her great-great-grandfather failed to pay the demanded lobola for his bride (a magnificent bull owned by a white farmer), she has decided to buy the bull herself—which brings her into trouble, that is, she is swept away by the crowd of protesters which is shot at by the apartheid police.

The novel stretches across three generations. In the first generation, Gershon Cohen witnesses the death of his father, who is killed 1938 in Dresden by the Nazis in the course of the Kristallnacht pogroms. Gershon, severely traumatised, escapes to South Africa, where he meets the hare-lipped Rosa, whom he marries after some time. Rosa bears him a daughter, the beautiful Lilianna, who later becomes pregnant with twins without being married. A botched-up abortion results in the survival of one twin—Reuben—and Lilianna decides to take her life: she drowns herself in a river.

Gershon can never forget what he saw during the Kristallnacht in Dresden, witnessing the death of his father.

> He realized that the only way he could carry on living and conversing with others would be to close up his past for ever. From that first morning in Auntie Pearl's guestroom, Gershon kept his horror tightly sealed in his heart, where it would remain, surfacing only in nightmares that would plague him periodically, in the dark hours before dawn, for the rest of his life. (p. 68)

He is unable to talk about his feelings, but his silence becomes the 'elephant in the room' that traumatises everybody else. Although Gershon tries to leave his old life behind, the past keeps catching up with him:

> Gershon left Europe by ship, but he never really left it behind. He crossed the sea, but his nightmares were always of Dresden fragmented into glittering glass. He reached Africa, but he never arrived; not in any true sense. He tried to forget and begin again, but the past haunted him and would not let him subdue the soldiers and the glass and the terror. (p. 134)

His grandson Reuben is traumatized in more than one way: he shares the intergenerational trauma of the Jewish people, and as a Jew in South Africa, whites and blacks treat him with contempt; his twin brother is killed in his mother's womb; he never gets to know his mother and father but grows up a Jewish orphan in a Roman-Catholic boarding school; the killing of four black youths by the SADF in which he takes part traumatises him even further.

The beautiful quilt, which Rosa made for his mother Lilianna, becomes the central symbol of the novel and gives it its title: *A Quilt of Dreams*.

> He would lie on her double bed, on the beautiful patchwork quilt Rosa had made for her, and try to invent her, try to make a mother out of the adoring snippets his grandparents had given him.

> Her name was Lilianna. She had long black curls. Her cheeks were like petals. Her voice was a bird's song. She was lovely beyond words. The sun once rose each morning only on her account.

> 'Hold me,' the boy would whisper into his mother's pillow. 'Come back to me so that I can sleep here and not at the orphanage. Come to me, Mamma. I am waiting for you,' and he would attend with bated breath, his eyes closed as he anticipated a heaviness on the bed to signal that she was lying there next to him, ready to take him in her arms. (p. 45)

Lying on his mother's quilt is a means of relating to her. The death of his mother and the absence of his father create a trauma from which he has to suffer for the rest of his life. For Reuben, the quilt functions as transitional object, a surrogate or mother 'Ersatz' by which he is able to connect with her in his fantasy. Like the quilt is constructed from bits and pieces of different cloths, he tries to put together the image of his mother by the bits and pieces of information given by his grandparents.

On the story level, then, the quilt plays an important role: it illustrates Reuben's isolation and loneliness, provides consolation, and is an important requisite in the mourning process by which he tries to cope with his bereavement. With regard to Rosa who produces this work of art in the first generation, it illustrates her unfulfilled dreams, her unconsummated love for the itinerant salesman Emmanuel Levy who visits the family now and then and whom she secretly loves. He brings her fabrics that "come from all corners of the earth, some ancient and some just old; all of them exquisite" (p. 55). He takes quilting really seriously and instructs her so that she becomes an expert in it. For Rosa, the art of quilting is a sublimation of her unfulfilled erotic desires. On the political level, the quilt is also a central symbol: it consists of precious materials in various colours and make-ups that come from different parts of the world and have unique histories. Rosa sews them together, joins them so that they finally form an organic whole. "This is going to be an organic work, Mrs Cohen, a slow-growing work. We are going to make something of a stained-glass window out of the finest of woven fabrics" (pp. 105f.). The quilt thus stands for everything that is opposed to apartheid and becomes a symbol of humanity.

> Over the years, while the country's apartheid regime strengthened and its policies became more cruel and divisive, the quilt had slowly grown towards a harmony of types and unison of different colours. It was now complete, fully backed and lined except for one last square to be placed in the right-hand corner. (p. 112)

The "last square to be placed in the right-hand corner" needs a lot of consideration. It reminds one of Virginia Woolf's *To the Lighthouse*, where Lily Briscoe towards the end of the novel finishes her painting with one stroke of her brush. On the level of discourse, the quilt (quilting, sewing, joining) symbolizes the art of narration. Each cloth that Emmanuel Levy brings to Rosa has its own history: "The stories he told Rosa were really those of humankind, the beautiful ones" (p. 106). In so far as the narrator of this novel is also stitching together, joining the life stories of people of different colour and ethnicity, trying to give them coherence, forming them into a whole, quilting is a metaphor for novel writing. Even the herringbone stitch, which Emmanuel Levy favours and recommends to Rosa, has narratological implications: Schonstein is reflecting about emplotment, about how to draw the different parts of the story together. The herringbone is simple but effective, and the neat crossing of threads creates a decorative pattern that has an aesthetic quality of its own. In *A Quilt of Dreams*, the different life stories are neatly woven together, their crossing seems to happen accidentally but is actually the result of the author's planning, her intentionality, her 'stitching'.

This is also illustrated by the episode of the carved wooden bull, which Reuben gives to the injured Vita as a present. The artist who produced it is Reuben's father, whose own life story remains peripheral to the novel's plot but is of course important with regard to Reuben's trauma. Reuben's father carved it in hospital where he had to undergo psychiatric treatment after Lilianna's suicide. When Reuben receives the bull from Nicodemus, a black man who had been working in the shop of his grandparents and whose son was in hospital together with Reuben's father, he is at first unwilling to accept it and does not want to hear its story. But when he hears that his father van Tonder carved it and gave it as a present to Nicodemus' boy Pious (who later dies in prison) he suddenly gets interested (cf. pp. 302-307). Nicodemus returns the bull to "his family" because "a white man … had befriended my youngest son, my last-born" (p. 303).

As Reuben confesses to his psychiatrist, the bull he received from Nicodemus had an unexpected effect on him:

> 'It was night when I went back in. I locked myself inside and went to lie on my mother's bed. On her quilt. And then I started to cry. I cried and cried like a damn baby. Holding on to that bull. Fucking kissing the bull…' (p. 306)

Again we are dealing with a transitional object, the bull carved by Reuben's father. In the same way as the quilt represents the absent mother, the bull stands for the absent father. Lying on the quilt and holding on to the bull, Reuben cries like a baby, letting out his sorrow, mourning his loss. The two transitional objects help him in this mourning ritual, and his tears signify a slackening of tension and beginning relief.

The story of the bull is there from the beginning of the novel, and like the quilt dominates the first strand of plot, the bull dominates the second, that of Vita's family. The novel begins with the mythic tale of the rescue of the Xhosa chief Maqoma by his favourite bull, Jingqi, from Robben Island in 1873. The second plot strand continues with the grandmother's tale about the failed quest for lobola, the bull of a white farmer. This is followed up by Vita's attempt to 'heal' this family misfortune by buying the bull in the present, getting injured in the course of the events. It finds its solution in the novel when Reuben gives the bull carved by his father to Vita as a present.

The two plot strands are interwoven in a careful way, first loosely, at the end tightly: Vita's mother works as 'maid' for the Cohen family; Reuben takes part in the killing of Vita's brother Boniface (whom he doesn't identify as Vita's brother). When Reuben at the end saves Vita's life by taking her to a white hospital ward, and gives her the bull as a comforter, the two plot strands become one: apartheid is defeated, not only in reality (it is 1989), but also on the level of plot.

For Reuben, the wooden bull is a precious keepsake, something through which he can relate to his father whom he never got to know. Nevertheless, he gives it to the injured Vita whom he has rescued and taken to hospital, thus overcoming his egotistic sorrows and problems and turning to the other in a generous gesture of self-conquest. The concept of 'transitional object' hereby takes on a different shade of meaning. When Vita wakes up from her coma with the carved bull in her arms, and her father who has been released from prison by her bedside, a dream seems to have come true: the black family has finally succeeded in acquiring the white man's bull after all—at least symbolically. Subsequently, the curse is lifted from Vita's family, and the end of apartheid is dawning. The artificiality of this tale, the fairy-tale-like quality of its ending, is also an implicit comment on what art can do. The ending may be compared to the last patch of cloth in the quilt, which has to be placed carefully in the right-hand corner, so that the whole becomes an aesthetic work of art. Lily Briscoe would have appreciated it, and aestheticism is triumphant.

Conclusion

Sewing, quilting, or knitting are traditionally female occupations. Making whole what is torn, separated, ripped apart seems to be the female lot—at least according to the novels I have analysed.

On the story level, traumatised characters who cannot speak about the 'unspeakable' use cloth art—sometimes unconsciously—as a means of relating to themselves and to others, of communicating their feelings, in a non-discursive manner. Their art comes from suffering, and by the help of their art, they relate to their traumas. Sculpting, quilting, sewing, poetry in this way contribute to the process of 'working through' one's trauma, of recovering one's self, of redefining one's identity.

On the level of discourse, the different art forms are employed to reflect about the role of art as such in the coping process, which includes the art of novel writing. Novel writing, too, is a way of relating to the past, and of coming to terms with the present. The authors I have been dealing with answer the question of what art can do with regard to trauma in a positive way. In the third generation, the intergenerational cycle of trauma is broken, the protagonists lift their heads and begin to see their own future with new eyes. They start to tackle life again, and they are not to be defeated by the traumas that have accompanied them for the greater part of their lives. Even if they have not got rid of their traumas entirely, they have learned to live with them, 'entangled' but coping.

References

Primary Sources

Fedler, Joanne (2005). *The Dreamcloth*. Johannesburg: Jacana.
Schonstein, Patricia (2007). *A Quilt of Dreams*. London: Black Swan.

Secondary Sources

Benedetti, G. (2003). Trauma und Kunst aus dem Leiden. In R. Hampe, P. Martius, A. Reiter, G. Schottenloher & F. von Spreti (Eds.), *Trauma und Kreativität. Therapie mit künstlerischen Medien* (pp. 39-49). Bremen: Universität Bremen.
Bryant-Davis, T. (2005). *Thriving in the Wake of Trauma: A Multicultural Guide*. Westport, CT: Praeger Publishers.
Cape Town Jewish Board of Deputees (2012). *About the Jewish Community*. Retrieved March 9, 2015, from http://www.capebod.org.za/about-the-board/about-the-jewish-community
Gilbert, S. (2010, Spring/Summer [New Series]). Jews and the Racial State: Legacies of the Holocaust in Apartheid South Africa, 1945-60. *Jewish Social Studies*, 32-64.
Mengel, E. (2012). Trauma and Genre in the Contemporary South African Novel. In E. Mengel & M. Borzaga (Eds.), *Trauma, Memory, and Narrative in the Contemporary South African Novel* (pp. 143-175). Amsterdam: Rodopi.
Shain, M., & Mendelsohn, R. (2008). *The Jews in South Africa: An Illustrated History*. Jeppestown: Jonathan Ball Publishers.
Tischer, A. (2008). *Die weibliche Stimme im englischen Frauenroman des 18. Jahrhunderts*. Frankfurt: Lang.
Volkan, V. D. (2009). The Next Chapter: Consequences of Societal Trauma. In P. Gobodo-Madikizela & C. van der Merwe (Eds.), *Memory, Narrative and Forgiveness: Perspectives on the Unfinished Journeys of the Past* (pp. 1-26). Newcastle: Cambridge Scholars.
Winnicott, D. W. (1971). *Playing and Reality*. Routledge, London.
Young, R. M. (1994). *Mental Space*. London: Process Press.

Chapter 13
Handing Down the Holocaust in Germany: A Reflection on the Dialogue between Second Generation Descendants of Perpetrators and Survivors

Beata Hammerich, Johannes Pfäfflin, Peter Pogany-Wnendt, Erda Siebert, Bernd Sonntag

Members of the Study Group on Intergenerational Consequences of the Holocaust

Introduction

Our intention in this chapter is to make a personal contribution to a better understanding of the psychological mechanisms involved in the transmission of Holocaust experiences, both on the part of victims and of perpetrators. A core element in this understanding is the dialogue among descendants of both sides.

After the end of the apartheid regime, the TRC in South Africa made possible a direct confrontation between victims and perpetrators in the generation of those affected—a confrontation that never occurred in Germany. Therefore, we are particularly interested in comparing the timely South African process of addressing and exposing a dictatorial system to the delayed process in Germany involving transgenerational carry-over into the second and third generation.

In Germany, even as recently as the 1990s, with very few exceptions, neither the psychological conflicts emerging from transgenerational transmission of the Holocaust nor the prerequisites for a constructive dialogue among descendants of victims and perpetrators were studied systematically. The situation was dominated by silence and speechlessness (Opher-Cohn et al. 2000).

This prompted a group of Jewish and non-Jewish psychotherapists and members of other professions to found, in 1995, an organisation devoting its attention to these problems. More than ten years of work in the Study Group on Intergenerational Consequences of the Holocaust have been characterised by the systematic pursuit of personal dialogue, topical work groups and public discussion forums that have, in part, been evaluated for research. In the course of these analyses and the confrontations they encompassed, it became increasing apparent that victims and perpetrators in the generation that was directly affected unconsciously handed down their unresolved experiences to their children and grandchildren, charging them as surrogates with the task of resolution. These commissions involved "undigested" feelings of mourning, anger, guilt and shame. Some aspects of this process within our group have also been described elsewhere (cf. Opher-Cohn et al. 2000; Volkan 2000; Volkan, Ast and Greer 2002).

The ongoing dialogue among PAKH members has provided insight into the unconscious tradition of the victim–perpetrator dynamic, which is an essential determinant of dialogue in the second generation after the Holocaust.

The following text employs examples of such vital experiences to describe and reflect upon the work of PAKH. The process of dialogue in the second generation is depicted from the perspective of a victim's and a perpetrator's child and related to their respective life histories. From this contrast, conclusions are drawn and discussed.

To understand the process of the group, it is important to know that we are a group of five psychotherapists in our late forties to early sixties, and we belong to the second generation after the holocaust. Two of us are children of perpetrators, two are offspring of Jewish families that survived in Czechoslovakia and Hungary. One of us is the son of a father who joined the army at seventeen but was not actively involved in Nazi misdoings.

Transgenerational Consequences of the Holocaust from the Point of View of a Child of Survivors

(Perspective of Beata Hammerich)

My participation in PAKH meant for me, first and foremost, making my Jewish origins public. This was nothing short of breaking a taboo since, in my family, we had never let anyone know the truth about our history. This way, no one was overly cautious towards us, and we were able to recognise prejudices more easily. Even now, the very idea of speaking openly about my origins makes me feel as if the ground were sinking beneath my feet.

Given the background of my mother's life history, I fully understand why she urged me "not to tell". She survived the major part of the war as a baptised Jewish child in a convent in Slovakia. It was drummed into her, "Don't you ever tell anyone anything, or you will get us all killed", and indeed, at the time, this threat was real.

This left an indelible impression on my mother, and its influence carried over into later life—still capable, after decades, of triggering something like a breakdown. Once I was telling her about a supervisory session with my teaching analyst, who was Jewish. The topic had been the significance of my Jewish origins for my therapeutic work with a particular patient, a woman whose father had been in the SS. Suddenly my mother glared at me, a shocked expression in her eyes; she turned pale, sat down and asked me full of dismay, "And you told him who we are?"

As an adult and trained analyst, I realised immediately what had happened. I called her attention to the difference between the past and present, and my mother said with relief, "That gave me such a terrible fright." What had happened? And how often had something similar gone unnoticed in the course of my childhood? I would like to expand this point with reference to a psychoanalytic concept.

Fonagy (Fonagy et al. 2004, chap. 4 passim) describes the importance of appropriate affective reflection on the part of the mother for the development of affective regulation in the child. If emotions are mirrored insufficiently or inappropriately—for example, if they are intermingled with the mother's own anxieties—this seriously inhibits the process of the child's development of a sense of self. Fonagy corroborates what Khan (1974, quoted in Grubrich-Simitis 1979, 1006) tried to characterise in children of survivors in the concept of "cumulative trauma". With this term, Khan denotes a disturbance in the non-verbal relationship of mother and child in which low-profile empathetic deficits, hardly noticeable when they occur, are cumulated over a long period of time and lead to traumatic effects.

Insufficient empathy on the part of the parents emerges from a capacity that, for many, was a key to survival but later could not be cast off: they built up protective "armour" around the ego, learning to disavow or to invert feelings. When a mother cannot reflect emotions adequately, the child—who naturally tries to empathise with the mother—develops a "false sense of self".

This inhibition of empathy, a result of an emotional numbness necessary for survival, is the key factor in transgenerational transmission of trauma and in the ensuing identity disturbances in children of survivors. Overcoming this numbness involves becoming aware of the losses suffered, allowing all the associated feelings of pain, grief, anger, shame and so on to surface, and enduring these feelings without being broken by them. The less successful this "re-vitalisation" through mourning, the more burdensome will be the task passed on as a legacy to the next generation.

Taking differences of historical circumstance into account, these observations can be generalised to apply to any dictatorship. I experienced that same notion of "you're not allowed to tell" as a child, growing up in Prague under the communist regime. My mother had retained the Christian faith from her convent, and she raised my sister and me as Christians, despite the dangers this implied within the communist system. She did not tell us that we were Jews. I can recall once meeting a schoolmate in a place where we were not supposed to be—in a church. Each of us looked the other way; we were embarrassed rather than feeling like allies. Anxiety is the instrument of power in all dictatorships, and the force of this mechanism is made clear by this seemingly banal situation. It would have been very risky not to follow the rule of silence—"keep quiet and keep covered"—for example, it could have endangered our parents' jobs.

After the occupation of Czechoslovakia in 1968, my family immigrated to Germany. There I first learned of my Jewish origins, quite by chance, from my cousin. She was astounded: "Don't you know that we're Jewish?" I pretended that I had known it all along, and felt mortified. It was not until years later that I was able to articulate to my mother how she, by her very effort to protect me, had put me into a very difficult situation.

It still shocks me to think of how long I lived in Germany without being aware that I was on friendly terms with former perpetrators and their children. The extent of this denial is difficult for me to grasp, even today. It can only be comprehended through careful consideration. Thanks to my identification with my mother—reinforced by my own experiences under the communist regime—I had internalised to the point of denial all the anxieties and the protective mechanisms of "keeping covered". Compulsively, I devoured books about the Holocaust, but this encounter took place in absolute isolation. Meanwhile, I visited my girlfriends at their homes frequently—never noticing anything, never looking for anything, definitely not asking any questions or talking about my background. Long after there was any necessity for it, we still believed we had to hide.

All the same, I felt a strong need to belong. In Czechoslovakia I had not belonged because I was a Christian, with no inkling of my Jewish origins. In Germany I was an immigrant. Finally, in 1980, I made an important discovery. I came across the book by Helen Epstein (1980), Children of the Holocaust. I realised that there were others like myself. I was not alone with my life story and my feelings, even if I did not know any of the others personally! Or so I thought.

First Phase: Establishing Contact with the Jewish Members
Struggle for Acceptance

I first learned about the PAKH group while attending the PAKH symposium in 1998. Initially, the Jewish participants had the greatest significance for me.

I chose Peter as a contact person. His story touched me most deeply. He talked about his unconscious sadness, which had been pointed out to him by his daughter—a sadness that he himself, as a child, had perceived in his father.

At the root of my wish to take up contact with other Jewish children of survivors was my need to find out whether they would accept me or reject me when I disclosed my identity as a baptised Jew. For me, this was a question of life and death. As opposed to my mother, I had consciously seen myself as a betrayer. Now, I no longer wanted to hide out in a lonely place.

I felt guilty for denying my real identity, and was alone with my guilt until I heard Peter's story. When his family immigrated to Germany, his parents had resolved not to let it be known that they were Jewish. Before getting married, Peter decided to reveal the secret once and for all. He did not want to start a family of his own and then have to hide his own life story from his children. He was expecting vehement reproaches from his parents. In a one-on-one talk, he told his father about this decision and to his amazement, his father nodded, with tears in his eyes—visibly relieved and proud.

On my entry into the group, the non-Jewish participants played a secondary role, although I appreciated their heartfelt welcome. During the same period, together with my Jewish analyst, I was working through my complicated identity. This was a decisive factor enabling me to reveal myself and to accept the recognition of the Jewish members of the group. I felt as if I had finally found a home.

Second Phase: Approaching the Non-Jewish Members Overcoming Anxiety and Inner Resistance

When Erda Siebert came into the group, I was frightened and immediately had a strong impulse to leave. My sentiment was, "If she stays, then I have to go". I already knew Erda, but at that point knew nothing about her history. I did not understand myself, and I forced myself to stay.

The more I learned, the more distinct were my feelings—at first predominantly a feeling of inhibition, followed by empathy and then by the anxiety that I might be perceived as an accuser, merely because I was the child of a survivor. A personal conversation with Erda was a milestone for me; here, we told one another about our life stories. This was the first time that such an exchange did not leave me with the unpleasant feeling that I had "dropped my cover". It became clear to me that this surprising fact was due to Erda's genuine interest and empathy. Encouraged by her questions, I had the courage to ask her a few questions, too.

This initial phase of feeling liberated and relieved was followed by a difficult period. In the group, we now directed our full attention towards the perpetrators. I was flooded by inward resistance, I felt overtaxed and criticised myself for that. I also felt guilty for refusing to empathise. When I managed to articulate the difficulty I had in getting so deeply involved in the personalities of prominent perpetrators, it was Erda who backed me up with her understanding.

Viewing the television documentary film My Father, the Murderer (Tatari 2003) at a public event held by PAKH in 2003, together with the daughter of a Gestapo boss, I was overwhelmed by my empathy with her burdensome fate and my admiration for her bravery in confronting her own situation as the daughter of a culprit. I kept quiet, because I felt that I had no right to speak out, since I myself did not have such a terrible load to carry. This feeling of having no right to speak resulted from a number of encounters with survivors who said one should not express opinions on things one had not experienced oneself. How many times had survivors told me, "You haven't got a clue, you haven't been through anything!"

Within me, gradually a feeling which I did not understand at the time took the upper hand—a feeling of, "I'll have nothing to do with it all". My refusal to become involved emerged whenever the children of perpetrators brought forth positive aspects of their parents and their mutual attachment. I insisted that the perpetrators be regarded as perpetrators, while their children struggled to accept their own parents. Erda made it clear to me why it was so important that the children of the perpetrators be able to acknowledge positive qualities in their parents.

Hearing Pumla Gobodo-Madikizela and Eva Mozes Kor speak publicly at the Institute for Advanced Study in the Humanities in Essen in 2005 brought to the fore the themes of forgiveness and reconciliation. Pumla's impressive depiction of her meeting with Eugene de Kock deeply affected us all. Eva Mozes Kor's account of her "reconciliation" with her tormentor in Auschwitz, Hans Münch, left us with many unanswered questions. Very helpful for me was the encounter with Hillel Klein's (1992 [1983]) thoughts on responsibility. He emphasises that if a survivor forgives his would-be murderer, it is tantamount to accepting the Holocaust and avoiding the necessary task of grieving. This leads to disastrous consequences for the following generation, because without mourning, there can be no empathy. Trauma is thus handed down to children through their experience of their own relationships with their survivor parents. Alongside everyday reality, the children inhabit a "second world" in the traumatic past, and in their imagination carry out a futile struggle to overcome it on behalf of their parents. Above all, they take on the parents' affective burden of feeling constantly exposed to the threat of death.

Laub (Laub, Peskin and Auerhahn 1995) coined the term "second holocaust" to describe this phenomenon of repetition across the generations. In the struggle to overcome the trauma of the "second holocaust", coming to terms with one's own inner representation of parents is a prerequisite to developing an integral sense of self. The children of survivors face the conciliatory task of accepting their destiny: that they have parents who have been damaged, and that they as children must deal with the ramifications. Only after releasing themselves from a duty to fulfil the impossible task passed on to them by their parents can the children assume responsibility of their own.

Third Phase: The Confrontation Takes on Contours, Intimacy and Distance

At present, I see myself in a third phase of my interaction within PAKH. It fluctuates between an experience of similarity and closeness with the children of perpetrators on the one hand, and on the other an experience of differences and inability to comprehend. Sometimes the differences appear to be insurmountable, but to a certain extent they are realities that cannot be altered.

Grünberg (2000, 1019) describes how inappropriate and dangerous it is to equate victims and culprits. Neither their suffering nor their silence can be compared. The same applies to the second generation: like the children of survivors, children of perpetrators are marked and burdened by the Holocaust, but in completely different ways. Problems that may appear to be similar are, in fact, not identical and cannot be reduced to a common denominator.

I find that Klein (2003, 289) has expressed this most adequately:

> The children of the tormentors, who are not guilty of the actions of their murderer fathers but who nevertheless, in their own lives, cannot deny the lasting burden of responsibility, correlate tragically in this respect to the children of survivors, who in their own continuity take on the burden of their parents' fate.

We, the children of survivors and perpetrators, have done no harm to one another. Therefore, we do not need to be reconciled: there is nothing we need to forgive. However, our personal contact is burdened by the trauma that occurred and that survivors and perpetrators have handed down to us. The fact that our parents either suffered grievances or inflicted them and thus became laden with guilt can have a destructive effect on our relationships with one another. However, we can, if we assume our individual responsibility as children of either survivors or perpetrators, enter into a genuine dialogue. Such a dialogue would require us to confront one another, to admit that irresolvable differences exist and to live with them.

One step in that direction—to quote Dan Bar-On (Braunschweiger Zeitung, August 23, 2006)—would be "if the children could get to know and respect the other side's narrative of history, without abandoning their own narrative".

This dialogue is encumbered by an inner conflict: standing up to my own life history would imply identifying the perpetrators for what they are. In doing so, I would be accusing the fathers of my friends and colleagues, who would thus be damaged. Moreover, I would see myself in the role of the accuser, the perpetrator, the culprit. The reason why I have avoided this became clear to me in retrospect: I recognise my own behaviour as an attempt to placate the children of the perpetrators, to gain their recognition. It is a gesture of submission. I was not aware of my dependence on them, and it is certainly not yet entirely overcome.

I have repeatedly experienced this dialogue as being endangered. Only through a permanent process of introspection and clarification can the obstacles be surmounted. When I am able to open myself, encouraged by the openness of others, then we can carry on with our dialogue.

My conclusion is that we, the children of survivors, are called on to come to terms with our inner representation of our parents and to grant ourselves remittance from the impossible tasks they have handed down to us. That is the prerequisite if we are to assume individual responsibility. Only in this way can we avoid passing on the same inheritance—capable of destroying identity—unfiltered, to our own children. Only in this way can we enter into a genuine dialogue with the children of perpetrators, a dialogue which can further promote our inner process of development. A genuine dialogue, in my eyes, implies that we allow ourselves to be truly moved by one another, while accepting that some distinctions between us cannot be overcome.

Transgenerational Consequences of the Holocaust from the Point of View of a Perpetrator's Child

(Perspective of Erda Siebert)

Before I focus on my process in the PAKH group, I would like to look briefly at how I see my own development in the context of German society after the Second World War.

The Beginnings

My father was born in 1906 and joined the National Socialist Party at the age of twenty-five. Two years later he joined the SS and, by 1942, had advanced to the rank of "SS-Obersturmbannführer". From 1938 onwards, he must have been responsible for serious crimes, particularly after 1941 when his unit was active in Eastern Europe. I do not have any precise information and so can only speculate. I do, however, have some positive memories of him from the first six years of my life; my parents were divorced after the War and I did not see him again before he died in 1974.

I myself was born in Dresden in the East of Germany, but my mother fled the bombed city in the winter of 1945 with me, aged eleven months, and my two brothers. We came close to death several times during three air raids. In Northern Germany we found a new home with my grandparents as a refugee family.

Many children had no idea of the crimes their fathers had been involved in. Fathers—including my father—went into hiding after the war. Families were afraid and fled to avoid discovery, and so the children's loyalty to their crisis-ridden and apparently persecuted families was inevitable. As a result, the development of our individual identities was undermined.

After the war, the occupying Allies enforced a process of informing people about the Nazis and democratising society, but in many families this went hand-in-hand with a continuation of the national socialist ideology. My brother remembers a situation as late as the 1950s, when he was ten: he was apparently threatening to show some "unmanly" feelings when my mother snatched him up, saying, "Hands at your sides, and be a hero!" That was how the second generation learned to deal with feelings of guilt, shame and grief. Worse still was a fundamental diffusion of identity, in which we learned to regard as alien what was in fact our own and belonged to us (for example, in the recurrent dream of a patient that as soon as she became pregnant, she was compelled to abort her child). Instead, parental introjections were perceived as the way life was to be lived (Shengold [1979] speaks of "soul murder", Hardtmann [1995] of "being a stranger in one's own house"). Moreover, there always lurked an existential angst that the "destructive tumour", the cruel perpetrator within ourselves, might develop against our own will and erupt like a volcano (Hardtmann 1995).

These introductory remarks are intended to make clear what a complicated blend of culprit/victim roles was imbibed by the second generation as it grew up and how this contributed to making it impossible, for many years, to process one's personal family history.

The '68 Movement

From 1968 onwards and into the 1970s (the so-called '68 revolt), information began to seep out about the involvement of fathers in the atrocities of the national socialist era, and that a significant number of them had smoothly re-assumed positions of power and authority. The Jewish author Ralph Giordano calls this "the second guilt":

> Any second guilt presumes a first—in this case, the guilt of the Germans under Hitler. The second guilt: the suppression and denial of the first, after 1945. It has significantly influenced the political culture of the Federal Republic of Germany until today—a mortgage that will take a long time to repay. (Giordano 1987, 11)

With this development, the parents' "silent generation" suddenly gave way to the "raging generation" of their children. Battle was now openly declared against this "second guilt", against the duplicity and hypocrisy to be found at almost all levels of public life.

With hindsight, the fierce and committed struggle for a better society and the protest against the silent, paralysed parents were, in the final analysis, once again a struggle to maintain an "intact ego ideal" that united both generations and produced a solidarity of silence about the evil and murderous past. As a result, inwardly the perpetrators' children remained indivisibly united with their parents and developed, on the one hand, the narcissistic ego ideal which the parents had lost, and, on the other hand, a cruel and punishing super-ego if they were unable to realise these ideals (Schneider 1993; Franzen 1999).

The Period Following Reunification (1989) and Its Consequences

Upon the reunification of Germany and the fall of the Berlin Wall, the American government permitted public access to the Berlin Document Centre and gave us the first opportunity to obtain documents about our fathers that had previously been kept secret. The upshot of this for me—and no doubt for many others like me—was a sudden confrontation with the facts of a reality that, until then, I had been able to play down in my imagination. So, forty-five years after the end of the war, I gradually began to get some idea of the extent of my father's criminality and guilt.

During the 1990s, along with many other offspring of perpetrators, I felt an urgent need to engage in dialogue with persons in a situation similar to mine. The inner loneliness I had felt due to not being able to speak openly often seemed quite overpowering. The general public for the most part was still imprisoned in their mindset of hypocrisy and denial of their involvement in national socialism, be it as bystanders or perpetrators. Groups came into being to foster dialogue among the descendants of victims and perpetrators, as well as to make contacts with people in Israel. At that time, in 1998 after the PAKH symposium (see Opher-Cohn et al. 2000), I joined the PAKH group.

I would like to turn now to the process that other descendants of perpetrators and I went through within PAKH, differentiated into three phases.

First Phase: Anxiety and Resistance

In the beginning of the PAKH dialogue work, before I entered the group, the emphasis lay on the suffering of the victims and their families and on literature by Jewish authors. That meant that the non-Jewish Germans, children of perpetrators or bystanders, had not yet confronted the aspect of the culprit in themselves.

At that time Johannes, also a perpetrator's child, described his situation as follows:

> I looked for and found the problem in the others. I regarded myself as the good person who was a victim of circumstances. My past and present became increasingly intermingled in me, as I allowed the past to surface. Suddenly I felt as if I myself were a Nazi criminal and had to defend myself in relation to the other Germans in PAKH, for instance Erda, who presented herself from the start as the daughter of a perpetrator.

For me personally during this phase of angst and resistance, two events were essential.

Firstly, in the literature circle of PAKH consisting of victim's and perpetrator's children we were discussing a book by Anna Maria Jokl (1997), a Jewish psychoanalyst who was then practising in Berlin. She had had a young male Jew and a young male German in therapy at the same time. The Jew had fled from the ghetto with his mother and the German was the son of a SS officer. Anna Maria Jokl describes how their life histories converged at a central point in the psychoanalysis: namely in their nightmares about vermin, destruction and death. Each of them revealed both victim and perpetrator aspects. Both had been damaged at the root of their personalities by the national socialist ideology.

In our group the courageous but also daring comparison of these two 25-year-olds led to a heated discussion about whether and how a (moral, human, ethical) boundary had been crossed by bringing together victim and perpetrator in this way.

This brings to mind Pumla Gobodo-Madikizela's book A human being died that night (2003), in which the central issue was likewise the breaching of both an external and an inner psychological boundary between victim and perpetrator, good and evil.

To return to Anna Maria Jokl: her book had already strengthened in me the hope that the children of perpetrators, too, can and will be allowed to experience not only profound feelings of guilt but equally profound sorrow. The discussion of the book pushed the group towards a crucial decision: namely, whether it was willing to accept this concept and, with it, me as a perpetrator's child with such feelings and as a fully acknowledged member of the group. The discussion was very difficult for everyone and in the end I was so tense that I was in tears, leaving me with an intense feeling of shame. I was concerned that a sacrosanct barrier had been breached that evening—and that I had thereby turned the literature circle into a self-experience group and was imposing myself on the others. This can only be understood by explaining the problem that our literature circle, consisting of both victim's and perpetrator's children, ran the risk of becoming too emotional and of losing its rational basis.

The second key occurrence was the documentary film (Tatari 2003) about the daughter of the head of the Gestapo in Belgrade/former Yugoslavia (Bruno Sattler), which we viewed and discussed in her presence. This event confronted the German non-Jewish participants with perpetrator elements within themselves—about which they were in denial—and led to massive resistance. There was a critical lack of openness and empathy during the discussion, as if there was a wall between her and the group.

Later it emerged that the group had split in two: the Jewish members fell more and more silent and left the discussion to the offspring of the perpetrators. The latter were increasingly caught up in their own anxiety defence structures: denying their anxiety, they tried to defend their critical opinions. This was perhaps also because, in my opinion, the film depicted a heroic daughter who, without sparing herself, had embarked on uncovering the trail of her father's cruel and awful crimes, and was doing so without any visible angst or ambivalence.

Initially, the film induced in us resistance and a sort of dissociation. Later, a letter from our guest revealed her disappointment about the course of the discussion. Then, suddenly, it became clear to me why I had been unable to face the film and the discussion more openly: I had experienced it as a challenge to me to follow up my father's trail in a similar manner. I did not have the confidence that, were I to undertake a similar search, I would be able to separate my life from my father's; in this way, the threat inherent in the message of the film became clear to me.

Second Phase: Cautious Approach and Coming to Terms with the Victim Position

This second phase was triggered by a so-called "Saturday conversation". It was only open to members of the group and was an annual event. In small groups we would narrate and re-experience our own personal life stories. In our group there were three women (including Beata Hammerich and myself) who took part in intensive, if cautious, exchanges. The questions put to Beata did not probe deeply and I, too, felt I was being treated with great consideration. However, for the first time, I experienced a very close confrontation with the victims' side. I saw that the group was in a position to cope equably with our different life histories and to listen to them respectfully and empathetically one after the other, and that each of us had a moving story to tell. This fed into the literature circles and intervision groups that took place afterwards. There was an increasing trend to differentiate less between Jewish and non-Jewish participants, and closeness and trust spread throughout the group.

In this context, a noteworthy process developed between David, a Jewish survivor—one of the few from the first generation—and Johannes, a second-generation perpetrator's child, as a result of their experience of each other. At the outset, Johannes perceived David as perplexing, but then tried to establish contact with him. Johannes was afraid of confrontation and an intensely demanding attitude from which he could not distance himself. He feared it might provoke in him a massive counter-reaction in which he would devalue David. The human support that Johannes experienced from Jews of his own generation in the group helped him, as he said, to correct "the prejudiced image of Jews I had inherited". It enabled him to acknowledge David's autonomy and dignity. David, for his part, reminded us that he was a Jew but first and foremost a human being and that he wished to be accepted on the basis of his humanity and his own personality.

To me David is the bearer of the real experiences of the Holocaust and a living example of reconciliation to us all. One outcome of these shared experiences is his recent project in which he told ten-year-old schoolchildren about the Holocaust and his life under the Nazis. "How can I do that without scaring the children?" he asked Johannes beforehand. The moving answer can be found in a booklet created by the schoolchildren themselves, containing pictures and texts about this project (Kloecker and Reusmann 2005).

During the period from 1990 until today, German society has become more open in this respect. People have been publishing documents, novels, biographies and films (often about their own families) as an attempt to recreate the continuity of family histories, accepting the perpetrators as "our fathers". There may be hope now of closing the gap in social and family history.

Third Phase: Confidence, Beginning Acceptance of One's Own Unconscious Involvement in the Crimes, Shared Grieving

Johannes Pfäfflin reported the following about me:

> When Erda entered the literature circle, she wished to talk about a book that she wanted us all to read, one about the children of perpetrators and how they dealt with the heavy burden they have inherited. That Erda was the daughter of a perpetrator immediately put a gulf between us. Her openness and at the same time her inner crisis, which for me was very noticeable, brought me once again into contact with the perpetrator side of me; which I had indeed always blocked out as part of my identification with my father. Embarrassing and dangerous images arose in me, but ones that from now on should be permitted to have a place.

The climax of this more trusting and open phase was brought about by another film we viewed in our literature circle, The lost children of Cologne by Jürgen Naumann (2006) who showed it to us in person; it led to a profound discussion. During the film there was a moving scene during which, as far as I could see, almost all those present were weeping. I experienced a strong feeling of thankfulness in sharing this grief with my Jewish and German colleagues.

Personally, the gradual experience of allowing myself to feel trust in the group, and the encounter with Pumla and her book two years previously in South Africa, was something new for me. Reading A human being died that night opened a door inside me, which a deep paralysis had kept firmly closed until then. To me, now, the title of the book could well be A human being was born that night because it opened up the opportunity for me to perceive my "monster father" differently, and to give him a human face. Interestingly, through the book and our dialogue in PAKH it became possible for me to differentiate between the "good" and the "bad" father and to give up the inner splitting within myself. A mourning process had taken place that allowed me not only to perceive emotionally my father's "human" life to see him as a human being who himself had gone through childhood, had parents and experienced a development but also to realise my feelings of shame and grief that this father had been capable of committing such atrocities.

In summary, it seems to be vital that we, the offspring of perpetrators, should come to terms with the atrocities committed by our fathers and, moreover, should confront the parental introjections in ourselves. In so doing we can differentiate between our fathers' guilt and our own shame and responsibility in order to rebuild our own autonomy. Furthermore, it helps to restore the missing human links between the generations that all family traditions need.

Conclusion

In the course of our dialogue over many years in PAKH, we were confronted with the unconscious dynamic of victim and perpetrator. We, the children of the victims and the children of the perpetrators of the Holocaust, are charged with addressing the unmourned suffering of our victimised parents or the guilt for which our victimiser parents did not want to assume the responsibility.

If this dynamic remains unrecognised, then it will unfold its destructive energy. Reflecting on the process of dialogue has led to an important insight: by taking on the unsolved tasks of our parents we are bound into unconscious roles, either as victims or perpetrators, through which we define ourselves.

At the beginning of PAKH, the dialogue was significantly influenced by these roles. To illustrate: shortly after the founding of PAKH, the core group—consisting of three German, non-Jewish members and two Jewish non-German members, one born in Rumania and one born in Hungary—organised a symposium. During the preparations, tensions became apparent in the group. In some situations, the Jewish members reacted extremely aggressively to their German colleagues, whereas on other occasions they behaved in a submissive manner. Similar fluctuations could be observed in the behaviour of the non-Jewish Germans. Unconsciously, the Jews perceived the Germans as "Nazis", while the Germans regarded the Jews as "victims".

Vamik Volkan, our supervisor at that time, described the process as follows:

> The members of the PAKH core group were psychoanalytically trained colleagues, people with similar interests and not enemies. However, their German and Jewish parents, grandparents and relatives had lived in completely different circumstances. They had been enemies, victims and perpetrators—and the next generation had carried forward this ill-starred heritage on both conscious and unconscious levels. Although in the meantime, half a century had passed, they carried within themselves the inexpressible trauma of the war and of annihilation. (Opher-Cohn et al. 2000, 32)

Nowadays, PAKH-Members are more successful in making visible the unconscious roles of victims and victimisers so that they can be handled better. The question is, what led to this change? Our thesis is as follows: through long-term work in the encounter with one another, we increasingly succeeded in disavowing the roles of victim and perpetrator. With that, the dialogue became less determined by these roles.

We will now try to sketch this process briefly in four phases.

Phase 1: Search for Protection, Recognition and Sense of Security from One's "Own Side"

In the above-mentioned core group, the members oriented themselves emotionally in their early days at PAKH in a way similar to that described by Beata and Erda: they tended to bond with their "own side", from which they hoped for protection, recognition and a sense of security. At the same time, relations with the "other side" were shaped by anxiety, mistrust and bias. As the dialogue in the group was very much determined by these roles, some crises nearly broke the group up.

Phase 2: Cautious Approach to the "Other Side"

This was able to occur in the course of further development of PAKH after each person had been accepted into their "own group" and felt supported by them. This step was always accompanied by very ambivalent feelings.

The wish for "reconciliation" which arose during this period was accompanied by the serious danger of falling into a destructive dependency on victim–perpetrator roles and being unable to surmount this. The child of a victim assumes its parents' feelings of having lost their dignity and self-respect. Subsequently, the child unconsciously believes that only the offspring of a perpetrator, as a representative of the Nazi-victimiser, can restore his dignity. By contrast, the perpetrators' child wants the victims' child to forgive him the legacy of guilt. Since neither "restoring dignity" nor "release from guilt" is possible between the offspring of culprit and victim, the two are caught in an emotional trap: each of them expects "release" from the other. The feelings of hate and revenge that are thereby repressed, as well as the disappointment about the non-fulfilment of the desired "release" lead to the development of an interaction which, in the long term, is destructive in nature.

Phase 3: Moving Beyond the "False" Feeling of Reconciliation

This step is necessary to enable the unfolding of a dialogue that is not handicapped (or even entirely undermined) by the dependency trap. The protagonists must differentiate and separate themselves from the "other side" and again focus on themselves. This is necessary because the offspring can only overcome the respective victim and perpetrator roles on their own, as an autonomous action. Toward this end, they have to give back the "unfulfillable tasks" to their parents. This can only be attained by dealing with their internal representations, and it presupposes painful mourning. It is a very difficult process, since feelings of betrayal towards the parents and strong feelings of guilt are bound to arise.

This step is not one of reconciliation as such, but rather of coming to terms with one's internal images of the parents and refusing to fulfil unrealisable tasks, which can then lead to giving up unconscious burdening roles.

Phase 4: Independent Dialogue

Depending on the extent to which victim and victimiser roles can be relinquished, the dialogue can become more "normal" and less dependent, that is, less determined by the delegated dynamic of victim and perpetrator.

If this occurs, the Holocaust increasingly loses its character as a "chosen trauma", the term Volkan gives to humiliating trauma that, unmourned, goes through transgenerational transmission with appalling consequences. Thus, it need no longer be transmitted as a "virulent", emotionally uncontrollable phenomenon, but can instead be passed on to the coming generations as narrative and remembrance.

Over the years in PAKH, there have been very moving encounters between individual members. On some occasions we were able to feel the pain of the other; at other times it was aggression, unconscious hatred or desire for revenge that determined our dialogue. In spite of all this, though, we were to some extent able to reflect such feelings and to continue the dialogue. We became aware of the destructive dynamic which lies in the deepest layer of the dialogue between the two poles of the second generation of the Holocaust: at this level we are confronted with murder and survival, gas chambers and the hills of corpses, also with hatred and revenge, bare destruction and naked inhumanity.

We have attempted to describe our experiences in PAKH concerning the dialogue between the offspring of the perpetrators and the offspring of the victims of the Holocaust as a flowing and lively process that has been going on for years. Personal narratives that are shared shape the group's process. A constructive dialogue is only possible to the extent to which the protagonists are able to give up their delegated roles as victims or perpetrators. If they succeed in that, they will allow themselves to be affected by the narratives of the others.

This process requires an attempt to come to terms with the past of our parents and includes painful mourning. In this way, the impossible tasks that were handed down to us can be abandoned and given back. Reconciliation is not necessary because neither have the offspring of the victims themselves experienced persecution, nor do the offspring of the perpetrators have blood on their hands. In a work published in 1946, the French existentialist Jean Paul Sartre commented: "To blame the grandchildren for the mistakes of the ancestors, one must have a very primitive concept of responsibility" (Anti-Semite and Jew, 1946). Our responsibility consists in maintaining the memory of what took place, without transmitting the fateful and destructive dynamic of hostility to our children. Insomuch as we do not fulfil our "tasks", we fulfil them.

References

Epstein, H. 1980. *Children of the Holocaust*. New York: Bantam Books.

Fonagy, P., G. Gergely, E. L. Jurist, and M. Target. 2004. *Affektregulierung, Mentalisierung und die Entwicklung des Selbst*. Stuttgart: Klett-Cotta.

Franzen, G. 1999. Diktierte Reue. Unerwünschte Trauer. Marginalien zur individuellen, literarischen und psychoanalytischen Schuldpolitik. *Freie Assoziation* 29: 211-220.

Giordano, R. 1987. *Die zweite Schuld oder Von der Last Deutscher zu sein*. Hamburg: Rasch und Röhring Verlag.

Gobodo-Madikizela, P. 2003. *A human being died that night: A story of forgiveness*. Cape Town: David Philip Publishers.

Grubrich-Simitis, I. 1979. Extremtraumatisierung als kumulatives Trauma. *Psyche* 33: 991-1023.

Grünberg, K. 2000. Zur Tradierung des Traumas der nationalsozialistischen Judenvernichtung. *Psyche Sonderheft*: 1002-1037.

Hardtmann, G. 1995. *Die Schatten der Vergangenheit. In Kinder der Opfer, Kinder der Täter: Psychoanalyse und Holocaust*, ed. M. S. Bergmann, M. E. Jucovy, J. S. Kestenberg, 239-261. Frankfurt am Main: S. Fischer Verlag.

Jokl, A. M. 1997. *Zwei Fälle zum Thema "Bewältigung der Vergangenheit"*. Frankfurt am Main: Jüdischer Verlag im Suhrkamp Verlag.

Khan, M., and R. Masud. 1974. *The concept of cumulative trauma. The Privacy of the self*, ed. M. Masud and R. Khan, 42-58. London: Hogarth.

Klein, H. 1992 (lecture held in 1983). Von Schuld zu Verantwortung. *Psyche* 46: 1177-1186.

Klein, H. 2003 (posthumous). Überleben und Versuche der Wiederbelebung: Psycho-analytische Studien mit Überlebenden der Shoah und ihren Familien in Israel und in der Diaspora, ed. C. Biermann, and C. Nedelmann. *Jahrbuch der Psychoanalyse*, Beiheft 20. Stuttgart: Frommann-Holzboog.

Kloecker, C., and D. Reusmann. 2005. *Nie die Hoffnung verlieren*. Düsseldorf: self-published.

Laub, D., H. Peskin, and N. C. Auerhahn. 1995. Der zweite Holocaust: Das Leben ist bedrohlich. *Psyche* 49:18-40.

Naumann, J. 2006. *Die vergessenen Kinder von Köln*. 60-minute documentary film. Cologne: Westdeutscher Rundfunk, broadcast November 1.

Opher-Cohn, L., J. Pfäfflin, B. Sonntag, B. Klose, and P. Pogany-Wnendt, eds. 2000. *Das Ende der Sprachlosigkeit? Auswirkungen traumatischer Holocausterfahrungen über mehrere Generationen*. 2nd ed. Gießen: Psychosozial Verlag.

Schneider, C. 1993. Jenseits der Schuld? Die Unfähigkeit zu trauern in der zweiten Generation. *Psyche* 47:754-774.

Shengold, L. L. 1979. Child abuse and deprivation: Soul murder. *Journal of the American Psychoanalytic Association* 27: 533-559.

Tatari, J. 2003. *Der gute Vater—Eine Tochter klagt an*. 90-minute documentary film. Cologne: ARD/WDR/3sat, broadcast August 31, 2003.

Volkan, V. D. 2000. Die Anatomie der Vorbereitungen für das Symposium "Das Ende der Sprachlosigkeit?". In *Das Ende der Sprachlosigkeit? Auswirkungen traumatischer Holocausterfahrungen über mehrere Generationen*, ed. L. Opher-Cohn, J. Pfäfflin, B. Sonntag, B. Klose, and P. Pogany-Wnendt, 23-49. Gießen: Psychosozial Verlag.

Volkan, V. D., G. Ast, and W. F. Greer. 2002. *The Third Reich in the unconscious: Transgenerational transmission and its consequences*. New York: Brunner-Routledge.

Chapter 14
Confronting the Past, Engaging the Other in the Present: The Intergenerational Healing Journey of a Holocaust Survivor and his Children

Jeff Kelly Lowenstein, Dunreith Kelly Lowenstein, Edward Lowenstein

Harvard University

Introduction

In May 2012, Edward Lowenstein returned to his hometown of Essen, Germany for the first time since 1939 when at the age of 4 he was put on a train to England as part of the Kindertransport. Dr. Lowenstein was invited to Essen as part of German teacher Gabriele Thimm's attempt to teach her students about their country's troubled past. Thimm played a critical role in shaping the experience into an opportunity for understanding and healing for both sides. Lowenstein was accompanied on the trip by two of his sons and one of his grandsons. The trip illustrates many key elements involved in breaking intergenerational cycles of trauma transmission for family members and the Essen community. A subsequent trip in June 2013 to present an award created in the family's name for children who act with tolerance and justice helped advance this process and to begin to forge a new and different story for the town that moved away from shame, guilt and denial and into an honest reckoning with its genocidal past. This paper will explore the trauma experienced by the Lowenstein family, its generational transmission, and the impact the return to Germany held for both the Lowenstein family and the community of Essen, and will place the trip and ensuing activities in the context of other scholarly, autobiographical and artistic works that address similar themes.

The Holocaust is one of humanity's greatest atrocities. The state-sanctioned murder of 6 million Jews, including more than 1 million children, and more than 5 million other victims inflicted physical and psychic wounds with which Jews and non-Jews alike continue to grapple.

As with nearly all, if not every, Jewish family of German descent, the genocide directly affected the Lowensteins of Essen-Steele, an upper-middle class, religiously observant and culturally integrated family who had lived in the community for at least 140 years by the time Adolf Hitler and the Nazi regime came to power in early 1933.

Many members of the family were murdered by the Nazis, including patriarch Joseph Lowenstein, who had been a much-respected and loved physician in Steele, his son Rudolf, also a physician; his daughter-in-law Margarethe and his grandchildren Klaus-Martin and Clara.

The Nazi regime also affected Lowensteins who were able to escape its murderous clutches. Edward Lowenstein, who was born in 1934, and his older brother Ralph, born in 1932, were two of them. Both boys were sent on trains called Kindertransport, or child transport, to England. The Kindertransport was established by the British government in the aftermath of the Kristallnacht pogrom in November 9 and 10, 1938 that injured and killed many Jews, destroyed thousands of Jewish synagogues, homes and businesses across Germany. The goal of the program was to give sanctuary to 10,000 Jewish children from Germany, Austria, Poland and Czechoslovakia,

The Lowenstein boys were able to flee the country due to the advocacy of an English relative in England and the courage of their parents, Max and Hilde Lowenstein, in sending the young children away.

Ralph, who was 7 years old at the time, went first. In his Shoah interview close to 60 years later, he recalled how agonizing it had been for his father to let him go.

Edward, who had not turned 5 years old, followed a few weeks later. His departure was delayed by appendicitis. Max, an injured World War I veteran, had taken his son around the town in an effort to find someone who would perform an appendectomy, but no one would operate on a Jewish boy. Eventually, Max's father Joseph found a non-Jewish doctor who was willing to perform the procedure and carried it out on the kitchen table on the first floor of Joseph's three-story house. Just weeks after having a life-threatening condition that required emergency surgery, Edward was sent away from his parents for a period of unknown duration.

Edward remembers little of his time in Germany-a lack of memory that perhaps was due to the combination of his tender years and the traumatic nature of the experience.

The boys stayed in the country near Southampton, England for about 18 months, under the watchful and loving care of Ruth Stern, headmistress of a country school who never married or had children. In later life, both Edward and Ralph spoke about their attachment to Stern, while she described the transformative experience for her of caring for them.

In the spring of 1940, Max and Hilde were able to leave Germany via Genoa, Italy, a port city in a country whose government was a Nazi ally, and to depart from there for the United States. The boys left from England shortly thereafter, arriving in New York City October 4, 1940. Thus, just 18 months after having lost contact with their parents, Ralph and Edward experienced the second loss of Ruth Stern, the primary parental figure who had cared for them after they left Germany.

After a few months, the refugees moved from New York city, where they had been staying with Hilde's brother Eric Goldberg and his wife Ilse both of whom had immigrated to the United States in 1937, to Cincinnati, Ohio. Once there, the parents set about the task of learning the language and adapting to life in the country that had given them safe haven.

It was no easy task.

As opposed to Germany, where the family was known and respected in the community and lived in material comfort, the family was unknown, poor and depended upon the kindness of others. In Germany, Max and another brother were lawyers, while his two other brothers were doctors. The loss of his professional status was particularly painful for him.

The Trauma

Trauma was a defining element of the Lowenstein family´s experience during these years. There was Max's physical trauma of having been arrested and beaten as well as having loved ones murdered by the Nazi regime. There was the material trauma of having lost home, money and careers. There was the emotional trauma of having lost the respected place they held in the community, the security of living in a country where one spoke the language, had roots and understood the culture, and, perhaps, some guilt at having survived where so many others did not.

As many German Jewish families did, and, indeed, as many trauma survivors do, the family adopted a number strategies to deal with their trauma. The most important of these was focusing on moving forward in their new home, not looking back at where they used to live. Hilde and Max concentrated on caring for their children, earning a living and establishing a community in an unfamiliar nation where they did not have history, language or cultural bearing.

Although Max and Hilde socialized with other German Jewish émigrés, they did not talk much about what had happened in Germany with their children. One can speculate about their motivation, and it is possible that several factors were at play. The first was that sharing of this nature was not within their pre-existing cultural framework. The second was that they may have been trying to shield the children from the pain they had experienced. And a third may have been that the challenges as new arrivals left little time for reflection and sharing of this type.

Regardless of the reasons for their silence, Hilde and Max indeed did not share much about their lives in Germany with their boys. As a result, whether consciously or unconsciously, they passed on the practice of not speaking openly about traumatic events.

In short, then, Germany changed from a much-loved home and site of family connection and tradition, albeit interspersed with episodic antisemitism, to a place from which one was totally cut off, about which there was little information, and from which one had to flee to save one's life.

Edward and Ralph grew up, married and had children of their own. Edward adopted the same approach with his three sons toward his and the family's past that his parents had done with him.

He did so in the face of evidence that the subject clearly troubled him.

Jeff had a memory of watching the first episode of the mini-series Holocaust. The show had barely aired for 20 minutes when Edward, distraught, silently shut off the television. Yet when Jeff and his brothers asked what was upsetting him, Edward insisted that nothing was wrong.

This disjunction between the stated words, the lack of information and the emotional distress impacted each of the boys in different ways.

Jeff in particular thirsted to know more about his father and that period. After graduating from college, he initiated a series of actions to fill the void he felt within himself. These included visiting and interviewing family members from the previous generation like Ilse Goldberg and Ernie Lowenstein, a paternal uncle of Edward's who played a major role in his decision to become a doctor. Jeff read many books about the Holocaust, identified with oppressed people of different backgrounds, and, in 2004, took a trip sponsored by the German government to see new Jewish life in the country.

At the end of the trip, he tacked on several extra days to visit sites of family significance, visiting the two apartments his father, uncle and grandparents had lived in and meeting a non-Jewish family who had held the Lowenstein family bible at great personal risk for a quarter century. A member of the non-Jewish family also gave Jeff a copy of a notebook she had assembled that contained more than 100 pages of correspondence between the two families collected over 65 years.

The supplying of information, the visiting of sites where his family had lived and the meeting people who had known key family members all were sources of comfort and healing for Jeff, who returned with the notebook, shared its contents with the family and spoke about his hope that the entire family might return with Edward and/or Ralph to see the hometown they had left so many decades ago.

Jeff also wrote about the experience in a three-part series for a Jewish publication. In 2008, at a national journalism conference, he met a representative from the German government who, after hearing the story, expressed interest in publishing the piece on the federal website. (This happened later in 2008.)

Gabriele Thimm read the article on the site while searching for Lowenstein family members as part of her planning a memorial event for the Jewish community in Essen. She then contacted Jeff.

It is impossible to overstate the importance of the role Gabriele Thimm played in the project. As a teacher deeply committed to teaching her students the true nature of her nation's history, she has worked tirelessly to provide in-school learning as well as outside of school, "real-life" situations that have taken the educational activities out of the classroom and into the community. She has thereby provided a vehicle for the students to take concrete and constructive action based on what they have learned about the Nazi genocide and the possible involvement of their forebears.

In 2006 Thimm worked with the students to have Stolpersteine, or stumble stones, placed outside the home on Alte Zeilen, which had been owned by Lowenstein family patriarch Joseph Lowenstein. Bronze stumble stones are placed just below the standard level of stone, thus causing the person who walks not to fall, but to have their normal gait interrupted by the fact of history. Individual stones record the name, year of birth, and year and location and manner of death for the people who lived at the address.

Gabriele and her students participated in the laying of the stones for Joseph, Rudi, Margarete and Clara, who among them represented three generations of Lowenstein family members who were murdered during the Holocaust. (The students' parents sponsored Klaus-Martin's stone.)

Rudi Lowenstein, no longer able to make a living as a physician due to Nazi regulations, had moved back to his father's home. He chose not to pursue sending his children on the Kindertransport, believing they would be better off staying together in Germany. Sadly, all five family members ultimately perished in Auschwitz.

In Thimm, then, the students have the example of a ceaseless advocate not only for providing them with an unblinking look at Germany's murderous history, but of someone who is equally committed to providing them with opportunities to engage in constructive activities based on their newly acquired knowledge.

Thimm applied both of these qualities during the Lowenstein family trip with the family itself, with the students with whom she worked, with her colleagues at the Realschule Uberruhr and with other members of the Essen community.

The initial contact with the family came through virtual communication. In her email Thimm explained that she was organizing a memorial ceremony for the Jewish community and that one of the planned stops was going to be at home of Joseph Lowenstein, the family patriarch for whom Jeff was named and a highly respected doctor in the community who was murdered in Auschwitz.

She invited family members to attend the event, which was to be held on the 73rd anniversary of Kristallnacht.

> "I think, it's our responsibility to teach the children/pupils about the German history in the time of National Socialism (Hitler) and the history of the Jews in Germany," she wrote.

Lowenstein family members were unable to attend the event in person, but did send pictures that were projected onto Alte Zeilen, a three-story yellow stucco building.

The family also sent the following statement to be read during the ceremony:

> Dear Ms. Thimm, parents, teachers, and members of the Essen-Steele community,

> It is with gratitude and respect that we write this note to register our appreciation of the commitment you have shown to confront the dark chapter in Germany's past and to commemorate the lives of residents in the community who were killed during the Nazi era.

> Ms. Thimm, we honor the courage, character and persistence you have shown in undertaking this project, and we also want to acknowledge the support you have received from your supervisors and the other members of the community in making a public and permanent acknowledgment through these memorials of what happened here during the period when Adolf Hitler ruled the country.

> This memorial and the ongoing teaching of the children about what occurred represents an important act of acknowledgment that has, in its process and substance, contributed to a healing process. It is also a critical, but not sufficient, element in allowing young people to emerge into adulthood with a full understanding of what has been part of their nation's past, but what need not be again should they act with the same decency and humanity demonstrated by so many of the people who are gathered here today.

> We regret that we are not able to join you on this momentous occasion, but want to be emphatically clear that our inability to attend in person does not in any way signal a lack of awareness, appreciation and respect for what you have done and what you will continue to do this in this area.

We look forward to the day, hopefully this spring, when we will be able to meet and express our gratitude to you in person. In the meantime, we hope the ceremony goes well today. Please know that it is deeply appreciated by us.

Sincerely,

The Lowenstein Family

Jeff Kelly Lowenstein wrote about the buildup to the ceremony and the event itself for (http://www.huffingtonpost.com/jeff-kelly-lowenstein/kristallnacht-anniversary_b_1082302.html) the Huffington Post, a blog network to which he contributes, as well as on his own blog.

Thimm sent a description of the event, which included stops at three houses where Jewish people used to live, a description of the Jewish community in Essen, an explanation of what happened during the Nazi era, the reading of the statement, and a display of old and new family pictures. The final part of the presentation was music and the message, "Life goes on."

In December 2011 Jeff Kelly Lowenstein spoke to the family about taking the trip to Germany, and, for the first time, Edward Lowenstein agreed. The topic had been one that the family had discussed at various points over the years, even to the point of talking about dates for tickets. In fact, he had been reluctant to return to his birthplace even to the point of declining to get off a train stopped there during a trip to Europe in the mid-1960s. He felt it had "nothing to do with his life."

Jeff and Gabriele were the point people in the planning process, which was an important element in establishing trust and building a connection between people on both sides. Both took care to be inclusive of the people with whom they were communicating, to provide new information whenever it surfaced and to ensure that people on both sides were comfortable with the schedule and events. The communication took place largely through email with occasional Skype calls.

During these conversations Gabriele spoke English and Jeff spoke German. Although this possibly made the communication less efficient and involved both people speaking in a language in which each had less proficiency, it also was a sign of respect and an effort to engage the other. They also began to build a personal relationship that extended beyond the logistics of the trip to learning about each other's children and even cats. Jeff's wife Dunreith participated in the conversations, too.

The planning process itself stimulated significant conversations on both sides. A concern surfaced on the Lowenstein side about whether Gabriele was to be trusted since she kept asking for additional information about the family. This perspective was understandable, given the family's previous experience. But part of breaking the intergenerational cycle of repetition was developing confidence that the person on each side was indeed to be trusted.

At the same time, the period before the 2012 trip also sparked discussion and sharing of Ralph's trip to Essen in 1977 with his family-a trip during which he visited his father's former law office and met the non-Jewish family who had kept the Lowenstein family bible. Thus, Ralph was happy to share his experience with family members but more guarded about sharing it with an as yet unknown German teacher.

One key effort of the planning by each side was an effort to be as inclusive and open as possible.

This meant sending a myriad of emails to all members of the family, including those who were not going on the trip, answering questions and informing everyone of the latest developments. It also meant being as clear as possible with Gabriele about what was happening on the family's side. Gabriele did the same for the community.

In designing the week Gabriele and Jeff tried to strike a balance between having activities that would be meaningful, but the pace of which would not be overwhelming.

The family members who eventually went on the trip were Edward, Jeff, Dunreith, Aidan and Jon. Edward's partner Lee accompanied them.

The goals of the trip were to provide a series of experiences for the family that would help them learn about their roots, that would be comfortable for Edward during his return and that would also create a forum for learning and healing for the community and family. The emphasis of the ceremony was to be on life, not on the destruction that had occurred. They were therefore entitled, "A Celebration of Life."

The Trip

The trip had five distinct types of experiences for the family: return for Edward; those that extended the family's knowledge; those that involved a family connection with a non-Jewish German family; celebrations; and a pair of public events that emphasized community and youth education.

Return

Three events were related to return for Edward. The first two consisted of going to the two apartments where he had lived before he left Germany in early 1939, while the third involved going to Alte Zeilen, the former home of his grandfather Joseph and the site of his appendix operation on the kitchen table.

Gabriele had organized for a local historian, Dr. Ludger Heid, a historian at the University of Duisburg-Essen, to attend the apartment visits with the family. While the visits were planned, no contact had been made with the people who lived there. Fortunately, residents were present in both apartments.

The first apartment was on Roonstrasse in Duisburg. A resident of the floor below where Edward had lived was home and, after hearing the explanation of the family's reason for visiting, welcomed them into his home.

Edward had very few remaining memories of being in Germany. However, standing in the window and looking across the street produced a visceral feeling that he had been there. Dr. Heid informed him that there had been a Hitler Youth camp across the street. This for the first time gave Edward the realization that the nightmares of green men marching ominously that he had experienced for many years while young in England and Germany might well be related to the marching of Hitler youth.

The man who lived in the apartment, Michael Frohling, was professionally involved in arts education and even contacted the family later to see about having a Stolperstein put in outside the home to commemorate the family's living there. (After some discussion, the family decided against it because they felt the intent of the Stolpersteine was to note the presence of people who had lived there and later been killed by the regime.) Frohling spent time with them, showed the backyard and pledged to keep in contact.

The second visit was an entirely different experience. This was on Lotharstrasse, and also a place Jeff had visited in 2004. The name Winkelmann was still there. After ringing the bell, the family discovered that Mr. Winkelmann was no longer alive, but his widow was.

Mrs. Winkelmann's manner was almost the complete opposite of Mr. Frohling. She asked for identification before allowing the family to enter the apartment, did not show them around and went to great lengths to share a story that presented her family's actions in a favorable light, but that proved impossible to have taken place. According to her, her father had stretched himself to give Max Lowenstein, Edward's father, a good deal when he bought the apartment from Max in the late 1930s. Max had returned after the war to ask for money. Like her late husband, Mrs. Winkelmann clearly considered Max Lowenstein's price distasteful. Again, as her husband had done with Jeff eight years earlier, she searched for documents that ultimately she could not locate that she asserted would have proved the veracity of what she was saying.

There were at least three factual errors in Mrs. Winkelmann's story. The first was that the Lowensteins were renters and never owned the apartment. The second was that there were no documents. The third was that Max never returned to Germany after the war.

After a visit of about 30 minutes, Mrs. Winkelmann showed the family around the Square and pointed out a wall plaque that noted the destruction of the synagogue in November, 1938 caused by Kristallnacht and shared her memories of having walked, as a scared little girl, hand in hand with her mother watching the fire.

While less emotionally gratifying, the visit to the Winkelmann house contributed to a deeper understanding of the generational transmission of trauma in several ways. To begin, it showed the abiding unease and suspicion with which many people live many decades after the war's end. Through her anecdote about Kristallnacht, Mrs. Winkelmann demonstrated how, even as her family had benefited from Jewish suffering, she carried with her a self-concept as a victim of that era based in part on her disturbing childhood memories.

The interaction provided the family an understanding of how the issues of trauma transmission exist on both sides of the historical divide and also helped place the generosity and extraordinary level of welcome by Gabriele and many others in the community in a larger cultural context. It also illustrated the need that many people who have benefited unfairly have to explain their actions in a way that casts them in a positive light, even if it requires telling a story that is untrue and easily disproved.

The first two visits occurred without advance notice for the people living there. The third was the most planned and had the warmest sense of welcome.

The family visited the residents of the first floor of 22 Alte Zeilen, a stately yellow three-floor building where Joseph Lowenstein had lived and where Edward had been operated on shortly before leaving on the Kindertransport.

The Fuchs family could not have created a more inviting environment. The table was beautifully set, and Mrs. Fuchs had baked cakes from her favorite recipes, including one of her mother's.

The Fuchs family also presented the Lowensteins with a series of gifts, each of which conveyed the Fuchs' desire to help them understand and feel connected to their past. These included a floor plan Mr. Fuchs had obtained in his capacity as a civil servant, a copy of the bill of sale from Joseph Lowenstein to an unknown butcher and an actual piece of the house that had become dislodged during a repair project. Each was offered with generosity and without hesitation. Dirk Fuchs later communicated in writing to Jeff his pleasure in the house and his desire that the Lowensteins also have information about his family.

Angelika, a woman who owned the second-floor unit, also joined the gathering. She started crying when she shared her feelings of guilt and shame after she had learned about how the house had previously been owned by Jewish people and what had happened to them.

Lowenstein family members explained to Angelika that they did not hold ill will toward her, and she appeared comforted by that. She invited the family upstairs, and, before they left, said, "It's the family's house. We are just visiting."

On one level, it was the ultimate statement of welcome. But on the other hand, her statement raised important questions of reparations and the state of what would happen should the family have actually wanted to live there.

While the three visits did not result in sparking new memories for Edward, they did allow the family to have a shared experience of a range of welcome, a greater understanding of where they had come from and a connection to the people who live there now.

Extend Family Knowledge

The family had two experiences that extended their knowledge of their roots beyond what they known before. The first was a visit to the local Jewish cemetery in which four generations of Lowensteins were buried, while the second was a surprise visit to a farm family members used to own.

Gabriele arranged both for the family to have access to the Jewish cemetery, which remained intact during and after World War II even though half of the Jewish community had been murdered, and for the experience to be a guided one.

Dr. Uri Kaufmann, a Swiss scholar who headed the former old synagogue and current cultural center, was the guide. He showed the family five points in the cemetery where Lowensteins had been buried, including a blank stone where the last relative had been buried in 1940.

The graves were of varying size and prominence, showing both the family's deep roots and position in the community. The decreasing size and elaborateness of the graves over time demonstrated the family, like the rest of the Jewish community, had seen their status decline during the Nazi regime. Dr. Kaufmann also gave the family information that extended beyond the Holocaust and the experience of profound rupture and disruption.

The second event occurred during a surprise birthday party for Edward, when Norbert Mering, who hosted the event with his wife Hanni, informed the family that they used to own a nearby farm called Hemmerhof, and invited them to go see it.

The family did, and, after a short drive, arrived at the main house.

Mering knocked on the front door, and presented the family to a woman in her late 30s or early 40s. She nearly went into shock, ran over to another house on the property and joyfully summoned her in-laws. Her father-in-law had been born in the house, and was the direct descendant of the Roemling family who had purchased the farm and the house from the Lowenstein family in the early part of the 20th century, decades before the Nazi era. The two families visited and chatted before the Lowenstein family returned to the party. Members of the Roemling family later joined them.

Both of these incidents showed the family that they indeed had deep roots in the community. Through documents, people, property and graves, they gain a broader sense of the family´s history in the community and were able to place the Holocaust era in greater historical perspective.

Family Connection: Meeting the Non-Jewish Family

During the week the Lowenstein family also met the non-Jewish family. The husband's father Karl had owned a print shop and been a patient and friend of Joseph Lowenstein. Joseph had visited Karl shortly before being deported to Theresienstadt, and later to the Auschwitz death camp. During that visit Joseph entrusted for safe keeping until he returned a copy of the Lowenstein family bible that had a hand written family tree that went back to 1791, along with books of classical literature. Karl had held the bible for a quarter century before Ernest Lowenstein, one of Joseph´s sons, returned in 1968 to retrieve it.

Jeff had visited Karl's son and his wife in 2004 and had learned that the wife, a former secretary, had kept a faded blue notebook in which she had compiled correspondence between the two families. The documents began in 1931, when Karl printed the death notice for Joseph´s wife Clara, and continued until the present.

The couple welcomed the family to their home and showed the family the notebook over more sweets and tea. The husband told the family that Karl had urged Joseph many times to leave the country, but Joseph had not wanted to do so until it was too late. The husband also shared memories of receiving care packages the Lowenstein family had sent after the Second World War, while Edward shared memories of making the packages and considered that experience responsible for learning to wrap presents.

The visit to the family allowed Edward to meet a member of the family who was responsible for saving the family bible and for the rest of the family to know someone whose ancestors had not blindly complied, but instead actively resisted, the dictates of the Nazi government.

Celebration

The week contained official and unofficial celebrations.

They began at Gabriele's home, where this indefatigable host had prepared bountiful food and provided copious amounts of wine that she and her college-age children, Gawain and Gloria, shared with the Lowenstein family. She did this several nights, enabling all to begin to truly know each other. The dates included the evening of May 28, which at midnight marked the beginning of May 29 and Edward's birthday.

Other meals and sweets were also sites of unofficial gatherings during which participants chatted and built their relationship in a setting that was less formal and more conducive to relaxed conversation.

The community also gave Edward a surprise 78th birthday party at Hanni and Norbert Mering's home the evening of the first ceremony. It was an idyllic setting with plenty of green space Norbert had cleared by hand, honey he had gathered from his hives, tasty food, a champagne toast, gifts and, later, a roaring bonfire. The evening was an official tribute to Edward to thank him for returning 73 years after he had last left.

These celebrations provided the settings in which relationships and friendships could develop and conveyed the diametrically opposite message from that which he and his family had received during the Nazi era.

Ceremonies Centered on Youth and Education

The most public and communal element of the week was a pair of ceremonies held at the Old Synagogue and, the next day, at Realschule Uberruhr, the school where Gabriele taught.

Gabriele had worked with her students for months on both events.

The first was attended by hundreds of people and included statements by dignitaries welcoming the family and thanking them for their participation in the event. The program consisted of students reading, singing, showing pictures and taking the audience through the history of the Jewish people, the history of the Jewish community in Essen, the history of the Lowenstein family and the destruction that occurred after the Nazis' rise to power.

A young woman named Melina explained the perspective that the students brought to the presentation:

> "This is neither because we feel like offenders nor because we feel like victims, but because it is our concern to remember those people who lived in Essen as respected citizens, as friends, as acquaintances, as sport comrades, as parents, as employers and employees, in fact as citizens of the city of Essen," she read.

Edward Lowenstein answered questions in both ceremonies; some in German though mostly in English. When asked what he thought of Germany, he said that it was the country where some of the worst events in human history had taken place, but it was also the country that had done more to face its past than any other.

Edward also made a statement in which he explained that, rather than accept the honorarium he had been offered, he and the family had spoken and had decided to offer to create an award in the family's name that would be awarded annually to students to promote tolerance and justice.

Jeff spoke in German about how being there was a dream coming true for the family. He talked about the gifts the community gave the family through their presence and complimented the young people who had done so well during the ceremony.

He also said that the adults understood that it is not easy to be a young person, but that they were there for the youth, they believed in the youth and they know young people can learn not just from history's bad parts, but from people like the non-Jewish family who had helped the Lowensteins.

Each ceremony had key elements of symbolism. The first was held in the Old Synagogue, a building that Kaufmann explained had been desecrated during the same Kristallnacht pogrom that sparked the establishment of the Kindertransport program on which Edward and Ralph had escaped the country.

People the family had met throughout the week, like the Merings and the Fuchs, all attended the ceremony.

The second had a Stammbaum, a green cardboard family tree that was empty at the beginning of the celebration. Students who had been given signs with names of family members were called forward to place them on the tree. Thus, in a short time, seven generations of Lowenstein family members' names were added, literally building the tree as the ceremony progressed.

Each event also contained an injunction from Gabriele for the students and all attendees to recognize that the work of building a better world had only been begun, not completed:

> Dear Dr. Löwenstein, may I ask you to join me once more. I want to reveal to everybody here that Dr. Löwenstein celebrated his birthday yesterday, on 29th May. He was 5 years old when he had to leave Essen to survive, and now, after 73 years, he is back for the first time. Almost everything has changed—and fortunately, many things have improved.
>
> But even today, we don't live in a land of milk and honey.
>
> We still have to create our own paradise.
>
> Knowing history and remembering is the only way to make sure people can work on future freedom, security and peace. While antisemitism increases and there are frequent menaces to extinguish Israel, we still won´t give up hope that young people will learn to think on their own and withstand indoctrination and manipulation to live a life in freedom.

The events were not identical.

Geared to a younger audience, the ceremony at the school was more interactive and included frequent stops by the older students conducting the ceremony to ask the younger students in the room for the answers to questions they posed to the group. The second event also included information about Edward's professional accomplishments. This allowed the students to understand that his life was not solely defined by being a Holocaust refugee who returned 73 years later with some family members. Rather he was a highly accomplished Harvard professor and medical doctor who not only had not allowed the turbulence in his childhood to deter him, but instead who had displayed values of compassion and a commitment to helping others who had been less fortunate than him. The inclusion again highlighted the trust, dialogue and openness to feedback that characterized Gabriele´s interactions with the family the entire time.

These events and the family´s response provided the most public and communal forum for healing helped to forge a new and different chapter to a story that had been shrouded for decades in guilt, shame, and death. It is important to note that the future-oriented approach did not for one second imply that what took place did not happen or did not matter. Instead memories of the past should be an active stimulus to learning and preventing such atrocities from happening again.

Post-trip Presentation and Return for the Award

In August 2012, family members applied and gained acceptance to present about the trip at the third Engaging the Other conference in Bloemfontein, South Africa. The presentation summarized the background to and events during the trip, and included in-person presentations by Dunreith and Jeff Kelly Lowenstein, Dunreith reading a statement that Gabriele had prepared, Edward Lowenstein participating via audio conference and Jon Lowenstein participating by sharing a sample of the photographs he had taken during the trip.

A member of PAKH, or Arbeitskreis für intergenerationelle Folgen des Holocaust, a German dialogue group of psychiatrists who are either the children of Nazi perpetrators or of Holocaust survivors, facilitated the session.

The presenters, shared their thoughts and perspectives, then opened the audience to questions.

In response to one of these, Edward replied that while the trip had had many benefits for him, it had not led him to a place of forgiveness. This statement sparked a vigorous discussion around the topic of forgiveness, including specifically about who has the right to confer it and to what degree, if at all, people should be held accountable for the actions of their parents or ancestors. (The unanimous consensus among the family was that they should not.)

After the session ended, audience members from South Africa, Germany, Rwanda and Israel all shared their gratitude for the substance and method of the presentation.

The conference was important for family members because it allowed them to see, listen to, learn from and talk with people engaged in similar efforts throughout the world. The experience expanded the perspective, which had initially been limited to a private family journey of return, to joining a global community dedicated to reconciliation work. Furthermore, they learned that the family´s project resonated powerfully with people from countries that had no direct connection to either the Holocaust, Judaism or Europe.

Following the conference presentation, Dunreith and Jeff Kelly Lowenstein, and Jon Lowenstein met with Dr. Mary Harvey, a psychologist who has done important work around communities healing from violence. Harvey introduced family members to Lesley University faculty. Family members and Gabriele participated in an event on the Lesley campus in Cambridge, Massachusetts in February 2014 that began a yearlong series of events titled, "Violence Transformed." (The event included showcasing the work of Manuel Schroder, an artist affiliated with Michael Frohling, the gentleman who lived in the same building as one of Edward Lowenstein's apartments. Frohling connected Schroder to the family, who then in turn put him in touch with Harvey.)

In June 2013 Edward Lowenstein and Jeff Kelly Lowenstein returned to Essen to present the Lowenstein Family Award for Tolerance and Justice to the first winners.

The presentation of the first annual Lowenstein Award took place during the tenth birthday celebration of Realschule Uberruhr, and again saw dignitaries express their gratitude to the family for having made the journey to return and show the community the importance of the work they were doing.

Edward Lowenstein made a statement in German, reading from a translation by a teacher who had been unable to attend the previous year's event: "We hope that students make Justice and Tolerance a part of your lives every year, and in turn teach your children, family and friends," he said. "The future is the hands of the youth, in your hands."

He also presented the awards to students who had participated in the 2012 as well as to the winners selected by a jury of three community members-Andreas Bensch, a student teacher, retired middle school teacher Ute Kuntzsch, and Gabriele Thimm-who chose from the 19 essays submitted by students on a broad range of topics. The winning essay was by student Eva Sander, who wrote about the poverty in the world with her own ideas for poverty reduction. Lowenstein's statement and the student's recognition both elicited hearty applause.

Student acts also included a rap about the family created by 14 young people that told the story of the family's history, and a video. The video started by showing black and white pictures of children holding suitcases, wearing numbers around their necks and waiting to board a Kindertransport that would take them to safety. Ensuing text explained that Edward and Ralph Lowenstein were two of the 10,000 children who were part of the program. The video then showed pictures from the previous year's ceremony at the Great Synagogue, explaining that Edward Lowenstein had returned with his family after 73 years and the family had created the award that would be given out for the first time that evening.

The family's presence was noted at other points in the school. Pictures from the previous year's ceremony were displayed in a case on the school's second floor, and at least one student had made the family the focus of a major school project that was displayed among other examples of meritorious work.

Importantly, much of the focus had to do more with the principles of tolerance and justice than with the family's specific history. The school's art teacher had, with his students, built a mural that stretched around three interior walls of a building that bordered a concrete section of the students' playground. The teacher and his class had designed, then painted the mural, which had many bright colors and which spelled the words "Tolerance" and "Justice" letter by letter. The letters were made of puzzle pieces put in place by human-like characters, each of whom at most could create a single piece and many of whom were doing other activities like swinging on a swing or playing. The mural's message signified the importance of the components of tolerance and justice and suggested that everyone has a part to play in its becoming a lived reality for all. Principal Frau Elvira Bluemel expressed the thought that words were not enough; rather, the students had created a visual reminder of the standards to which she and other community members need to hold themselves and the children.

In addition to the acts and mural, the family also learned of the impact of the project by meeting and talking with the people whom they had met in 2012.

People like Mr. and Mrs. Roemling and Norbert Mering.

They related that Mering was building two plaques with the family's name on it. One will be on a wall at the school and will have the name of the prize winner engraved each year. The second plaque is a historical one that the Roemling family has given permission to display permanently near the front of the house after it had been completed.

Mering's action was one of several that suggested that the experience had been a positive, and even healing, one for second-generation members of the Essen community. Dirk Fuchs, the owner of the first-floor unit at Alte Zeilen, wrote to Jeff Kelly Lowenstein. In his letter he said that he had appreciated the family's visit to their home, that he wanted to spend some time introducing his family to Kelly Lowenstein and that the home had been a place of joy for his family.

Members of the third generation seemed positively affected by their participation in the project, too. Gabriele Thimm's children Gawain and Gloria said they felt enriched by participating in the project in a supportive role, a number of her students told her in 2012 that the Lowenstein family's visit had been one of the highlights of the year for them, and several of the young men who had written the rap went with Thimm to greet Edward Lowenstein and Lee Kass at the train station when they arrived in June 2013.

The second visit and award presentation cemented many ties that had been established. It also allowed the family and the community to engage with each other in a way similar to the one that the student at the first ceremony had described; aware of and sobered by the past, but living in the present with an eye toward the future.

"Children need repetitions," Gabriele Thimm wrote about the family's second visit. "They need tradition. So you can install the awareness of their own responsibility for a better world. In retrospect, I realize what has happened with the students. Before our project nobody talked about his own family-history. But today more and more children know about their own family and they tell about it. So they get an empathically feeling for each other. This is a beginning for understanding and also for working together—I hope."

Further Expansion and Development of the Project

The project has continued to expand and grow.

In November 2013, students from Realschule Uberruhr spoke about the Lowenstein Family Award and performed the rap in front of 250 people, including Essen mayor Reinhard Pass, delegates from many political parties and Bishop Matthias Ring, at the 75th anniversary commemoration of Kristallnacht in Essen.

The number of students at Realschule Uberruhr participating in the second award competition was about double from the first year; the year's theme was "Life in a multi-cultural community: the people of Essen."

In late December 2013 Gabriele Thimm suggested that the family consider establishing a non-profit association in order to be able to present the award at more schools and to ensure its continuation after she retired from the Realschule Uberruhr. The family agreed, and both Edward and Ralph Lowenstein enthusiastically pledged financial support for this endeavor.

Also in December Pumla Gobodo-Madikizela, a former member of South Africa's Truth and Reconciliation Commission and convener of the 2012 conference Dunreith and Jeff Kelly Lowenstein attended, visited Essen to better understand the project. She went to the Lowensteins' former apartment, met Gabriele Thimm and Frau Bluemel, spoke with students at the school and heard the rap performed. Subsequent to her visit, Gobodo-Madikizela began discussions with the family about winners of the award and a teacher being sponsored to attend a youth conference in South Africa in 2016.

Thus, the project has rapidly expanded beyond the original parameters to one involving people of good will from three continents.

Key Themes, Unique Elements

Many others have grappled with and written about the themes of memory, intergenerational transmission of trauma, the hunger to know one's family's past, and the desire for dialogue and mutual understanding among members of post-atrocity generations that were among the most central of the Lowenstein family's trip and ensuing project.

Indeed, there is an emerging, increasingly rich body of works that tackle the themes of the intergenerational transmission of trauma to the children of survivors and perpetrators.

In *Haunting Legacies: Violent Histories and Transgenerational Trauma*, literary scholar Gabriele Schwab connects her personal experience growing up in postwar Germany with those of her countrymen on both sides of the genocide. Schwab also delves into the "disappearances" that happened in South American countries like Chile and Argentina and explores these issues in South Africa during the apartheid era.

The late psychologist Dan Bar-On's interviews with the children of former Nazis, several of whom were high-ranking officials, formed the basis for his significant work *A Legacy of Silence*. Both books address the themes of shame and the desire on both sides to puncture the silence that is one of the chief vehicles of transmission and enforcement of trauma.

Others have written about the experience of returning to one's former home or site of detention. In "We Would Not Have Come Without You": Generations of Nostalgia, professors and spouses Marianne Hirsch and Leo Spitzer chronicle their return with her parents to Czernowitz, Romania. In 1995, Elie Wiesel returned to the Auschwitz death camp, the place where he had lived and his father has died, and memorably implored a merciful God to "not have mercy on those who had no mercy on Jewish children." In a related but different vein, Helen Epstein describes her efforts to go beyond the single photograph she possessed and learn about her mother's experience in Where She Came From: A Daughter's Search for Her Mother's History.

There have also been numerous projects and works about dialogue between the children of Nazis and the children of survivors. Psychology Professor Florence Kaslow writes in the Journal of Family Psychotherapy about one such effort in the article, *A Holocaust Dialogue Continues: Voices of Descendants of Victims and Perpetrators*.

The members of PAKH have been in regular dialogue for more than 15 years. The topic has inspired works of art like *The Lost Childhood*, an opera based in part on survivor Yehuda Nir's memoir by the same name. The work depicts conversation and confrontation between a Holocaust survivor and post-war German, each of whom struggles with the past's emotional burdens.

The Lowenstein family trip bears similarities to the central concerns of these works, yet also has a number of distinctive elements. The first is the unique presence of Gabriele Thimm and her role in helping to transform what was initially a personal journey of family return into a public forum for healing. Hirsch and Spitzer conclude their article about her parents' standing in their former community and thanking their daughter and son-in-law for giving them the strength to return to their former home. No one from present-day Czernowitz is interacting with them. By contrast, Thimm's actions, from initiating contact with the family, inviting them to the November 2011 ceremony, planning the week with Jeff Kelly Lowenstein, working with the students to carry out the pair of ceremonies in 2012, administering the first award contest, suggesting the formation of an association, and hosting Pumla Gobodo-Madikizela all played a vital role in helping the family feel welcome and creating a space for intergenerational learning on both sides.

The presence of three generations of Lowenstein family members is another element that distinguishes the trip from other similar journeys, which at most involve two generations. Aidan Kelly Lowenstein's being able to witness the return of his grandfather is both rare and a powerful story of survival and resilience.

Edward Lowenstein and the family's decision not just to return and engage in dialogue with the community, but to confer an award designed to honor those students whose written work reflects a commitment to tolerance and justice is a third unique aspect of the Lowenstein family trip. Lowenstein spoke openly with the community about the atrocities that had occurred in the country and that for many decades had made him unwilling to return to his former home. Yet he also took the honorarium that had been offered to him and gave it back to the community. "The purpose of this is to try to do a little to ensure that such acts as occurred in Germany in the 1930s and 1940s are never again performed," he said at the ceremony at the Great Synagogue in May 2012. He added that the family would work with school and community leaders to determine a mutually acceptable content and form of the award. Thimm and family members decided that the goal of the award would not be so much to focus on the past, but rather to use the lessons of the past to consider the present moment and give students tools to help construct a better future.

The visit by Gobodo-Madikizela and the possible participation of Israeli educators and students constitute a fourth unique element of the project. Previous dialogue projects have primarily remained with the framework of the original country where the trauma or atrocity occurred. Gobodo-Madikizela's speaking to students about South Africa and subsequent offer of at least one spot in a 2016 youth conference for a Lowenstein Family Award winner provided the opportunity for students and educators to place their experience in a larger, more global context, and to consider the simultaneous emotional similarities and cultural and historical differences between their situation and that of post-apartheid South Africa. This process is likely to continue and extend for all sides.

Finally, it is worth noting the incremental, organic and unofficial manner in which the project began and has grown. No one involved on either side envisioned an award with an association, students from two countries and participation from people in three continents, yet that is precisely what has evolved thus far. The substance and process of the project sends a powerful message both about the role that each individual can play in bringing something unknown into existence and the powerful energy that is unleashed and to which people respond when one establishes a space for young people inheriting a painful past to move in a different direction.

Potential Challenges, Limitations and Developments

At the same time, it is important not to paint an overly rosy picture of the experience, as extraordinary as it was.

Indeed, there were a series of challenges associated with it.
To begin, it took Edward Lowenstein months to reckon and come to terms with the completely opposite treatment he received from the German people in the community when he returned to Essen with the lifelong negative associations he had held in his head and heart. He arrived at a sufficiently peaceful place by the following June to make a return trip, though it was not an easy process for him.

Gabriele Thimm expressed the concern that many Germans observe Holocaust commemorations, but are doing so from political correctness rather than because the sentiment is coming from their hearts. She also talked about the importance of not separating the past from the present. "Only both together can build a better future," she wrote.

Building that future will be a stiff challenge, according to Thimm, citing rising antisemitism in Germany, the indoctrination of many Muslim children against Jews through Koranic schools, parents and Arabic television shows.

"The few Jewish children we have at school keep secret about it," she wrote.

The potential participation of the Israelis sparked discussion among family members about whether the award was specifically designed to focus on German children and the Holocaust or whether there are more universal messages. With the growth of the project come questions of funding, organizational structure and criteria by which other schools and nations can meaningfully participate. Finally, while the goal of young people not being burdened by the past is arguably a laudable one, approaching that state can also raise the specter of complacency, indifference and even forgetting.

As significant as they are, these problems occur within the context of a real and viable entity that as of May 2012 simply did not exist. (As Edward Lowenstein noted in the opening words during the 2013 award ceremony, "A year ago we didn't know each other. You didn't know us and we didn't know you.")

At the same time, the difficulties within the community that Thimm described provide additional motivation for Lowenstein family members and Thimm to expand and grow the project.

Although not undertaken with the intention of serving as a model for other groups or communities to emulate, the project's development raises the possibility a number of elements might well be worthy of consideration for others interested in doing similar work.

These include the building of respect and trust through regular communication, continuous sharing of new information, and checking to see how a person on the "other side" is feeling, the importance of planning while retaining flexibility, and the recognition that each person in this situation has something valuable to give the other, even as the meaning that each person derives is different. The importance of structuring time that includes a range of activities, including time for socializing and celebrating, is important, too.

The goals were also enhanced by having a tangible, youth-oriented project that used the creation of a public and detailed description of the history of both sides that combined elements of acknowledging the past, living in the present and working to create a better world in the future.

"I think ... that the story of the Lowenstein family makes history alive," wrote Gloria, Gabriele's daughter in an email message, "I think many of the learners were very touched when they met you first. I think such personal stories are a good sign for young people ... that you didn't talk about guilt but that you were in a dialogue with them. People have to understand that it's not possible to turn back time, but that we have to look to the future and try our best to have good and deep relations" (G. Thimm, personal communication, February 17, 21014).

References

Schwab, G. (2010). Haunting legacies: Violent histories and transgenerational trauma. New York: Columbia University Press.

Bar-On, D. (1989). A Legacy of silence: Encounters with children of the Third Reich. Cambridge: Harvard University Press.

Hirsch, M., & Spitzer, L. (2002). "We would not have come without you": Generations of nostalgia. American Imago, 59(3), 253-276.

Epstein, H. (1997). Where she came from: A daughter's search for her mother's history. Teaneck, NJ: Holmes & Meier Publishers.

Nir, Y. (2002). The Lost Childhood: A World War II memoir. New York: Scholastic Press.

Kaslow, F. W. (1998). A Holocaust dialogue continues: Voices of descendants of victims and of perpetrators. Journal of Family Psychotherapy, 9, 1-10.

Chapter 15
Breaking Cycles of Trauma and Violence: Psychosocial Approaches to Healing and Reconciliation in Burundi

Wendy Lambourne, David Niyonzima

University of Sydney, Trauma Healing and Reconciliation Services, Burundi

Introduction

As one of the poorest countries in the world, Burundi is struggling to recover from 40 years of political and genocidal violence, including a civil war during which approximately 300,000 people died and many more were wounded, internally displaced or became refugees. This paper argues that addressing the cycles of trauma produced by these cycles of violence is critical to peacebuilding and prevention of further violence. By examining the work of the Burundian non-government organisation THARS (Trauma Healing and Reconciliation Services) and other local Quaker organisations, we explore how combining locally-developed trauma healing and reconciliation methods with principles of capacity-building and self-help, can assist in building social trust and community resilience.

The chapter also considers how Burundians are preparing for the Truth and Reconciliation Commission (TRC) that was agreed as part of the Arusha Peace and Reconciliation Agreement of 2000, and the likely psychosocial impact of the TRC, based on research conducted by THARS in 2012. Our overall aim is to further understanding of how approaches to transitional justice and peacebuilding can be more localised, holistic and transformative through addressing psychosocial needs and priorities with a particular emphasis on trauma healing and reconciliation. But first, an account of the causes and consequences of the politically motivated ethnic violence illuminates the challenges and opportunities facing the Burundian people as they seek to rebuild their country through dealing with the legacies of the past.

Ethnic Tensions, Genocide and Civil War

Burundi, together with its more well-known neighbour, Rwanda, was colonised by Germany as part of German East Africa in 1890, and following World War I it became a League of Nations mandate, and later following World War II a trust territory, of Belgium. The kingship structure and geographical boundaries of Burundi remained relatively unchanged since the mid-19th century, with a very high population density in a country less than the size of Belgium (Watt, 2008, pp. 23-4). In pre-colonial Burundi, rank and privilege were determined largely from social status rather than ethnic identity as such, although these tended to coincide (Lemarchand, 1996, p. 10), and there were no wars or conflicts between the majority Hutu and minority Tutsi groups (Uvin, 2009, p. 7). The political system was relatively stable, and the Hutu/Tutsi divide remained more fluid in Burundi even under Belgian colonial rule, compared with neighbouring Rwanda, with the result that post-independence in 1962 a mixed government emerged in Burundi (Lemarchand, 1996, p. 1). However, political stability quickly eroded over the next four years, with an increase in Hutu/Tutsi differences and a number of coup d'état, resulting in Tutsi military rule from 1966 until the beginning of the civil war in 1993 (Uvin, 2009, p. 9).

Like Rwanda, Burundi has experienced genocide, but the history of power dynamics, political coups and violence since independence has been more volatile and complex. In 1972, approximately 200,000 Hutu were massacred by the Tutsi army in response to a violent Hutu uprising against Tutsi rule, and up to an estimated 300,000 Hutu refugees fled to neighbouring countries. It was after the genocide of 1972 that the Hutu/Tutsi divide became more widely and deeply entrenched. Hutu were thereafter almost totally excluded from political and military leadership, education and business (Uvin, 2009, p. 10), and the memories continued to haunt the Hutu masses creating a collective trauma driven by fear of another 'holocaust' (Lemarchand, 1996). In 1988, a small violent uprising incited by extremists afraid of impending liberal reforms, was followed by a localised but still vicious revenge massacre by the Tutsi army, which added further fuel to Hutu fears (Watt, 2008, p. 41).

Efforts towards democratisation resulted in a brief period of Hutu-led government which was abruptly ended when the President was killed in a coup d'état in 1993 (Uvin, 2009, p. 11-14). An estimated 50,000 Tutsi lost their lives in revenge killings, and a further 700,000 Hutu refugees fled in fear of reprisal massacres (Watt, 2008, p. 48). The civil war had begun.

Peace, Reconciliation and Transitional Justice

Violence had become a political strategy in Burundi, with coups a regular occurrence when any hint of political stability seemed on the horizon. Factional splits in the Hutu rebel movement resulted in a number of rebel groups emerging to fight the Tutsi-dominated security forces and the local Tutsi militia, whilst divisions amongst the Tutsi elite also fuelled the violent approach to political power (Lemarchand, 1996; Taylor, 2013). The internationally mediated Arusha Peace and Reconciliation Agreement was signed on 28 August 2000, and the United Nations provided a peacekeeping mission which supervised the election of a power-sharing government in 2005 (Penklis, 2011). The fighting continued, however, until December 2008 when the last of the rebel groups, Palipehutu-FNL, finally agreed to disarm, but only after reassurances that they would not be arrested and prosecuted (Vandeginste, 2012, p. 4). Other transitional justice issues which were discussed during the final peace negotiations included the release of combatants and prisoners of war, integration of former combatants into the security forces, and the rebels' preference for a 'Truth, Forgiveness and Reconciliation Commission' (Vandeginste, 2012, p. 3).

The 2000 Arusha Agreement had already provided a framework for transitional justice in Burundi, including the establishment of a Truth and Reconciliation Commission in order to investigate the crimes committed in Burundi, promote reconciliation, and clarify and rewrite the country's history (Taylor, 2013, p. 4). It called for an educational program on peace, democracy and ethnic tolerance and the promotion of reconciliation and unity amongst Burundians. It also stipulated that the transitional government would request the UN Security Council to set up an international judicial commission of inquiry which would be followed by a request for an international criminal tribunal for Burundi should evidence be found that acts of genocide, crimes against humanity or war crimes had been committed (Vandeginste, 2012, p. 2). Legislation for the establishment of the TRC was adopted in December 2004, but it was not implemented, and negotiations between the UN and the Burundian government to establish a judicial mechanism also foundered based on disagreements about the relationship between the two proposed bodies (Vandeginste, 2012, p. 2). Instead, agreement was reached for national consultations on transitional justice which were conducted in 2007, and the findings released in 2010.

The national consultations revealed majority support for the establishment of a TRC with a mixed national and international composition and a mandate to investigate the full range of crimes from independence in 1962 until the end of the civil war in 2008, as well as provision for reparations (Impunity Watch, 2013, p. 2). Following repeated commitments by the President, the creation of a technical committee, release of the Kavakure report and several versions of a draft law with guiding principles for the proposed TRC, the law to establish the TRC was finally promulgated in May 2014. At the same time, the UN has continued to include a mandate to support transitional justice in its political missions, most recently the UN Office in Burundi (BNUB) which includes a Transitional Justice Unit (TJU) tasked with supporting civil society engagement in transitional justice through the creation of FONAREC/JT (Forum National des Relais Communautaire en Justice de Transition, or Forum of Community Facilitators in Transitional Justice) and support for the protection of witnesses once the TRC is created.

International and local non-government organisations in Burundi have established a Reflection Group on Transitional Justice (Groupe de Réflexion sur la Justice Transitionnelle or GRJT) which, along with the UN and other local civil society groups, has commented on the Kavakure report and subsequent versions of the draft law for the establishment of the TRC. These comments have included criticisms that the draft law fails to comply with international standards and does not reflect the findings of the national consultations. The third draft of the law which was presented to Parliament in December 2012 included amendments which provide for pardon in exchange for confessions (conditional amnesty), and give the Burundian government the sole authority to nominate and select the commissioners instead of opening the process to public participation (Impunity Watch, 2013). This is disturbing but not surprising given that the government comprises a number of former rebel leaders who could be accused of genocide, war crimes and crimes against humanity through the TRC, and who thus have a vested interest in maximising their control of the Commission. It is therefore a challenge for civil society in Burundi to have a meaningful say in the proposed TRC, despite the national consultations and UN presence. Essentially, the design and implementation of the TRC and any other national transitional justice process is in the hands of the Burundian government which is unlikely to support a robust investigation through a truth commission, far less prosecutions through the establishment of a special tribunal.

Trauma and the Truth and Reconciliation Commission

In the absence of any formal transitional justice institutions or processes of reconciliation, local civil society organisations, led by THARS, have focused on addressing the legacy of psychological trauma in the Burundian population, and on preparing the population from a psychosocial perspective for the planned TRC. It was evident that, while a peace agreement had been reached and armed conflict had ended, Burundians faced many peacebuilding challenges in the context of extreme poverty and political indifference at the national level, as well as the psychological scars and social breakdown resulting from 15 years of civil war and mass population displacements. Despite intensive involvement of the UN in peacekeeping and peacebuilding, the focus on political and economic development at the macro level has failed to address the psychosocial impacts of genocide and cycles of trauma on individual and community well-being and ability to engage constructively across the ethnic divide. As argued by Gutlove and Thompson (2006), "social reconstruction is a strand of humanitarian activity that complements physical reconstruction and political reconstruction" that by focusing on community reconciliation aims to restore social trust and hope within a community and to support cooperative behaviour and the development of shared values and expectations (p. 187).

THARS' emphasis on understanding the role of trauma in the Burundian population and the means to promote healing has been driven by a Quaker belief that for peace to be lasting, you have to start on the healing process because healing lays the ground for creating peace in the country. It also draws on Western psychological theories about trauma and therapeutic approaches to healing, which will be elaborated in the following section. We argue that unhealed trauma is a driving force in perpetuating cycles of violence, which in turn produce more trauma, and that this affects the decision-making of political elites as well as relationships and therefore peace and development in local communities. The work of THARS is aiming to redress past experiences of transitional justice processes in other countries (such as the South African TRC), where there has been minimal recognition of trauma, its impact on participation in transitional justice, and the impact of transitional justice on trauma.

Trauma has been defined in the Western context as the sense of being completely overwhelmed by a very stressful event in which the ordinary systems of care that give people a sense of control, connection and meaning are destroyed; attachments of family, friendship, love and community are shattered, and the belief systems that give meaning to human experience are undermined (Herman, 1997). In response to real or perceived threat to the survival of an individual, a support system, or a larger community or culture, trauma leads to changes in the brain and nervous system that are essential to survival but potentially detrimental to ongoing sense of self, engagement in relationships and productive involvement in learning and work (Kantovitz & Riak, 2008). Collective trauma has been identified as a form of trauma which permeates a group living in an environment of fear and institutional failure, direct and/or structural violence.

In Burundi, a new word was created in the Kirundi local language to express the meaning of trauma resulting from the cycles of genocidal violence and civil war: ihahamuka, which conveys the sense of running, being afraid and out of breath. The term means 'being overwhelmed by what is inside me'. It attempts to capture the state of being completely overwhelmed and unable to cope or integrate the ideas and emotions involved with the traumatic experience.

THARS started by investigating the level of trauma in the Burundian population, to provide a baseline for developing a project of sensitisation and psychosocial accompaniment during the process of transitional justice and in preparation for the TRC in particular. It is important to recognise here that we are not only talking about the trauma experienced by victims, but also the trauma produced by perpetrating mass violence. Surveys were conducted in 2012 to ascertain the level of trauma in the Burundian population, as well as to gauge the level of knowledge about transitional justice, and to understand the fears and needs of Burundians in relation to transitional justice. The study found that 25% of the population were traumatised according to clinical definitions of trauma or post-traumatic stress disorder (PTSD), but this does not mean that the rest of the population who experienced the cycles of violence in Burundi do not also suffer from some symptoms of traumatic stress which could impact on their psychological well-being and social effectiveness.

There are those who are living in the streets or sometimes with their families, who exhibit extreme symptoms of trauma, unable to cope at all with a normal life. In addition to psychological symptoms, such severe trauma or PTSD causes physical symptoms including confusion, nightmares, exhaustion, lack of appetite and sleeplessness which may be experienced immediately after the traumatic event and can continue to recur over many years (Hayner, 2011, p. 152). Others may appear to be coping, but the underlying trauma can be triggered when they see the person who harmed them or their families in the past, or they may not be able to interact on a daily level with those from the other ethnic group or political party. If the memories, pain and trauma remain repressed and unexpressed, it is likely that family and social relationships will continue to be affected and economic productivity may also be impeded (Hayner, 2011, p. 146). It is the latter impact of trauma which is mostly what trauma healing workshops and other community-based psychosocial interventions aim to address by providing a safe space for people to talk about their suffering, while the more serious cases of PTSD are referred to individual psychological counselling or psychiatric interventions when such services are available.

The trauma experienced by Burundians during the historical cycles of genocidal violence has had a particularly devastating impact because of the targeted nature of the violence based on ethnicity and the identification of an enemy group which has 'deliberately inflicted pain, suffering and helplessness on its victims' (Volkan, 2009, p. 1). According to Volkan (2009), the transgenerational transmission of trauma can result in the evolution of a 'chosen trauma' which refers to the 'shared representation of an event in a large group's history in which the group suffered a catastrophic loss, humiliation and sense of helplessness at the hands of enemies' (p. 15). In the case of the Hutu majority in Burundi, their chosen trauma is the 1972 genocide, while for the Tutsi minority it is the massacres of 1993 combined with the impact of the 1994 genocide against the Tutsis in neighbouring Rwanda. The repeated or ongoing experience of trauma for an individual and their ethnic group over long time periods, meanwhile, is likely to affect individual health and resilience, as well as social or community resilience, the success of development projects and the ability to continue life with hope for the future (Yoder, 2005, p. 27). The impact of trauma induced by such extreme political violence as occurred in Burundi can also be reinforced by the chronic traumatic experience of living in poverty and facing severe economic and social challenges which can impede the healing process (Hayner, 2011, p. 152).

A truth and reconciliation commission has the potential to enable group mourning and begin to heal the chosen traumas of each group if it allows the stories of both victims and perpetrators to be heard and acknowledged, recognising that both groups have suffered loss and trauma (Volkan, 2009; Minow, 1998). This was the approach taken by the South African TRC, where both black and white victims and perpetrators of violence during the apartheid era were able to tell their stories, to forgive and reconcile at an interpersonal level in order to support the national reconciliation process. The transformative potential of acknowledgement via a TRC could thus be critical for Burundians to begin to heal their historical wounds and collective trauma (Green, 2009). Following safety and freedom from fear of recurrence, acknowledgment is the second stage identified as part of the process of trauma recovery or healing (Herman, 1997). This potential benefit of the TRC will depend on all political parties and ethnic groups involved in the conflict participating and being willing to contribute to determining the factual/forensic truth as well as sharing their personal/narrative truths, in order to create a social/dialogical truth and as a result the opportunity for promoting a healing/restorative truth at the individual, community and national levels (Boraine, 2006).

If the TRC is able to provide a safe and respectful space for victims and witnesses to tell their stories and express their feelings, and previously denied events and responsibility are acknowledged, the process of recovery and healing may thus be supported. However, the TRC could serve to retraumatise individuals through the retelling of stories of pain, humiliation and suffering, and reinforce collective trauma if the political leaders of Hutu or Tutsi groups fail to acknowledge their role in perpetuating the cycles of violence (Brounéus, 2010). Burundians also fear that by revisiting the past it will reignite the hatreds and undermine the potential for reconciliation. Indeed, the evidence that truth commissions can promote reconciliation is far from clear (Gobodo-Madikizela, 2009, p. 150). By focusing on the importance of psychosocial accompaniment, THARS is seeking to reduce the chances of retraumatisation as a result of the TRC, and by combining this approach with sensitisation, trauma healing and reconciliation programs in local communities, the aim is to strengthen individual and community resilience and social trust in a culturally appropriate manner in order to maximise the potential of the TRC to promote healing and reconciliation. As pointed out by Hayner (2011), 'a truth commission is not therapy' (p. 151) and THARS recognises that positive and sustainable impact will only be achieved if TRC staff are trained in trauma awareness and psychological support is provided for those who testify, along with ongoing community-level psychosocial programs. Healing is a process that requires time and support in order to build resilience and guard against relapses.

A number of Burundians have expressed strong misgivings about the likelihood that the TRC will be successful in this aim as the political party in power is making unilateral decisions about its structure, composition and functioning. It seems unlikely at this stage that there will be a representative expression of the truth in a way that would acknowledge the pain and loss of all Burundians from different ethnic groups and political parties. The TRC has thus been described by some Burundians as a commission to protect the politicians rather than the people. The work of THARS and other organisations promoting psychosocial healing and community level reconciliation and unity thus becomes more important to counter the potentially divisive and retraumatising impact of the TRC.

THARS has produced a brochure and a training program on transitional justice which include an emphasis on healing, forgiveness and reconciliation and as part of the Quaker Peace Network in Burundi (QPN Burundi) has developed a Burundian model of transitional justice. This model translates the UN's four pillars of transitional justice (prosecutions, truth recovery, reparations and institutional reform) into more culturally and contextually sensitive processes. The QPN Burundi model was launched in June 2014 at a public event attended by representatives from a number of local as well as international civil society organisations, the media, government and United Nations. The model includes reference to the need for healing and other psychosocial processes such as community dialogue and reconciliation which can improve social cohesion and thereby contribute to the prevention of the reoccurrence of socio-political atrocities. It also calls for removal of the cultural and other barriers to finding the truth as a means to healing the pain and hurt caused by the war and thus to support justice and forgiveness, good relations and a sustainable peace (QPN Burundi, 2014, p. 6). During the discussion and exchange of ideas after the QPN model was launched, a consensus emerged that the work of QPN was commendable as a tool to foster healing and reconciliation even though it did not fully address the justice component.

Trauma Healing and Peacebuilding

By contrast, at the macro-level of United Nations-led peacebuilding and national development, limited attention is paid to the role of trauma healing and psychosocial services (Lambourne & Gitau, 2014). There is a perceived disconnect between the individual, the community and the state which is not breached in traditional peace processes and theories of development which focus on political and socioeconomic change. Trauma diagnosis and healing are seen as belonging in the realm of psychology, psychotherapy and counselling, and in the Western context this means professional training in specific skills and techniques. Processes of healing, forgiveness and reconciliation are associated with personal, spiritual transformation which is not considered appropriate to include in the political, economic or development spheres at community, national or international levels.

At the micro-level, however, faith-based civil society actors recognise the critical role of individual and collective healing for peacebuilding and development. In the aftermath of mass violence, the psychological process of healing is intimately bound up with the social context, requiring 'social transformation aimed at rebuilding the shattered political, economic and social relationships' (Hamber, 2001, p. 131). Especially in African contexts such as Burundi, where religion and spirituality play a prominent role in individual beliefs and community life, healing and reconciliation are supported as priorities for community development. World Vision, for example, has developed a model of transformational development underpinned by an understanding of the links between trauma healing, peacebuilding and development (Kantowitz & Riak, 2008). According to this model, individual and collective trauma inhibits survivors' ability to engage in post-conflict reconstruction and development, so there is a need to focus on agency and empowerment, and meeting basic needs. Inspired by his experience working with genocide survivors in Rwanda, Gasana (2008) proposed three stages of the trauma healing journey which are necessary for overcoming poverty and building peace: journey of energy recovery, journey of hope renewal, and journey towards togetherness and connectedness (pp. 157-9).

Our research has supported the observation that participation in development is adversely affected by a lack of hope, trust and resilience in communities after mass violence. And community healing has been found to directly address the restoration of the social fabric that has been destroyed as a result of mass violence and contribute to the relational health of the society as a whole (Gutlove & Thompson, 2006, p. 185). Reconnection with society is the final stage of trauma healing advocated by Herman (1997). Gutlove and Thompson (2006) advocate the embedding of trauma healing within a program of psychosocial support that is 'synergistic with related humanitarian and reconstruction efforts' (p. 193). THARS has therefore focused its work on healing linked with relationship and capacity-building in order to foster reconciliation, social trust and productive engagement in livelihoods. This approach directly addresses the root causes of direct and structural violence in order to counter ongoing trauma, and thus to interrupt the cycles of violence.

This practice is underpinned by a process of healing and reconciliation through the creation of transformative relational spaces that enable a healing of the gap between self and other. This idea is linked to the concept of intercommunal reconciliation, described by Andrieu (2010) as unfettered dialogical processes building spaces in which participants would be able to discuss the causes of conflict and its societal consequences. It also builds on Gasana's model of community life in which three primary spaces of communication, solidarity-building and conciliation intersect in four new spaces of social interaction: transformed relationships, healing and wholeness, truth telling and unity-building processes (Gasana, 2008).

Burundians tend to be reticent by nature, and this cultural tendency is exacerbated by the impact of traumatic wounds which people may be afraid to speak about. Many people do not understand why they are having intrusive thoughts or behaving strangely, perhaps thinking that their trauma symptoms are the result of 'demonic attacks or the work of ancestral spirits' (Watt, 2008, p. 125). The methods used by THARS and others to promote healing and reconciliation share some common principles, including the provision of a safe space for people to share their stories and their trauma, so that they feel heard and the psychological barriers separating them from others begin to be eroded. Workshop participants come to realise that they are not alone, and start to reach out to others in friendship as their fear, anger and suspicion is relieved and transformed.

THARS has a number of projects and programs which support its overall mission: 'to contribute to the healing and peacemaking in the Great Lakes Region of Africa in general and Burundi in particular, using a holistic approach which brings people of all walks of life to psychosocial healing and resolution of differences' (THARS, 2010-2011). These projects and programs include trauma healing training workshops; alternatives to violence workshops; building 'listening rooms'; support groups for women who were once victims of war-related atrocities; self-help groups to empower the poorest women; healing of memories workshops; conflict mitigation and reconciliation; rescue and reintegrate children; transitional justice and Truth and Reconciliation Commission preparations; and development of the THARS centre in Gitega (the second largest town in Burundi).

The THARS listening rooms apply a particular technique of group counselling or therapy with a trained facilitator ('listener') and with a specific focus on listening. Participants in THARS workshops are educated about the impact of trauma on brain functioning and the ability to express what has happened to them. Individual responses in these workshops include saying: 'Yes—that is what happened' … 'Me too' and 'me too'. The workshops and listening rooms help people to feel empowered and raise their self-esteem so they are able to make healthy choices and be responsible for the choices they make.

The THARS intervention model provides a parallel with the three stages identified by Herman (1997) which trauma victims move through in the healing process: safety, acknowledgement and reconnection. Trauma healing aims to give victims (and perpetrators) a feeling that they have control over their lives again. Healing programmes guided by these processes foster resilience in the survivors, defined as 'the capacity to positively or successfully adapt to external problems or threats' (Chandler, 2012, p. 217). This capacity is both at an individual level and at a community level; individual resilience contributes to building community resilience, and vice-versa.

One of the specific methods used by THARS in Burundi is the conduct of AVP (Alternatives to Violence Project) workshops in rural settings where there are political and ethnic tensions. AVP is a program developed by the Quakers to encourage and train people to use creative, non-violent strategies for handling conflicts which might otherwise lead to violence. The guiding principle of AVP is the potential of 'transforming power' which is explored through experiential, interactive exercises that focus on affirmation, cooperation, personal sharing, trust-building, community-building, role playing, humour and confronting and accommodating differences among members of the group (Garver & Reitan, 1995, p. 4).

THARS has also run Healing of Memories workshops as developed by Father Michael Lapsley in South Africa (www.healing-memories.org). Comments from participants in these workshops in Burundi indicate how they contribute to promoting trauma recovery, reconciliation and trust:

> I hadn't realized how serious the workshop was at the beginning. It enabled me to review my whole life and face issues from the past that I had been avoiding.

> I was able to discover some of the feelings I had been avoiding and have not been aware of different ethnic groups can share together how they have been affected.

> I liked the freedom of expression right through the workshop; it enabled us to trust and made us willing to share our feelings.

THARS support groups involve women who have been victims of war-related atrocities coming together to complete their healing processes through manual activities and a little commerce, including making quilts, baskets, soap, bags and jewellery. The emphasis is on practical activities, making things with their hands and working together, which helps in addressing the neurological impacts of trauma, as well as making an income from what they produce so they can become helpful and productive in the family. In these groups, and the self-help groups for the poorest women to realise their hidden potential, there is a focus on the mentality of self-reliance and ownership, as well as relationship-building, which helps to restore hope, dignity, well-being and social trust. The self-help groups are based on three principles of empowerment: economic, social and political empowerment, which aim to facilitate improved life conditions for the women and their children. The approach taken by THARS is thus consistent with the claim by Gutlove and Thompson (2006) that 'healing societal trauma involves the development of support groups that employ a facilitated process whereby individuals heal in the context of a group' (p. 192). It also illustrates how 'empowerment is an important by-product of reconnection' that enables survivors to re-engage within a functional society (Gutlove & Thompson 2006, pp. 193 & 211).

Another Quaker organisation which operates on a similar philosophy in Burundi is Healing and Rebuilding Our Communities (HROC), which was created in partnership with the African Great Lakes Initiative of the Friends Peace Teams in 2003. HROC workshops bring together participants from the different ethnic groups in order to build trust, deepen psychological healing and thereby contribute to rebuilding communities. Each workshop involves three steps: education about trauma, understanding and relating to others' experiences of trauma, and working together to build more peaceful communities through developing joint projects if participants wish to do so. Such projects have included joint goat-raising and joint crop farming on shared land. HROC programs address the psychological trauma of individual participants at the same time as supporting community peacebuilding through joint income-generation projects. HROC workshops have also been run only for the Twa minority group to help them understand and heal from intergenerational trauma, and to assist them with training in kitchen gardening and nutritional health. These psychosocial interventions thus directly assist in building sustainable peace and development.

Ministry of Peace and Reconciliation under the Cross (MiPAREC), another member of the Quaker Peace Network in Burundi, has focused on creating peace committees in rural communities throughout Burundi. MiPAREC was the first of the Quaker organisations to start peace work in Burundi, and it has recently become very involved in making sure that principles of peace and reconciliation are included in the transitional justice process in Burundi. The QPN Burundi model for transitional justice includes reference to the potential contribution of local peace committees to building good relations as a basis for peace, security and community development (QPN Burundi, 2014, p. 7).

THARS workshops and programs enable Hutu and Tutsi to come together, shake hands, laugh together, realise that they are one people, and discover that the violence was based on political manipulation so that their fear can be dispelled. The Twa are also included in workshops, sometimes as facilitators, which contributes to reducing discrimination against this most marginalised group. THARS' approach specifically aims to be inclusive and holistic, focusing on relationship-building and empowerment to help build both individual and community resilience. In this way, localised approaches to reconciliation and community development through individual and collective healing can assist in providing the basis for the prevention of further violence and thus for a more sustainable peace.

Conclusion: Planting the Seeds of Peace Through Healing

> The seeds of tomorrow's wars grow in the soil of today's unhealed traumas. The seeds of tomorrow's peace grow in the soil of today's healing and reconciliation.—THARS website (www.thars.org)

In this chapter, we have begun to explore how psychosocial transformation through individual and collective trauma healing can contribute to building sustainable peace. As argued by Hart (2008), peacebuilding in traumatised societies requires attention to challenging the emotional as well as structural causes of mass violence. Trauma healing interventions such as those conducted by THARS in Burundi specifically focus on the individual psychological as well as relational aspects of micro-level peacebuilding. Combining this inner transformation and relational transformation with macro-level political, economic and legal structural transformation can provide the foundation for transformative peacebuilding, the restoration of social order and economic development from the ground up (Lambourne, 2009). Daly and Sarkin (2007) similarly argue that conceptualising reconciliation as an inclusive process of social restructuring, rather than focusing on restoration of relationships between enemies as such, can promote new cultural values and a broad vision of a peaceful future.

LeBaron (2003) emphasizes the importance of engaging people in post-conflict societies in ways that address their psychological, spiritual, emotional, and physical needs—a holistic approach, combined with flexibility and creativity (pp. 168-9). This kind of approach helps to build resilience and coping strategies to enable traumatised survivors of mass violence to re-imagine and re-engage productively in life and work (de Jong, 2011). As outlined by de Jong (2011), resilience enables individuals and groups 'to restore a new balance and related worldview' which enhances the ability to cope with the political, socioeconomic and physical conditions of the post-conflict peacebuilding context. This observation is reinforced by the South African experience where the Khulamani self-help group has continued to grow and provide community support for survivors of trauma, and according to some 'provided a much greater sense of healing than the (TRC) itself' (Hayner, 2011, p. 158).

As discussed, the TRC in Burundi is unlikely to be successful in promoting a full acknowledgement of the truth and a supportive environment for healing and reconciliation without significant political transformation. The QPN model of transitional justice for Burundi proposes a culturally contextualised and comprehensive approach to addressing these socio-political deficits with its emphasis on developing leadership, positive relationships and community empowerment supported by psychosocial reintegration. In the absence of an effective TRC, local community programs are making an impact on psychological healing and reconciliation in Burundi. As argued by Gutlove and Thompson (2006), psychosocial healing 'promotes the psychological and social health of individuals, families and community groups' and thus contributes to the 'relational health of the society as a whole' (p. 185).

The work of THARS and other Quaker organisations in Burundi illustrates the potential significance of a psychosocial approach to ending cycles of violence through culturally appropriate trauma healing programs at individual and community levels, and reinforces the critical role of psychologists and faith-based actors in a transformative holistic approach to transitional justice and peacebuilding.

References

Andrieu, K. (2010). Civilizing peacebuilding: Transitional justice, civil society and the Liberal paradigm, *Security Dialogue*, 41(5), 537-558.

Boraine, A. (2006). Defining transitional justice: Tolerance in the search for justice and peace in Boraine, A. & Valentine, S. (Eds) *Transitional justice and human security*. Cape Town: International Center for Transitional Justice, 22-37.

Brounéus, K. (2010) The trauma of truth telling: Effects of witnessing in the Rwandan gacaca courts on psychological health, *Journal of Conflict Resolution*, 54(3), 408-437.

Chandler, D. (2012) Resilience and human security: The post-interventionist paradigm', *Security Dialogue*, 43(3), 213-229.

Daly, E. & Sarkin, J. (2007) *Reconciliation in divided societies: Finding common ground*. Philadelphia: University of Pennsylvania Press.

de Jong, K. (2011) *Psychosocial and Mental Health Interventions in Areas of Mass Violence: A Community-Based Approach*. Guideline Document. 2nd edn, Amsterdam: Médecins Sans Frontières.

Gasana, S. N. (2008) Confronting conflict and poverty through trauma healing: Integrating peace-building and development processes in Rwanda in Clark, P. & Kaufman, Z. D. (Eds), *After genocide: Transitional justice, post-conflict reconstruction and reconciliation in Rwanda and beyond*, London: Hurst & Company, 145-169.

Gobodo-Madikizela, P. (2009) Working through the past in Gobodo-Madikizela, P. & Van Der Merwe, C. (Eds), *Memory, narrative and forgiveness: Perspectives on the unfinished journeys of the past*. Newcastle-upon-Tyne: Cambridge Scholars Publishing, 148-169.

Green, P. (2009) The pivotal role of acknowledgement in social healing' in Gobodo-Madikizela, P. & Van Der Merwe, C. (Eds), *Memory, narrative and forgiveness: Perspectives on the unfinished journeys of the past*. Newcastle-upon-Tyne: Cambridge Scholars Publishing, 74-97.

Gutlove, P. & Thompson, P. (2006) Using psychosocial healing in postconflict reconstruction' in Fitzduff, M. & Stout, C.E. (Eds) *The psychology of resolving global conflicts: From war to peace*, Volume 3: Interventions, Westport, Con.: Praeger Security International, 185-213.

Hamber, B. (2001) Does the truth heal? A psychological perspective on political strategies for dealing with the legacy of political violence in Biggar, N. (Ed.) *Burying the past? Making peace and doing justice after civil conflict*, Washington, DC: Georgetown University Press, 131-148.

Hart, B. (2008) The way forward in Hart, B. (Ed.), *Peacebuilding in traumatized societies*, Lanham, Maryland: University Press of America, 319-325.

Hayner, P.B. (2011) *Unspeakable truths: Transitional justice and the challenge of truth commissions*. New York: Routledge.

Herman, J. H. (1997) *Trauma and recovery*. New York: Basic Books.

Impunity Watch (2013, January). *Policy brief: Burundi's draft law on the proposed TRC*, Bujumbura: Impunity Watch.

Kantowitz, R. & Riak, A. (2008) Critical links between peacebuilding and trauma healing: A holistic framework for fostering community development' in Hart, B. (Ed.), *Peacebuilding in traumatized societies*, Lanham, Maryland: University Press of America, 3-26.

Lambourne, W. (2009) Transitional justice and peacebuilding after mass violence, *International Journal of Transitional Justice*, 3(1), 28-48.

Lambourne, W. (2012) Outreach, inreach and civil society participation in transitional justice' in N. Palmer, P. Clark & D. Granville (Eds) *Critical perspectives in transitional justice*, Cambridge, UK: Intersentia, 235-261.

Lambourne, W. & Gitau, L. W. (2014) Psychosocial interventions, peacebuilding and development in Rwanda', *Journal of Peacebuilding and Development*, 8(3), 23-36.

LeBaron, M. (2003) *Bridging cultural conflicts: A new approach for a changing world*. San Francisco: Jossey-Bass.

Lemarchand, R. (1996) *Burundi: Ethnic conflict and genocide*. Cambridge, UK: Woodrow Wilson Center Press.

Minow, M. (1998) *Between vengeance and forgiveness: Facing history after genocide and mass violence*. Boston: Beacon Press.

Niyonzima, D. (2001) *Unlocking Horns: Forgiveness and Reconciliation in Burundi*. Newberg, Oregon: Barclay Press.

Penklis, D. J. (2011) *Implications of the 1993 to 2008 Burundi peace process for United Nations peacekeeping operations*, unpublished PhD Thesis, University of Sydney.

Quaker Peace Network Burundi (2014, June) *QPN Burundi Modele de Justice Transitionelle'*, Bujumbura: QPN. [translated from the French by the author]

Richters, A. (2010) Community-based sociotherapy in Rwanda' in Kapteigns, L. & Richters, A. (Eds) *Mediations of violence in Africa: Fashioning new futures for contested pasts*. Leiden: Brill, 74-90.

Taylor, D. (2013) Truth under the avocado trees: Local needs and Burundi's TRC: Whither the Truth?, *Journal of East African Studies*, 7(3), 450-470.

THARS & GIZ ZFD (2012) *Study of the needs in psychosocial accompaniment for victims during the process of transitional justice'*, Bujumbura: THARS.

Uvin, P. (2009) *Life after violence: A people's story of Burundi.* London: Zed Books.

Vandeginste, S. (2012) Burundi's Truth and Reconciliation Commission: How to shed light on the past while standing in the dark shadow of politics', *International Journal of Transitional Justice*, 6(2),355-365.

Volkan, V. (2009) The next chapter: Consequences of societal trauma in Gobodo-Madikizela, P. & Van Der Merwe, C. (Eds), *Memory, narrative and forgiveness: Perspectives on the unfinished journeys of the past.* Newcastle-upon-Tyne: Cambridge Scholars Publishing, 1-26.

Watt, N. (2008) *Burundi: Biography of a small African country.* London: Hurst & Company.

Yoder, C. (2005) *The little book of trauma healing.* Intercourse, PA: Good Books.

Chapter 16
Breaking Cycles of Trauma through Diversified Pathways to Healing: Western and Indigenous Approaches with Survivors of Torture and War

Shanee Stepakoff

California Institute of Integral Studies

Introduction

For the past two decades, professionals working in settings affected by war and ethnopolitical violence have debated the usefulness of Western-oriented psychotherapy approaches, such as psychodynamic and cognitive-behavioral therapies (Stepakoff et al., 2006). Some practitioners (e.g., Wessells, 1999; Wessells & Monteiro, 2004) have maintained that community dialogues and alternative healing rituals such as purification ceremonies may be preferable to psychological care. Others (e.g., LeRoy, 2002) have argued that traditional healers provide valuable services for war-affected populations. The importance of social-systems interventions such as livelihood support, conscientization, and collective action has also been emphasized (Wessells, 2008). Often, these debates have been characterized by a failure to recognize the possibility of blending Western and indigenous approaches to healing, in order to more effectively address the psychological suffering that is often a part of daily life for survivors of large-scale trauma.

The aim of this chapter is to challenge that polarization by discussing two psychosocial programs in which psychological counseling and indigenous healing methods were successfully combined. Both programs were developed by the same international nongovernmental organization (NGO)—the Center for Victims of Torture (CVT), but were implemented in very different settings: (1) refugee camps in a remote rural region of Guinea, West Africa, serving war-traumatized Liberians and Sierra Leoneans; and (2) an urban clinic in Amman, Jordan, serving Iraqis who had fled ethnopolitical violence in their homeland. I spent two years with CVT (one year in each of these programs), as a clinician/trainer on an international team of mental health professionals. We recruited, trained, and supervised teams of Liberian and Sierra Leonean paraprofessonal counselors in Guinea, and a team of professional Iraqi, Palestinian, and Jordanian counselors in Amman. We worked closely and collaboratively with the local counselors as they learned to facilitate group sessions; we provided live, on-site supervision in a large percentage of the sessions; and we met with the local counselors regularly to plan and debrief the therapy sessions. Though there were a number of similarities in the programs, for the purposes of this chapter each of the programs is considered separately, below.

Guinea

In the refugee camps, in addition to suffering based on difficulties obtaining adequate food, physical health care, shelter, and so forth, a substantial proportion of the refugees reported psychological suffering, including grief, lethargy, feelings of hopelessness, difficulty sleeping, and painful intrusive memories of the war-related events (Hubbard & Pearson, 2004; Stepakoff, 2007). Many questioned whether they could still make meaningful contributions to their families and communities. Most found it difficult to imagine rebuilding their lives.

As discussed in a previous publication (Hubbard & Pearson, 2004), the program in Guinea had three main objectives: (a) the provision of psychological services to address mental health problems experienced by refugees, (b) the enhancement of community capacity to meet the mental health needs of the refugees through the training and supervision of local refugee counselors, and (c) the raising of awareness about torture, war trauma, mental health, and related issues throughout the camps through camp-wide sensitization campaigns, including outreach to community leaders.

This chapter focuses mainly on the clinical services component. (For a more detailed examination of the clinical model, readers are referred to Stepakoff et al., 2006.) CVT established and administered four community mental health centers in the refugee camps of Guinea, each serving an average of 300 clients per year. Given the particular context, it was important to be able to reach large numbers of people without compromising on quality of care. Moreover, it was necessary to enhance clients' capacity to form meaningful interpersonal relationships and establish new social support systems. CVT's approach was designed to effectively address these realities.

A variety of clinical services and modalities were offered, with supportive group psychotherapy as the primary approach. The theoretical foundations for the model included elements of psychodynamic, relational/interpersonal, cognitive-behavioral, narrative, and expressive/humanistic psychotherapies. The building and encouragement of interpersonal connections was the primary aim. Another key idea was that there are psychological benefits to representing intense emotion-laden experiences in words or other symbolic forms (e.g., drawings, drama, songs).

The local counselors regularly visited vulnerable clients in their homes to reduce isolation, monitor well-being, and encourage renewed participation in the community. A hallmark of the program was the combination of Western and African approaches. Circular mud-brick huts with thatched roofs, built with locally procured materials and in a traditional style, served as "counseling huts", designed to provide a sense of safety, comfort, and familiarity for the clients. The fact that the paraprofessional group counselors were themselves Liberian and Sierra Leonean refugees living in the camps helped to ensure that the treatment methods would be culturally sensitive. Elements of traditional West African culture that were incorporated into many of the groups included healing rituals, symbols (e.g., offering kola nuts to welcome newcomers), folktales, drumming, chants, rhythmical clapping (for example, a specific clap was used to mark transitions within a group session, and sometimes to begin or end a session), and song.

Most groups met for 10 weekly sessions of about two hours each, although the exact number of sessions was tailored to the participants' needs as well as exigencies of life in the camp. Groups typically comprised 9-10 clients (with an average attendance of 7-8 members per session), and were led by two local counselors, one of whom also served as a language interpreter for the supervising clinician. Groups were formed according to age (e.g., children, teens, adults), gender, and commonality of traumatic experiences.

From the orientation session on, we sought to support clients in developing safe, caring relationships with each other. In contrast to many traditional Western group psychotherapy approaches, which restrict contact among group members outside of sessions, in our groups contact among members between sessions was encouraged. This seemed important, given that most of the clients no longer had access to the social support networks they relied on in their home countries. For example, in many instances people who had lived in cohesive neighborhoods or villages dispersed as a result of a violent attack. Further, for many of the refugees, multiple members of their immediate and extended family had been killed or were unaccounted for.

Cultural stories were incorporated into the group counseling sessions. Sometimes clients chose to share a folktale as a way of conveying important truths about their experiences and feelings, but more often stories were told by the counselors, as a way of inviting exploration of important topics

(Stepakoff, 2007). The most common themes of these stories were: the dangers of violating confidentiality; the importance of hope and faith; heroes or role models who embody positive attributes; the experience of renewal following loss; the benefits of making and keeping friends; the ability to overcome adversity; communal beliefs about moral versus immoral behavior; and the value of peacemaking, forgiveness, and reconciliation.

Among Liberians and Sierra Leoneans, songs are among the most common and valued means of expressing emotions and coping with fear, sorrow, or stress (Stepakoff, 2007). A review of the wide variety of songs used in the counseling groups indicated that songs served a variety of psychological and social functions: to welcome newcomers; express grief and sorrow; convey messages about acceptable and unacceptable behavior; renew energy; help people get to know each other (e.g., learn names); transition from one part of a session into the next; bring about calmness and relaxation; foster an attitude of faith, hope, and persistence; encourage peace and reconciliation; inform about important historical events; and say goodbye (e.g., at the end of a group cycle). A typical example was a Liberian song consisting of the following two lines, designed to be repeated numerous times so that they have an effect similar to that of an incantation: *Never never you give up in this world—life should go ahead.*

Group counseling sessions almost always began and ended with a song. Most of the time, the songs would be initiated by the clients. Typically, one client would begin singing the song, and the others would quickly catch on and join in. There is a strong tradition of call-and-response songs among Liberians, so the most common situation was one in which a client would initiate the call portion of a song, and the other clients would sing the response. At times, songs were initiated by the counselors, generally with a particular therapeutic objective in mind. Clients seemed to appreciate and enjoy the opportunity to learn a new song and sing it with fellow group members during the session.

We combined these traditional West African healing approaches with methods derived from contemporary psychodynamic, cognitive-behavioral and humanistic/expressive psychotherapies. While cognizant of the need to avoid an arrogant or imperialistic attitude about the usefulness of Western mental health approaches in a refugee camp context, we nevertheless felt that it would be patronizing to assume that Liberian and Sierra Leonean refugees could not benefit from the insights or tools of contemporary psychotherapeutic methods.

One simple yet meaningful set of exercises we engaged in focused on supporting clients in finding and using precise, accurate words to describe their own emotions and those of others. In many ethnic and linguistic groups in Liberia, it is common to use general terms such as feeling "bad" to describe a very wide range of emotions. We found that supporting clients in developing a capacity to choose more specific verbal representations of their internal states would contribute to a sense of relief and a possibility of being more accurately understood by others. The medium of language could give form and containment to otherwise overwhelming sensations and emotions.

Though over the past decade there has been much debate in the professional literature about whether it is useful to draw upon concepts such as "posttraumatic stress" when working with clients in non-Western settings, we consistently found that clients appreciated gaining new knowledge about common reactions to torture and war trauma. They were relieved to learn that their struggles with nightmares, startle reactions, hyperarousal, and intrusive recollections were normal given the events they had endured. Clients appreciated the opportunity to compare and contrast their reactions with those of their peers, and to learn practical means of managing these difficulties more effectively (for example, mindful breathing and other grounding techniques). Clients expressed appreciation for these coping tools, and reported continuing to utilize them even after the group cycle ended.

We used a variety of methods for building connections among group members, and between the counselors and group members. The local counselors endeavored to serve as models of empathic interpersonal communication. When a group member would share, the facilitator might ask the other group members, "what touched your heart most in what s/he just told us?", and the other participants would share their responses.

In order to help clients more fully grasp the technique of replacing negative self-talk with positive self-talk, the co-facilitators sometimes performed a skit called "The Two Hearts" (in Liberian English, "heart" refers to one's mood or state of mind), which depicted a person who felt torn between an encouraging attitude about his/her life and a discouraging, self-defeating attitude, and who ultimately is able to choose the former. A variation on this was an exercise called "Talking Back to Discouragement", which drew on principles from psychodrama and from narrative, body-oriented, and dance/movement therapies. In this version, participants would first generate a list of negative thoughts which they acknowledged as exacerbating their despair, and a facilitator would then embody Discouragement, approaching each group-member one at a time while giving voice to the pessimistic thoughts that s/he had listed (e.g., "things will never get better", "the situation is hopeless"). Group members were invited to rise and push against the facilitator's hands while "talking back" to him or her in a strong tone (e.g., "You're wrong! I have survived hard times before, and I will survive this too"). The local facilitators reported that this exercise appeared to have a special cultural resonance, as many of the clients' indigenous traditions featured supernatural entities (e.g., "bush devils") that personified particular attributes.

The middle part of the group cycle focused on emotional, cognitive, and verbal processing of traumatic memories, and included narrating the trauma story in the presence of compassionate witnesses, and allowing oneself to feel a range of emotions associated with it, in a contained environment (i.e., the group). There was considerable debate amongst clinicians about how much trauma narration should be done within the groups (versus in individual sessions) and how it should be managed. Ideally, this task was only attempted after a reasonable measure of safety had been established. The particular interventions and techniques at this stage varied according to the needs and composition of the group.

In some groups, clients were invited to share about "a time they had felt afraid", or about their "most difficult moment." Sometimes we would propose that they depict this first in a drawing, and then use the drawing as a basis for sharing. The drawings helped to provide focus and containment in comparison to a purely oral approach. We could not use drawings in every group, however, because many clients (especially the women) had never been to school and thus were not familiar with using pencils. In these groups, the facilitators would ask open questions in order to help the clients explore their memories and emotions. As clients would answer, facilitators would listen, paraphrase the essence of what had been shared, validate and normalize their emotions, and express empathy, while also providing group members an opportunity to express empathy for one another.

At the same time, the facilitators were implicitly conveying the idea that nothing is too scary to be talked about. We believed that the events would be less overwhelming if they could be talked about, and if the trauma narratives could be borne by the facilitators and other group members. In addition, in order to reduce feelings of stigmatization and shame, and to strengthen connections among the group members, it was helpful to highlight the commonalities among them. Although trauma is a very individual experience, there were usually important similarities in their stories.

Loss and grief comprised another key area that we addressed midway through the cycle. Refugees from Liberia and Sierra Leone suffered massive losses from the wars. Many lost several close relatives, and some lost their entire immediate families. Most also had relatives who remained missing. Although nothing can completely erase the pain of such losses, in the group counseling sessions we offered a safe, contained space within which clients could feel, and express, their grief. Grief tends to be more overwhelming and terrifying when people feel isolated and unsupported. By contrast, when the bereaved are provided with empathy and support, the pain can become more bearable and they can usually regain a capacity for hope and a sense of meaning and purpose in their lives.

In contexts of war, mourning is a precondition for psychological wholeness, thus we attempted to facilitate processes whereby clients could begin to mourn their losses. Clients appeared to benefit from having a safe space and at least one other person who was willing to listen to and "hold" their expression of fear, anger, shock, and despair. Once the grief was expressed, the intensity of the anguish tended to slowly lessen and the client could usually find interest in life once again. Also, we attempted to support clients in remembering as much as possible about the lost person's life as a whole, and in particular, in revivifying a positive, life-affirming internal representation of their loved ones as they truly were in life, thereby counterbalancing the horrific, violence-laden images with multisensory images of being nurtured and loved.

Usually, it was also important to allow time for clients to explore their feelings about not having been able to perform traditional ceremonies and rituals following their loved ones' deaths. As a result of the constraints of the war situation, in which the survivors themselves were typically captured, injured, struggling to survive in the bush, or attempting to flee into refuge, it was often impossible to carry out the rites that would normally be expected in peacetime, such as a proper funeral and burial. Some clients expressed a desire to perform some type of bereavement ritual in the camp. We encouraged them to fulfil this desire to the extent that they were able in the refugee camp setting, in which traditional religious leaders and sacred objects were usually lacking.

More often, however, drawing on the idea that words could serve as a substitute for action, we verbally explored the mourning practices and rituals that each group-member would have performed if s/he had not been robbed of the opportunity. Group members appeared to enjoy being able to share about their ethnocultural bereavement practices, and to learn about those of others. They gained some relief from representing these practices in words, even without being able to actually implement them.

The interventions we chose to use in supporting clients to explore their losses and grief were informed by African cultural beliefs concerning the continuation of consciousness after physical death, and were also informed by a contemporary Western view of bereavement, developed over the past two decades, referred to as "continuing bonds" (Klass, Silverman, & Nickman, 1996). In this view, the bereaved do not typically "de-cathect" their lost loved ones as was believed in previous psychological models of grief, but rather search for meaningful and culturally appropriate ways of remembering and honoring connections with them for the rest of their lives. Thus, we supported clients in developing a sense of a positive bond with a lost loved one.

Although in many Western settings this might be experienced as an "as if" type of process, in which the positive representation is perceived as internal and subjective, the Sierra Leonean and Liberian clients tended to experience an authentic and potent sense of actual spiritual connection with the soul of the lost one. We used a variety of specific techniques to achieve these therapeutic aims. One was inviting each client to write a letter saying whatever s/he would like to say to the lost person, and then write a letter to himself/herself, in the persona of the lost one. The messages or letters may then be shared with the group. Yet many of our clients lacked basic literacy skills. Thus, a more widely applicable approach was a guided visualization in which group members close their eyes and imagine that they are speaking to their loved one, and that their loved one is speaking to them in reply. They would then share these messages with the group.

A third approach, derived from a Gestalt therapy technique, was an exercise in which two chairs would be placed in the center of the hut, facing each other, and each client would take a turn sitting in one chair and facing the empty chair while imagining that his or her loved one was seated there; the client would say whatever s/he wished to say to the loved one, and then switch to the empty chair and imagine himself or herself as the lost one, looking across at himself or herself in the empty chair and responding in the persona of the loved one. Aspects of this exercise were consonant with the indigenous practices of many of the clients, in which during funerals and other ceremonies there is often a spokesperson who directly addresses the spirit of the deceased.

In the latter part of the group cycle, clients would begin to redefine themselves in the light of their traumatic experiences, place these experiences in the broader perspective of their total life story, and reinvest in life and the future. This includes forming new relationships and reintegrating into the community. They would also begin to reclaim a sense of their own resilience and worth.

One of the themes explored in this stage was referred to as "Stories of Survival." We hoped to support clients in developing a more positive self-image, namely, as survivors rather than victims and as persons who had shown courage and a capacity to endure; to enhance their awareness of coping strategies they had employed in the past and might therefore employ in the future; to contribute to the restoration of a capacity to trust other human beings by remembering that other people had helped them survive; and to help group members learn to recognize and validate each other's strengths.

A variety of techniques were used to accomplish these goals. In some groups the facilitator would tell a traditional folktale about a protagonist who had endured terrible hardships by a combination of ingenuity and determination. Clients would comment on the lessons conveyed in the story, and then share their own stories. Facilitators would pose questions such as "What qualities in yourself did you draw upon when things became especially hard?"

During the latter part of the group cycle, we also drew on the healing power of images. In the African context, as in many cultures, trees are a powerful and resonant symbol. Thus, perhaps not surprisingly, a technique that was consistently well-received was the utilization of a poster-size painting of a tree that had lost many of its branches and leaves but which was still standing, possessed strong roots, and showed signs of inchoate life (e.g., buds, or a few tiny flowers). This poster was used as a catalyst for exploring themes of loss and renewal, and their inherent dignity and value as human beings. In response to the poster and discussion, clients would usually arrive at the idea that even when a tree has lost most of its branches and leaves, if it still has roots and the inner core of a tree, and a capacity to grow and produce new blossoms, then it is still a tree. They would relate this idea to themselves, often culminating in a discussion about a person's indestructible "core" or soul, sometimes leading to a guided visualization in which they would close their eyes and allow themselves to receive a message from their "inner core."

Survivors of torture and war trauma tend to be very preoccupied with the past. This trauma-related difficulty envisioning or planning for the future was exacerbated by the overwhelming challenges of daily survival in the camps. Thus, in the last part of the group cycle, another theme we sought to explore was "facing the future." Through a combination of discussion and creative techniques, we attempted to help clients generate realistic goals, begin to prepare for future challenges, and think about ways to rebuild their lives.

Very often, in preparation for the final session, clients would express a desire to perform some type of ritual signifying their completion of the cycle. We felt that in many instances, rituals could contribute to the process of reinvesting in life. The clients had many creative ideas for ways to acknowledge the ending of their group experience. These included sharing favorite proverbs or songs; planting a palm tree or a flower garden together near the counseling hut; bringing scraps of fabric, needle, and thread, and using them to sew something special together (in one group, participants sewed a cat, to represent the Liberian view that cats have "seven lives" and therefore, symbolizing their own capacity to survive hardship and adversity); and building a miniature wooden boat in which group members placed messages expressing their wishes and dreams for the future and which they then released on the river in the direction of Sierra Leone.

A ritual that was often used in the final session of a cycle, which was originally developed by an expressive arts therapist in the United States yet resonated easily and comfortably with the Liberian and Sierra Leonean clients and counselors, was to invite the group members to go outside and find an object that symbolized hope and healing. Clients would then return to the counseling hut, and take turns showing the object, and explaining how and why they had chosen it. For example, one client presented a stone, and said that it represented indestructibility; another presented a green leaf, and said that it represented the possibility of new life; another presented a pencil, and said that it represented her hope of obtaining an education; and so forth. Clients tended to be very moved and engaged during this process.

The most common closing ritual was to share a simple meal together at the end of the final session. Among the clients, it was commonly believed that once people have partaken of food together they will never injure or betray one another in the future. In many groups, when they shared a meal in the final session, consistent with West African traditions they set aside a small portion of food in memory of their lost loved ones. Sharing a meal was also a way of expressing feelings of connection and mutual respect among group members.

After a group cycle was over, clients usually continued to stay in touch with each other, often becoming significant sources of both emotional sustenance and practical assistance for one another. Many former clients showed an interest in building greater community awareness about torture and war trauma. This interest seemed consistent with the goal of regaining the capacity for meaningful participation in public life. Often, this also involves a desire to help other survivors, and to be part of collective efforts at prevention, awareness, justice, political transformation, and truth-telling.

An example of the ways that public truth-telling was both an indicator of and a contributor to trauma recovery occurred each year on June 26th, the United Nations International Day in Support of Victims of Torture. One year, as a creative means of bearing witness to ethnopolitical trauma, we used the "Story-Cloth and Liberian Time Line." The method had conceptual roots in narrative approaches, which emphasize the psychological importance of being able to think of events in a coherent sequence. Participants were first invited to collaboratively recall key political events from the beginning of the unrest to the present. These events were written on a "timeline" of modern Liberian history, beginning with the 1980 "rice riots" which preceded the first coup. Participants were then provided with square pieces of fabric of various colors and were asked to think of a loved one who was tortured or killed, and to write the person's name, as well as the date, place, and manner in which s/he was victimized, on the cloth.

Next, with the empathic support of the facilitators, each person was invited to share his or her story with the other participants. Finally, each person placed his or her loved one's square on the timeline cloth, matching private tragedy to the corresponding political event, thereby "peopling" the history. For many participants, this was the first time that they had ever linked their personal stories to a larger historical and political context, thereby becoming better able to make sense of traumatic experiences that had previously seemed incomprehensible. The cloth functioned as a "container" that allowed the survivor to stand outside the story and bear witness to it, rather than being imprisoned by it, and also served as a physical space in which survivors could both memorialize loved ones who were killed and acknowledge those who survived.

Moreover, there soon emerged, beyond the images of the tragic losses of specific beloved individuals, a powerful representation of massive collective losses that had resulted from repeated, large-scale civil wars. Thus, pain that had seemed purely personal was discovered to be part of the larger, collective phenomenon of ethnopolitical persecution. This realization can contribute to reconnection with the community, thereby deepening the work of the last stage of healing (Herman, 1992).

Throughout the duration of the program, the paraprofessional counselors were trained and supervised in conducting psychosocial assessments, and in using assessment to inform treatment. Measures of psychological symptoms, social support, and daily functioning were re-administered at one month, three months, six months, and twelve months post-intake. Statistical analyses of the data consistently showed both significant and meaningful reductions in trauma symptoms, and increases in social support and daily functioning, during and after participation in the therapy groups. After the wars in Sierra Leone and Liberia ended, and the refugees were repatriated, the local counselors went on to establish similar services and programs in their home countries.

Jordan

CVT's Jordan program began in 2008, and continues to the present. The clients were initially Iraqi survivors of torture and war trauma who had fled their homeland to seek refuge in Jordan, though since 2011 the program has also served large numbers of Syrian refugees. As with the West Africa work, the program model was based on capacity building, with a focus on training and on-site clinical supervision of Iraqi, Palestinian, and Jordanian counselors.

The group therapy model had many similarities with the model used in the above-described Guinea program, but with modifications for the differences in population and setting. In Jordan, hot tea is served in all groups, as in Iraqi culture offering tea traditionally signifies a welcoming, respectful attitude. Most of the Iraqi clients had good literacy skills, thus many of the counseling groups in Jordan successfully incorporated methods from poetry therapy. Poetry therapy—one branch of the larger field of creative arts approaches that comprise music, dance, art, photo, and drama therapies—relies on the utilization of poetic language to promote therapeutic aims such as insight, empowerment, interpersonal connection, and healing.

Methods that rely on the creative utilization of language are particularly salient for survivors of ethnopolitical trauma. Most survivors do not readily find words to describe their experiences and emotions, particularly at the earlier stages of recovery. In addition, larger sociocultural and political forces discourage—and even actively suppress—the verbal narration of the violations they have endured. This silence often leads survivors to feel isolated, burdened, and overwhelmed (Stepakoff & Ashour, 2011). In the context of a safe, caring relationship, gradually moving from silence toward speech paves a pathway for reconnection with self and restoration of the capacity to connect with other human beings (Stepakoff et al., 2011).

Critics might argue that the utilization of Western-style poetry therapy approaches with Iraqi clients in an Arab country (Jordan) is a form of cultural imperialism. However, the recognition and utilization of the transformative power of literature has ancient antecedents in Arab culture, especially in Iraq. Indeed, words were written for the first time in human history (around 3200 BCE) in Mesopotamia—the early civilization located in the site of modern-day Iraq.

In all of the monotheistic faiths practiced in Iraq, the reading of verses from sacred texts, either silently or aloud (e.g., in the form of chanting), is used to foster comfort and inner strength. Among Muslims, strong value is placed on being able to read the Koran and commit Koranic verses to memory. Moreover, the rhythmical and linguistic properties of the Koran are believed to enhance the positive psychological impact of reading it or hearing it read aloud.

Though the counseling model in Jordan was based on a variety of approaches, in many of the individual and group sessions we were able to successfully incorporate methods derived from poetry therapy. This was not merely a Western approach imposed on Iraqi clients. Rather, stories, poems, and writing are an integral part of Arab culture in general and Iraqi culture in particular. Of course, there are important differences between the indigenous use of verbal-artistic expression and the formal practice of the expressive therapies. Nevertheless, most of the clients welcomed opportunities to work with traditional literary forms.

In particular, Arabic proverbs from ancient sources were used as a basis for supporting clients in exploring important concerns. For example, in one session, as a springboard for discussing a client's dignity and intrinsic worth, counselors used a poem by Ali Ibn Al-Jahm Al-Sami, an Arabian poet who was based in Baghdad (born around 804 A.D., died in 863): *Be like the date tree in its generosity and its pride: people throw stones at it and it gives them the best dates.*

In another group, a group counseling session was designed around a rhyming couplet by Al-Mutanabbi, an Arab Iraqi poet who lived from 915-965 A.D.:

> *Not all that person desires does he or she obtain:*
> *The winds blow without regard for the wishes of the ships.*

We typed these lines (in Arabic) on a sheet of paper, and distributed it to each of the group members. The Iraqi facilitator read the poem aloud three times, in order to enhance its impact. Clients were then invited to respond by "free-writing." "Free-writing" is a technique in which clients are asked to write non-stop for a specified number of minutes, without thinking, without censoring themselves, and without lifting their pens from the page.

Below are two examples of clients' free-writing from the session (the excerpts below were originally published in Stepakoff et al., 2011).

> The future was mine and now I am set in oblivion. I do not know where my future lies nor that of my family, and I have a sense of fear, of being terrified and unstable and without safety....My thoughts have become hazy and I have no clue what to do. ("Jalen")

> *This proverb reminds me of the current situation we live in, where fate plays the larger role in our lives: fate is similar to the strong wind that wreaks havoc and pushes all boats off their course. Despite the ship's plan to reach a shore that had*

been intended by the captain, the winds lead it to deviate from its course to another shore, which may be a safe shore that one may stay on for a lengthy period, but it may also turn out to be a barren island without water or vegetation and you will be forced to stay there and wait for a glimpse of hope by the passing of other ships or a rescue boat. The proverb makes me think of the plans for the future that we used to imagine, plans for a happy and pleasant life for the whole family, but this is not what has occurred. ("Laith")

We were struck by the strong responses engendered by this couplet-poem.

We continued to use this proverb and this method in several other groups, with consistently positive effects. In the above example, the therapists chose the literary material. Sometimes, however, clients brought in poems, proverbs, or songs that they wished to share, either spontaneously or in response to an invitation by the therapists. Material that clients brought to counseling sessions rarely mentioned torture or war directly, but instead tended to capture particular aspects of the experience of suffering, loss, and grief. For example, in a counseling group for men, "Burhan", whose brother had been brutally murdered for ethnopolitical reasons, had rigid psychological defenses against discussing his emotions about his brother's death, even when other group members shared about their losses. About midway through the group cycle, Burhan, though he still had great difficulty talking about his feelings directly, shared the following passage from a poem by Al-Khansa, a renowned seventh-century Arab female poet whose brother had been killed in war in the year 615 A.D. Burhan had memorized the poem, and as he read it aloud it became clear that by sharing the poem, Burhan was able to express his own feelings more fully and precisely than he had been able to do on his own:

Every sunrise reminds me of my brother, Sakhar
And I continue remembering him until the sun descends
And if it were not for the presence, all around me, of so many other people
who are also mourning their brothers
I would kill myself.

Hearing this preexisting poem led to a fruitful group discussion of the experience of grief, and of the ways that forming connections with others who are grieving, and thereby feeling less alone in one's sorrow, somehow made the anguish more bearable. Though the above examples used preexisting literary sources as a catalyst, oral and written self-expression are also important components of the counseling groups. Therapeutic letter-writing is an expressive technique that can be systematically incorporated into group sessions. Usually, the counselors give the clients a suggestion regarding to whom the letter should be directed and/or what issues it should explore. In Jordan, we used letter-writing in a variety of ways, particularly as a tool for working with traumatic grief. It is important that clients not only write a letter in which they express their own thoughts and feelings, but also that they imagine how the person receiving the letter would reply.

There appears to be an archetypal healing function in the psyche that is activated during the imagined reply. More specifically, almost always, the responses are reparative and life-affirming. Typical messages include remarks such as "Take good care of the children", "I want you to be happy", "I forgive you", "I'm sorry", "I am not with you physically but I remain with you spiritually", and so forth.

Below is an example of a letter that a client, "Nafeeza", wrote to her deceased brother, "Zafir", who had been tortured and killed in Iraq. After composing the letter and the imagined reply, the client read both letters aloud in the sixth session of a women's counseling group (the excerpt below was originally published in Stepakoff et al., 2011):

My beloved and dear brother:
First of all I wish to tell you that I've been missing you very very much. I miss your laughter and gentle joking, I miss seeing your beautiful and bright face and how you always entered the house with the tastiest of foods even if it cost you all the money you had on you. I want to tell you that I am sorry that I was not there with you when they captured you and took you away. I cannot stop thinking about you and of how they tortured you. I remember how sometimes you used to say the phrase "Oh Brother!" if something hurt you, and this time something hurt you and none of your brothers was with you to respond. Why has all this happened? What is your crime? Is your crime your name, or your love for people, or your high morals or your tenderness? I wish I knew why they did this to you, for you were like a blossoming flower spreading your fragrance to everyone around you....I tell you that I remember you every day and I shall never forget you and the same goes for my son, who always asks when you'll be back whenever he sees your picture that is hanging on the wall. Even though he only remembers a little about you as he was young at the time [you were captured], he will never forget your love for him or your compassion.
"Nafeeza"

Nafeeza's imagined reply from her brother:

My dearest sister:
I wish you knew how much I miss you and how sorry I am for...all the pain I have caused you, and especially for the pain of my mother and father. But this is what God had in store for us and we must bear His will. I want you to always be strong and to endure and to keep your faith in God, and I want you to know that I am comfortable, though I miss seeing you, and this will happen one day, God willing, sooner or later, for we will meet [in paradise]. I send my kisses to you and also to

Mom, Dad, all my brothers and friends, and especially to my beloved nephew, your son.
"Zafir"

We also used letter-writing in counseling groups for child survivors of torture and war trauma. In one such group, the children were invited to use the letter-writing as an opportunity to address anyone to whom they had something to express. Some of the children chose to write to their perpetrator, articulating in the letters their feelings of anger and betrayal. Others chose to write to their lost loved ones, giving voice to their feelings of grief and longing. In one group, a particularly creative and precocious 12-year-old boy decided to write the letter to himself (the excerpt below was originally published in Stepakoff et al., 2011):

Dear "Talib",
You've lost everyone who you like, toys, love, freedom, and friends, you've lost the person who was the most beloved and important to you. You have been beaten, and cursed, and you've been made to feel ashamed...You've been displaced, you had to leave your country, and your heart was very close to your country....I wish for you a pleasant life, and to overcome all the obstacles and problems, and for you to find someone who can help you to solve those problems....I wish for you new friends, like the friends you have found in this group. I wish you a happy life, and I wish peace and renewal for your country, and I wish you success in your hobbies. Thank you my secret friend, I know that you live in my heart.

Conclusion

In the aftermath of mass trauma, survivors from a wide range of cultures appear to have a psychological need to tell their stories and share their truths. Though nearly all human beings seek to give symbolic form to the emotions and images they carry inside, and to tell of their experiences of suffering and violation, the ways that these needs are channeled may be culturally specific. In this chapter, I have attempted to show that by drawing on a creative combination of Western and indigenous approaches, survivors of torture and war find wider possibilities for overcoming the silence and isolation that are among the most destructive sequelae of ethnopolitical trauma. By diversifying the pathways by which healing can occur, to encompass the best of contemporary and traditional healing methods, we can maximize the opportunities for recovery from the wounds of war.

References

Herman, J. (1992). *Trauma and recovery*. New York, NY: Basic Books.

Hubbard, J. & Pearson, N. (2004). A psychosocial program to address community violence experienced by refugees from Sierra Leone. In K. Miller & L. Rasco (Eds.), *The mental health of refugees: Ecological approaches to facilitating healing and adaptation* (pp. 1- 30). New Jersey: Lawrence Erlbaum Associates.

Klass, D., Silverman, P., & Nickman, S. (1996). *Continuing bonds: New understandings of grief*. Washington, DC: Taylor & Francis.

LeRoy, J. (2002). How can participation of the community and traditional healers improve primary health care in Kinshasa, Congo? In J. de Jong (Ed.), *Trauma, war, and violence* (pp. 405-440). New York, NY: Kluwer.

Stepakoff, S. (2007). The healing power of symbolization in the aftermath of massive war atrocities: Examples from Liberian and Sierra Leonean survivors. *Journal of Humanistic Psychology*, 47, 400-412.

Stepakoff, S., & Ashour, L. (2011). Reading and writing: Working with traumatic grief among Iraqi refugees in Jordan. *The Forum: Quarterly Publication of the Association for Death Education and Counseling: Special Issue on Expressive Therapies in Thanatology*, 37, 22-23.

Stepakoff, S., Hussein, S., Al-Salahat, M., Musa, I., Asfoor, M., Al-Houdali, E., & Al-Hmouz, M. (2011). From private pain toward public speech: Poetry therapy with Iraqi survivors of torture and war. In E. G. Levine & S. K. Levine (Eds.), *Art in action: Expressive arts therapy and social change* (pp. 128-144). Philadelphia, PA: Jessica Kingsley Publishers.

Stepakoff, S., Hubbard, J., Katoh, M., Falk, E., Mikulu, J., Nkhoma, P., & Omagwa, Y. (2006). Trauma healing in refugee camps in Guinea: A psychosocial program for Liberian and Sierra Leonean survivors of torture and war. *American Psychologist*, 61, 921-932.

Wessells, M. (1999). Culture, power, and community: Intercultural approaches to psychosocial assistance and healing. In K. Nader, N. Dubrow, & B. Stamm (Eds.), *Honoring differences: Cultural issues in the treatment of trauma and loss* (pp. 267-282). New York, NY: Taylor & Francis.

Wessells, M. (2008, Sept.). *Trauma, peacebuilding and development: An African region perspective*. Paper presented at the Trauma, Development and Peacebuilding Conference, New Delhi, India, hosted by the International Conflict Research Institute and International Development Research Centre.

Wessells, M., & Monteiro, C. (2004). Healing the wounds following protracted conflict in Angola. In U. P. Gielen, J. Fish, & J. G. Draguns (Eds.), *Handbook of culture, therapy, and healing* (pp. 321-341). Mahwah, NJ: Erlbaum.

Chapter 17
Acting Together to Disrupt Cycles of Violence: Performance and Social Healing

Polly Walker

Juniata College, Pennsylvania

"In effect, we human beings act together because the meaning of our lives springs from our relationships with others." *(Febres, 2011, p. ix)*

"My desire to join the theatre during the sunset of the last military regime stems directly from the realization that only through creative work would I be able to heal and rebuild after so much destruction." *(Varea, 2011, p. 155)*

Introduction

The quotations above illuminate the entanglement of interrelatedness, creativity and healing. Drawing on these concepts, this chapter explores the role of performance in the collective healing of social groups that have been fragmented by intense and protracted violence. Performance, in the form of ritual and theatre, is uniquely situated to collective healing. Ritual and theatre are collective endeavours: leaders of ritual, theatre artists and directors have a long history of crafting performances that engage audiences and participants in bringing injustices to light, envisioning more peaceful societies, and providing healing for those who have been traumatized by violence. Performance engages more than verbal, rational analysis: it engages people's bodies, emotions, and sense of spirituality and has the potential to facilitate more holistic experiences of healing. Nevertheless, it is only recently that theatre artists and scholars have joined with scholar-practitioners of peacebuilding to develop a conceptual framework that would facilitate a more rigorous engagement with the transformative potential of performance. This has occurred in part through the international collaboration known as the Acting Together network.

The seeds of the Acting Together peacebuilding performance project were sown through a collaboration in 2005 between Roberta Levitow of Theatre Without Borders and Jessica Berns, director of Coexistence International at

Brandeis University, who joined forces to explore ways in which theatre builds peace in divided societies around the world (Levitow, 2011, p. xv). Levitow and Berns soon brought Cynthia Cohen (1997) into the network, building on her seminal work on the aesthetic mediation of conflict. Under the direction of Cohen, the Acting Together Project was born, bringing together 24 theatre artists, directors and peacebuilding scholar-practitioners to create a two-volume anthology on the creative transformation of conflict. The texts include 13 multi-vocal chapters from more than 15 different countries, curated by authors who integrated a wide range of case studies and highlighted a number of diverse voices. In conjunction with the anthology, Cohen (2011b) also produced a related documentary *Acting Together on the World Stage* in collaboration with filmmaker Alison Lund and members of the acting together network.

The Acting Together Project drew on John Paul Lederach's (2005) concept of the moral imagination, defined as the ability to stay grounded in the realities of ongoing violence while at the same time envisioning a more peaceful future. Lederach maintains that peacebuilding requires four essential disciplines: acknowledging interdependence even between opponents, engaging with paradoxical curiosity, making space for the creative act and the willingness to risk moving beyond conflict toward peace (pp. 34-39).

The editorial team of Acting Together, Cynthia Cohen, Roberto Varea and myself, engaged with chapter curators over six years, facilitating dialogues, workshops, and collaborative writing and editing sessions. We were seeking a deeper understanding of both the strengths and limitations of performance in transforming conflict in the midst of violent conflict, in the aftermath of violent conflict, and in building just and sustainable communities. Through an analysis of the many performances featured in the anthology, we found that peacebuilding performances facilitated: the expression of silenced and repressed experiences, the restoration of capacities damaged by violence, and the enacting of the moral imagination in relation to issues of identity, through acts of resistance and memory, and in the quest for justice (Cohen, 2011, pp. 171-182).

We did not focus specifically on healing as a central aspect of the analytical framework in the Acting Together Project. Nevertheless, there is ample evidence that performances can be skilfully crafted to disrupt repetitive cycles of violence and trauma. A number of scholars emphasize the healing potential of performance. Richard Shechner (1988), one of the founders of performance studies, names healing as one of the central functions of performance. Healing of self, others, and social groups, what Varea (2011) calls "mending the torn social fabric," (p. 154) has become a persistent thread in the project as the Acting Together network continues to work with the assembled materials and with the wider network of artists and scholars.

In this chapter, I analyse some of the performances featured in Acting Together in relation to social healing, "the capacity of communities and their respective individuals to survive, locate voice, and resiliently innovate spaces of interaction that nurture meaningful conversation and purposeful action in the midst and aftermath of escalated and structural violence" (Lederach & Lederach, 2010, p. 208). Lederach and Lederach (2010) maintain that this collective voice "creates social echo that simultaneously moves inward and out," linking individual processes of healing with wider national processes of reconciliation (p. 208).

Resiliently Innovating Spaces for Meaningful Conversation

Creating innovative spaces of meaningful communication in settings of intense and protracted violence involves the creation of safe space for communication between enemies and/or former opponents; the restoration of meaning to societies reeling from the senselessness of mass atrocities, and the expression of formerly unspeakable experiences. These are neither easy nor straightforward tasks, particularly for opponents or former enemies living side by side in the same communities. Nevertheless, this proximity requires that people meet face to face with members from all sides of the conflict in order to engage with the legacies of violence and to find ways to work toward justice, reconciliation and sustainable peace. Performances provide such spaces, and the artists and scholars in the Acting Together network describe both ways of creating safe space and the kinds of meaningful dialogue that can take place within those containers. The discourse within those spaces would often not be considered as 'safe' outside the performance space; rather, the aesthetic excellence and discipline of the performers seem to create a sense of beauty and resonance that removes the performers, at least to some extent, from the legal sanctions that exist outside the performances.

In creating safe space, peacebuilding artists and scholars stress the importance of integrating "symbolic distance," innovative ways of engaging with the reality of people's experiences of violence without recreating the immediacy and trauma those events have occasioned. For example, Jo Salas (2011), one of the founders of Playback Theatre, maintains that stories which include traumatic experiences should not be enacted literally. In contrast, symbols, gestures or other indirect means can be utilised to maintain a safer distance from the violent events for audience members and performers. Another example of using symbols to create some emotional distance from the violence portrayed in performances can be seen in the work of Grupo Cultural Yuyachkani in Peru. Yuyachkani created the performance piece *Kay Puncu* to address the culture of impunity surrounding Peruvian soldiers' rape of women. Lepri (2008) explains that when Yuyachkani presented street performances of Kay Puncu, the rape scene depicted a group of uniformed soldiers, each one yanking a strip of scarlet cloth from beneath the legs of the many women lying prostrate before them. The scene was powerful, evocative, and beautiful, clearly depicting the violent assault in a symbolic way that has enhanced witnesses' capacities to speak about and work toward ending sexual violence in the military.   Another powerful example of the creation of innovative spaces of social healing can be seen in the work of DAH Theatre in the former Yugoslavia. Dijana Milosović (2011) founder of the theatre company, describes a piece, *This Babylonian Confusion*, that they performed in the streets of Belgrade to draw attention to the fact that their country was engaged in a war, although the public was forbidden by the government at that time to use that term in regard to the violence that was occurring (pp. 30-32). Up to a third of the audience for these street performances were armed militia, yet not one of them turned their guns on the actors in the streets (Kneživić, cited in Milosović, 2011, p. 31). Milosović (2011) maintains that this safe space was created through the "commitment and the artistry of the actors" protecting them from the violence they might have otherwise expected (p. 32).

The safe space of peacebuilding performances creates a container in which performers and audience members may strengthen their willingness and capacity to resist violence and injustice and to disrupt ongoing cycles of violence. Artists and audience members have engaged in critiques of government policies that would be disallowed, or even illegal, outside the performance space. Performance scholar Mads Palihaptiya (2011) explains that in Sri Lanka some theatre pieces performed after the war between Sinhalese and Tamil groups allowed artists and audience members to engage with biting critiques of public figures and government policies. Although these kinds of public expression were technically illegal, no performers were punished. Palihaptiya describes these spaces as "…an oasis—in which people could interact on physical, intellectual, and spiritual levels, and explore their values and their perspectives on the war" (p. 75-77), engaging in discourse that was silenced in other arenas.

Pauline Ross (2011) founder of the Derry Playhouse, describes the safe spaces created within the Theatre of Witness in Northern Ireland in which performers explored the violence that plagued communities during The Troubles: "...It was as if the performance had prepared the ground, a safe, sacred place for public discussion of very private stories of grief and pain. Performers and police officers all faced death threats for participating in performances" but none were ever killed or attacked for performing in, or witnessing the plays (pp. xiii-xvi).

Concerns for the safety and wellbeing of performers and audience members are of the highest importance when creating performances in the midst of, and in the aftermath of, intense and protracted violence. High aesthetic quality, symbolic distance from violence and finely honed performances attuned to the deeper needs of audience members seem to provide some level of protection from the kinds of sanctions that may be exercised outside of performance spaces.

In addition to the creation of safe space, peacebuilding performances have demonstrated ability to restore meaning destroyed by war and other mass atrocities. Varea (2011) explains how violence disrupts the processes that give meaning to our lives: "Perhaps nothing threatens our ability to create meaning more than becoming victims of violence. In its many shapes and forms, violence interrupts the telling of the story and our ability, as survivors, to make sense of it, rendering us helpless" (p. 154). Intense, protracted violence affects the ability of societies and individuals to understand the complex dynamics of conflict, making it even more likely that violent conflict will continue: "...the peoples or social groups who have suffered deaths, genocide, slavery, or other forms of oppression carry with them the stigma of having been erased from history. Thus we understand that violence is the destruction of meaning, a disorder that contaminates the very symbols with which we build our lives in communion with others. And because it corrupts meaning and reduces our humanity, violence often appears as an inexplicable act, almost impossible to understand at the very time it occurs" (Febres, 2011, p. x). In contrast, performance builds artists', ritual leaders', audience members' and participants' ability to build a deeper, more nuanced, collective understanding of the violence they have experienced, enhancing their agency to heal, rebuild relationships and reform structures that are keeping violence in place.

Restoring meaning to situations of seemingly meaningless suffering, alienation and despair involves more than language. One aspect of performance that makes it uniquely suited to this restoration is that it is embodied, engaging memories that are not always easily recalled verbally but that may be accessed through "creative work that engages the body" (Cohen, 2011, p. 166). Performances' restoration of meaning happens in part in the out-of-awareness aspects of human experience, as conflict resolution scholar Michelle LeBaron (2003) explains: "ritual and ceremony touch the unconscious parts of the self where identities breathe, and meaning is made" (p. 276).

The restoration of meaning through performance is in part accomplished through giving expression to the atrocities and horrors of violent conflict that people may be unwilling, or unable, to discuss. Varea (2011) further explains that "Performance creates a complex but accessible language to speak the seemingly unspeakable. The capacity to continue on with the construction of meaning after traumatic violence is a founding principle of theatre, ritual, and also of peacebuilding" (p. 154).

The restoration of meaning can also be seen in rituals that restore respect and honour to ways of knowing and being that have been disrupted by mass violence. An example of these processes can be seen in the Nez Perce Memorial Ceremonies which take place annually in the United States at Ft. Vancouver, Washington, where members of the Native American Nez Perce Nation join with non-Native settlers, local government officials and members of the United States Army stationed at Ft. Vancouver. Meaning is restored in part through respectful engagement with Native American religious ceremonies which were banned, and made illegal in the United States until 1978. This marginalization of many cultural rituals that were meaningful to Native Americans meant the ceremonies were disrupted or driven underground, some no longer performed, others not spoken about publicly. The Nez Perce Memorial includes a number of these Native rituals: the pipe ceremony, signifying peaceful relations; gift giving, signifying interdependence and generosity of spirit; and the empty saddle ceremony, paying respect to those who have died. The empty saddle ceremony involves a number of Nez Perce warriors in full regalia, who honour the dead of all those present at the ceremony, bringing into symbolic relationship descendants of both Native and Settler peoples who opposed each other in the War of 1877.

These public rituals that engage former enemy groups in collaborative endeavours have assisted in restoring the Nez Perce 'way of the horse' At the end of the War of 1877 the United States Army shot and killed over 6,000 Nez Perce horses in an attempt to destroy the military might of the tribe. To the Nez Perce, this loss was much more than a blow to their military strength. They did not consider their horses to be weapons, rather relatives, with reciprocal relationships of respect and care similar to those they had with their human relations (Axtell, personal communication, March 13, 2009; Scott, personal communication, March 13, 2009). This loss, carried over the ensuing years, had broken the younger generations' connection to the 'Great

Horse Nation.' Nez Perce spiritual leader Horace Axtell (personal communication, March 13, 2009) and Wilfried Scott (personal communication, March 13, 2009), chairman of the tribe at the time of the first memorial, explain that the ceremonies and related activities have restored the younger generations' involvement with the 'way of the horse', restoring meaning to their connections with their more-than-human relationships, which were disrupted by the war.

In addition to restoring meaning, performances have been crafted to literally restore some losses sustained in mass atrocities. Varea (2011) describes performances in Argentina that restored children of the disappeared to their grandparents, the wider community, and to the nation as a whole, mending the social fabric in tangible ways. HIJOS, an organization of young Argentinian men and women, joined forces with Mothers and Grandmothers of the Plaza Mayor, identifying the biological parents of over a hundred children and reuniting these children with their birth families (pp. 160-163).

Social healing also requires processes that allow audience members and ritual participants to talk about what was formerly unspeakable. Catherine Filloux (2011) created a performance, *Photographs from S-21*, which has allowed audience members to discuss formerly repressed experiences of the Cambodian genocide that took place at the hands of the Khmer Rouge. She created the play in part to give voice to people who were represented in a de-contextualised installation of photos from S-21, which was a notorious site for the execution of people being held there. In Filloux's play, a young man and woman, who have been murdered in the detention centre, come down from their photos at night when the museum is closed, and begin to share their experiences that had never been voiced. Filloux explains that in dialogue sessions after the performance, audience members also have shared their stories of trauma during the Cambodian genocide, experiences which they had been unable to share previously. For example, when the play was performed at Brandeis University in 2006, the Cambodian-American who played the part of the young man told the audience that after the play, for the first time his parents had spoken with him about the genocide. These shared memories re-connect audience members with the past, allowing them to grieve and to move into the future (pp. 207-211).

Purposeful Action

The previous section of this chapter explores ways in which peacebuilding performances have created safe spaces, restored some measures of meaning to individuals and societies damaged by violence, and facilitated the expression of experiences that formerly had been unspeakable. The social healing effected through performance also builds people's capacities for purposeful action designed to enhance their capacity and will to effect some measures of justice and to move beyond fixed, polarized identities, creating possibilities for relationships with former opponents.

There are a number of ways in which performance facilitates audience members and ritual participants' engagement with restorative justice. The public performance of one's story, if handled well, may itself be an act of justice. Through restoring meaning and collective memory, performance at times is "a form of justice that cleanses and vindicates our species in a universal way" (Febres, 2011, p. xi). Judith Hermann (cited in Salas, 2011) explains that this type of performance "represents a transition toward the judicial, public aspect of testimony" (p. 119). Witnessing people's lived experiences enacted on stage encourages listeners to take action to redress the injustices they now understand more fully (Rivers, cited in Salas, 2011, p. 119). Perhaps this is due, in part, to the enhanced capacities of the witnesses of the testimonies, to connect in a personal and embodied way with those experiences, to empathize as if the pain of the stories also belongs to them (O'Neal, 2011, p. 126).

The shared experience of pain facilitated through performance may also unite audience members with performers, building solidarity and thus capacities for effecting social change. This process is eloquently described by Salomon Lerner Febres (cited in Varea, 2011), the President of the Peruvian Truth and Reconciliation Commission:

> The experience of theatre is also for the spectator, who is as much a part of the event. Just as in art, if there is no observer, the work of art remains just here like another object. In some way, this 'objectifying' of pain through the agency of art can cut the knot that ties it to us, and also that silences us. Because ultimately we understand that, even if unfortunately, this is not just our personal experience, but a shared experience. It does not belong only to us. The search for justice in our own personal matters implies the externalization of what was felt, what was lived, and what occurred. (p. 175)

The kinds of justice effected through performance address losses and traumas that retributive justice processes are unable to fully redress. For example, in performances, loved ones who have been killed may be symbolically restored to their families and communities. Ana Correa (cited in Varea, 2011), a founding member of Grupo Cultural Yuyachkani, created a theatre piece that has helped to effect justice and heal trauma through a form of symbolic restoration. Her play *Rosa Cuchillo* is the story of an alma viva, a living soul, who travels to the land of the dead, searching for her son who has been disappeared. Rosa is reunited with him and at the end of the play she returns to the living to share her testimony. Correa explains that this play is one of solidarity, healing, memory and agency: "a way to help people overcome fear and begin to heal from forgetfulness ... and create space to contextualize the possibility to deal with the forces that hurt us" (pp. 171-173).

Performances have facilitated engagement with other, more formal justice process. For example, Varea (2011) describes how Yuyachkani's work has supported transitional justice through a collaboration with the Peruvian Truth and Reconciliation Commission (TRC). The TRC enlisted Yuyachkani to create performances designed to facilitate more effective encounters between them and the remote Andean communities who had suffered the most violence and trauma. Yuyachkani's performances created a stage for the restoration of public memory of atrocities and trauma that had occurred during the dictatorship, and held these memories within rituals of remembrance that provided some measures of individual and social healing. Yuyachkani's performances were able to support justice initiatives through dignifying and honouring victims, and empowering people to speak publicly, first in response to the performance, and then to the TRC (Varea, 2011, pp. 166-167).

Another act of restorative justice effected through Yuyachkani's performances involves the symbolic restoration of a dismembered person, both to his own body and to the social imaginary of his community. Augusto Casafranca created the play *Adios Ayacucho* as the story of a peasant who had been disappeared, dismembered and buried beside the road. In search of justice, the man's spirit inhabits the body of a Quechua ritual dancer and travels to the capital to demand justice. This play illuminates the wounds sustained in protracted violent conflict, "the layers of personal, societal, and mythical trauma involved in the disappearances. A person is denied his bones, and a whole people is denied inclusion in the body politic of the nation" (Varea, 2011, pp. 169-170). At the end of the play, the peasant through his symbolic re-membering finds a dignified death. Casafrana (cited in Varea, 2011) explains that he created the play to encourage the people most affected by the violence to voice their own truths, strengthening their ability and willingness to testify before the TRC and supporting efforts to bring perpetrators to justice. Performances that transform individual memories of trauma into collectively held memories have also been acts of restorative justice, restoring a sense of collective agency to groups immobilized by trauma. Hjalmar-Jorge Jaffre-Eichorn (2011), working with playback theatre in war-torn Afghanistan, describes the ways in which playback theatre deals with memories. He argues that storytellers' memories, when they are publicly enacted by skilled, trained actors, "transgress the boundaries" of the individual and are relocated in the bodies and minds of performers and audience members. Although these stories are painful, the public performance of traumatic experiences may help victims reconnect with the wider society. When governments and other ruling powers have been the source of, or complicit in, mass atrocities, performance has the potential "to create spaces of trust and respect in which those who have been silenced by the historical narrative can legitimize and document their own experiences" (pp. 114 -115). This more immediate and personal connection contrasts with the more objectified processes of formal justice processes that may seem remote and relatively meaningless to those living face to face with perpetrators of violence.

A type of restorative justice can also be seen in performances that re-centre an oppressed people's ways of knowing and being. For example, in Uganda, theatre pieces have been created that integrate local, indigenous ontologies and epistemologies into professional theatre, disrupting the hegemony of the colonial influence in that country (Mulekwa, 2011, pp. 46-49). Charles Mulekwa (2011) describes the ways that he and other Ugandan playwrights are redressing the "epistemological assault" of the British marginalisation and suppression of Ugandan forms of performance that impacted negatively on Ugandans' well-being and identity (pp. 54-55). Similarly, performance scholar Daniel Banks (2011) explores the ways in which hip hop theatre in Ghana and South Africa creates a "new psychic space in which to work, one owned by the participants, often in contrast to hegemonic and/or Eurocentric practices," drawing on "a porous pedagogy that relies on local knowledge, practices, values, and concerns" (pp. 68-69). These ways of restoring respect and agency to local, indigenous ways of knowing and being have been significant justice endeavours to oppressed peoples, impacting in positive ways on the wellbeing of their societies.

Purposeful action related to performance and social healing in situations of racism, genocide or other atrocities also requires redressing power imbalances and unacknowledged privileges. John O'Neal (2011) one of the founders of the Free Southern Theatre during the Civil Rights Era in the United States, explains the importance of critiquing power structures that keep injustices in place and that perpetuate trauma: "Our idea was that we had a larger mission than simply to entertain those who had achieved a certain measure of comfort in a hostile environment. The larger purpose of art in the context of injustice is to challenge the norms of those who are benefiting from the injustice" (p. 138). O'Neal claims that social healing must be designed to disrupt complacency and hopelessness, awakening a sense of agency among members of oppressed groups. Alex Mukulu's Ugandan play *Thirty Years of Bananas* critiqued the apathy and complicity of the Ugandan populace, as well as the corruption of their leaders, and called for individual and collective agency in healing and rebuilding after years of despotic rule (Mulekwa, 2011, pp. 57-62). Facilitating a stronger sense of agency assists oppressed or marginalised people to create a vision for engaging more actively with justice initiatives, as Sri Lankan playwright and scholar Ranjini Obeysekere (cited in Palihapitya, 2011) explains: "The seemingly 'passive' participation of audiences in a dramatic performance gives them a sense of power, however temporary and symbolic, over the political evils in the world outside. They can laugh at them, and in the laughter reaffirm that the world can be different from what it is now" (p. 75). This sense of empowerment also translates into purposeful engagement with issues of justice outside the performance space.

Restorative justice is also seen in performances that re-story people by replacing dominant, external narratives with personal, authentic stories of their experiences. Re-storying returns a fuller sense of agency, and resists the marginalisation and suppression inherent in many official government accounts. Nora Strejilevich (cited in Varea, 2011) describes the restorative justice effected through rewriting and publicly performing her story of being disappeared by the Argentinian dictatorship:

> I was not only sharing the account of my kidnapping in the very place where I had become a desaparecida, I was basically re-writing myself. Terror had wanted to turn me into a victim and, instead, I had turned into a creator of my own life/text. A story that had been imposed on us in order to destroy our humanity was being turned upside down... (pp. 156-157)

Social healing through performance facilitates engagement with fluid and interdependent identities that contrast starkly with the kinds of fixed, oppositional identities that characterise intractable conflict. Victor Turner (1977), one of the seminal scholars of ritual, maintains that ritual performance creates a liminal space in which the participants are able to move from one state of being to another. Within this liminal space, people can temporarily set aside their own identities, and try on another, even that of enemy or former opponent. In so doing, performance facilitates audience members' and ritual participants' ability to move beyond dualistic and alienated identities, exploring interconnections with 'the other.' There are a number of ways performances facilitate awareness of and engagement with interdependence: through developing rigorous empathy and through creating interdependent relationships that continue to exist outside the performance space.

Rigorous empathy is recognizing the humanity of former opponents or members of enemy groups, acknowledging the complicity of members of one's own group in violence, and yet at the same decrying and redressing injustices. Palihaptiya (2011, pp. 83-86) describes a performance in Sri Lanka designed to facilitate empathy. After the civil war, Dharmasiri created a rendition of the *Trojan Women* that allowed Sir Lankans to grieve with women, as mothers, wives and sisters of those who had been killed in the area. Many had become numbed to the violence, and unable to empathize with the ways in which women are adversely impacted by the losses of war. It also served to encourage the development of a superordinate identity in which both Sinhalese and Tamils could see themselves as people who had been adversely impacted by war and who were committed to redressing injustice and building peace.

Identifying solely with fixed, rigid identities is a characteristic of intractable conflict and repeated cycles of violence and trauma. In contrast, engaging with fluid, multiple identities is a crucial aspect of conflict transformation. Ruth Margreff (2011), performance studies scholar, describes awareness of, and engagement with, multiple identities as a crucial aspect of redressing ethnic and sectarian violence. Margreff describes what she terms as a Ziskian split which allows audience members to identify both with members of their own group and those of opposing groups. She analyses the performance *Hidden Fires* that was created to address the Gujarat massacres of 2002, in which Hindu extremists killed around two thousand Muslims. *Hidden Fires* challenges audience members to complexify their allegiances and to grapple with their own complicity in violence rather than identifying an "evil other" to whom to ascribe the violence.

> The 'split' then is the experience of holding both ethnic identities within the actor's one body at the same time, so that the actor is saying (with her body) 'I am a Hindu artist, I am a Hindu extremist/rioter/complacent-media-person, and I am also a Muslim victim.' And to the extent that the acting is convincing and the audiences are identifying with the characters, audience members experience these splits as well (p. 194).

This more complex engagement with the identities of the actors, and by extension audience member's identities and allegiances, strengthens audience members' agency to address acts of violence that they previously may have ignored.

Relationships that are 'performed' in the liminal space of rituals may continue to exist outside the performance space, creating alliances and collaborations aimed at disrupting historical and contemporary cycles of violence. In reconciliation ceremonies involving Indigenous and Settler peoples in Australia and the United States, participants have moved beyond identities of descendants of victims and perpetrators into more interrelated identities (Walker, 2011). For example, in regard to the Nez Perce Memorial Ceremonies, Royce Pollard (personal communication, April 14, 2009), former commander of Fort Vancouver stated, "We have moved beyond reconciliation, we are in relationship." More fluid identities regarding Indigenous and Settler peoples can also be seen in the rituals of the Myall Creek Massacre Memorial in Australia. Sue Blacklock, descendant of the Aboriginal survivors, extended a kinship relationship to Beulah Adams, descendant of one of the perpetrators of the massacre, saying "We are now sisters" (Adams, personal communication, June 11, 2008). Likewise, in the *Two Rivers Powwow*, Methow Indians have conducted naming ceremonies for two non-Natives, inducting them into a relationship of rights and responsibilities within their community. These individuals who formerly identified as white Australians or white Americans are now also adopted members of Indigenous groups.

Limitations of Performance in Social Healing

Performances have demonstrated strengths in terms of social healing, as seen in the numerous case studies in the Acting Together Project. Nevertheless they also have a number of limitations in this regard. The outcomes of performance are neither linear nor causal, and in situations of violence where a specific outcome is needed quickly, the more liminal spaces of performance may prove ineffective and/or dangerous.

The outcome of performances is unknown, relying on the resonances of interaction that occur between audience member and actors, or between participants and leaders of ritual. Performance therefore, facilitates a transformation of some type, but not always in the direction of social healing or peace. Performances, with their abilities to engage powerful emotions, build resistance and strengthen participants' agency, have also been used to exacerbate and to legitimate violence. There is therefore no guarantee that a performance will disrupt cycles of violence and trauma.

Even when performances are crafted with strong peacebuilding frameworks, the outcomes are in part reliant on audience members' openness and readiness to engage the issues raised in the performance. Attempting to humanize the experiences of diverse peoples may resonate very differently with members of opposing groups, some of whom may see such performances "as a threat to the personal, cultural, or national narrative they hold dear" (Nasrallah & Perlman, 2011, p. 141). In such cases, enmity divides may be exacerbated or maintained by performances.

Another limitation of performance in social healing is the relative difficulty of addressing ways in which members of a performance group are themselves constrained by institutionalised violence such as racism, gender bias or homophobia. In his chapter on theatre and racism in the United States, O'Neal (2011) describes his struggles to address racist dynamics and other forms of power imbalances within theatre collaborations in which he has been involved (pp. 130-133). At times theatre companies and participants in rituals find it easier to address direct and structural violence that occurs in the world outside the performance space, while finding it threatening and distressing to address such forms of violence within performance groups.

There are also tensions between a healing exchange of stories and the potential for re-traumatizing the participants by bringing complex, vivid emotions and experiences to the stage. In her work with playback theatre Salas (2011) points out that given the fluidity of the liminal spaces of performance, it can be challenging to ensure that audience members are not re-traumatized. In the aftermath of genocide and other mass atrocities, performance alone is not capable of effecting the kinds of social healing needed to disrupt ongoing cycles of violence. Performances designed to address injustices and facilitate social healing need to be linked with wider societal process of justice, healing and conflict transformation. Nevertheless, restrictions from funders and policy makers often limit the kinds of interdisciplinary endeavours that would support a more robust engagement with sustainable peace and justice processes.

Also, performances may be resisted by social groups when those performances challenge chosen narratives and deeply held beliefs, increasing peoples' resistance to change and encouraging them to elide engagement with issues of healing and justice. Performance scholars Aida Nasrallah and Lee Perlaman (2011) explain that peacebuilding performances "... require a willingness on the part of audiences to confront unsettling questions about the society in which they live and their role in perpetuating the status quo. For the citizens, theatre artists, and theatregoers in Israel, as in most other societies, it is easiest just not to know" (p. 116).

Furthermore, rituals that are performed for the social healing of one group to a conflict, although often necessary and effective, may be perceived by opposing groups as efforts to strengthen the enemy. Palihiptiya (2011) describes Tamil rituals that were held in Sri Lanka after the civil war where Kandasamy Sithamparanathan formed the Theatre Action Group (TAG) which created seven day intensive ceremonies for Tamils. TAG's rituals strengthened participants' capacities to mourn losses, deal with traumas build solidarity, and restore agency. "Instead of telling people what to think, TAG helped people who had been politically divided and badly traumatized regain their ability to think clearly for themselves" (p. 89). Nevertheless, some Sinhalese perceived the power that Tamil participants developed through the performances as a threat of renewed violence.

At times, performances are crafted in such ways that the worldviews of the artists or ritual leaders' obscure issues that are of critical importance in audience members or ritual participants' worldviews. The marginalisation of a people's worldview is a form of epistemic violence that may render performances less meaningful. Even the terminology employed in this chapter, that of social healing, may obscure many interrelationships that are critical in a number of Indigenous worldviews. For example, in traditional Native American and Aboriginal Australian worldviews, one's 'self' is not a discrete, skin-bounded individual, rather is embodied both in a number of human kin (both living, deceased and not yet born humans), and in relationships with other living beings and features of the natural world. In these worldviews, the concept of healing extends beyond human beings into what philosopher Dave Abram (1997) calls the more-than-human-world. People holding these worldviews tend to conceptualise healing as relational healing which extends the processes of meaningful interaction and purposeful action to include ancestors, generations to come, and to the natural world.

Examples of relational healing can be seen in rituals of the Two Rivers Powwow, a collaborative performance of both traditional Native rituals and newly designed reconciliation rituals involving both Settlers and Natives. It occurs annually in Twisp, Washington in the USA. The Powwow is a form of cyclical restorative justice, in which Methow Indians are formally welcomed by descendants of Settlers into places from which, in 1866, the Methow were forcibly removed by the United States Army. In the Powwow, traditional Methow rituals involving drumming, gift giving, and giveaway ceremonies are interwoven with new rituals that integrate both Methow and Settler descendants: telling the silenced histories of the Methow people and their removal from the valley, apologies on the part of Settlers, and the enacting of new relationships through symbolic gift giving and through public affirmations of new relationships. John GrosVenor (cited in Stamper, 2009), an Echota Cherokee, describes the reconnections that the rituals establish with the more than human community: "When we dance, in theory, every time a foot hits the earth, it's a prayer, and the singing, eating and drinking are also part of that spiritual connection to the land." The rituals in the Two Rivers Powwow also renew connections between Native peoples and their ancestors, as well as to the coming generations. Stephen Iukes (as cited in Mitchell, 2007), a Colville Indian elder, describes the role of departed loved ones in the contemporary reconciliation processes: "The Ancestors of these ones from the valley are still here, the Spirits are still here. By singing these songs we sing that they might be awakened again, to know that they are not forgotten." These rituals of reconnection with land, animals, and plants of significance to Native peoples effect some measures of relational healing.

Purposeful action to redress injustices can also extend to the more than human world. Participants in Indigenous/Settler reconciliation ceremonies in Australia and the United States describe the ways in sites of violence themselves can be transformed through rituals and ceremonies of healing and reconciliation. The places where these ceremonies are held have been described as "wounded space," as places that have "been torn and fractured by violence" (Rose, 1997). In relational healing, these spaces that have suffered violence can also be transformed. For example, John Brown (personal communication, June 12, 2008), one of the settler Australian founders of the Myall Creek Memorial explains the healing that has taken place through the rituals at the massacre site as reconnecting participants with the spirits of those who have died, and with the land itself.

Conclusion

In the aftermath of violence, societies must create spaces and processes of social healing, which require "that losses be mourned, and adversaries invited to empathize with each other's suffering, even across lines of enmity and power. Memories must be dignified, but at the same time, people need to begin to imagine and create a safer, more secure future, where conflicts can be addressed constructively" (Cohen, Varea & Walker 2011b, p. 147). These kinds of interdependent relationships can be facilitated through well-crafted performances of high aesthetic quality that create a kind of resonance between performers and audience members and between leaders and participants of ritual. These resonances are one example of what Lederach and Lederach (2010) call "social echo": linking collective healing of social groups with individual healing and national justice and reconciliation initiatives (pp. 211-224.)

Social healing incorporates action aimed at both justice and the coexistence of former opponents. Performances have been shown to build people's agency and capacity to disrupt cycles of violence and trauma.

Performance can, as Charles Mulekwa (2011) states, "put a knife through the matter and cut it open, helping people who have been oppressed, traumatized, or broken to face their condition and imagine something better ….. when people think critically about their lives, they can be activated" (p. 62). As Salomon Lerner Febres (2011), maintains, performances designed to witness the evils of mass atrocities, to develop collective narratives and deeper understandings are "a sort of therapy that returns to us, mended and sensible, a broken and stunned reality" (p. xi).

References

Abram, D. (1997). *The spell of the sensuous: Perception and language in a more-than-human world.* N.Y.: Random House.

Cohen, C. E. (1997). *A poetics of reconciliation: The aesthetic mediation of conflict* (PhD thesis). Retrieved on Dec. 1, 2013, from http://www.brandeis.edu/ethics /peacebuildingarts/pdfs/poetics.pdf

Cohen, C. E. (2011). The permeable membrane and moral imagination: A framework for conceptualizing peacebuilding performance. In Cohen, C. E., Varea, R. G., & Walker, P. O. (Eds.) *Acting together: Performance and the creative transformation of conflict. Volume II. Building just and inclusive communities.* (pp. 161-189). Oakland, CA: New Village Press.

Cohen, C.E. (Producer) & Lund, A. (Director). (2011). *Acting together on the world stage.* [Motion Picture]. United States: New Village Press.

Febres, S. L. (2011). Foreword: The rebellion of the masks. In Cohen, C. E., Varea, R. G., & Walker, P. O. (Eds.) *Acting together: Performance and the creative transformation of conflict. Volume II. Building just and inclusive communities.* (pp. ix-xi). Oakland, CA: New Village Press.

Filloux, C. (2011). Alive on stage in Cambodia: Time, histories, and bodies. In Cohen, C. E., Varea, R. G., & Walker, P. O. (Eds.) *Acting together: Performance and the creative transformation of conflict. Volume I. Resistance and reconciliation in regions of violence.* (pp. 201-223). Oakland, CA: New Village Press.

Marcy Stamper, M. (Aug. 17, 2006). Getting to the heart of the Methow, *Methow Valley News,* 3.

LeBaron, M. (2003). *Bridging cultural conflicts: A new approach for a changing world.* San Francisco: Jossey-Bass.

Lederach, J. P. & Lederach, A. J. (2010). *When blood & bones cry out: Journeys through the soundscape of healing & reconciliation.* St. Lucia, Qld: University of Queensland Press.

Lepri, C. (Oct. 6, 2008). *The Heights.* Accessed 12/18/2013 at: http://www.bcheights.com/ 2.6177/kay-punku-bears-witness-to-peruvian-women-1.905940#.UqSZrxaPfS8.

Milošević, D. (2011). Theatre as a way of creating sense: Performance and peacebuilding in the region of the former Yugoslavia. In Cohen, C. E., Varea, R. G., & Walker, P. O. (eds.) *Acting together: Performance and the creative transformation of conflict. Volume I. Resistance and reconciliation in regions of violence.* (pp. 23-43). Oakland, CA: New Village Press.

Mitchell, R. (Producer). (2007). *Two Rivers.* [Motion Picture]. United States: Greenleaf Street Productions.

Mulekwa, C. (2011). Theatre, war and p[eace in Uganda. In Cohen, C. E., Varea, R. G., & Walker, P. O. (eds.) *Acting together: Performance and the creative transformation of conflict. Volume I. Resistance and reconciliation in regions of violence.* (pp. 45-71). Oakland, CA: New Village Press.

Nasrallah, A. & Perlman, L. (2011). Weaving dialogues confronting harsh realities: Engendering social change in Israel through performance. In Cohen, C. E., Varea, R. G., & Walker, P. O. (eds.) *Acting together: Performance and the creative transformation of conflict. Volume I. Resistance and reconciliation in regions of violence.* (pp. 123-144). Oakland, CA: New Village Press.

O'Neal, J. (2011). "Do You Smell Something Stinky?": Notes from Conversations about Making Art while Working for Justice in Racist, Imperial America in the Twenty-First Century. In Cohen, C. E., Varea, R. G., & Walker, P. O. (eds.) *Acting Together: Performance and the Creative Transformation of Conflict. Volume II. Building Just and Inclusive Communities.* (pp. 125-159). Oakland, CA: New Village Press.

Palihapitiya, M. (2011). The Created Space: Peacebuilding and Performance in Sri Lanka. In Cohen, C. E., Varea, R. G., & Walker, P. O. (eds.) *Acting together: performance and the creative transformation of conflict. Volume I. Resistance and reconciliation in regions of violence.* (pp. 73-95). Oakland, CA: New Village Press.

Rose, D. B. (1997). Rupture and the ethics of care in colonized space. In Bonyhady, T. & Griffiths, T. (eds.) *Prehistory to Politics: John Mulvaney, the humanities and the public intellectual.* Carlton: Melbourne University Press.

Ross, P. (2011). Preface: Speak to the past and it will heal thee. In Cohen, C. E., Varea, R. G., & Walker, P. O. (eds.) *Acting together: Performance and the creative transformation of conflict. Volume II. Building just and inclusive communities.* (pp. xiii-xvi). Oakland, CA: New Village Press.

Salas, J. (2011). Stories in the moment: Playback theatre for building community and justice. In Cohen, C. E., Varea, R. G., & Walker, P. O. (eds.) *Acting together: performance and the creative transformation of conflict. Volume II. Building just and inclusive communities.* (pp. 93-123). Oakland, CA: New Village Press.

Schechner, R. (1988). *Performance studies: An introduction.* London: Routledge.

Turner, V. (1977). *The ritual process: Structure and anti-structure.* NY: Cornell University Press.

Stamper, M. (2006, August 17). Heart of the Methow brings cultures in the confluence of Two Rivers. *Methow Valley News,* p. 4.

Varea, R. G. (2011). Fire in the memory: Theatre, truth, and justice in Argentina and Peru. In Cohen, C. E., Varea, R. G., & Walker, P. O. (eds.) *Acting together: Performance and the creative transformation of conflict. Volume I. Resistance and reconciliation in regions of violence.* (pp. 153-177). Oakland, CA: New Village Press.

Walker, P. O. (2011). Creating a new story. In Cohen, C. E., Varea, R. G., & Walker, P. O. (eds.) *Acting together: Performance and the creative transformation of conflict. Volume I. Resistance and reconciliation in regions of violence.* (pp. 225-251). Oakland, CA: New Village.

Epilogue
"They Did Not See the Bodies": Confronting and Embracing in the Post-Apartheid University

Jonathan Jansen

University of the Free State Bloemfontein

Introduction

I want to conclude this outstanding anthology of research and thought on the subjects of trauma, forgiveness, reconciliation and justice where Donna Orange's brilliant Prologue to this book started, with a gut-wrenching story about bodies. The author makes reference to a horrific film made by Alfred Hitchcock that was never shown but is now available. When the allies entered the Bergen-Belsen concentration camp towards the end of the Second World War they found well-fed Germans in their quarters living alongside the dying and decaying corpses of Jews succumbing to hunger and disease. You literally see the bones pushing out against the off-white skin, and swollen heads with large eye sockets and sunken eyeballs. Jewish inmates were literally dying on each other within walking distance of the quarters of the Nazi officers.

Even more striking is that the film first takes the viewer into and through the surrounding town with its manicured lawns and peaceful suburban housing where ordinary Germans lived. They must have known of the miniature Holocaust down the road, but life went on as normal. On the camp site and around it, there was another world even though the chimney smoke going up from burning bodies and the smell of decaying human flesh in the open air must surely have betrayed the genocide down the road.

Then something remarkable happens. The Allied forces require the Nazi officers to touch, lift and carry the dead bodies against their own bodies to deposit into trenches dug by the German soldiers themselves. It is a gut-wrenching site to witness on this black and white video the emotionless guards of the Reich loading bodies onto trucks and carrying them against their naked upper bodies, arms and legs dangled around their warm necks, flailing, and then slid down the sand embankment into a hole.

But it is the next set of slides that took my breath away. The public officials and elders from the town of Bergen-Belsen, as well as ordinary German citizens, are lined up around the open trenches with layers of Jewish bodies, forced to see the bodies killed. In that moment neat conceptual distinctions between perpetrator and bystander become grey and dark, and the redeeming excuse "I did not know" is no longer available to the Germans. They saw the bodies.

The Knowledge of Evil

Here is the problem of white South Africans at large, the defensive claim that "I did not know" or, in the carrying metaphor of this story, they did not see the bodies. In many ways this is true. State censorship of all the main media, including print media and television, not only sought to discourage black people and the black resistance in particular from knowing about white losses and grief in the battlefield, it also shielded white citizens from the horrors perpetrated by so-called civilized Christian men against black and white opponents of the regime.

It is clear to me that the parents of the white "born-frees," as they are erroneously called, did not know fathers were raping civilians on the Namibian border while fighting SWAPO and the ANC; ordinary white citizens had no knowledge of the brutality of torture routinely conducted in John Vorster Square police station in Johannesburg or Caledon Square police station in Cape Town. The gunning down of defenceless school youth from Atteridgeville in the North to Athlone in the South largely bypassed white consciousness. Inside the censored world of apartheid, everything looked normal. They did not see the bodies.

When these stories of conflict did break in the news it was in the form of unrelenting propaganda. "Terrorists" were killed and "terrorist attacks" thwarted. Prisoners jumped to their death or slipped on soap and fell down stairs or hanged themselves all on their own. Every encounter of war was a victory over godless communists wanting to destroy white civilization and "our Christian way of life"—the stock response even today to state terror on opponents.

Yet to present the "no knowledge" response in such clear and absolute terms is of course disingenuous. Here the memorable response to this problem by a former apartheid cabinet Minister turned Human Rights Commissioner is revealing when he declared that "the defence that I did not know is not available to me, for in many ways I did not want to know." This is an important insight for as much as the apartheid state censored white reality, black and white lived too closely together in the intimacy of their intertwined lives not to have seen the bodies, in the manner of speaking.

White lecturers who taught on black campuses saw the bodies; white teachers who taught in black high schools bore witness to police brutality. White madams saw the grief of the domestic whose children were shadowed away in the dark of night. White employers of black labour saw the beaten bodies from weekends in detention. White policemen, soldiers, spies, volunteers killed directly and came home with the scars of war on the streets of the townships or the infiltration of homes in neighbouring states.

Still, it was only during the TRC's open sessions that many South Africans "saw" the bodies of victims so openly day after day. Yet I do not believe that ordinary white citizens dwelt on that channel or read the reports of mainly black bodies shaking and wanting to know what happen to their children. Not only did white citizens not show up at the TRC to own up to the dead and disappeared bodies, many flatly dismissed the commission as biased against them, an ANC plot to make whites feel guilty about something they did not do.

Back to the Future

As the black Rector of a former white university two decades after apartheid, this is the heart of the dilemma. How do you deal with white alumni (parents from the apartheid era) who behave as if there were no bodies? How do you teach white students (children born after apartheid) who become very angry and aggressive, especially young white males, at the slightest hint of any reference to historical bodies? Not only do many white students and their parents not want to talk about bodies, they want things to remain as they were under apartheid, especially in relation to apartheid symbolism.

The problem with symbols in the post-apartheid university is that they are visual reminders of our divided past. In a place like the University of the Free State (UFS), those symbolic reminders are everywhere. When I flip open the university's graduation programme in 2014, there is a long list of every man (until recently, only males) who received an honorary doctorate from our university. On that list appears the most destructive apartheid politicians like HF Verwoerd, PW Botha and BJ Vorster, but also every major and minor administrator of the apartheid government, including Geoff Cronje who was the academic architect of apartheid's racial classification system. The main building of the Law School is named after CR Swart, an apartheid President. Student residences bear the names of white supremacists and segregationists like JBM Hertzog and NJ van der Merwe.

For those singular universities which, believe it or not, still run majority white campuses in South Africa, the question of bodies is less likely to come up. But at an institution like the University of the Free State, where a majority of students are black, the question is posed all the time and in the following way—those symbols are divisive, they remind us of our violent past, and they makes us feel excluded even in the present. Put differently, even if you did not want to talk about bodies those symbols bring up the subject in the minds of especially black students.

The Political and Pedagogical Project

South Africa did not have a revolution. We entered into a negotiated settlement where the white apartheid government sat down with the black liberation movements and drafted a Constitution that ensured a place for all in the future of the country. Led by Nelson Mandela, the reconciliation narrative was written prominently across the political script that birthed the new South Africa. Invariably, this was taken to mean that while a black majority would lead the country, the kind of governance and administration would be generous and inclusive, and give due recognition to the rights of white citizens in respect of things like culture, language and property. The very anthem, containing lines in Afrikaans from the apartheid *volkslied* (national anthems), is a clear if awkward example of the extent to which recognition and reconciliation was carried forward in the symbolism of this new country.

The problem is that Mandela did not leave behind a manual or a guide book for how we work out the grand narrative of reconciliation and social justice in the day-to-day encounters between black and white South Africans as we shave up against each other in places of learning, living and labouring. We have to do that work ourselves within the broad framework set by Mandela and others, and this is the challenge of post-apartheid leadership in a public institution like the University of the Free State.

It is impossible, as the chapters in this book show, to build and sustain a post-conflict society without talking about those invisible bodies. This requires extraordinary skills of teaching across the disciplines. Such skills of compassion when there are "bodies in the middle of the room" (Elbaz-Luwisch, 2004) and competence in the discipline cannot come easily from professors whom themselves were military conscripts on behalf of the apartheid regime. While many have come to terms with the new country, and are indeed committed to teaching black students with passion and dedication, deep belief systems do not change that easily and academics across the world are not prepared as teachers, let alone teachers in a post-conflict society.

In this respect the UFS established an Institute for Reconciliation and Social Justice as well as a Centre for Teaching and Learning tasked, in part, to begin building a campus of compassion and embrace, on the one hand, and on the other, a teaching corps of academics versed in the facilitation of difficult dialogues. Those who become part of these two entities benefit greatly, but it is a minority in a voluntary suite of programs on offer. Still, there is a place where students and faculty can come to confront historical and present "bodies" that otherwise remain unspeakable. The many seminars, conferences, workshops, special lectures, and more, are all designed to create open spaces for constructive dialogue about how we deal with the bodies.

All first-year students taking the core curriculum called UFS 101, encounter the bodies of both young white men executed in the Anglo-Boer War, as it was called, and young black men executed in the anti-apartheid struggles. This history module, which I teach with hopefully both empathy and challenge, generated considerable anger among young white men especially in the smaller tutorial sessions. No matter how the subject matter was presented, the very mention of bodies from the past is enough to evoke deep, deep anger among those who were born after apartheid. Why? Because they had already learnt from their parents and peer groups, from *dominees* (ministers in the Afrikaans churches), rugby coaches, and other significant adults in their lives, to react negatively, sometimes violently, against any mention of historical bodies. This makes the pedagogical task of teaching difficult, it makes the psychological burden of healing hard, and it makes the political task of social cohesion very challenging.

Here institutional context matters. It would be much easier, though not without difficulties, taking on discussion of bodies in historically black universities or the liberal white universities. But in century-old institutions like the UFS, where white Afrikaans speaking students and black students occupy common ground, the children of historical enemies do not come to the table easily or without angst for they have inherited memories that come as divided and divisive as those who have direct knowledge of the bodies. And that is what makes the discussion of symbolic reparation such a challenge.

Should JBM Go?

One of the old male residences with a significant number of white Afrikaans students is named after a prime minister of the then Boer republic, the Orange Free State, one JBM Hertzog. It was this residence which welcomed me as new Rector in 2009 with a swastika painted against the wall visible from where I was sitting during the introductions.

My Dean of Students had started a discussion with the residence and during one of those visits to JBM Hertzog, he told a house meeting that their name would change. A student with a hidden recorder taped this message and sent it to the local Afrikaans newspaper. All hell broke loose. What in another context would have been a non-event became a fiery attack on the Dean and the university leadership in general; how dare we even consider changing that name? The regional Afrikaans newspapers picked up the story and angry, vicious letters followed for weeks on end.

I received a set of anonymous letters with some of the worst racist bile I had ever encountered in my life; it was cutting, and personal with racist and ethnic insults against my person that I had not even encountered during the worst of the apartheid years. Death threats came with the correspondence. All because one of my Deans dared to express his view that the name of the residence should change. His view, because name changes are in fact made by the governing body of the university and not by an individual in the middle management of a large, multi-campus institution.

A few white men demanded a meeting of Convocation, a derelict body that had last met in 2007 to vote against racial integration on campus. It turned into an evening of abuse as right-wing men spat abuse and insult at the university leadership on all kinds of things but, at its heart, was the transformation of the institution and, in particular, the threat of name changes to a men's residence.

What would unleash such a torrent of intolerance and barely concealed racist abuse from a few white, Afrikaans men? Quite simply, they did not see the bodies. Here racial arrogance stalks the land among a few who clearly do not believe there was a violent, apartheid past captured and retained in these alienating symbols on a changing campus. These are men who generated the bodies as military service men and as civilian policemen. They saw the bodies, and yet these bodies do not exist because of their emotional, physical and spiritual distancing from those events.

At a psychological level what you witness in such public behaviour is a profound sense of loss and receding sense of control over "their" last remaining institutions on which they can claim ownership—the white university. They lost control over the institutions of state; before you could call your Member of Parliament, now you call your local Afrikaans newspaper which outlet I have often described as a receptacle for white anxiety. You feel vulnerable in this new country where you live with the Afrikaans press telling daily, front-page stories of the horror of farm murders and home invasions as if the target is white Afrikaans citizens as opposed to all South Africans. You witness ongoing stories about government corruption, and there is nothing you can do about it except that it confirms for the racists everything they knew about black people.

That anger is now inflected inwards on the one Afrikaans institution also threatening to slip forever beyond your control—the university. This is the place that formed you and where you have deep emotional, spiritual and ethnic bonds. And it wants to challenge and change the memories and remembrances of that treasured past.

The Leadership of Change and Conciliation

What then is the pedagogical task inside former white institutions in a black majority country that came into being through a negotiated settlement that sought to balance reconciliation and social justice? In this formulation of the question lays three critical variables for change leadership.

First, in a black majority country, unlike the United States of America, for example, it is a matter of time before institutional change happens anyway. The still-white dominant professorship will change in all 25 public universities and most of the students in the few still-white dominant campuses will be black. This means that the leadership of change requires patience but also generosity.

Second, the spirit of reconciliation exemplified in our first president, Nelson Mandela, demands an approach that does not steamroller over the memories and emotions of the vanquished. Our national anthem with its clumsy but necessary language and ideological blend is the most glaring example of such an approach. What this means in an institution such as the UFS is that there needs to be a delicate balance between changing and retaining the symbols that mark this century-old institution. We have maintained Afrikaans as a university language, alongside English.

We continue to engage this challenge through leadership actions that "add to" the extant symbolism of an old university in meaningful rather than contradictory ways (such as the new African artworks along campus pathways); to withdraw offensive symbols and exclusive traditions (such as practices of Dutch Reformed Calvinism in public ceremonies); and to establish conciliatory traditions (such as the annual Reconciliation Lecture). It will remain an uneasy truce with pressure from black and progressive white students to change all, and pressure from white alumni to hold onto treasured symbols from the past.

Third, the devastating history of colonialism and apartheid demands social justice especially in a white-exclusive university that was central to the maintenance of white supremacy over a century. This means being clear, from the top down, about what the university stands for in terms of social justice and institutional reparation. The employment of senior black professors and administrators is not simply a matter of compliance with government legislation but communicated through the logic of social justice. The same applies to acts of symbolic reparation and social responsibility towards disadvantaged communities. Community outreach, always done in the ideological framework of religious upliftment of the uncivilized is now done in the political context of social justice for the oppressed; this is a significant shift in institutional motivation and requires further elaboration in another place.

Conclusion

The challenges for leadership in the aftermath of conflict are many, such as how to manage the lingering claims to martyr memories on both sides of a conflict (chapter 3) or how to conduct "second generation" journeys into the past in ways that create more promising futures (chapter 5) or how to build shared spaces out of volatile segregated ones (chapter 8). The question these chapters pose, in various ways, is whether there is a future, and if so what kind of future, after traumatic conflict?

South Africa has not yet escaped inclusion in the lament of Leon Uris (1976: p. 751) in Trinity—"Ireland has no future only the past happening over and over." This book, on the other hand, offers a wealth of comparative research and knowledge on how post-conflict states everywhere can yet build promising futures out of broken pasts.

References

Elbaz-Luwisch, F. (2004). "How Is Education Possible When There's a Body in the Middle of the Room?" *Curriculum Inquiry, 34*, 9-27.
Uris, L. (1976). *Trinity: A Novel of Ireland.* New York: Doubleday Publishers.

Author Biographies

JACO BARNARD-NAUDÉ is Professor in the Department of Private Law at the University of Cape Town (UCT) where he teaches post-apartheid jurisprudence. He holds degrees in BCom (Law), LLB and LLD from the University of Pretoria and an MA in creative writing from UCT. He is also a past recipient of the UCT Fellows' Award. He has spent time on research fellowships at the Max Planck Institute for International Private Law in Hamburg and as Honorary Research Fellow at the Birkbeck Institute for the Humanities, University of London. He is a director at the Institute for Justice and Reconciliation and at the Triangle Project in Cape Town. His research interests include post-apartheid aesthetics, deconstruction, psychoanalysis and literary criticism, all of which he brings to a re-treatment of law in the postcolony.

JESSICA BENJAMIN teaches and supervises at the Relational Track at New York University Postdoctoral Program as well as the Stephen Mitchell Centre for Relational Studies. She is the author of *The Bonds of Love*; *Like Subjects, Love Objects*; and *Shadow of the Other: Intersubjectivity and Gender in Psychoanalysis* and the frequently cited article *"Beyond Doer and Done to: an Intersubjective view of Thirdness"* (Psa. Quarterly 2004). Her forthcoming book on recognition theory will discuss the clinical and social application of the concept of the Third and the role of acknowledgment in relation to trauma.

JULIET BROUGH ROGERS is an Australian Research Council Fellow, a Senior Lecturer in Criminology in the School of Political Sciences at the University of Melbourne, and Adjunct Professor at Griffith Law School, Queensland. Prior to her academic career she was a therapist in the trauma field. She has recently been a Visiting Fellow at the European University Institute, Yale Law School, UCT Law School, Queens University Law School, Belfast and at the University of Bologna, TRaMe Centre.

SARAH DAVIES CORDOVA is currently a Senior Research Fellow at the University of Johannesburg and teaches Francophone literatures and cultures at the University of Wisconsin-Milwaukee. Her interdisciplinary work focuses on representations of dance and the socio-political in 19th-21st centuries French, Antillean and sub-Saharan colonial and post-colonial texts, and examines the conscientizing role of literature and performance in their intersections with memory and history of migrations, dictatorships, genocide and conflict.

GRAHAM DAWSON is Professor of Historical Cultural Studies and Director of the Centre for Research in Memory, Narrative and Histories at the University of Brighton, England. He is author of *Soldier Heroes: British Adventure, Empire and the Imagining of Masculinities* (1994), and *Making Peace with the Past? Memory, Trauma and the Irish Troubles* (2007), and co-editor of collections on the politics of war memory, trauma, and contested spaces of conflict.

KATHLEEN DOLL studied Psychology, Political Science, and Women's Studies at Chapman University. She has been a research fellow in the Henley Lab where she explored the intersections of politics and psychology. Doll has also published on body objectification. She is currently completing a term of national service with AmeriCorps in Austin, Texas working on democratizing access to higher education. Doll pursues graduate studies in Evaluation Science at Claremont Graduate University in California.

PUMLA GOBODO-MADIKIZELA is senior research professor at the University of the Free State. She won the Alan Paton Award in South Africa, and the Christopher Award in the United States for her book, *A Human Being Died that Night: A South African Story of Forgiveness*. Her other books include *Narrating our Healing: Perspectives on Healing Trauma*, as co-author; *Memory, Narrative and Forgiveness: Perspectives on the Unfinished Journeys of the Past*, as co-editor.

BEATA HAMMERICH is a psychologist and psychoanalyst in private practice in Cologne, Germany. She was born in 1957 in Prague, Czechoslovakia, and fled with her family to Germany in 1968. She is a member of the board of the Study Group on Intergenerational Consequences of the Holocaust.

JONATHAN JANSEN is the Rector and Vice-Chancellor of the University of the Free State. He is the Honorary Professor of Education at the University of the Witwatersrand and Visiting Fellow at the National Research Foundation. For his book *Knowledge in the Blood* (2009), Professor Jansen was awarded the Nayef Al-Rodhan Prize by the British Academy for the Humanities and Social Sciences, and an outstanding book recognition award from the American Educational Research Association. His other books include *Diversity High: Class, Color, Character and Culture in a South African High School* (2008), *Curriculum: Organizing Knowledge for the Classroom* (2009), and *How to Fix South Africa's Schools* (2014). His most recent award is the Chivas Humanitarian Award.

ANGELIKI KANAVOU is a Tobis Fellow at the Interdisciplinary Centre for the Study of Ethics and Morality at the University of California, Irvine. She has taught Peace Studies at the University of Notre Dame and Chapman University and has been Interim Director of the Program for Peace Studies at Chapman. Kanavou has a Ph.D. in international relations from the University of Southern California. She has been a fellow at the Program on Negotiations at the Harvard Law School and at the Joan B Kroc Institute for International Peace at the University of Notre Dame. Kanavou has published in the area of ethnic conflict and currently works on post-conflict social adaptation of perpetrators and survivors and their children and intergenerational trauma transmission.

ROSANNE KENNEDY is Associate Professor of Literature and Gender, Sexuality and Culture at the Australian National University. Her research interests include trauma, testimony, and memory and its re-mediations in cultural, literary, and human rights texts and contexts. Recent articles have been published in Memory Studies, Australian Feminist Law Journal, Comparative Literature Studies, Biography, Studies in the Novel, Australian Humanities Review and Australian Feminist Studies. Her chapter "*Moving Testimony: Human Rights, Palestinian Memory, and the Transnational Public Sphere*" appears in *Transnational Memory: Circulation, Articulation, Scales*, Eds. Chiara De Cesari and Ann Rigney, Berlin and Boston, Walter de Gruyter, 2014. She is currently working on a book titled *Moving Testimonies: Art, Advocacy and Transnational Publics*.

BJÖRN KRONDORFER is Director of the Martin-Springer Institute and Endowed Professor of Religious Studies at Northern Arizona University, USA. His fields of expertise are religion, gender and culture, (post) Holocaust studies, reconciliation studies, and Western Religious Thought. His publications helped to define the field of Critical Men's Studies in Religion. He currently explores connections between traumatic memory, restorative justice, and moral repair. He has been guest professor at the Institute of Theology/History of Religion at Berlin's Free University, Germany, and has been Faculty Affiliate at the University of the Free State,

South Africa. He facilitates intercultural encounter seminars, most recently in Israel/Palestine.

WENDY LAMBOURNE is Deputy Director, Centre for Peace and Conflict Studies, University of Sydney. Her research on transitional justice and peacebuilding after genocide and other mass violence has a regional focus on sub-Saharan Africa and Asia/Pacific. Recent publications include chapters in *Transitional Justice Theories* (Routledge, 2014) and *Critical Perspectives in Transitional Justice* (Intersentia, 2012) as well as articles in the *Journal of Peacebuilding and Development, International Journal of Transitional Justice, Genocide Studies and Prevention* and *African Security Review*.

EDWARD LOWENSTEIN is the Dorr Distinguished Professor of Anaesthesia and Professor of Medical Ethics at Harvard Medical School. A German Kindertransport child, he and his brother reached England in spring 1939. Cared for lovingly by Ruth F. Stern, a secular Jewish headmistress, they were reunited with their parents October 1940 in the United States. A pioneer in cardiac anaesthesiology who became interested in the ethics of end of life care though this profession, his recent interests include universal access to medical care and the reallocation of medical care resources to social determinants of health.

DUNREITH KELLY LOWENSTEIN is an Educational consultant and Freelance writer who is particularly interested in stories of resilience and creative expression in the face of adversity. A long-time educator, she most recently was a member of the senior leadership team of Facing History and Ourselves. Her chapter, *"Every Stitch a Memory"* is included in *Stitching Resistance: Women, Creativity and Fiber Arts* (2014). She holds degrees from Williams College and Smith College.

JEFF KELLY LOWENSTEIN is a Lecturer in the Journalism Department at Columbia College Chicago. His work has been published by The New Yorker, and the Chicago Tribune, among many other publications, and has received local, national and international recognition. A Fulbright Teacher, Scholar and Specialist, Kelly Lowenstein holds degrees from Northwestern University and Stanford University. He has written two books and writes for the Huffington Post and on his own blog.

EWALD MENGEL is Professor of English Literature and New English Literatures at the University of Vienna. He has published books and numerous articles on the eighteenth-century novel, the historical novel, twentieth-century drama, Harold Pinter, and translation and adaptation. He is the co-editor of *Weltbühne Wien/World Stage Vienna* (2010—2 volumes). His recent research interest focuses on trauma and the contemporary South African novel. *Trauma, Memory, & Narrative in South Africa: Interviews (with Michela Borzaga and Karin Orantes)* appeared in 2009, a collection of essays Trauma, Memory, and Narrative in the Contemporary South African Novel (with Michela Borzaga) was published by Rodopi (Amsterdam) 2012.

DAVID NIYONZIMA is a Part-time lecturer and Executive Director of Trauma Healing and Reconciliation Services (THARS) in Burundi. David holds an MA (Counselling) and Doctoral degree from George Fox University, USA. David has more than twenty years of experience in psychosocial activities and peacebuilding in the African Great Lakes Region, with THARS and as General Secretary of the Burundi Yearly Meeting of Friends (Quakers). He is co-author with Lon Fendall of *Unlocking Horns: Forgiveness and Reconciliation in Burundi* (Barclay Press, 2001).

DONNA ORANGE is a Clinical Professor in the Relational Track, Post-doctoral Program, New York University. She also teaches at the Institute for Psychoanalytic Psychology of the Self and Relational Psychoanalysis, Milano and Roma. Educated in both philosophy and clinical psychology, she runs study groups in philosophy, in the history of psychoanalysis, and in contemporary relational psychoanalysis. She is author of *Emotional Understanding: Studies in Psychoanalytic Psychology; Thinking for Clinicians: Philosophical Resources for Contemporary Psychoanalysis and the Humanistic Psychotherapies*, and *The Suffering Stranger: Hermeneutics for Everyday Clinical Practice* (2011). With George Atwood and Robert Stolorow she has written *Working Intersubjectively: Contextualism in Psychoanalytic Practice* and *Worlds of Experience: Interweaving Philosophical and Clinical Dimensions in Psychoanalysis*. With Roger Frie, she co-edited *Beyond Postmodernism: Extending the Reach of Clinical Theory*.

KOSAL PATH is an assistant professor of political science at Brooklyn College. He is a survivor of the Cambodian genocide (1975-79). As a researcher for the Cambodian Genocide Program at Yale University and the Documentation Center of Cambodia from 1995 to 2000, he helped document the atrocities of the Pol Pot regime. His main teaching interests are international relations, foreign policy analysis, human rights and genocide. He has published on Sino-Vietnamese relations and genocide studies.

JOHANNES PFÄFFLIN is a Group therapist and Psychoanalyst in private practice in Erkrath near by Düsseldorf/Germany. He is an Institutional Supervisor as well as Member and former Chairman of the Study Group on Intergenerational Consequencs of the Holocaust (previously PAKH e.V.).

PETER POGANY-WNENDT is a Psychiatrist and Psychotherapist in private practice in Cologne, Germany and founding member and chairman of the Study Group on Intergenerational Consequences of the Holocaust, formerly known as PAKH e.V. He was born 1954 in Budapest, Hungary. His parents, both Jewish, survived the Holocaust. During the Hungarian Revolution he fled with his family to Chile, relocated to Germany in 1970, and studied medicine.

JEFFREY PRAGER is a Professor of Sociology at the University of California, Los Angeles (UCLA) and Former Dean and Senior Faculty Member at the New Centre of Psychoanalysis, Los Angeles. He is the author of many books and articles, including Presenting the Past: Psychoanalysis and the Sociology of Misremembering (Harvard 1998). His current research focuses on topics concerned with trauma, racism and social repair, in the United States, South Africa and elsewhere. His most recent publication is entitled "*Melancholia and the Racial Order: A Psychosocial Analysis of America's Enduring Racism.*" He has been the recipient of many honours and awards including a Best Teaching award from UCLA.

ERDA SIEBERT is the Vice Chairperson of the Study Group on Intergenerational Consequences of the Holocaust (previously PAKH e.V.). She was born 1944 in Dresden (East Germany) during World War II and fled with her family to North-West-Germany in 1945. She is working as Psychoanalyst in private practice.

BERND SONNTAG is a Psychiatrist and Psychotherapist from the Department of Psychosomatics and Psychotherapy, Deputy Medical Director, Specialist for Psychosomatic Medicine, University Hospital of Cologne, Germany and founding member of the Study Group on Intergenerational Consequences of the Holocaust (previously PAKH e.V).

SHANEE STEPAKOFF is a clinical psychologist in private practice in New York City and Adjunct Professor in expressive arts therapy at the California Institute of Integral Studies.. She also holds a Masters of Fine Arts in creative writing. She was the psychologist for the UN-backed war crimes tribunal in Sierra Leone for over two years. She spent two years as psychologist/trainer for the Centre for Victims of Torture, first in Guinea and later in Jordan. She has conducted trainings in Liberia, Cambodia, and the United States.

POLLY O. WALKER is Assistant Professor of Peace and Conflict Studies at Juniata College. She is of Cherokee descent, a member of the Cherokee Southwest Township. Her research, teaching and practice focus on peacebuilding and the arts, ritual, Indigenous knowledge systems, cross cultural conflict transformation, and systems theory and conflict. She also lectures for James Cook University in the Conflict Management and Resolution Program. Polly has published a wide range of articles and chapters in peer reviewed journals and texts.

ANDRÉ WESSELS is a Senior Professor in, and Head of, the Department of History at the University of the Free State, Bloemfontein, South Africa. His main research focus is the military history of twentieth-century South Africa. He is also interested in aspects of the cultural history of South Africa. He is the author of more than a hundred peer reviewed academic journal articles; the author, co-author or editor of eight books, as well as many other publications.

Index

a condition of the other 49

accountability 21, 44, 96, 99, 109, 114, 131, 175

acknowledgement 4, 10, 22, 27–31, 51, 73 ff., 131 f., 150, 154, 199, 297, 301, 305

acting out 175

Acting Together Network 325 ff.

Adolphe, Madame Max 215, 232

aesthetic mediation 326

aestheticisation of politics 62

affective community 201

affective identification 204

affective reflection 249

Afrikaner nationalism 162, 167

Afrikanerdom 167

alienation 18, 56, 118, 147, 170 f., 190, 329

Allen, Danielle 24

alternative healing rituals 308

American slavery XIV, 124

amnesic toolkit 49

Anglo-Boer War 160–172

Anglo-Boer War museum 168

anxious mutism 221

apartheid policy 168

apartheid symbolism 345

Aramin, Bassam 71

archaic expectations 208

attachments to the past 156

Bayardo memorial 149 f.

being-in-the-world 56, 66, 96

beneficiaries 4, 64, 111, 125, 131, 202

Berlin Wall 140, 257

bitterness XVI, 7, 161 f.

black bodies 345

Black nationalism 167

Bloody Sunday 31, 138

body-oriented movement therapies 312

Boer women 168, 170

Bonhoeffer, Dietrich XII

born-frees 344

Botha, PW 345

Bringing Them Home Report 194–202, 204 ff., 208

British Unionist 139

Center for Victims of Torture 308

chosen trauma 264, 297

civic life 66

cloak of denialism 5, 50

co-birth 228, 232

co-created space of shared rhythms 72

cognisant nemesis 229

collective memory 124, 200, 332

collective remembering 21

collective trauma 1, 8, 75, 131, 178, 191, 199, 234, 292, 296 ff., 300, 304

Combatants for Peace 5, 71, 79, 81

conflicting histories 156

constructive dialogue 247, 264, 347

containing function 38

corruption 113, 181, 191, 335, 349

Cradock 4 29, 41 ff.

creative potentiality 5, 52, 54

Cronje, Geoff 345

cultural stories 310

cultural texts 205, 210

cumulative trauma 249

Cupar Way 140

cycles of destructiveness 7, 15, 21, 191

de Kock, Eugene 30, 123, 252
de la Rey, General Koos 165
de Wet, General Christiaan 165
deadening silence 214
death dance 2
dehumanization 14, 79, 120, 124, 169, 177
delegated dynamic 264
dependency trap 263
deproblematised story-telling 145
Derrida, Jacques XV, 37, 50, 58 f., 68
dialogical models 90
dialogical processes of healing 67, 300
dictatorship's hubris 226
diegetic memory 216
dissociation 74–78, 83, 86, 259
Dúchas Archive 154 f.
Duvalier, jean-Claude 213 ff., 217–223, 228, 230 ff.

East Belfast Oral History Archive 155
embodied knowledge 225
empathetic deficits 249
Enniskillen bomb 138
ethical action 87
ethno-sectarianized space 149
exhaled pain 239
exhausted discourse 62 f.

fantasy reparation 204 f.
fictionalised real time 216
first awakening 43

Gandhi XVI
Gasana's model of community life 300
genuine remorse 4, 29, 44
geographical divisions 156
gerontocratic view 196

ghost of the undecidable 50
global archive of suffering 200
Great Trek 160, 171
Gugulethu Seven 30, 129 f.
guided visualization 315 f.

hands-uppers 167
Hani, Chris XVI f.
healing journey 267–290, 300
Healing of Memories workshops 301 f.
healing power of images 316
hegemonic inscription 38
Heidegger, Martin 53 ff., 58, 63
Hertzog, JBM 345, 347 f.
historical consciousness 56
historical trauma X, 1, 3–9, 90, 94–100, 103, 105–108, 117, 119, 124, 131, 135
historicised diegesis 222
history-making 154, 156
Hitchcock, Alfred XIV, 343
Hobhouse, Emily 167 f., 170
honest reckoning 267
horizontal allegiance 66
Human Rights and Equal Opportunity Commission, HREOC 194, 199 ff.
humiliation 27, 85 f., 114, 122, 131, 161, 297 f.

identity-masking 152
incorporation 19 ff., 98, 125, 215, 220, 310, 319 ff., 340
inner representation 253 f.
institutional perpetrators 31
intergenerational cycle X, 1, 3, 8, 24, 162, 172, 246, 267, 274
intergenerational learning 287
interior landscapes 152
interior monologue 223, 226

internal cohesion 80
internal dialogue 119, 223
internal goodness 77
internal obstacles 109
internal representation 14, 119, 263, 314
internal unity 109
internal witness 40, 45
interrelatedness 325
intersubjective psychoanalytic theory 72
introjection 19 f., 256, 261
intrusive memory 15, 21 f., 309

Jonker, Ingrid 62
jouissance 29, 44
journey of return 8, 282

Kathrada, Ahmed XVI
Kavakure Report 294
Khmer Rouges/KR cadres 174 ff., 178 f., 182, 184, 187–191
Kindertransport 8, 267 f., 271, 276, 280, 283, 354
Kohut, Heinz 22, 121, 126
Kristallnacht pogrom 241 f., 268, 272 f., 276, 280, 285
Krog, Antjie XV, 32, 34–37, 52 f., 59, 64, 67, 75

Lalo, Fyèt 216, 226, 232
large-group identities 90, 95 f., 98 ff., 106, 109
last outpost of the British Empire 160
liminal moment 17
Lincoln, Abraham XVI f.
linking objects 235
listening exercises 109
loss of thirdness 74
Lucas, Graham 72

Madiba XII, XV
Mandela, Nelson XI ff., XV–XIX, 62, 114 f., 170, 346, 349
Mars, Kettly 215 f., 231
martyr memories 350
material reparation 49, 65
maternal identifications 85
Mbeki, Thabo 50
mediated affect 195
melodrama 197, 208, 210
memorial sites 22
mental maps 141, 151 f.
metaphors for narrative construction 236
metaphysical guilt 66
Mississippi Burning 43
monologic historicising project 227
moral imagination 326
mother/child bond 235
Moving Beyond Violence Film 71, 75, 87
mythological intertexts 236

narrative trajectory 210
narratives of suffering 107
national recognition 201
Nazi extermination camps 163 f.
necklace murders 1 f.
negotiated settlement 346, 349
nemesis 217, 220 f., 226–229, 232
new South Africa 13, 17, 62, 346
non-verbal relationship 249

official forgetting XIII f.
oiesis 55, 59
omniscient judge of childhood fantasies 39 f.
over-identification 21

palimpsest memoryscapes 137, 218
peacebuilding 9, 291, 295, 299 f., 303 ff., 325–331, 337 f.

Plaatje, T. 167
plurality 5, 66
poetic stance 61, 64, 66
poetics of survival 7, 131, 194,
    196 f., 205, 207, 211, 217
political conjuncture 215
positive representation 315
post-apartheid citizenship 64
post-apartheid university 34, 345
post-conflict spaces 135 ff., 155
post-segregated society 24
previously repudiated other 5, 72
prosthetic memory 205
protection XIX, 19, 122, 152, 169,
    189, 195 f., 262, 294, 329
Protestant 139, 148–153
psychodrama 312
psychological burden of healing 347
psychological paradigm of
    recognition 71

Queen's Island 145 f., 148, 156
quilting 241, 243, 245

raging generation 256
reactive position 81
re-awakening of the divine 54
re-cognition 236
reconciliatory exoneration 106
reenactment of torture 29
reflexivity 64
reframing 110
regeneration 135, 142, 144, 175
re-imagining 105, 135, 142
re-lating 236
remaking of the self
re-membering 333
Remorse 4, 6, 16, 27–31, 37, 40 f.,
    44, 46, 102, 113, 118–123, 126,
    128 ff., 131, 188, 224
remorseless 224

reopening the coffin 16
reparative citizenship 5, 49, 52, 57,
    59 f., 64, 66 ff., 132
re-positioning of the perpetrator 40
Republicanism 135
resentful silence 221
resituating understanding 96, 99,
    110
resonant symbol 316
return to humanity 30
revenge 13, 16, 81, 85, 119, 127,
    176, 237, 263 f., 292
Robben Island XII, XV ff., 244
Rudd, Kevin 31, 194

sacred texts 319
Saisons sauvages 215, 231
sculpting 241, 245
sculpture 109 f.
second guilt 256
second holocaust 253
secret wounds 227 f.
sectarianized spatial practices 151
self and other 6, 16, 22, 38, 73, 83,
    120, 122, 125, 177, 188, 221,
    300
self-ness 65
self-reflective awareness 98
sentimental poetics 211
Shakespeare, William XVI f., 121
shameful past 12, 17
Shankill Road bombing 30
Shapira, Itimar 71
shared historical present 195
shared representation 297
shared spaces 142, 146, 148, 156,
    350
shock of the new 196, 209, 211
silent generation 256
sincerity XVII, 30
Singer, Irris 71 f., 76, 81

single identity enclaves 139
Sisulu, Walter XII, XVI
situation tragedy 208
Small, Adam 52 f., 58 f.
social body 110
social echo 327, 340
social rationality 61
social solidarity 107
Sorry Books Campaign 201
soul murder 256
space of dialogue 5, 72
spaces for constructive dialogue 347
spaces of fear 141, 149 ff., 156 f.
spatial consequences 135
spatial knowledges 155
spatial manifestations 135
speechlessness 213, 247
spiritual connection 315, 339
standing in the spaces 84
Stolen Generations inquiry 200
Story-Cloth 317
surrogates 247
Swart, CR 345
swastika 348
symbolic distance 327, 329
symbolic re-enactment 3
symbolic reparation 347, 350

Taylor, Eric 4, 10, 27, 29, 41 ff.
temporal dimensions of conflict
    transformation 136
testimonial methods 200
testimonial process 200
Titanic Quarter 145 f., 148 f., 154
tonton macoutes 213, 215, 218, 221,
    229, 231 f.
transformational process 87
transgenerational trauma 8, 172,
    286
transitional objects 235, 244
transpositional ploys 216

trauma novels 7, 234
Traumatic transmission 18
traumatised character 236, 245
treasured past 349
trilateral trust-building 93
tropological encounter 221
Truth and Reconciliation
    Commission, TRC XIII, 1, 3 f.,
    9 f., 13, 17, 23, 25, 28, 30, 32,
    38, 41, 43, 47 ff., 113–117, 121,
    123 f., 126, 128 f., 131, 161, 170,
    191, 221, 247, 285, 291, 293–
    299, 304–307, 332 f., 345
Tutu, Desmond XI, XIII, XV, 51,
    75, 117, 123
twin-speed economy 142, 149

ubuntu XV, XIX, 75, 115 f.
Ulster loyalism 135
unaccountability 175, 310
undigested feelings 248
unfulfillable tasks 263
unhealed trauma 295, 304
unrootedness 223
unsettling possibility 98

vengeance 6, 81, 115, 221
Verwoerd, HF 169, 345
virtual witnesses 201
visionary vocabulary 64, 67
visual reminder 248, 345
Vorster, BJ 344 f.

way of the horse 330 f.
Western Front 140
white consciousness 344
Winnicott, Donald 22, 26, 117 f.,
    130, 235 f.
Women's Memorial 168
wounding 90 f., 96

Zéphirin, Frantz 213

Printed in the USA
CPSIA information can be obtained
at www.ICGtesting.com
LVHW081417310823
756645LV00013B/1341